THE

MICHIGAN BOOK

ANN ARBOR
1898

The Inland Press
Ann Arbor

CONTENTS

FORMER SEAL OF THE UNIVERSITY.

CHAPTER I

OUR ALMA MATER

By an act of Congress passed in 1804 one township of land in the prospective Territory of Michigan was set apart for the support of a seminary of learning. Twenty-two years later Congress enlarged the grant to two townships. In the year 1817 the Governor and Judges of the Territory enacted a marvellous bill drawn by Augustus P. Woodward, Presiding Judge, whereby was established the "Catholepistemiad or University of Michigania". This statute decreed that the University should be composed of thirteen professorships, each called a didaxia, the didactors or professors to be appointed by the Governor. Two "didactors" at salaries of $12.50 each were appointed, and a primary school and a classical academy were established in Detroit; but in 1821 the act of 1817 was repealed, and a new act was passed for the establishment at Detroit of the University of Michigan, to be managed by twenty-one trustees. This board was legislated out of office by the Michigan statute of March 18, 1837, entitled "An act to provide for the organization and government of the University of Michigan", and passed only two months after the admission of the State into the Union by Congress. To the Rev. John D. Pierce, a graduate of Brown University and of Princeton Theological Seminary, who in the summer of 1836 had been appointed Superintendent of Public Instruction, is due the framing of this law under which the final organization of our Alma Mater was effected. As closely as possible the German idea of an university was followed, instead of imitating Yale and Harvard, themselves copies of English institutions. Michigan's University was to crown the educational system of the commonwealth, and to "provide the inhabitants of the State with the means of acquiring a thorough knowledge of literature, science, and the arts". The business affairs of the University were to be managed by a Board of Regents appointed by the Governor of the State and approved by the Senate. Two days after the passage of the organizing act the legislature adopted another statute locating the University at Ann Arbor, "upon such site or lot of ground as shall be selected by the Regents of the University and conveyed to them by the proprietors . . . free from cost . . . which site or lot of ground shall not be less than forty acres". One day later the Regents appointed by Governor Mason under the new law were approved by the Senate. The Board held its first meeting in Ann Arbor, June 5, 1837. In 1839 Governor Mason saved the University from destruction by vetoing a bill which had passed both houses of the legislature for the sale of the endowment lands at a price far below their value.

From 1837 to 1841 branches or preparatory schools were established in different localities throughout the State, and five buildings,—four dwellings and what is now the north wing of University Hall—were erected at Ann Arbor for the use of the collegiate department, which was finally opened in September, 1841. George P. Williams, Vermont '25, and the Rev. Joseph Whiting, Yale '23, constituted the active Faculty when collegiate instruction began. The number of students increased from six, in September, 1841, to eighty-nine in 1847-48.

THE CAMPUS—NORTHWEST ENTRANCE.

In 1848 the assistance of the University was withdrawn from the branches. This had the effect of depriving the institution of most of its preparatory schools, and in consequence the attendance diminished. Still more effective in checking growth was the secret-society struggle, which ultimately led to the entire reorganization of the University, and to constitutional changes whereby the Board of Regents became an elective body, charged by the fundamental law with "the general supervision of the University, and the direction of all expenditures from the University interest fund". In October, 1850, the Department of Medicine and Surgery was formally opened.

In August, 1852, Henry P. Tappan, Union '25, was by the new Board of Regents elected President of the University. It has been customary to attribute to this illustrious man whatever eminence the University attained in its earlier career, and it has been said somewhat extravagantly "His administration begins the history of the University as an educational power in Michigan and in the Northwest". The truth is that during its first decade, notwithstanding the disastrous society-war, our Alma Mater flourished as no other Western institution had ever flourished, and as no Eastern institution had flourished in the period of infancy. Michigan's first ten classes, all of which had been matriculated and eight of which had been graduated before Dr. Tappan's advent, gave a roll of 141 alumni; the first twenty classes of Yale and the first twenty of Harvard graduated only 102 and 136 respectively. The original lines of the University were laid upon the Prussian plan, to which Chancellor Tappan adhered; and the institution prior to 1852 had become such an "intellectual power" that it drew to its doors the representatives of the best families in Michigan, who thus were prevented from going East for their education. Whoever cares to contrast the first ten years of Michigan with the first ten of any other state university will find abundant evidence not only that our University was on the whole ably managed from the outset, but that it was successful beyond all precedent. Nor should it be forgotten that the alumni graduated before Dr. Tappan's time are not less renowned than those whom he trained.

Nevertheless the University owes to its first President an incalculable debt. He gathered around himself a Faculty equal to any in the country—such men as Boise, Frieze, Brünnow, White, and Watson; he introduced the scientific course; he opened the laboratory and the law department; he procured the erection and equipment of the astronomical observatory; and he imparted to the students and to the people of the State true ideas of what a University should be.

That the arbitrary and impolitic removal of President Tappan by the Regents did not wreck the University was due to the tact and energy of his successor, Erastus Otis Haven, who from 1863 to 1869 held the presidential office. During Dr. Haven's time a new course, the Latin and scientific, was organized; a course in pharmacy was arranged; additions were made to the laboratory, the observatory, and the medical building; the library was enlarged and rendered serviceable; the number of students so increased as to exceed the enrolment of any other institution of learning in the country; and, more than all else, an annual appropriation was obtained from the legislature, thus controverting these words of *The Nation* "The people will never consent to a general tax for the purpose of instructing a small body of men in Yale or Harvard or the University of Michigan". It was in 1867, when the University was only twenty-six years old, that George William Curtis, the Chairman of the Committee on education in the Constitutional Convention of New York, said of Yale, Harvard and the University of Michigan: "They are the three great institutions of learning in this country".

Upon the resignation of Dr. Haven in 1869, Professor Henry S. Frieze became Acting-President. In his brief but exceedingly important administration of two years the graduates of approved high schools were admitted upon presentation of diplomas, thus unifying the educational system of the State. The annual roll of academic graduates became very long for those times, and far surpassed the class lists of the struggling colleges of Michigan and the surrounding states. In January, 1869, women were permitted to enter the University.

At Commencement in 1871 James Burrill Angell, L. L. D., who had resigned the control of the University of Vermont, and whose student life at Brown had ended twenty-two years before with his delivering the valedictory for his class, was inducted into the presidency. Among the results of Dr. Angell's long administration, which covers nearly half of the active existence of the University, have been the occupying of our campus with commodious buildings, the erection and equipment of a splendid gymnasium, the acquiring of a field for athletic exercises, the broadening and strengthening of the curriculum, the doubling of the time required for graduation in law and medicine, the development of graduate courses, an extraordinary increase in the number of students and graduates, and the obtaining from the state of a fixed and fairly liberal annual income. All this has been accomplished in spite of great obstacles, and notwithstanding untoward episodes against which no foresight could guard.

Twice the active service of Dr. Angell has been interrupted by his absence from Ann Arbor owing to public duties as Envoy of the United States, first to the court of Peking from 1880 to 1882, and second to the Ottoman Porte, from 1897 to 1898. During the earlier of these absences Professor Frieze again became Acting-President; and at the present writing Harry B. Hutchins, '71, formerly Dean of the Law Department, has charge of affairs, he being the first of the graduates of the University to act as its chief executive.

The square tract of forty acres now called the campus was given to the Regents in 1837 by the Ann Arbor Land Company a thrifty association which had persuaded the legislature to overrule Detroit and other cities in favor of Ann Arbor as the site of the new University. Notwithstanding the advice of President Tappan, who was in favor of buying the land clear through to the river, the campus itself never has been enlarged, the tracts purchased for the observatory, the hospitals, and the athletic field being separated from it by considerable distances.

Elaborate plans for beautifying the college grounds were adopted more than fifty years ago; but these were soon abandoned, and the forest growths of which the campus had been deprived before it passed to the Regents were replaced without any set design. There was planting of trees in 1845, 1847, and 1854, and much more from 1858 to 1860. "Tappan Oak" which stands east of the south wing has survived most of the maples placed around it, and notwithstanding the terrible versification to which it has been subjected it bids fair to live to a great age. Among the memorials on the campus are the class stone of '58 at the foot of the Tappan Oak, the huge boulder left by '62, "calico rock" the offering of '69, the statue of Benjamin Franklin contributed by '70, and the broken column which commemorates the virtues of Professors Whiting, Houghton, Fox, and Denton.

CHANCELLOR TAPPAN.

In the autumn of 1870 a new fence was placed around the campus. This was so often injured by "rushes" and otherwise that in 1889-90 the remains of it were removed, and the grounds were thrown open. Old pictures of the University show a walk in front of the campus, but no such thing existed before 1890. In that year artificial stone was laid all the way along State street, and in the year following the other sides of the campus received like attention. As these sidewalks are not in the street proper, but occupy University ground, they are not within the city ordinance concerning bicycles, and one who takes to them jeopards his life. As for the old tar walks in the campus they have been replaced gradually by cement flagging, and the grounds themselves, formerly devoted to the Secretary's cow and to the raising of an annual crop of hay, have been levelled, sodded, and otherwise cared for.

In 1839 a magnificent plan for the erection of buildings was adopted by the Regents. This would have involved the spending of half a million of dollars, nearly as much as has been realized from the sales of the endowment lands; and it failed to receive the approval, then necessary, of the Superintendent of Public Instruction. Since then the principle that the first requisite of an university is great teachers rather than magnificent buildings has been recognized. Michigan has flourished because its funds have been put less into brick and stone and more into professorships.

Four two-story houses of stuccoed brick, designed as residences for professors, and costing about eight thousand dollars, were erected in 1839–40, two on the north side and two on the south side of the campus. These, the first buildings of the University, still remain. One is the President's House, which was greatly enlarged and improved five years ago at an expenditure of twelve thousand dollars. Another of these houses, the one east of Dr. Angell's residence, was occupied by Professor Frieze until 1877, when it was given to the dental school. A wing was added in 1879, and in 1891–92 the building was enlarged for the classes in engineering. Of the two dwellings on the north side of the campus the one towards the east was given in 1869 to the medical department for hospital purposes. It was enlarged in 1875 by a frame pavilion, and in 1879 by an ampitheatre for surgical operations. Similar additions were made in 1879 to the northwest dwelling, which since 1875 has been used by the homœopathic college. The dental school was a joint tenant of the same building from 1875 to 1877; then it occupied the southeast dwelling; and since 1891 it has held the house formerly used by the "regular" medical hospital.

What is now the north wing of University Hall was finished in 1841, and south college, the counterpart of it, was completed eight years later. Both are of brick, stuccoed. When built they were thought to be very handsome, and certainly they were equal if not superior to the generality of collegiate edifices of that day. At first these buildings were used in part as dormitories for the academic students. Each set of apartments consisted of a study, two sleeping chambers, and a room which was both a lavatory and a place of storage for luggage and wood. To each suite were assigned three and sometimes four students. Upperclassmen had the first choice of suites and generally took the highest floor. We are told that the furniture usually found in the rooms was a table or two, a lounge, a few chairs, a supply of hard-oil lamps or candlesticks, beds, occasionally a carpet, and now and then a clock. In 1856–57 the dormitories were abolished, the space they occupied being needed for other purposes.

The western part or front of the medical building, begun in 1848, was finished in the summer of 1850. It cost about nine thousand dollars, and in 1864 more than twice that sum was spent in enlarging it to its present dimensions.

In 1853–54 the astronomical observatory was built upon ground situated northeast of the campus. Citizens of Detroit contributed most of the money which went into this building. An addition to the observatory was made in 1865. The chemical laboratory, or rather the nucleus of it, was erected in 1856-57, and was enlarged in 1861, 1866, 1868, 1874, 1880, and 1890.

Thirty-five years ago was built the structure of red brick trimmed with yellow which continues to disfigure the northwestern part of the campus. Until 1872 it held the general offices, and until 1883 the library, of the University; and prior to 1872 the chapel exercises of the literary department were held in the large lecture room of its second story. Since 1883, however, the law school has had full possession of the building. In the summer of 1892 the sum of twenty-seven thousand dollars was spent in putting up an extensive addition with a tower. In March, 1898, work was begun upon a still larger addition toward the south. The tower is to be taken down, the rest of the building is to be remodelled, and there is to be an entirely new front, of which the lower story will be of light-colored stone, while the second and third story will be of pressed brick. Fifty thousand dollars will be spent upon these improvements.

University Hall, occupying the space between north college and south college, was building from 1871 to 1873, and cost $108,000. Like the wings it is of brick covered with stucco. It contains a hall capable of seating three thousand persons. In the winter vacation of 1895–96 the wooden dome was removed, and it will not be replaced until a new roof shall have been constructed.

In the rear of the north wing of the main building is the central boiler-house erected in 1879, now used for storage purposes. That same year was built the museum, a structure of red brick which cost forty-two thousand dollars, and which underwent important repairs in 1894. The library, one of the best of the buildings in the campus, was begun in 1881. It was dedicated December 12, 1883, by public exercises in University Hall, and it cost one hundred thousand dollars.

The first section, forty by eighty feet, of the engineering laboratory, was built in 1885. Another section was added in 1888 and a third in 1892, making the total expenditure fifty thousand dollars. In 1888 the physical laboratory and the anatomical laboratory were erected. New hospitals—large brick buildings near Catherine street, northeast of the campus—were finished for the two medical schools toward the close of 1891. Three years later Tappan Hall was built for the purpose of relieving the crowded class-rooms of the literary department. It cost thirty thousand dollars. In 1894 was reared the stone structure whence light and heat are supplied to the other buildings in the campus.

Of all the University buildings the one most desired by the students was the Waterman Gymnasium. The University Chronicle of October 17, 1868, said: "Each class here, within the last thirty years, has asked 'shall we ever have a gymnasium?' Faculties have promised, Regents have promised, legislatures have promised, and the people have promised, but some of those old college boys are growing gray." In April, 1869, the Regents appointed President Haven and Professor Tyler a committee "to obtain plans for the construction of a building not to cost more than $5,000;" and The Castalia for 1868-69, in its editorial welcome to the class of '72, said: "Before you graduate you will see in all likelihood, a new gymnasium completed." But it was found that the sum mentioned was inadequate; other needs of the University were deemed more pressing; and for long the gymnasium consisted of the campus itself, with two upright posts, a cross-bar, and a rope, for equipment.

UNIVERSITY HALL.

Twenty years ago the growing interest in athletic sports led to an energetic revival of the gymnasium project. A fund was started by the students, and to it were added contributions from friends of the University and the profits from football and baseball games, from college publications, from student entertainments, and from the sales of college songs. Yet the sum realized in twelve years from all sources was little more than six thousand dollars; and as aid had been sought in vain from the state, the prospect of securing a building seemed remote. In the college year 1889-90, Mr. Joshua W. Waterman, Yale '44, a prominent citizen of Detroit, who during the sixties had taken much interest in field sports at Ann Arbor, and whose son-in-law, Dr. Ernest T. Tappey, was a Michigan graduate, offered to give twenty thousand dollars to the gymnasium fund if a like sum were raised by others. This condition was met in April, 1891, and in 1894 the building was completed and opened. The sum realized from savings and subscriptions was about forty-nine thousand dollars, sixteen thousand less than the expenditure upon building and equipment. Large gifts from former Regents Hebard and Barbour, and contributions from others, have made it possible to add to the gymnasium a wing for the use of women students; but enough money to complete the interior of the new part has not been raised.

The twenty buildings owned by the University, and the arrangements for heating and lighting them, represent a total outlay of a million of dollars. An extensive addition to the library, and a separate building for the fine-art collection, have became necessary; and it is hoped that before many years shall have passed University Hall and the museum building will be replaced by structures worthy of our Alma Mater.

There are in all the libraries of the University about 123,000 bound volumes, 18,000 unbound pamphlets, and 1,400 maps. The law library contains about 14,000 volumes, and the library of the medical department has about 8,000. The libraries include special collections of great value, such as the McMillan Shakespeare library, the Parsons library of political economy, the Goethe library, and the Hagerman library of history and political science.

In the museum are collections illustrative of natural history, the industrial arts, chemistry, materia medica, archæology, ethnology, and the fine arts. The works of art belonging to the University are in galleries in the library building. Among them are the original casts of the works of the late Randolph Rogers, the six hundred paintings—some of them of considerable value—of the Lewis art collection, and many good casts from the antique.

The annual income of the University is now about $400,000,

of which amount the sum of $164,000 is derived from students' fees. The fixed income from the fund held in trust by the State and from the annual one-sixth mill tax is about a quarter of a million of dollars—equivalent to the interest, computed at five per cent, upon an endowment of $4,500,000. Yet the requirements of the institution are far in advance of its income. Money is needed for books, for buildings, for graduate scholarships, and for fellowships. A million a year could well be spent by the University; and the State of Michigan would profit by giving the University that amount to spend.

Venerable for the eighty-one years through which it has been transmitted to us, and honorable for the official connection which it implies with one of the greatest of the American sovereignties, the name of our Alma Mater has not satisfied all persons. Just as Canadians speak of "The States", a term never used by educated persons in this country, so men who should know better talk and write of "Ann Arbor University"; and the substitution of the latter title for "University of Michigan" has been advocated with apparent seriousness in the columns of an undergraduate magazine. If a short title is needed, "Michigan" suffices. The Latinized name "Universitas Michiganensium" appears in the catalogue of 1848; and diplomas awarded to graduates use the title "Universitas Reipublicæ Michiganensium". In a catalogue of the Delta Phi society the name is Latinized thus: "Universitas Michiganiensis".

The original seal of the University is rather less than two inches in diameter. It represents the Goddess of Wisdom directing the attention of an ingenuous youth to the Temple of Fame perched upon a lofty mountain; below is the explanatory legend "Minerva monstrat iter, quaque ostendit se dextra sequamur"; around the whole within concentric circles are the words "University of Michigan". This seal never was engraved for printing—at any rate no representation of it appears in the catalogues or other publications of the University—but impressed upon paper of a light-green hue it adorns thousands of diplomas. From 1858 to 1878 the coat-of-arms of the State appeared upon the cover or the title-page—frequently upon both—of the annual catalogue.

December 14, 1894, the Regents adopted an entirely new seal, an inch and three-fourths in diameter. This displays a shield charged with a lighted antique lamp set upon an open book, which itself rests upon a closed volume; below the shield, in a scroll, is the motto "Artes Scientia Veritas". For crest there is a rising sun with rays which fill the back-ground of the inner circle of the seal. The shield bears the horizontal lines that in heraldry indicate blue; and presumably the lamp and the books are intended to be of gold, thus utilizing the distinctive colors of the University. A likeness of this seal, having a diameter half an inch shorter than that of the original, has been engraved for printing, and appears upon the title-pages of the catalogues from 1895 to 1898.

Our college colors were chosen at a meeting of the literary department held in the chapel on Saturday, February 12, 1867, when Milton Jackson, '67, Albert H. Pattengill, '68, and J. Eugene Jackson, '69, the committee appointed for the purpose, reported a resolution in favor of "azure-blue and maize", which was adopted. In about ten years the colors came to be styled, as they are now styled, yellow and blue. The original blue was neither light nor very dark, and the yellow was decidedly golden. Never has there been any warrant for the sickly yellow and the faded blue furnished by some of the tradesmen of Detroit and Ann Arbor.

THE PRESIDENT'S HOUSE.

Of course the colors are made much of in all possible ways. The best of our songs is called "The Yellow and Blue", and one of the college papers had the same name. They are used in college buttons, a yellow ground with blue letters "U of M" or yellow letters in a blue field; or the letters may be blue and yellow counter-charged on a field divided by a diagonal between the colors. Minute pennants attached to stickpins and enamelled to show the colors and "U of M" or "Michigan" are often seen.

Two years after the adoption of the colors a discussion concerning college caps began. Class caps were of earlier origin. Finally, after prolonged debate, the students of the academic department—nobody dreamed in those days of consulting other students—voted by a large majority at a meeting held in the chapel, Saturday morning, November 27, 1869, to adopt a cap. Professor Williams and Acting-President Frieze strongly favored the movement, the latter declaring that a cap which he could wear without reference to changes of fashion would be most acceptable to one of his slender income. The cap selected was not the Oxford cap—the regular mortar-board. It was made of fine blue cloth, with square top, to the centre of which was attached a black tassel. Above the moveable visor were the letters U M, and just beneath them the class numeral. The failure to designate to what department the wearer belonged was soon noted, and on other grounds it was felt by not a few students that the thing desired had not been found. The caps arrived in January, 1870, and were donned by a majority of the Faculty and by many students. But the sophomores, who had previously obtained the class-caps, would not adopt the University affair, and before long those who had the latter grew tired of it. The Chronicle of November 5, 1870, said "At present it is a meaningless oddity, and, unless more generally worn, ought to be discarded entirely". In January, 1877, another cap, a genuine mortar-board, was adopted, but The Chronicle of March 3, 1877, declared "Thus far only about one-fourth of the literary students have purchased them, and the demand is on the decline". Six months later the same paper said "The Oxford Cap has already become a stranger in our streets, an early victim of the fickleness of the students' preferences".

Following the not altogether dignified custom of the students of other institutions of learning, a peculiar cheer or "yell" has been adopted—or, more accurately speaking, has been developed—by our undergraduates. According to The Chronicle of April 28, 1883, the "yell" at that date was "Rah, rah, rah! U-of-M!! rah, rah, rah, rah!!!". More dangerous to the ear, and therefore more effective, is the present cheer: U. of M., rah, rah, rah, rah! U. of M. rah, rah, rah, rah!! Hoo rah, Hoo rah, Michigan, Michigan, rah, rah, rah!!!

CHAPTER II

GRADUATES AND FORMER STUDENTS

An official list of the graduates of the University was first printed in 1848, as an appendix to the annual catalogue of that year. It is headed "Alumnorum Catalogus", and contains four classes, thus: '45, eleven men; '46, seventeen; '47, twelve; '48, sixteen; total, 56 alumni. This corresponds with the roll as published in the general catalogue of 1891, except that '45 is credited in the latter book with twelve men; Mr. W. B. Wesson making the twelfth because of his *nunc pro tunc* degree given in 1873. Of the 56 men graduated 1845-48, thirty-two have died.

The general catalogue has passed through three editions, those of 1864, 1871, and 1891; and to these should be added the admirable catalogue issued in 1880 by Theodore R. Chase, with the approval of the Board of Regents. Forty pages containing the names of 999 graduates made up the edition of 1864. Of the alumni proper, the graduates of the collegiate department, nineteen classes, from '45 to '63, with 428 members, were enrolled. The thirteen graduated classes of the medical school were credited with 363 men, and for the law school four classes and 144 graduates were given. Sixty-four graduates, forty-four of whom belonged to the literary department, were marked with the "fatal star". No account of non-graduates was taken by the general catalogue of 1864; residences were not designated; and the biographical notes were few and meagre.

The general catalogue of 1871—misnamed "Triennial"—was much like its predecessor, except that it included eight additional classes and the names of about 2,000 recent graduates. It was a pamphlet of eighty-eight pages. "The Michigan University Book" edited and published in 1880 by Theodore R. Chase of '49, is a fine volume of 400 pages. It includes the graduates of 1880, gives the names and classes of non-graduates, and presents a total of 7,542 names, the total number of graduates enrolled being about 6,000. Mr. Chase's book is especially valuable for its geographical index, a feature omitted from the general catalogue of 1891. The latter contains 472 handsomely printed octavo pages bound in cloth boards with gilt top. According to the figures of this catalogue the total number of persons (up to and including Commencement in 1890) who had received degrees was 10,127, the number of those upon whom the ordinary degrees of the collegiate department had been conferred being 2,524. A count shows that the number of non-graduates enrolled in this catalogue is about 9,400, of which total the college proper claims 2,500, the medical school 4,300, and the law school 2,050.

Thus far about 14,000 persons have been graduated from the University. The number of those who have received the ordinary collegiate degrees is 3,990. The degree of M. D. has been conferred upon 3,190 persons, that of LL. B. upon 5,765, that of Ph. C. upon 744, that of D. D. S. upon 738, that of M. D. (Homœopathic) upon 323. It would seem that the number of academic non-graduates is about equal to that of the graduates, that degrees are received by not more than forty per cent of the medical matriculates, and that about two-thirds of the law-school men finish their course. The total number of those who have received instruction in the halls of our Alma Mater is about 27,000. It is supposed that about 1,500 of the graduates have died. Edmund Fish is believed to be the sole survivor of the oldest graduated class, that of '45, George E. Parmelee, also of that class, not having been heard from for many years. Eighty-two of the 145 graduates of the first ten classes are known to have passed away.

THE HURON RIVER.

Any attempted list of those alumni and former students who have been especially prominent in the various walks of life must necessarily be both defective and invidious. The names to be dealt with are so numerous, our graduates are so widely dispersed, and changes occur so frequently, that mistakes of fact are not merely possible but certain. And even when the facts are known the problem is one of selection; a few must be chosen to represent many; and errors of judgment are inevitable. It must be remembered also that many alumni who never have held political, judicial, or educational offices, who have done little that can be summarized in print, may as successful lawyers, doctors, bankers, or manufacturers be the leaders of the communities wherein they reside. This much having been said by way of forestalling criticism, an effort will be made to name the distinguished sons of our common Alma Mater.

In the Senate of the United States the University has been represented by Adonijah S. Welch, A. B. '46, Thomas W. Palmer, '49, Cushman K. Davis, A. B. '57, Ozora P. Stearns, B. S. '58, LL. B. '60, Arthur Brown, A. M. '63, LL. B. '64, Calvin S. Brice, '67 *l*, John B. Allen, '68 *l*, and Lucien Baker, '70 *l*. Messrs. Davis and Baker are members of the present Senate. Oddly enough none of the eight served in the House before entering the other branch of the National legislature.

The following Ann Arbor men have sat or are sitting in the Federal House of Representatives: William W. Phelps, A. B. '46; J. Logan Chipman, '47; John S. Newberry, A. B. '47; Byron G. Stout, A. B. '51; Henry A. Reeves, '52; Jay A. Hubbell, A. B. '53; Jasper Packard, A. B. '55; Edwin Willits, A. B. '55; Levi T. Griffin, A. B. '57; Augustus H. Pettibone, A. B. '59; Byron M. Cutcheon, A. B. '61, LL. B. '66; Jonas H. McGowan, B. S. '61, LL. B. '68; Seth C. Moffatt, '64, LL. B. '63; Justin R. Whiting, '67; Horace G. Snover, A. B. '69, LL. B. '71; William C. Maybury, '70, LL. B. '71; Roswell P. Bishop, '72; John F. Shafroth, B. S. '75; Ben T. Cable, B. S. '76; Charles A. Towne, Ph. B. '81; John J. Lentz, A. B. '82; John B. Rice, M. D. '57; Henry F. Thomas, M. D. '68; Walter I. Hayes, LL. B. '63; John H. O'Neall, LL. B. '64; Edwin W. Keightley, LL. B. '65; James W. Owens, '66 *l*; Edward P. Allen, LL. B. '67; Adoniram J. Holmes, LL. B. '67; Samuel R. Peters, LL. B. '67; Thomas J. Wood, LL. B. '67; Marriott Brosius, LL. B. '68; William H. Harries, LL. B. '68; George Ford, LL. B. '69; S. S. Kirkpatrick, '69 *l*; John C. Tarsney, LL. B. '69; Solomon G. Comstock, '70 *l*; Melvin M. Boothman, LL. B. '71; William F. L. Hadley, LL. B. '71; James Laird, LL. B. '71; John A. Pickler, LL. B. '72; Timothy E. Tarsney, LL. B. '72; John D. White, LL. B. '72; Thomas A. E. Weadock, LL. B. '73; Nils P. Haugen, LL. B. '74; Theobald Otjen, LL. B. '75; James S. Gorman, LL. B. '76; Samuel W. Smith, LL. B. '78; Winfield S. Kerr, LL. B. '79; George D. Meiklejohn, LL. B. '80; Ferdinand Brucker, LL. B. '81; Edward E. Wilson, '81 *l*; David H. Mercer, LL. B. '82; William S. Mesick, '82 *l*; Joseph M. Kendall, '83 *l*; Edgar Wilson,

LL. B. '84; Benjamin F. Shively, LL. B. '86; William H. King, LL. B. '87; and Marion DeVries, LL. B. '88.

Two of our number—David Mills, LL. B. '67, and William F. Roome, M. D. '67—have been members of the Canadian Parliament.

In the President's Cabinet our Alma Mater has had these representatives: Edwin F. Uhl, A. B. '62, Secretary of State; Don M. Dickinson, LL. B. '67, Postmaster-General; J. Sterling Morton, '54, Secretary of Agriculture; and William R. Day, B. S. '70, the present Secretary of State. Other important posts at the national capital have been filled by the following alumni: Eugene Willits, A. B. '55, Assistant Secretary of Agriculture; George Chandler, LL. B. '66, Assistant Secretary of the Interior; George D. Meiklejohn, LL. B. '80, now Assistant Secretary of War; Bluford Wilson, '65, Solicitor of the Treasury; Charles H. Aldrich, A. B. '75, Solicitor-General of the United States, and Lawrence Maxwell, Jr., B. S. '74, his successor in the same office; Mark W. Harrington, A. B. '68, Ex-Chief of the Weather Bureau; and Henry T. Thurber, A. B. '74, President Cleveland's Private Secretary.

The following children of the University have held important positions in the diplomatic and consular service of the United States: Edwin F. Uhl, A. B. '62, Ambassador to the German Empire; Thomas W. Palmer, '49, Minister to Spain; William E. Quinby, A. B. '58, Minister to the Netherlands; Richard Beardsley, B. S. '59, Consul-General at Cairo; and William K. Anderson, A. B. '68, Consul at Hanover.

The Ann Arbor men who have been governors of states or territories, are: Thomas B. Cuming, A. B. '45, Acting Governor of Nebraska, 1856-58; Cushman K. Davis, A. B. '57, Governor of Minnesota, 1874-76; Lyman U. Humphrey, '68 *l*, Governor of Kansas, 1889-93; Ridgley C. Powers, '63, Military Governor of Mississippi, 1871-74. Although the chief magistracy of Michigan has not yet been exercised by any graduate (O. M. Barnes, A. B. '50, having been defeated by his Republican opponent in the election of 1877), yet the office of Lieutenant-Governor has been held by Dwight May, A. B. '49, and by Thomas B. Dunstan, '73 *l*, both former students at Ann Arbor; and State Senator Joseph R. McLaughlin, B. S. '77, recently acted as Lieutenant-Governor. Henry A. Conant, '65, was Michigan's Secretary of State, 1883-87. Edward H. Butler, '61, Benjamin D. Pritchard, '62 *l*, and James M. Wilkinson, '64, LL. B. '64, have all served Michigan as State

Treasurers. William C. Stevens, LL. B. '68, was Auditor General, 1883-87, and the post of Attorney-General of Michigan has been held by Dwight May, A. B. '49, Fred A. Maynard, A. B. '74, LL. B. '76, S. V. R. Trowbridge, '76, Byron D. Ball, LL. B. '61, Isaac Marston, LL. B. '61, Jacob J. VanRiper, '62 *l*, and Moses Taggart, LL. B. '67. The alumni who have held like offices in other states are too numerous to mention. Among the alumni to whom large cities have turned for good government are Isaac M. Weston, '67, formerly Mayor of Grand Rapids, William C. Maybury, '70, LL. B. '71, now Mayor of Detroit, and Cyrus P. Walbridge, LL. B. '74, recently Mayor of St. Louis.

Our University has trained nearly a score of college presidents, including Charles Kendall Adams, A. B. '61, formerly at the head of Cornell University, but now the President of the University of Wisconsin; Harry B. Hutchins, Ph. B. '71, Acting President of the University of Michigan; Austin Scott, A. M. '70, President of Rutgers College; Lewis R. Fiske, A. B. '50, President of Albion College, 1877-97; Mark W. Harrington, A. B. '68, recently President of the University of Washington, over which institution William F. Edwards, B. S. '90, now presides; Henry Wade Rogers, A. B. '74, President of Northwestern University; George G. Groff, '78, President of Bucknell University, 1888-89, and now in the Faculty there; Hosmer A. Johnson, A. B. '49, late President of the Chicago Medical College; Adonijah S. Welch, A. B. '46, Edwin Willits, A. B. '55, Lewis McLouth, A. B. '58, and Oscar Clute, '67, all of whom have governed agricultural colleges; Park S. Donelson, A. B. '49, now deceased, President of the Ohio Wesleyan Female College; and Mrs. Alice Freeman Palmer, A. B. '76, President of Wellesley College, 1881-87.

PRESIDENT HAVEN.

Of course our Alma Mater has drawn heavily upon her own sons to fill her Faculties, until many of the leading chairs are occupied by men who formerly were students here. Without attempting to give a complete list these may be named: Alfred DuBois, A. B. '48, Assistant Professor of Chemistry, 1857-63; Edward P. Evans, A. B. '54, Professor of Modern Languages and Literature, 1863-70; Levi T. Griffin, A. B. '57, Fletcher Professor of Law, 1886-97; James C. Watson, A. B. '57, Professor of Astronomy, 1863-79;

Bradley M. Thompson, A. B. '58, Jay Professor of Law since 1888; Charles Kendall Adams, A. B. '61, Professor of History, 1865-85; Martin L. D'Ooge, A. B. '62, Professor of the Greek Language and Literature since 1870: Joseph B. Davis, C. E. '68, now Professor of Geodesy and Surveying; Isaac N. Demmon, A. B.'68, Professor of English and Rhetoric since 1871; Mark W. Harrington, A. B. '68, Professor of Astronomy, 1889-93; Albert H. Pattengill, A. B. '68, Professor of Greek since 1889; Joseph B. Steere, A. B '68, Professor of Zoölogy since 1881; Edward L. Walter, A. B. '68, Professor of Romance Languages and Literatures since 1887; Wooster W. Beman, A. B. '70, Professor of Mathematics since 1887; Richard Hudson, A. B. '71, Professor of History since 1888, and Dean of the Literary Faculty since 1897; William J. Herdman, Ph. B. '72, Professor of Practical Anatomy since 1888; Volney M. Spalding, A. B. '73, Professor of Botany since 1886; Victor H. Lane, C. E. '74, LL. B. '78, Professor of Law since 1897; Jerome C. Knowlton, A. B. '75, LL. B. '78, Marshall Professor of Law since 1889; Victor C. Vaughan, M. S. '75, M. D. '78, Professor of Hygiene and Physiological Chemistry; Alexis C. Angell, A. B. '78, Professor of Law; George Hempl, A. B. '79, now Junior Professor of English; Andrew C. McLaughlin, A. B. '82, now Professor of American History; Jacob E. Reighard, Ph. B. '82, now Professor of Zoölogy; Fred N. Scott, A. B. '84, now Junior Professor of Rhetoric; Joseph H. Drake, A. B. '85, now Assistant Professor of Latin; John O. Reed, Ph. B. '85, Assistant Professor of Physics; Edward D. Campbell, B. S. '86, now Junior Professor of Analytical Chemistry; Frederick G. Novy, B. S. '86, Junior Professor of Hygiene and Analytical Chemistry; Fred M. Taylor, Ph. D. '88, Junior Professor of Political Economy and Finance; Dean C. Worcester, A. B. '89, Assistant Professor of Zoölogy; Frederick C. Newcombe, B. S. '90, Assistant Professor of Botany; George E. Frothingham, M. D. '64, Professor of Materia Medica, etc., 1880-89; Albert B. Prescott, M. D. '64, Professor of Organic Chemistry since 1874; Oscar LeSeure, M. D. '73, Professor of Surgery in the Homœopathic College; Eliza M. Mosher, M. D. '75, Professor of Hygiene, and Women's Dean in the Literary Department; G. Carl Huber, M. D. '87, Assistant Professor of Histology; Thomas A. Bogle, LL. B. '88, now Professor of Law; Elias F. Johnson, LL. B. '90, Professor of Law; Otis C. Johnson, Ph. C. '71, Professor of Applied Chemistry; Alviso B. Stevens, Ph. C. '75, Assistant Professor of Pharmacy; Roy S. Copeland, M. D. '89,

Professor in the Homœopathic Medical College; and William H. Dorrance, D. D. S. '79, Professor in the Dental School.

How vast a debt the educational interests of our country owe to Michigan may be learned by reading the roll of those whom our University has sent to teach in other halls of learning. From Maine to California, from Cambridge to Berkeley, there is hardly a prominent college in which Michigan instructors are not found. Following is a partial list: Edmund Andrews, A. B. '49, for many years Professor of Surgery in the Chicago Medical College; Alexander Martin, A. B. '55, Dean of the Law Department of the University of Missouri; John E. Clark, A. B. '56, Professor of Mathematics at Yale College; Moses Coit Tyler, '56, Professor of English Literature at Cornell University; William J. Beal, A. B. '59, Professor of Botany in the Michigan Agricultural College; Volney G. Barbour, '64, Professor of Civil Engineering in the University of Vermont; Gabriel Campbell, A. B. '65, Professor of Philosophy in Dartmouth College; Amos E. Dolbear, M. E. '67, Professor of Physics and Astronomy in Tufts College; Willard B. Rising, M. E. '67, Professor of Chemistry in the University of California; Francis A. Blackburn, A. B. '68, Professor of English in the University of Chicago; John C. Freeman, A. B. '68, Professor of English Literature in the University of Wisconsin; Bernard Moses, Ph. B. '70, Professor of History and Political Economy in the University of California; S. Robertson Winchell, A. B. '70, Professor of Latin in the University of Illinois; Edwin L. Mark, A. B. '71, Professor of Anatomy in Harvard University; John B. Webb, C. E. '71, Professor of Mathematics and Mechanics in Stevens Institute; Charles L. Doolittle, C. E. '73, Professor of Astronomy in the University of Pennsylvania; Mrs. Mary Sheldon Barnes, A. B. '74, Assistant Professor of History in Leland Stanford, Jr., University; Calvin Thomas, A. B. '74, Professor of German in Columbia University; Rolla C. Carpenter, C. E. '75, Professor of Experimental Mechanics in Cornell University; Angie C. Chapin, A. B. '75, Professor of Greek in Wellesley College; A. V. E. Young, A. B. '75, Professor of Chemistry in Northwestern University; Archibald L. Daniels, A. B. '76, Professor of Mathematics in the University of Vermont; John F. Downey, '76, Professor of Mathematics and Astronomy in the University of Minnesota; William P. Durfee, A. B. '76, Professor of Mathematics in Hobart College, and Dean of the Faculty of the same institution; Lucy M. Salmon, A. B. '76, Professor of History in

Vassar College; John M. Schaeberle, C. E. '76, Astronomer of the Lick Observatory; George C. Comstock, Ph. B. '77, Professor of Astronomy in the University of Wisconsin; Mary E. Byrd, A. B. '78, Director of the Smith College Observatory; Eva Chandler, A. B. '78, Associate Professor of Mathematics in Wellesley College; Charles M. Gayley, A. B. '78, Professor of English Literature in the University of California; Jeremiah W. Jenks, A. B. '78, Professor of Political Economy in Cornell University; George W. Knight, A. B. '78, Professor of History and Political Economy in Ohio State University; Charles C. Brown, C. E. '79, Professor of Civil Engineering in Union College; Edward M. Brown, Ph. B. '80, Professor of Modern Languages and Literature in the University of Cincinnati; Katharine E. Coman, Ph. B. '80, Professor of History and Economics in Wellesley College; Willis Boughton, A. B. '81, Professor of English Literature in Ohio University; Carl W. Belser, A. B. '82, Professor of Latin in the University of Colorado; Douglas H. Campbell, Ph. M. '82, Professor of Botany in Leland Stanford, Jr., University; John J. Abel, A. B. '83, Professor in Johns Hopkins University; Lewis A. Rhoades, A. B. '84, Professor of German in the University of Illinois; Louis M. Dennis, Ph. B. '85, Associate Professor of Analytical Chemistry in Cornell University; Alexander F. Lange, A. M. '85, Associate Professor of English Philology in the University of California; Charles W. Dodge, B. S. '86, Professor of Biology in the University of Rochester; Lawrence A. McLouth, A. B. '87, Professor of German in New York University; Robert B. Moore, Ph. B. '87, Professor of Modern Languages in Colgate University; Pomeroy Ladue, B. S. '90, Professor of Mathematics in New York University; Robert C. Kedzie, M. D. '51, Professor of Chemistry in the Agricultural College since 1863; Charles Ambrook, M. D. '70, Professor of the Theory and Practice of Medicine in the University of Colorado; Laureston A. Merriam, M. D. '73, Professor of the Principles and Practice of Medicine in the University of Nebraska; George E. Morrow, LL. B. '66,

MEDICAL BUILDING.

Dean of the College of Agriculture of the University of Illinois; David Mills, LL. B. '67, Professor of International and Constitutional Law in the University of Toronto; Marshall D. Ewell, LL. B. '68, Professor in the Union College of Law, Chicago; Arthur L. Green, Ph. C. '72, Professor of Chemistry in Purdue University; Maurice J. Sullivan, D. D. S. '80, Professor of Dental Pathology and Therapeutics in the University of California; and Byron S. Palmer, D. D. S. '83, Professor of Dental Techniques in Northwestern University.

The list of our alumni who have been prominent in educational work by no means ends with those who have taught in college halls. The following graduates have been or are Presidents of State Normal Schools: William H. Beadle, A. B. '61: Edward Searing, A. B. '61; George S. Albee, A. B. '64; and John J. Mapel, A. B. '72. Herschel R. Gass, A. B. '73, was Superintendent of Public Instruction in Michigan from 1882 to 1885, as was Henry R. Pattengill from 1892 to 1896. Walter S. Perry, A. B. '61, was Superintendent of Schools at Ann Arbor from 1870 until his death in 1897. Duane Doty, A. B. '56, was for many years Superintendent of Schools in Detroit and Chicago. Cornelius A. Gower, A. B. '67, has been Superintendent of Public Instruction and also Superintendent of the State Reform School at Lansing. Among those who are prominent in the work of secondary education, the following may be named: George L. Maris, '67, Principal of the George School at Newtown, Pennsylvania; Charles A. Cook, A. B. '71, Principal of the Jefferson High School, Chicago; Judson G. Pattengill, A. B. '73, Principal of the Ann Arbor High School; Theodore H. Johnston, A. B. '74, Principal of the West Side High School, Cleveland; Albert J. Volland, A. B. '76, Principal of the Grand Rapids High School; Frederick L. Bliss, A. B. '77, Principal of the Detroit High School; Lawrence C. Hull, A. B. '77, Principal of the Lawrenceville School; James H. Norton, B. L. '82, Principal of the Lake View High School; Avon S. Hall, A. B. '84, Principal of the Calumet High School; and William A. McAndrew, A. B. '86, Principal of the Hyde Park High School.

The following librarians are graduates of Michigan: Hamilton J. Dennis, A. B. '58, State Librarian of Kansas; Henry M. Utley, A. B. '61, City Librarian of Detroit; Charles E. Lowrey, A. B. '77, Librarian of the University of Colorado; James P. Dunn, LL. B. '76, State Librarian of Indiana; and Raymond C. Davis, '59, Librarian of our University.

Hiram A. Burt, A. B. '62, was the first alumnus to become a member of the Board of Regents, to which body the constitution of Michigan entrusts the government of the University. Since his election in 1867, thirty others have been elected or appointed to seats in the Board, of whom the following have been students in the University: Jonas H. McGowan, B. S. '61, LL. B. '68, 1870–77; Claudius B. Grant, A. B. '59, 1872–79; Charles Rynd, M. D. '59, 1872–79; Byron M. Cutcheon, A. B. '61, LL. B. '66, 1876–83; Samuel S. Walker, B. S. '61, 1876–83; Jacob J. VanRiper, '62 *l*, 1880–86; Lyman D. Norris, '45, 1883–84; Charles J. Willett, A. B. '71, 1884–91; Charles R. Whitman, A. B. '70, LL. B. '73, 1886–93; Charles S. Draper, A. B. '63, 1887-92; Roger W. Butterfield, LL. B. '68, since 1888; William J. Cocker, A. B. '69, since 1890; Peter N. Cook, LL. B. '74, since 1891; Levi L. Barbour, A. B. '63, LL. B. '65, 1892–97; and Frank W. Fletcher, Ph. B. '75, since 1893. So it appears that of the thirty-one members chosen during the past thirty years, sixteen are sons of our Alma Mater.

Among the distinguished clergymen who have studied in our University the following may be named: David M. Cooper, A. B. '48, of Detroit; Justin D. Fulton, '52, S. T. D., of Brooklyn; the late Tillman C. Trowbridge, A. B. '52, for many years a missionary in Turkey; Edward G. Thurber, A. B. '57, Pastor of the American Chapel at Paris; William J. Darby, A. B. '69, one of the leaders of the Cumberland Presbyterian Church; Edward A. Horton, '69, of the Old South Church, Boston; and Joseph M. Gelston, A. B. '69, of Ann Arbor.

In the Federal Judiciary the University is represented by William B. Gilbert, LL. B. '72, Circuit Judge, and by Henry H. Swan, '62, William Story, LL. B. '64, and John A. Riner, LL. B. '79, District Judges. Of the Supreme Court of Michigan the following graduates have been Chief Justices: Claudius B. Grant, A. B. '59; Isaac Marston, LL. B. '61; Frank A. Hooker, LL. B. '65, and John W. McGrath, LL. B. '68; and Joseph B. Moore, '68 *l*, is one of the Associate Justices. In the Supreme Courts of other states and of the territories the following has been our representation: Albert H. Horton, '60, Chief Justice, Kansas; Theophilus L. Norval, LL. B. '71, Chief Justice, Nebraska; William Story, LL. B. '64, Chief Justice, Arkansas; John B. Cassoday, '57, Chief Justice, Wisconsin; Thomas Burke, and Thomas J. Anders, LL. B. '61, Chief '74, Justices, Washington; John C. Shields,

LL. B. '72, Chief Justice, Arizona; Timothy E. Howard, '59, and Allen Zollers, LL. B. '66, Associate Justices, Indiana; James H. Cartwright, LL. B. '67, and Joseph N. Carter, LL. B. '68, Associate Justices, Illinois; LaVega G. Kinne, LL. B. '68, Associate Justice, Iowa; James E. Riddick, LL. B, '72, Associate Justice, Arkansas; Orlando M. Powers, LL. B. '71, Associate Justice, Utah; William H. Barnes, A. B. '65, Associate Justice, Arizona; Charles N. Potter, LL. B. '73, Associate Justice, Wyoming; and Alexander Martin, A. B. '55, Judge of the Supreme Court Commission of Missouri.

The following, all graduates or former students of the University, have been or are Circuit Judges in Michigan: Jay A. Hubbell, A. B. '53; Jared Patchin, A. B. '53; James B. Eldredge, A. B. '55; William D. Williams, B. S. '57; John J. Speed, '58; Robert E. Frazer, B. S. '59, LL. B. '61; Claudius B. Grant, A. B. '59; Orville W. Coolidge, A. B. '63; Edward D. Kinne, A. B. '64; Herman W. Stevens, A. B. '66, LL. B. '68; Aaron V. McAlvay, '68, LL. B. '69; Frank Emerick, '70, '75 *l*; Victor H. Lane, C. E. '74, LL. B. '78; George S. Hosmer, A. B. '75; James B. McMahon, Ph. B. '75; Joseph H. Steere, A. B. '76; Norman W. Haire, A. B. '80, LL. B. '85; Dan J. Arnold, LL. B. '61; Levi L. Wixson, LL. B. '62; Henry Hart, LL. B. '65; Frank A. Hooker, LL. B. '65; Clement Smith, '67 *l*; Richmond W. Melendy, '67 *l*; Philip T. VanZile, LL. B. '67; George P. Cobb, LL. B. '68; Robert J. Kelley, LL. B. '68; Joseph B. Moore, '68*l*; Charles H. Wisner, LL. B. '71; John A. Edget, LL. B. '72; Silas S. Fallass, LL. B. '72; George Gartner, LL. B. '72; Luke S. Montague, LL. B. '72; Stearns F. Smith, LL. B. '73; John H. Palmer, '74 *l*; Rollin H. Person, '74 *l*; George W. Smith, '75 *l*; Peter F. Dodds, '76 *l*; William L. Carpenter, LL. B. '78; Samuel W. Vance, '78 *l*; Robert B. McKnight, LL. B. '79; Roscoe L. Corbett, LL. B. '80; and John W. Stone, '86 *l*. The late Lyman Cochrane, A. B. '49, and the late J. Logan Chipman, '47, were Judges of the Superior Court of De-

ASTRONOMICAL OBSERVATORY.

troit, and Edwin A. Burlingame, LL. B. '69, is Judge of the Superior Court of Grand Rapids.

It is not altogether uninteresting to note that our University claims three of the five Justices of the Supreme Court of the State (including the Chief Justice), twenty-two of the thirty-five Circuit Judges, and a considerable majority of the probate Judges.

Space fails for the recording here of all of our graduates who in other states have served as judges in courts not of last resort. The roll is long, and contains the names of many who soon will be sitting in courts of final jurisdiction. Suffice it to mention Alfred Spring, '74, of the Supreme Court of New York; John E. McKeighan, A. B. '66, of St. Louis, Missouri; Morris L. Buchwalter, '69, of Cincinnati; Carroll C. Boggs, '66, of the Circuit Court of Illinois; and John A. Shauck, LL. B. '67, Judge of the Second Judicial Circuit of Ohio.

It is impossible to name here more than a few of the alumni and former students who have become distinguished in the active practice of the law. Many of these are mentioned elsewhere in this book, and need not be recalled now. The following list, which includes no graduates of classes later than '76, is suggestive merely: Sidney D. Miller, A. B. '48, William A. Moore, A. B. '50, Henry M. Cheever, A. B. '53, Ashley Pond, A. B. '54, Levi T. Griffin, A. B. '57, Browse T. Prentis, A. B. '58, Henry M. Duffield, '61, Hoyt Post, A. B. '62, LL. B. '63, John Atkinson, LL. B. '62, Levi L. Barbour, A. B. '63, LL. B. '65, Don M. Dickinson, LL. B. '67, Edward E. Kane, A. B. '67, Charles F. Burton, A. B. '70, LL. B. '72, Harlow P. Davock, B. S. '70, the late George H. Lothrop, '70, Edwin F. Conely, '71 *l*, Charles K. Latham, LL. B. '72, Frank D. Andrus, A. B. '72, LL. B. '79, Edward W. Pendleton, A. B. '72, Samuel T. Douglas, Ph. B. '73, Henry Russel, A. B. '73, LL. B. '75, and George Whitney Moore, '73 *l*, of the bar of Detroit; Dan H. Ball, '60, of Marquette; Edwin F. Uhl, A. B. '62, William J. Stuart, A. B. '68, LL. B. '72, Moses Taggart, LL. B. '67, and Loyal E. Knappen, A. B. '73, of Grand Rapids; Edgar A. Cooley, A. B. '72, of Bay City; William B. Williams, A. B. '73, of Lapeer; O'Brien J. Atkinson, LL. B. '60, of Port Huron; Orlando M. Barnes, A. B. '50, and Samuel L. Kilbourne, LL. B. '60, of Lansing; Henry H. Barlow, A. B. '70, of Coldwater; Frederick L. Geddes, A. B. '72, Barton Smith, B. S. '72, and George P. Voorheis, A. B. '72, of Toledo; Lawrence Maxwell, Jr., '74, of Cincinnati; the late James M. Walker, A. B. '46, H.

H. C. Miller, A. B. '68, William H. Barnum, '61, Sidney C. Eastman, A. B. '73, Charles H. Aldrich, A. B. '75, James L. High, LL. B. '66, and M. D. Ewell, LL. B. '68, all of Chicago; Joseph V. Quarles, A. B. '66, Charles Quarles, '68, and Charles H. Hamilton, B. S. '69, of Milwaukee; Oliver H. Dean, A. B. '68, LL. B. '70, and Homer Reed, A. B. '72, of Kansas City; Charles L. Buckingham, C. E. '75, of New York; Melvin M. Bigelow, A. B. '66, of Boston; Walter S. Harsha, A. B. '71, of Detroit, Clerk of the Circuit Court of the United States for the Eastern District of Michigan; Darius J. Davison, A. B. '54, Clerk of the United States District Court for that District; and Charles C. Hopkins, LL. B. '76, Clerk of the Supreme Court of Michigan.

Not a few of the eminent physicians educated by the University have been named in the lists of college presidents and professors. Others follow: The late Edmund P. Christian, A. B. '47, of Wyandotte; Samuel P. Duffield, A. B. '54, the late Henry F. Lyster, A. B. '58, M. D. '60, Theodore A. McGraw, A. B. '59, the late D. O. Farrand, '62, James B. Book, '64 *m*, John D. Mulheron, M. D. '69, David Inglis, '70, Hal C. Wyman, M. D. '73, Howard Longyear, '75 *m*, and Rolin C. Olin, M. D. '77, all of Detroit; Samuel A. McWilliams, A. B. '61, of Chicago; Henry M. Hurd, A. B. '63, M. D. '66, now Superintendent of John Hopkins Hospital; James D. Munson, M. D. '73, Medical Superintendent of the Northern Michigan Asylum for the Insane; and Edward A. Christian, A. B. '79, M. D. '82, Superintendent of the Eastern Michigan Asylum for the Insane.

Many names familiar in science have been mentioned in the lists of college professors already given. To those may be added Asaph Hall, '60, Director of the United States Naval Observatory; Newton H. Winchell, A. B. '66, State Geologist of Minnesota; Charles F. Brush, M. E. '69, inventor of the electric arc-light which bears his name; Marcus Baker, A. B. '70, Geologist of the United States Geological Survey; and Robert S. Woodward, C. E. '72, Astronomer of that survey.

William E. Quinby, A. B. '58, of the Detroit Free Press; Almon L. Aldrich, B. S. '60, of the Flint Globe; James H. Goodsell, '62, President of the National Associated Press; Charles M. Goodsell, A. B. '65, of the Daily Graphic; Abram J. Aldrich, A. B. '65, Editor of the Coldwater Republican; Isaac M. Weston, '67, of the Grand Rapids Democrat; Stanley Waterloo, '69, of Chicago; Lucien Swift, M. E. '69, Manager of the

Minneapolis Evening Journal; and Newton McMillan, A. B. '79, Associate Editor of the Chicago Evening Post, are a few of the representatives of the University in journalism.

Among the bankers who spent their college days at Ann Arbor the following may be named: the late William B. Wesson, '44, Edward H. Butler, '61, Joseph C. Hart, A. B. '64, William A. Butler, B. S. '69, Hamilton Dey, Ph. B. '72, and Edwin F. Mack, A. B. '83, all of Detroit; George R. Gibson, '74, of New York; Luther Mendenhall, A. B. '60, of Duluth; James J. Hagerman, B. S. '61, of Colorado Springs; Oliver P. Dickinson, A. B. '66, of Kansas City; William N. Ladue, A. B. '60, of Salem, Oregon, and Archibald B. Darragh, A. B. '68, of Allegheny City. Jacob L. Greene, '61, President of the Connecticut Mutual Life Insurance Company, and Schuyler Grant, A. B. '64, General Agent for Michigan of the Mutual Life Insurance Company of New York, represent the University in insurance circles. Henry W. Ashley, A. B. '79, General Manager of the Ann Arbor Railroad, Charles B. Lamborn, A. B. '58, Land Commissioner of the Northern Pacific Railroad, Horace G. Burt, '73, President of the Northern Pacific, and James D. Hawks, '70, of Detroit, are types of the alumni who are interested in railroad matters. The Michigan roll embraces also such merchants, manufacturers, and business men as Eugene F. Cooley, A. B. '70, of Lansing; Charles A. Rust, B. S. '71, of Saginaw; Francis D. Bennett, '72, of Jackson; George H. Hopkins, '73, LL. B. '71, formerly Collector of Customs at Detroit; and Franklin H. Walker, B. S. '73, Charles H. Jacobs, A. B. '75, Walter S. Russel, C. E. '75, John H. Avery, Ph. C. '77, Frederick K. Stearns, '77, William C. Johnson, Ph. B. '78, and William H. Murphy, '79, all of Detroit.

T. W. PALMER, '49.

Nearly six hundred former students of the University were enlisted in the federal armies during the Civil War. Of these the only one who attained the rank of Brigadier General was a non-graduate of the collegiate department, Elon J. Farnsworth, '59. He was killed at Gettysburg. The following, sixteen in all, acquired the rank of Colonel: Dwight May, A. B. '49; Edward Bacon, A. B. '50; Jasper Packard, A. B. '55; William W. Wheeler, A. B. '56;

Frank Askew, B. S. '58; John W. Horner, A. B. '58; Ozora P. Stearns, B. S. '58; Charles F. Taylor, '59; Arthur T. Wilcox, A. B. '59; Byron M. Cutcheon, A. B. '61; Isaac H. Elliott, A. B. '61; William T. Frohock, '61; George D. Robinson, B. S. '62; James H. Kidd, '64; Norval E. Welch, LL. B. '60; and Henry H. Jefferds, LL. B. '61. Nearly all of these, and several Lieutenant-Colonels, were rewarded by the brevet rank of Brigadier-General.

Recapitulating the lists that have been presented we find that the roll of Michigan students includes eight Senators of the United States, fifty-nine Representatives in Congress, four Cabinet Ministers, three Assistant Secretaries (Interior, War, Agriculture), two Solicitors-General of the United States, one Ambassador, two Envoys Extraordinary and Envoys Plenipotentiary, one Consul-General, four Governors of Territories or States, one Federal Circuit Judge, three Federal District Judges, eleven Chief Justices and eleven Associate Justices of State or Territorial Supreme Courts, forty-two Judges of the Circuit Courts of Michigan, fifteen Presidents of Colleges, forty-two Professors in the Faculty at Ann Arbor, sixty-three Professors in important colleges, one Brigadier-General, and sixteen Colonels.

Forty years ago an organization somewhat informal in its nature was effected by the alumni of the literary department. On the 26th of June, 1860, a constitution was adopted for the society, which thenceforth was known as "The Association of Alumni of the University of Michigan". According to the preamble of the constitution the objects of the Association were "the improvement of its members, the perpetuation of pleasant associations, the promotion of the interests of the University, and through that of the interests of higher education in general". In June, 1875, the Association was superseded by an incorporated organization "The Society of Alumni of the University of Michigan", which had been formed in July of the preceding year. Notwithstanding the general name, membership is restricted to graduates of the collegiate department. Merchant H. Goodrich, '45, was the President of the literary alumni from 1859 to 1860, and his successor was Datus C. Brooks, '56. Among later presidents have been Charles W. Noble, '46, Lieutenant-Governor Dwight May, '49, Thomas W. Palmer, '49, O. M. Barnes, '50, William A. Moore, '50, Ashley Pond, '53, Charles Kendall Adams, '61, Martin L. D'Ooge, '62, Levi L. Barbour, '63, E. D. Kinne, '64, and William J. Cocker, '69. The most important business of the literary alumni has related to the thrice unfortunate "Williams Professorship Fund", which was started for the purpose of providing for the venerable Professor Williams. For the business meeting of the Society the morning of Alumni Day, the day preceding Commencement, is set apart, and the literary exercises, consisting of an oration and poem, are held in University Hall on the afternoon of the same day.

An association of the graduates of the law school was formed on the 29th of March, 1871. The society held its first reunion at Cook's Hotel, Ann Arbor, on the evening of Tuesday, March 26, 1872. Isaac Marston, '61, was the first president, and among his successors have been Byron D. Ball, '61, Byron M. Cutcheon, '66, George H. Hopkins, '71, George W. Moore, '73, and other well-known graduates.

Before many years all of the departments had graduate associations of their own. It must be admitted that the interest taken in these organizations was perfunctory. The annual meetings and literary exercises were poorly attended, and little enthusiasm was displayed. In view of these facts—which however are equally true of all other universities—it was decided to unite the societies; and on the day before Commencement in 1897 the consolidation was affected. "The Alumni Association of the University of Michigan" as the amalgamated society is called, has a Board of five Directors. The President is Levi L. Barbour, '63. All persons who have received degrees or who have been recommended for degrees from the University are members, and any person who has been in attendance in any department for a period of not less than one year may be elected as an associate member after the expiration of four years from such year of resident study.

One of the earliest efforts, perhaps the earliest effort, to organize a local association of alumni was made in Detroit, where, April 7, 1869, at the office of Wilkinson & Post, a meeting was held for the purpose of combining in one society the graduates residing in the chief city of Michigan. This meeting formed the "Michigan University Club of Detroit", with E. B. Wight, '57, as President, Levi T. Griffin, '57, as Vice-President, Duane Doty, '56, as Corresponding Secretary, W. A. Green, '58, as Recording Secretary, Darius J. Davison, '54, as Treasurer, and Henry F. Lyster, '58, Browse Prentis, '58, and Theodore A. McGraw, '59, as Directors. Notwithstanding this formidable array of officers the organization never enjoyed a very vigorous existence, and before long it became a memory. Once in a decade or so an attempt was made to start a new society in Detroit, but the nearness of the city to Ann Arbor seemed to render organized effort less necessary or less popular than in more distant localities. What promises to be a permanently successful society was organized on the last day of October, 1895. It is called "The University of Michigan Alumni Association of Detroit", and has already held two successful reunions. William E. Quinby, '58, is the present presiding officer.

Beginning in 1869 three attempts have been made to establish or revive a society of Michigan's alumni in the city of Chicago. James M. Walker, '46, was the first President of this organization, which in 1887 was incorporated under the laws of Illinois. During the past decade the Chicago Graduate Association has been unceasing in its efforts to promote the interests of the University. It established the Chicago concerts of the University Glee and Banjo Clubs; it arranged for the presentation in Chicago by Michigan students of a Latin play; it founded the annual football contest between the elevens of Michigan and Chicago; it contributed largely to the Waterman Gymnasium; it paid for two years the salary of a coach for the football team; and it founded a medal and testimonial for the winners in the annual oratorical contest at Ann Arbor.

CHEMICAL LABORATORY.

December 7, 1876, "The Ann Arbor Club of the Pacific Slope" was formed, and three weeks later forty alumni members had a reunion dinner in the Palace Hotel, San Francisco. The alumni in Grand Rapids organized an association in 1877. Two years afterwards the New England Alumni Association was instituted. On the 17th of March, 1882, the alumni in New York gave a dinner at Delmonico's to Judge Thomas M. Cooley, and constituted themselves into a society, and fourteen days later the graduates in Cleveland held a reunion which was followed by the usual feast. An association was formed at Minneapolis in 1883, with N. H. Winchell, '66, as the first President.

On the 18th of February, 1885, a meeting was held at Willard's Hotel in Washington, for the purpose of forming a permanent organization of the alumni residing at the national capital. After articles of association had been adopted, the fifty alumni partook of a dinner over which the first President of the Association, Senator Thomas W. Palmer, presided. In response to the first toast "The University", Professor Charles Kendall Adams spoke concerning the part of the University of Michigan in the work of higher education. The activity of the Washington alumni has been continuous and successful; and the annual dinner is attended by nearly all of the many congressmen who claim Michigan as their Alma Mater.

"The Central Michigan Alumni Association", with headquarters at Battle Creek, was formed in 1885. It has had several reunions. In 1887 the University of Michigan Alumni Association of Colorado was organized. The second annual reunion of that society was held March 27, 1888. In 1889 a graduate association was formed in Kansas City. During the present decade alumni clubs have been founded in Buffalo, St. Louis, Milwaukee, Macomb County (Michigan), Saginaw, and elsewhere. It is believed that the cause of the University will be strengthened greatly by these organizations.

CHAPTER III

THE DEPARTMENTS

From the opening of the University in September, 1841, until the organization of the Medical Department in 1850, all the students were united in the pursuit of academic studies. Had the conditions precedent to the study of medicine been made as rigorous as those imposed upon would-be matriculates in the college proper, and had the time required for graduation been the same in both, it is possible that the two branches would have stood from the first upon an equal plane in popular opinion and in student esteem. But with slight requisites for admission, and with only two years—those years of six instead of nine months as in the collegiate department—it was impossible for medical students as such to receive much consideration from their fellow matriculates on the other side of the campus. With the opening of the law school in 1859, the difference between the so-called "lits" and the "professionals" was accented rather than diminished. As the requirements for admission to the law department were nominal, and as the term examinations were by no means rigid, that seat of learning became a retreat for academic students and others who desired to enjoy the advantages of university life without labor of preparation or of daily study. Thus it happened that in addition to the large number of college graduates and of other well-equipped students to be found in the law classes, were men who never should have been matriculated, and whose conduct was not invariably creditable to the University. Moreover the professional school undergraduates of a generation ago paid less attention than their literary comrades paid, or than their own successors pay, to matters of dress and address. But whatever the reasons, the students in the college proper used to look upon "laws" and "medics" as creatures of an inferior mold.

During the interval between the departure of President Haven and the inauguration of President Angell literary prejudice against the professional students was at its height. University Day had its origin in a resolution passed by the University Senate at the instance of Judge Cooley in 1868, and the express object of it was to consolidate friendly relations between the departments; but before the arrival of the date set for the first celebration disputes arose about the order of the different schools in the procession, and about the selection of the chief officer of the day. Finally it was decided that medicine should precede law, and that literature should follow both. Orson W. Tock, '70 *m*, was chosen grand marshal. Notwithstanding the preliminary controversies the first University Day, November 17, 1869, was very successful. The public was impressed by the parade, and the University profited by the attention the affair attracted. For the second celebration, November 9, 1870, Preston C. Hudson, '71, was elected grand marshal. The order of march was law, literature, and medicine. Unfortunate arrangement! As the procession was returning from the exercises—which were held in one of the city churches—that part of the legal contingent in which was carried the beautiful blue-silk banner of the department came by some strange tactical evolution in contact with the under-class "lits". A wild "rush" followed; many combatants lost collars, cuffs, and even more important parts of their raiment; and the banner of the law was sadly torn. Betaking themselves to their lecture-room the law students made many fiery speeches, and adopted a series of incendiary resolutions. A third University Day was not attempted. Speaking of the departed celebration The Chronicle said "We doubt if a real, genuine, University feeling can ever be established, however desirable it may be. The ties are too slight by which the professional school men who constitute a majority in the University are bound to the institution, their connection with it too slight, to inspire any great enthusiasm. The connection between the three departments exists more in name than in reality".

LAW BUILDING, 1863–98.

A great passage at arms between literature and medicine occurred November 9, 1872. For that day a game of football between academic freshmen and sophomores had been scheduled, and the medical students determined to play at the same time on the same ground. A meeting was held the evening before, and the medical students decided to wear, as an appropriate badge of the department, a red ribbon around either their wrists or their necks, and to put off the ground every person not so distinguished. Without any such organizing by the college men the two parties assembled in the northeastern part of the campus. The doctors tried to play, but the noise and the confusion were too great. Then the literary boys challenged them to play football just as they were. They refused. A crowd soon gathered around two excited speakers; some one on the outside began to push; and the rush began. Seven hundred and more men pushed and shouted, and tugged and wrestled, the "lits" trying to carry the "medics" eastward and the latter seeking to force the former westward. The senseless struggle continued until both sides needed rest, so rings were formed, and the wrestlers of both parties met in the midst. This was not exciting enough, nor as yet was sufficient damage done; at it again went the whole mob, and the pushing and battering were renewed. Spectators from all parts of the city filled the campus around the ball-ground. And now a large area was formed, and more wrestling and more boxing took place. As darkness came on many of the medical students repaired to their boarding houses, since your true "medic" never allows himself to remain hungry for long. Taking advantage of this strategic error the college men rushed upon their weakened foes, and soon every one of the ebryonic doctors, his red badge torn from him, was over the fence and out of the campus. Then the literary students formed in a triumphal procession, arranged in the order of the classes, and marched down into the city, where cheers were given and songs sung.

What must be regarded as the first important step toward placing the different departments on the plane of equality which in theory they occupy, and which they really do occupy in the German universities, and in the University of Virginia, was the lengthening of the terms in the professional schools from six to nine months. Thus the Commencements of all the schools were in 1885 for the first time held on the same day. In 1880 the course in medicine was increased from three to four years, and since 1894 three years instead of two have been required for admission to the law school. These changes, together with advances in the requirements for admission, and with such rigid enforcement of work during term time that neither law nor medicine is alluring to the lazy student, have done much to rehabilitate the professional schools in collegiate opinion. Should it be found practicable to require a college diploma before matriculation in any school save the academic, the lines between the different departments may in time be obliterated as far as student feeling goes. At present the relations, though not intimate, are friendly. It should be added here that the Engineering Department, which in 1895 was carved out of the Department of Literature, Science, and the Arts, is still reckoned as part of the latter in social and class matters; and as the requirements for admission to it are sufficiently rigorous academic students are not likely to ostracise their former associates because of the arbitrary division made by the authorities.

W. E. QUINBY, '58.

Until 1876 the School of Pharmacy, the first class of which was graduated in 1869, was catalogued as a subdivision of the literary department. For a time the students of the school insisted that they were "lits" and they claimed—but were denied—the right as such to vote in the elections for editors of The Chronicle and for officers of the Students' Lecture Association. Indeed the feeling of the real "lits" against them never was so acrimonious as it was against the "medics" and the "laws". As for the College of Homœopathy and the Dental School, the relations of their students with the academic undergraduates have been slight. The advocates of homœopathy used to complain of unfair discrimination against them on the part of the professors and students of the "regular" school; but such complaints are rare.

Years ago departmental spirit was fostered by circumstances. The entire medical school was called together very often, the law school daily, to hear lectures; and compulsory chapel exercises assembled every morning all the academic undergraduates. Meetings of the literary department used to be held on Saturday after chapel, and on occasion, as in choosing colors and when adopting a University cap, those meetings legislated for the whole body of students. At a department meeting some one of the seniors was called to preside. In October, 1870, a full complement of officers, with Charles E. Gorton, '71, as President, was elected, and it was determined that a new choice should be made at the end of every college year. But a second election did not take place.

With the abolition of Saturday morning chapel department meetings ceased, or were held on extraordinary occasions only. In fact when attendance at chapel became voluntary the academic students, no longer brought together by any official exercise, lost much of their partisan feeling. That feeling, however, has been preserved in each of the other schools by the solidifying influence of a common profession. The law students in particular have always manifested a genuine regard for their school. When the old University custom of celebrating the birthday of Washington was discontinued, the undergraduates of the law department took it up; and they have made so much of it that the list of those who have delivered the twenty-second of February addresses includes the most eminent men in the country. Of late the law students have been very active—and correspondingly successful—in the elections wherein members of different departments participate.

THE MUSEUM BUILDING.

CHAPTER IV

THE CLASSES

Of all the institutions with which the Michigan student comes in contact the most important is the class. This the young matriculate helps to organize, through it he becomes a factor in college life, and in memory of it he returns to Ann Arbor long after student days have passed. If anybody cares, fifty-eight academic classes have been matriculated. William B. Wesson of Detroit, who entered as a sophomore in 1841, but who left college in 1842 on account of poor health, constituted the class of '44; and Judson D. Collins, Merchant H. Goodrich, Lyman D. Norris, George E. Parmelee, and George W. Pray, formed at the outset the class of '45, which, after receiving eight accessions during the four years of its course, and after losing three of its number, came up to Commencement with eleven men. These eleven included all of the original six except Norris, who took his degree in 1845 at Yale where he had spent the last two years of his course. One of the two non-graduates was Alexander M. Campau of Detroit, whose place in the University has been taken by his sons and grandsons. With the class of '46 twenty-two men were associated, and the class of '47 had twenty-five, the number of graduates in each being seventeen and twelve respectively. Twenty-three alumni and twelve non-graduates made up the class of '49, which kept the lead in numbers until surpassed by '57. The attempt of the Faculty to suppress the secret societies drove to other colleges eight members of the class of '50 alone, and the evil effects of it were not effaced until the entrance of the large class of '58, the strongest ante-bellum delegation. With that class eighty-nine men, of whom forty-nine received diplomas, were connected. The academic class of '61 graduated fifty-three men, but the Civil War caused the attendance to diminish, and not until the class of '68 with its fifty-four alumni was the record of '61

equalled or surpassed. In 1866 was matriculated the largest delegation known up to that time; one hundred and four men entered with the class of '70, which also—despite a serious conflict with the Faculty—graduated a number before then unprecedented, viz., seventy-six. Now came many large classes, foremost among them being '75, with which ninety-two men took degrees. For a long time '75 remained the largest of the classes if the number of graduates is regarded as the test; but '88 carried 109 men through the ordeal of Commencement. At present '96 with its record of 170 male graduates is the banner class. The number of women graduated with each academic class has varied from one in '73 to eighty-two in '96.

Coming to the professional schools one learns that '51, the earliest class in medicine, was also the smallest, for it graduated only six men. This number grew to forty-one in 1854, but the hard times of 1857 caused a relapse. Toward the close of the Civil War and thereafter the delegations increased, ninety-seven men being graduated in 1869. Notwithstanding the lengthening of the terms from six to nine months, the popularity of the school continued to grow, so that as many as 117 students received diplomas with '83. Probably that class will long hold the record, for the addition of a third year to the course so diminished class rolls that nine years passed before the old figures were approached; and since '92 the requirement of a fourth year has lowered the average annual graduation to sixty.

As for the law school, its classes increased every year from 1860, when twenty-four men were graduated, to 1868, when 150 took degrees. This record remained until 1876, in which year the graduates numbered 159. In 1879 diplomas were conferred upon 193 students, a number which was not equalled until the graduation of '90 with 212 members. The classes now grew so large as to be almost unmanageable—'93 finishing with 327, '95 with 301, and '96 with 324—and the extension of the course to three years became necessary. This had the effect of reducing the class for 1897 to fifty-one members, but it is believed '98 will graduate nearly 200.

Classes in the school of pharmacy have varied in size at the time of graduation from five in 1872 to forty-one in 1889. The first class ('69) had twenty-three members, the latest ('97) twenty-one. In the dental school the earliest class '(76) graduated nine students, and the largest class ('94) includes sixty-five alumni. As for the homœopathic medical school, its classes, beginning with '77, have ranged from twenty-five men in 1879 to one man in 1895; and the class of '01 is the largest, with one exception, ever matriculated. The engineering department began in 1895-96 to have classes of its own, but its students are regarded as classmates by their comrades in the college proper, and its classes are included in the figures given for those of the literary department.

In the early days when the students roomed in the college dormitory, and when all the members of a particular class met in the same recitation rooms day after day, class spirit was necessarily strong. This spirit, of which class badges, canes, caps, colors, publications, reunions, seals, and songs are the legitimate exponents, while "bolts", "hazing", and "rushing" are its abnormal outgrowths, has varied greatly in different classes. Of it '68, '70, and '73 had perhaps a superabundance, while '69 was thought to have but little. Gradually changes have been introduced which have done away with much that nourished special pride in and affection for one's class. The dormitory is no more; compulsory attendance at chapel, where all academic students used to meet daily, each class sitting by itself, has been abolished; the privilege of holding class meetings immediately after chapel has been withdrawn; oratorical exhibitions in which the class as such was interested, have been abandoned; the system of elective studies has destroyed the integrity of the class by throwing together men of all classes; and finally, the Faculty has, since 1880, ignored class distinctions altogether, the names of all academic students being printed in one alphabetical arrangement in the catalogue. Some of these changes were made with the intention of minimizing what was regarded as a dangerous force; and already many zealous friends of the University are questioning whether the force has not been lessened too much, and whether anything else is a substitute for it in producing that collegiate loyalty without which Alma Mater can profit little by her sons.

It is to be regretted that the official catalogue has given up the arrangement by classes. That arrangement could easily be made in accordance with the proportionate amount of credits held, and it would be very convenient for purposes of reference, especially as to men who leave college without degrees. The editors of the general catalogue of the University, published in 1891, carried the official abolition of classes so far as to print in one long alphabetical roll the names of all the non-graduates of each department, an arrangement whereby the member of '90 precedes the member of '45, and which is both unscientific and inconvenient. It should be noticed that ever since 1860 the annual catalogue has distributed the law students into classes, and that the medical students since 1880 have received like treatment. Of course the academic students have inofficially preserved as well as they could the class arrangement. In this the student annuals and the catalogues of the leading fraternities have assisted, so that it is probable the class of every non-graduate since 1880 can be ascertained. Names prior to that date are properly classified in the exceedingly useful "University Book" published by the late Theodore R. Chase, '49.

Of class organizations no record earlier than 1860 remains, although before that date a full set of officers must have been elected annually by each class. In the literary department considerable interest attaches to the choice of officers for freshman year, as the election constitutes a kind of introduction to the college public. Thirty years ago the positions of freshman president and freshman orator were regarded as quite important, but the annual supper being the chief exercise of the class as such, the toastmastership—now usually given to a fraternity man—is considered very desirable. Following is the list of the freshman academic presidents:

'64 W. B. Hendryx,
'65 F. W. Becker,
'66 J. V. Quarles,
'67 Richard Montgomery,
'68 E. C. Burns,
'69 O. J. Campbell,
'70 V. S. Lovell,
'71 P. C. Hudson,
'72 L. H. Jennings,
'73 V. M. Spalding,
'74 G. S. Baker,
'75 E. F. Laible,
'76 S. C. Fuller,
'77 G. A. Cady,
'78 G. H. Harrower,
'79 F. D. Haskell,
'80 B. S. Waite,
'81 F. C. Robbins,
'82 W. D. Robbins,
'83 P. B. Haid,
'84 S. A. May,
'85 W. E. Brownlee,
'86 H. J. Powell,
'87 J. H. Cotteral,
'88 H. G. Coburn, Jr.,
'89 C. U. Champion,
'90 Dugald Brown,
'91 C. D. Warner,
'92 W. C. Quarles,
'93 P. M. Day,
'94 J. W. Loeb,
'95 F. F. VanTuyl,
'96 W. N. Choate,
'97 O. H. Tower,
'98 F. C. Hyde,
'99 Allen Campbell,
'00 A. P. Cox,
'01 H. J. Idema.

The freshman orators in the literary department have been:

'64 J. C. Hart,
'65 L. W. Halsey,
'66 J. F. Lawrence,
'67 Amos Wakelin,
'68 E. L. Walter,
'69 H. B. Farwell,
'70 G. T. Campau,
'71 Joseph McGrath,
'72 M. W. Ward,
'73 H. A. Adams,
'74 F. A. Maynard,
'75 J. M. Barrett,
'76 D. H. Stringham,
'77 B. H. Colby,
'78 P. H. Hanus,
'79 F. D. Mead,
'80 F. G. Allen,
'81 J. D. Wilson,
'82 J. M. Smith,
'83 C. T. Wilkins,
'84 R. M. Dott,
'86 J. C. Shattuck,
'87 J. H. Patterson,
'88 C. H. Perry,
'89 Louis Boyle,
'90 H. R. Seager,
'91 E. W. Dow,
'92 S. B. Grubbs,
'93 Hugo Pam,
'94 R. A. J. Shaw,
'95 C. M. Holt,
'99 C. G. Roe,
'00 Charles Frank,
'01 C. VanKeuren.

The toastmasters of the academic freshman classes have been:

'64 N. J. Hotchkiss,
'65 J. I. Christiancy,
'67 Thomas Parker, Jr.,
'68 Adoniram Carter,
'69 W. C. Johns,
'70 Z. K. McCormack,
'71 Horace Phillips,
'72 C. C. Worthington,
'73 Henry Russel,
'74 W. H. Wells,
'75 E. W. Jenney,
'76 B. T. Cable,
'77 M. H. Brennan,
'78 C. M. Dougherty,
'79 H. T. Morley,
'80 A. S. Deacon,
'81 C. H. Kumler.
'82 J. E. Beal,
'83 F. J. Jennison,
'84 J. B. Whelan,
'86 J. C. Shaw,
'87 S. K. Pittman,
'88 H. W. Allport,
'90 W. B. Ramsey,
'91 J. A. Jameson, Jr.,
'92 J. B. Miller,
'93 F. L. Evans,
'95 G. B. Russel,
'96 E. M. Holland,
'97 Benjamin Townsend,
'98 H. W. Standart,
'99 Muir Snow,
'00 R. C. Apted,
'01 J. M. Wetmore.

Years have passed since the offices of the academic sophomore year were regarded as important. Those of junior year were neither sought nor shunned until a brilliant intellect in one of the classes of the seventies conceived that dangerous candidates for the positions of senior year could be killed off by electing them to junior places; it being regarded improper to elect the same officers for two successive years. This artless scheme failing, the junior-class offices were bestowed upon worthy men whom the enmity or jealousy of fellows of the baser sort picked out for what had come to be a mark of disrespect. Usually the men nominated felt too indifferent to resist, and the election went by default. Sometimes these contests were embittered by the attempts of one fraternity to elect members of another to the objectionable positions. When the class of '82 reached its junior year the faction which had oftenest succeeded in this particular kind of enterprise was worsted, and its men were chosen. However they managed to get even by calling a class election upon insufficient notice; then they resigned, and elected their enemies to the places they had left. The members of '83 after much pulling and hauling resolved not to cast a slur upon any of their number, and abolished junior offices. Their immediate successors, the class of '84, went a step further, and by formal resolution declared the offices of junior year to be honorable; but '88 declined to do this, and bestowed its junior presidency upon a member of the non-secret fraternity. In '87 there were no officers during the third year. A spirited conflict arose in the class of '89 between the fraternity-men and the "Independents", each faction trying to foist the junior presidency upon a member of the opposing crowd, but finally as a compromise a committee of three was elected to exercise executive powers.

As the principal officers of the senior class have parts in the public exercises of class day, their positions have long been regarded as among the most desirable of collegiate honors, the presidency and the oratorship being especially sought. Following are the names of the presidents of the senior academic classes:

'61 J. W. Wood,
'62 R. C. Powers,
'63 L. J. Brown,
'64 W. D. Hitchcock,
'65 J. B. Root,
'66 S. T. Chapin,
'67 J. O. Andrews,
'68 E. S. Jenison,
'69 B. L. C. Lothrop,
'70 G. E. Dawson,
'71 J. A. Mercer,
'72 Lester McLean,
'73 J. M. Hemingway,
'74 G. H. Jameson,
'75 C. S. Burch,
'76 B. T. Cable,
'77 J. S. Ayers,
'78 C. M. Daugherty,
'79 C. S. Henning,
'80 B. S. Waite,
'81 Wetmore Hunt,
'82 D. H. Campbell,
'83 H. A. Mandell,
'84 J. H. Tyler,
'85 T. C. Phillips,
'86 W. A. McAndrew,
'87 S. K. Pittman,
'88 J. H. Powell,
'89 W. S. Holden,
'90 W. J. Baldwin,

'91 R. P. Lamont,
'92 P. W. Ross,
'93 Hadley Baldwin,
'94 D. F. Lyons,
'95 R. R. Lyman,
'96 E. B. House,
'97 S. W. Smith,
'98 F. S. Simons.

The orators of the senior academic classes have been:

'61 J. C. Johnston,
'62 E. F. Uhl,
'63 O. W. Coolidge,
'64 E. D. W. Kinne,
'65 S. B. Ladd,
'66 Eleazer Darrow,
'67 G. E. Church,
'68 E. L. Walter,
'69 W. J. Gibson,
'70 Bernard Moses,
'71 H. B. Hutchins,
'72 J. F. Dutton,
'73 H. W. Gelston,
'74 C. T. Lane,
'75 B. C. Burt,
'76 R. J. Young,
'77 H. C. McDougall,
'78 F. A. Barbour,
'79 George Wright,
'80 W. W. Cook,
'81 C. A. Towne,
'82 J. F. Gallaher,
'83 W. B. Garvin,
'84 A. S. VanValkenburg,
'85 J. O. Reed,
'86 S. B. Todd,
'87 T. F. Moran,
'88 Moritz Rosenthal,
'89 E. C. Goddard,
'90 H. B. Dewey,
'91 W. H. Nichols,
'92 W. H. Dellenbeck,
'93 S. C. Spitzer,
'94 W. W. Wedemeyer,
'95 J. S. Handy,
'96 F. P. Sadler,
'97 B. H. Ames,
'98 Charles Simons.

The position of poet of the academic senior class has been held by the following:

'61 H. M. Utley,
'62 W. E. Nelson,
'63 N. H. Winchell,
'64 S. C. Stacy,
'65 Gabriel Campbell
'66 C. S. Fraser,
'67 D. N. Lowell,
'68 R. J. Reeves,
'69 A. E. Wilkinson,
'70 Edwin Fleming,
'71 R. E. Phinney,
'72 W. A. Brooks,
'73 A. L. Todd,
'74 T. H. Johnston,
'75 J. B. McMahon,
'76 H. S. Harris,
'77 W. J. Miller,
'78 George Horton,
'79 E. P. Anderson,
'80 A. J. Potter,
'81 I. R. Crosette,
'82 F. E. Baker,
'83 Kitty VanHarlingen,
'84 Elmer Dwiggins,
'85 Mary B. Putnam,
'86 Helen L. Osgood,
'87 A. G. Newcomer,
'88 Elsie Jones,
'89 Isabella M. Andrews,
'90 Grace E. Harrah,
'91 Maud Miller,
'92 Julia Herrick,
'93 A. H. Holmes,
'94 J. R. Nelson,
'95 F. P. Daniels,
'96 Euretta A. Hoyles,
'97 A. M. Smith,
'98 C. F. Gauss.

The office of historian has been held by the following academic seniors:

'61 E. L. Little,
'62 T. H. Hurd,
'63 C. W. Noble,
'64 J. C. Hart,
'65 Albert Jennings,
'66 H. W. Lewis,
'67 Artemas Roberts,
'68 E. L. Hessenmueller,
'69 Henry Lamm,
'70 W. B. Stevens,
'71 J. L. Gillespie,
'72 W. T. Underwood,

'73 Henry Russel,
'74 Calvin Thomas,
'75 Lorenzo Davis, Jr.,
'76 J. H. Steere,
'77 G. N. Orcutt,
'78 W. J. Jenks,
'79 I. K. Pond,
'80 C. M. Wilson,
'81 Allan Frazer,
'82 W. B. Cady,
'83 J. C. Moore,
'84 Hugh Brown,
'85 E. E. Powell,
'86 M. D. Atkins,
'87 A. G. Hall,
'88 J. N. McBride,
'89 E. B. Perry,
'90 J. A. C. Hildner,
'91 O. R. Hardy,
'92 A. J. Tuttle,
'93 Jennie Eddy,
'94 F. L. Osenburg,
'95 R. O. Austin,
'96 Annie L. Bacorn,
'97 Oceana Ferrey,
'98 C. H. Farrell.

The office of seer or prophet, a leading honor in the senior academic class, has been held by the following:

'61 T. B. Weir,
'62 H. D. Follett,
'64 W. S. Brewster,
'65 C. M. Goodsell,
'66 Sidney Beckwith,
'67 H. P. Churchill,
'68 I. N. Demon,
'69 T. O. Perry,
'70 C. G. Wing,
'71 S. S. Green,
'72 Hector Neuhoff,
'73 Wayne Hayman,
'74 H. R. Pattengill,
'75 G. S. Hosmer,
'76 C. A. Blair,
'77 V. J. Tefft,
'78 S. D. Walling,
'79 F. H. Coe,
'80 C. H. Campbell,
'81 N. A. Stanley,
'82 Laura Hills,
'83 A. M. Brown,
'84 Jennie Emerson,
'85 D. H. Browne,
'86 F. B. Wixson,
'87 Nettie Brown,
'88 Laura O. Tupper,
'89 Fannie Barker,
'92 Mamah Borthwick,
'93 Maude E. Merritt,
'94 Marian U. Strong,
'95 Mabel Colton,
'96 Florence Halleck,
'97 Inez C. Perrin,
'98 Florence H. Pomeroy.

In the law department class officers are eagerly sought, and often the contest over them in senior year is long and bitter. When the class of '76 came to choose officers for the finishing year an attempt was made to elect to the presidency a member who had held the same office in the preceding—junior—year. The candidate was the noted "Colonel" Burleigh, who since his graduation has been lawyer, state senator, actor—"everything by turns and nothing long". He was fiercely opposed, the secret society to which he belonged being openly divided upon the question of supporting him. He was defeated. In 1886 the class of '87 occupied the entire day in balloting for orator. Finally W. W. Davis was elected, his success being noticeable because, although a "one-year man" and a member of a fraternity, he overcame the obstacle of a two-thirds' vote rule. Five different meetings were held by the class of '93 before the list of senior officers was completed, the struggle over the position of valedictorian being particularly exciting. At the fourth meeting ten ballots were taken, none of the candidates being successful. At the fifth meeting, after fourteen ballots, a choice was made.

Prior to 1875 the class officers outside of the literary department are not mentioned in The Palladium, and as there is no other continuous record the lists here presented are not complete. The roll of senior-class presidents in the law department is as follows:

'62 W. D. Wiltsie,
'63 Hoyt Post,
'70 J. B. Steere,
'75 W. R. Taggart,
'76 M. P. Kinkaid,
'77 G. F. White,
'78 J. A. Stacy,
'79 Charles Chandler,
'80 I. L. Hillis,
'81 T. R. Shaw,
'82 B. N. Rooks,
'83 S. C. Blake,
'84 Frank Healy,
'85 E. A. Woodward,
'86 J. W. Hamilton,
'87 E. D. Black,
'88 W. S. Frost,
'89 A. F. Wingert,
'90 F. W. Moultrie,
'91 N. A. Phillips,
'92 A. C. MacKenzie,
'93 A. W. Jefferis,
'94 R. E. Minahan,
'95 E. M. Walsh,
'96 F. L. Ingraham,
'97 W. L. Hart,
'98 L. C. Thompson.

The orators of the senior law classes have been:

'63 Cholwell Knox,
'70 Louis Fockler,
'78 H. M. Campbell,
'79 H. M. Woodford,
'80 J. H. Bayes,
'81 J. W. Lounsbury,
'82 W. F. Paxton,
'83 N. P. Conrey,
'84 J. P. Elkin,
'85 F. R. Lander,
'86 I. N. Huntsberger,
'87 W. W. Davis,
'88 Marion DeVries,
'89 V. O. Hildreth,
'90 J. B. Chaddock,
'91 L. S. Baldwin,
'92 W. I. Manny,
'93 J. W. Wood,
'94 J. L. Poston,
'95 L. G. Long,
'96 E. D. Reynolds,
'97 J. S. Handy,
'98 R. L. Weaver.

Following are the poets of the senior classes in the law department:

'63 C. E. Yost,
'70 Fleming Rogers,
'78 H. S. Reed,
'79 L. K. Mihills,
'80 D. H. S. McClure,
'81 L. R. Taylor,
'82 W. R. Wood,
'83 H. M. Oren,
'84 Z. F. Wharton,
'85 Mary C. Geigus,
'86 Lettie Burlingame,
'87 Margaret L. Wilcox,
'88 Charles Alling,
'89 S. R. Ireland,
'90 C. T. King,
'92 J. H. Whitely,
'93 C. E. Dedrick,
'95 S. G. Baker,
'96 H. E. Northomb,
'97 Albert Kocourek.

The historians of the senior classes in the law department have been the following:

'70 J. W. Wood,
'80 T. M. Sloane,
'81 W. G. Sharp,
'82 G. W. Allen,

'83 C. I. York,
'84 T. C. Jones,
'85 H. W. Dickinson,
'86 J. A. Crawford,
'87 Absalom Rosenberger,
'88 P. F. Gosbey,
'89 F. A. Brown,
'90 O. C. Volkmor,
'91 H. D. Jewell,
'92 J. W. Dawson,
'93 C. K. Friedman,
'94 L. R. Herrick,
'95 J. W. Ferrier,
'96 D. R. Williams,
'97 H. N. Hayes,
'98 M. H. Abbott.

Prior to 1882 the senior law students seem not to have indulged in the luxury of a class prophecy. The list of the seers follows:

'82 O. F. Hunt,
'83 F. W. Smith,
'84 C. W. Miller,
'85 L. A. Springer,
'86 F. G. Higgins,
'87 E. L. Curtis,
'88 Almeda E. Hitchcock,
'89 O. S. Riggs,
'90 R. M. King,
'91 E. R. Sutton,
'92 J. G. Erdlitz,
'93 A. J. Hitchcock,
'94 D. J. Buckley,
'95 G. W. Dayton,
'96 A. A. Huseman,
'97 M. W. Babb,
'98 P. Y. Albright.

In 1891 the senior class in the law department devised a new office, that of valedictorian. It has been held by the following men:

'91 S. E. Low,
'92 J. E. Roberts,
'93 Milton Johnson,
'94 V. O. Coltrane,
'95 P. G. Burnham,
'96 E. P. O'Leary,
'97 E. C. Ryan,
'98 Robert Healy.

It is commonly supposed that in the medical department the strife for class offices is less bitter than in the college and in the law-school. Following are the names of the presidents of the senior medical classes, 1880–96:

'81 G. F. Heath,
'82 Eugene Baker,
'83 J. B. Siggins,
'84 T. L. Iddings,
'85 M. L. Eaton,
'86 W. B. Sexton,
'87 M. H. Clark,
'88 Henry Hulst,
'89 E. H. Parker,
'90 L. C. Bacon,
'91 G. L. Kiefer,
'92 LeRoy Southmayd,
'93 R. H. Wolcott,
'94 R. B. Armstrong,
'95 H. A. Haze,
'96 C. S. McIntyre,
'97 G. B. Wallace,
'98 G. M. Livingston.

The presidents of the senior pharmacy classes from 1873 have been:

'74 G. C. Henry,
'75 J. H. Salls,
'76 J. H. Ames,
'77 W. H. D. Lewis,
'78 W. A. Hasbrouck,
'79 R. F. Mull,
'80 Ferdinand Thum,
'81 E. E. Gatchell,
'82 E. E. Meredith,
'83 C. S. Koon,
'84 J. D. Muir,
'85 Henry Palmer,
'86 E. A. Ruddiman,
'87 E. R. Beal,
'88 F. B. Raynale,
'89 Mark Rockwell,

'90 C. C. Sherrard,
'91 A. W. Adams,
'92 Richard Fischer,
'93 C. O. Hill,
'94 M. S. Nichols,
'95 W. J. Teeters,
'96 F. H. Wilson,
'97 E. D. Benjamin,
'98 Edgar Schiller.

The presidents of the senior homœopathic classes since 1881 have been:

'81 W. P. Polhemus,
'83 J. B. Hubbell,
'84 W. H. Sawyer,
'86 H. B. Reynolds,
'87 S. G. Milner,
'88 E. W. Ruggles,
'89 E. C. Williams,
'90 L. A. Howe,
'91 A. W. Burdick,
'92 F. J. Peck,
'93 G. F. Clark,
'94 L. E. Peck,
'95 W. H. Atterbury,
'96 W. F. Holmes,
'97 C. M. Steele,
'98 S. P. Tuttle.

These have been the presidents of the senior dental classes:

'84 L. M. James,
'85 E. F. Randolph,
'86 E. K. Clements,
'87 William Saunders,
'88 T. S. Maxwell,
'89 Arthur Richardson,
'90 C. H. Farman,
'91 P. P. Nelson,
'92 C. L. Blunt,
'93 C. A. Hawley,
'94 M. P. Green,
'95 J. H. Neeley,
'96 J. W. Lyons,
'97 G. D. Edgar,
'98 R. J. Roper.

Several of the classes have left memorials of themselves upon the campus or in the college buildings. One of these offerings is the huge mass of jasper conglomerate weighing seven and a quarter tons which stands in the northwestern corner of the University grounds. It was found in a garden below the old county jail, and only what is now the east face of it was exposed. Professor Winchell, to use the words of Dr. E. H. Wells, '62, had just been pounding into the class all the strata of the universe, and some brilliant member of '62 suggested the removal for a class monument of this pebble which the great geologist declared had been carried from the far North by a glacier. As the boys were poor they did the excavating themselves. After much tugging the rock was loaded on a sledge, and with flags flying was drawn by ten horses over slushy snow to its present resting place, February 24, 1862.

After the class of '66 had immortalized itself by depositing in the museum a copy of one of Murillo's master-pieces, '69 reverted to the example of '62, and brought upon the campus the choice geological specimen which lies in front of University Hall. The juniors planned to carry away or bury this stone, which is much smaller than the '62 affair, but being prevented they made such feints as caused the seniors to stand guard over their memorial until after Class-Day. Still another stone, which lies under the Tappan Oak, was placed in pursuance of a resolution adopted by the class of '58 at its twenty-fifth anniversary. That class before its graduation set out trees in circles around the Tappan Oak, and while some of these have been cut down others have survived. Trees were set out by the class of '71 also. The class of '72 planted ivy close to the south wing in what seems to have been uncongenial soil.

Taking an entirely new departure the class of '70 on the afternoon of Class-Day dedicated to the University the statue of Benjamin Franklin which adorns the campus. As early as 1872 fears were expressed for the health of the venerable printer and diplomat, and a writer for The Chronicle went so far as to insinuate that he is of perishable cast-iron rather than enduring bronze. Benjamin has been taken twice from his pedestal, and has suffered sundry coats of whitewash, but he survives. Other memorials are: the bronze bust of Judge Cooley, presented by the law class of '95; the bust of President Angell given by the academic class of '95; a cast of the Triumphal Arch of the Emperor Trajan at Beneventum, presented by the literary class of '96; a portrait in oil of Professor J. C. Knowlton contributed by the law class of '96; and a sum of money left as the nucleus of a scholarship fund by the academic class of '97.

Class songs came into vogue at an early day. The University Magazine for March, 1862, contains the "Parting Song of '62" in ten stanzas to the tune of "Auld Lang Syne". Richard S. Dewey wrote the "Parting song of '68". The song of '69 was in three stanzas, and was sung to the air of "Benny Havens, O," which also was utilized by Charles A. Warren for the class of '74. Among the writers, not already mentioned, of class songs, are G. W. Seavey, '71, H. H. Lyons, '72, J. R. Goffe, '73, B. C. Burt, '75, M. L. Woolsey, '77, C. M. Gayley, '78, F. S. Bell, '79, W. E. Brownlee, '85, and R. G. Cole, '88.

With the class of '62 began the series of class seals which for a quarter of a century formed part of Michigan's collegiate insignia. Most of them were not real seals; that is, they were not impressions upon wax or paper, but were printed from blocks of wood or metal. However, the seal of '70 was a stamp, and was not engraved for printing until the issue of the class book in 1890. Programmes of class exercises, stationery used by enthusiastic classmen, and class rolls in the Palladium and Castalia, were adorned with these designs, which contained the numerals and the mottoes of the classes, and, usually, the name or the abbreviated name of the University. Very unfilially the class cuts of '64, '65, '68, and '70, made no reference to Alma Mater. The mottoes were these: '62, Juncti semper; '63, Sapientia, facetiæ, lætitia; '64, *Μετ' ἀγῶνα ϛτέφανος*; '65, Vivere sat vincere; '66, Droit et avant; '67, Unus amore, more, ore, re; '68, Palmam habeat qui meruit; '69, Virtute et labore; '70, Nec mora nec requies; '71, Per aspera ad astra; '72, *"Ιχνος οὐδὲν τοὔπισθεν*; '73, Scientiæ amor nos ducit; '74, Semper plus ultra; '75, *Μελέτη τὸ πᾶν*; '76, Respice finem; '77, Surgere tento; '78, *"Αχρι ἐς ἄκρα*; '79, Volens et potens; '80, Esse quam videri; '81, *Πρὸς μάθησιν ἐκπονῆσαι*; '82, Pudeat extremos rediisse; '83, Ne tentes aut perfice; '84, *Εἰς τελέαν ἀνδρείαν*; '85, Semper sursum. The series ended with '85, although the class of '93, some time after it had left college, made use of a design which displayed on a shield within a circle three crescents interfretted. The seals of '63, '67, and '73 are coats-of-arms, and those of '72, '75, '76, and '78 are shields imperfectly heraldic. It must be admitted that '63's design is a close copy of the arms of Brazil, and that '73's is very like the seal of the Yale class of '69. As for the seal of '84, it unblushingly adopts the wave-beaten rock and even the owl-and-fasces crest of the frontispiece of the catalogue of one of the secret

societies. The class of '65 had two seals, it choosing to discard the earlier and neater after its freshman year. Two experiments were made by '66 also, the first a characterless affair, the second a huge design which covered half a page of The Palladium; and neither was used after sophomore year. While the design adopted by '67 was by no means poor, yet '62's seal remained unrivalled until the St. George's cross adopted by '71 came into the field. This in turn was surpassed by '72's very neat vignette. The seal of '74 was said to mean that the angular freshman would be developed into the complete and well-rounded senior. At first the class of '75 adopted for its seal a likeness of the statue of Michigan; but this was discarded in favor of a less ambitious design. Only one appearance in The Palladium was accorded to the seal of '82, a design representing Pallas, her right arm resting on a shield which shows the numerals '82, while her left hand grasps a spear from which floats a long streamer inscribed with the class motto.

As considerable delay usually attended the selection of a design and the engraving thereof, and as the finished product was not infrequently unsatisfactory, it sometimes happened that the freshmen did not have their seal ready for The Palladium. The editors kindly supplied the freshmen of '77 with a cut of a donkey accompanied by the motto "In hoc signo vinces". This had the effect of bringing '78 and '79 to time, but '80, '82, '83, and '85, whether in default or not, were set forth with burlesque seals in the annual aforesaid. A boycott being threatened by '84 in the event of the omission of its seal, the class gained its point. In The Palladium of '83 and in later issues all the classes save the seniors received burlesque vignettes. Finally class cuts were given up altogether. This was due in part to the absurd notion, assiduously cultivated by vendors of college stationery, that seals and arms of societies or classes must be printed from steel plates to be truly artistic. With the decline of class spirit the expense necessarily involved put steel engravings out of the question. The Chronicle of Nov. 17, 1888, recommends the purchase of a seal by each class, which, it says, "would be a good custom and would beautify our college annual"; but the suggestion remains unheeded even to this day.

Colors have been adopted by many classes, but the record is defective. The following is a list of the selections made by some of the academic delegations: '73 and '87, blue and maize; '88, ruby and silver; '89, seal-brown and gold; '90, steel-gray and carmine; '91, old-gold and white; '93, cardinal and black. Pink and Nile-green were the colors of the law class of '89, red and white those of the law class of '94.

Class caps have with us been more popular than college caps. Early in October, 1869, the sophomores adopted for their special use a four-cornered affair of blue broadcloth encircled with a silver band, and bearing the figures '72. A small tassel gave the finishing touch. This cap was very neat, and the '72 men were so proud of it that they actually wore it, a most unusual thing to do with a college cap. They also had to battle for it, as the '73 freshmen from the top of the stairs leading to the chapel (then the law-lecture room) precipitated much flour upon such sophomoric heads as they could reach on the morning of its first appearance, thus bringing on one of the liveliest "rushes" ever known in Ann Arbor. From time to time other classes adopted caps. In the spring of 1881 distinctive head-coverings were observed on the campus: the seniors wore maroon fez caps with old-gold tassels, the juniors white "plugs", the sophs white derbies, the freshmen black mortar-boards with cardinal tassels, the senior medical students black silk hats, the senior law students straw derbies with band of blue and maize, the "pharmics" low Mackinac, straw hats with band of old-gold and cardinal. Most of the academic senior classes in the eighties had class caps, the prevailing style being the mortar-board, which, indeed, with the gown, is now quite a frequent sight in senior year. The sophomores of '85 and the freshmen of '87 are among the lower classes which have had peculiar caps.

The wearing of class badges is hardly a Michigan custom. However, the members of '74 quite generally wore during sophomore year, and even later, the interlaced triangle and circle displayed in their seal; and the law class of '86 had as a pin a plain monogram of gold with a chain and guard.

After spending three years in quiet and unpretentious devotion to college duties the class of '69 suddenly became an originator of a new custom; it adopted a class cane. This is described as a Malacca stick with an ivory handle and a gold band; '69 being carved in raised figures on the end of the handle, and the owner's name being inscribed on the band. The class of '70 brought into fashion the class "autograph cane", and its members gave much of their time each to carving his name on every other's walking-stick. When '73 attained its seniority this nuisance was abated, to be revived at intervals afterwards—as in 1877—but hardly with the old fervor which caused the instructors of '70 and '71 to despair of the republic.

Another line of activity in which the academic classes became interested at an early date was the public literary exhibition. The first affair of this kind was given in the old Presbyterian Church by the sophomores on the evening of Aug. 10, 1843. Four orations, four dissertations, four essays, and one poem, gave every member of the class a chance. By the same class, '45, the first junior exhibition was given Aug. 14, 1844. Many years passed before a freshman exhibition took place, the first being on the evening of May 28, 1869. It was given by eighteen members of the class of '72 who had been appointed by Professor Tyler; and it may be observed that only two of the eighteen were chosen to speak at Commencement. The second and last of the freshman exhibitions was held on the evening of May 31, 1870. Twenty-three appointments were made for this by Professor Tyler. Henry Russel, George Hopkins, and S. T. Douglas, now of the Detroit Bar, and V. M. Spalding, now of the Faculty, were among the speakers. The exercises consisted of declamations and recitals.

Sophomore exhibitions were revived in the spring of 1868 for the immediate benefit of the class of '70. Two of these affairs were given, the first in March, the second in May. The speakers were self-appointed. As was sagely remarked none but sophomores would volunteer for such a purpose. On the evening of April 29, 1870, the last of this species of entertainment was given by the class of '72. Possibly by preconcerted arrangement the class of '73 was on hand to study the methods of its hated foe. Much pleased by the speeches, which were inconceivably poor, the '73 men were vigorous in applause and prodigal of testimonials, the latter taking the form of grass bouquets. As the evening wore away the flagging interest of the audience was aroused by the descent of a rooster in a somewhat intricate curve from the gallery to the stage, where it lay at the feet of Acting-President Frieze. This induction of poultry into the Methodist Church was too much for the patience of the authorities. Four of the class were suspended for six months, others for a longer period, but all were restored in consideration of a pledge by the class that it would refrain during the ensuing year from the usual disorderly conduct of sophomores. Perhaps the class thought that the giving of an exhibition would necessarily constitute a breach of its agreement; at any rate no sophomore exhibition—of a literary character—has occurred since that April night. At '73's class-day exercises what was claimed to be the rooster above mentioned was produced, but the identity of the fowl was strenuously denied, it being claimed by '72 that the janitor of the church had killed and eaten the bird. Affidavits for and against were produced, and much interest was aroused by the discussion.

Junior exhibitions were deeply rooted in the traditions of the college, and many believed they would long survive their sophomore and freshman analogues. The speakers were elected by the academic Faculty (for law or medical students had nothing to do with these distinctly collegiate exercises), and were usually the leading men of the class in scholarship and literary ability. "Junior Exhibition", says The University Chronicle of Oct. 26, 1867, "is looked upon by the undergraduates as the most important event of the course, and its honors are coveted more than all others, more, even, than class-day positions or Commencement preferences; in fact it is the only thing in the nature of a prize connected with the University." Under the system which went into effect in 1867, an appointment to speak on Commencement Day became a greater honor than one for Junior Ex.; but the latter continued to be regarded as very desirable, although some of every class professed indifference. These exhibitions were characterized by the publication of mock programmes, of which Professor Frieze once wrote:

"A 'mock programme' afforded large opportunity to those members of the junior class who were not honored with an appointment to exercise their wit at the expense of their more lucky classmates, and of any others, whether officers or students, whom they might wish to ridicule. Members of the Faculty, especially such as had salient peculiarities, and sometimes the President, not infrequently found themselves advertised in doggerel lines to take part in the performance, while the exhibitors themselves were named and characterized in such a manner, and their themes also designated with such absurd titles, that when the poor victims appeared on the stage, the audience being plentifully supplied with the 'mock programmes' as well as the genuine, could hardly escape their influence. Many of the officers were indicated in these humorous documents by some nickname; even the venerable Dr. Williams was not spared. But beginning as they did, in a spirit of harmless mirth, just like the practice of hazing, they inevitably took on at last a more or less criminal character, not seldom outraging both morality and decency. For college life cannot avoid occasions of personal enmity, and the college community most always contain at least some bad characters; and the influence of both came naturally to show themselves in these anonymous programmes. Playful satire, if it becomes anonymous, soon becomes malicious satire. Attacking in the dark, in sport, leads to stabbing in the dark. The mock programme, therefore, like all anonymous writings of a personal nature, tended to breed in the authors of them an unmanly and dastardly spirit. Accordingly these programmes at last became a public nuisance; and President Tappan and the Faculty made every effort to suppress them. This was very difficult because of the facility with which the printing of them could be secured in neighboring towns, and of the ease with which they could be circulated in secret; but the temptation to make use of such a congenial instrument for venting malice and vileness from time to time led some of the more reckless to repeat the offence, and it can scarcely be said to have been abolished until the exhibitions themselves disappeared".

Rascally as many of these programs are, they make up not the most uninteresting part of the memorabilia Michiganiensia. The one which had to deal with the exhibition of the class of '62 was "The University Bedbug", and it is said that a member of that class aided in getting it out and received a suspension therefor. Martin L. D'Ooge, now of the Faculty, was in junior year connected with '62 (although he was matriculated with '61), and of him this was written in the Bedbug:

"I and the Profs, (a pome)—Mighty little 'D'Ogan.
God save this junior sent
To teach us virtue's bent,
And when his say is out,
God save him, let him went.
"Music—'Oh could we climb where D'Ooge stands.' (Sung by the Freshmen, en masse.)".

The mock programme of the exhibition of '63 measures 14 x 6 inches and is printed in two columns upon one side only of the sheet. It is entitled "Great Moral Exhibition of the Junior Class of Mich. University, Wednesday eve., March 26, 1862." Levi L. Barbour, recently Regent, and N. H. Winchell, afterwards of the University of Minnesota, are subjected to discourteous verses; and ten other speakers suffer.

The burlesque on the Junior Ex. of '64 took the form of a long play-bill headed "Unparalled attraction! The Wild Beasts of the Forest, or the Dogans of '64. For one night only". In the bill of particulars which follows much liberty is taken with the initials of the Christian names of the twelve victims; O. F. Drury becomes "Our Fool Drury", W. B. Hendryx is rendered "Woe Begone Hendryx", and E. D. W. Kinne is translated "Endless Drawling Windy Kinne". After the speaking comes "Music", viz., a "Dirge" in these lines:

"Now view the young as off the stage they pass,
And ask how Nature made so vile a class".

When '65 gave its public performance it was treated to a four-page programme, the outer cover of which read: "Public Degradation of the Class of '65. To take place at the Athens of the West, under the Direction of Mister 'Old Owl' and his Satanic Majesty. Tuesday Evening, March 29, 1864". Within is the "Order of Exercises, showing the different stages of degradation"; this begins with "Music—'Ain't you glad you come', By the Select Twelve". Toward the close we are told "the Sigs and Alpha Delts will appear in mourning because Bills and Williams were not appointed to spout".

An altogether outrageous eight-page pamphlet was required to illustrate the defects of the appointed juniors of '66. This was entitled "Happy Moral Combination of Dirty Dilutions from a demoralized Squad of the Class of '66; McIntyre's Presbyterian Ranch, Ann Arbor, Mich., March 28, 1865". The class of '67 was gratified by an alleged account of its prospective exercises the title of which covered half a page, and read: "Declamation and Composition by some of the Younger Members of Mr. Rast Haven's School for Boys at the Parthenon, Athens, March 27, 1866". An exceptionally vicious attack was made upon '68's Exhibition.

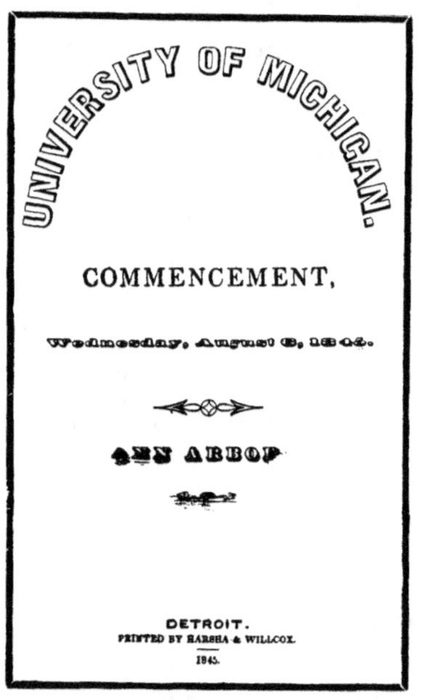
UNIVERSITY OF MICHIGAN.

COMMENCEMENT,

Wednesday, August 6, 1845.

ANN ARBOR

DETROIT.
PRINTED BY HARSHA & WILLCOX.
1845.

COMMENCEMENT PROGRAMME, 1845.

Tradition has it that the assault upon the Class of '69 by sophomores of '70 was so phenomenally atrocious that energetic efforts were made to discover the offenders, who, being found out, were expelled, thus more than decimating the class, and putting an end to the business of issuing mock programmes.

As the classes grew larger the difficulty, always great, of pleasing everybody with the annual list of speakers, increased. The problem became more intricate when public opinion compelled the cutting down the number of appointees. The marking system in vogue at all other important colleges had never been used by us, so that there was no actual written evidence of superiority in scholarship or literary merit. Consequently the reasons for a particular appointment were matters of opinion, and in a country where every one's opinion is as good as every other's, that test is apt to be unsatisfactory. For several years there was much quiet discontent; but '70, '71, and '72 managed to hold their Exhibitions in peace. When the elections for this important honor were made in '73, a class in which the delegations of the leading secret societies were at swords' points, it happened that the smallest delegation had the most appointments, and that certain worthy members of the other delegations were passed by. Some also of the non-society men felt slighted. No doubt there was ground for criticism, yet when, months afterwards, the names of the appointing committee transpired, the charge of intentional unfairness became ridiculous. But the appointees themselves cared so little about the matter that they offered their resignations, which were accepted. In accordance with the policy, adopted some years before, of giving up any custom which developed friction, Junior Exhibition was then and there discontinued.

ORDER OF EXERCISES.

Part 1.

1. Sacred Music.

2. Prayer.

3. Salutatory Address. — EDMUND FISH, *Bloomfield.*

4. Romance. — EDWIN LAWRENCE, *Monroe.*

5. The Power and Province of Rational Philosophy. — JUDSON D. COLLINS, *Lyndon.*

6. Music.

7. The Ideal. — THOMAS B. CUMING, *Grand Rapids.*

8. Intellectual Sovereignty. — MERCHANT H. GOODRICH, *Ann Arbor.*

9. Perfection of Philosophy. — P. W. H. RAWLS, *Kalamazoo.*

10. Music.

11. Claims of Agriculture on Science. — GEO. W. PRAY, *Superior.*

12. Lamech—A Fragment. — J. D. COLLINS, *Lyndon.*

Characters,
- Lambert, — *J. D. Collins.*
- Jarab, — *C. A. Clark.*
- Naphel, — *P. W. H. Rawls.*
- Sons of Lamech, — *T. B. Cuming, E. Lawrence.*

13. The Hire of Intellect. — EDMUND FISH, *Bloomfield.*

14. Music.

Part 2.

15. Greek Poem. — THOS. B. CUMING, *Grand Rapids.*

16. The proper direction of Intellectual Effort. — GEO. E. PARMELEE, *Ann Arbor.*

17. Physics and Metaphysics—Their Laws equally determinable. — JOHN MACKAY, *Calais, Me.*

18. Music.

19. Poem. The Nazarine. — P. W. H. RAWLS, *Kalamazoo.*

20. Connection between Faith and Knowledge. — CHAS. A. CLARK, *Monroe.*

21. Influence of the Crusades. — FLETCHER O. MARSH, *Kalamazoo.*

22. Music.

23. Degrees conferred.

24. Address to the Class.

25. Prayer.

Another kind of class exhibition was given on the Commencement stage from 1845 to 1878. The first Commencement of the University took place in the Presbyterian Church—not the present structure—on the sixth day of August, 1845. Professor Williams presided, and eleven students were graduated Bachelors of

Arts. Every member of the class delivered an oration, and two of them read poems in addition to their oratorical efforts. The nature of the rest of the exercises can be made out from the facsimiles herewith presented of the first three pages of the programme, which was a four-page affair, five inches in width and nearly eight inches in height, having the fourth page blank. Professor TenBrook made the closing address to the class. In the evening Mesdames Denton, Hawkins, and Page gave an entertainment in honor of the graduating class.

Not until the Commencement of '74 was the University able to hold the closing exercises of the college year under its own roof. Prior to the completion of University Hall recourse was had to the city churches, and, sometimes, to the hall of the Union School building. The Methodist Church was used from 1870 to 1873.

In early times each member of the graduating class in the literary department spoke on the Commencement stage. This necessitated in 1854 a morning and an afternoon session. When the large class of '61 was departing all of its members were required to write orations, and twenty-five speakers were chosen by lot. Beginning with '67 there was but one session on Commencement Day, and a comparatively small number of speakers was selected from the class by the faculty. Thereafter a Commencement appointment became the highest honor in college, and the desire to obtain one undoubtedly led to harder work on the part of the leading third of each class. From '67 to '77, both inclusive, 134 appointments were made, the proportion of appointments to graduates being about one in six. As was the case with Junior Exhibition, the selections made by the Faculty were not always exempt from criticism, yet on the whole they were fairly representative of the ability of the students as shown by their four years' records. The authorities gave '70 the option of making its own appointees, but after several meetings that wise class decided to let the speakers be chosen as before. In 1873–74 The Chronicle urged that "the standard of excellence to be attained, and the regulations of award, be fixed for this, our only college honor". After '75 had reached its senior year it asked that Commencement speaking be abolished; but the Faculty denied the request, and, perplexed by the great size and abnormal merits of the class, adopted the unprecedented plan of selecting twenty men by vote, and then of drawing by lot ten speakers from the twenty. As the names of the ten not drawn were not made public, every member of the class could flatter himself that he was one of the twenty even if his name did not appear among the ten; and it was jocosely reported that at least thirty men were individually and privately informed by members of the Faculty that they were among the worthy but unfortunate ten whose names were lost in the official lottery. No subterfuge of the kind was resorted to in '76 or '77, but with the departure of the latter class student speaking at Commencement ceased, and the plan of inviting some distinguished person to deliver a formal "Commencement Address" was inaugurated. Many alumni think that the Commencement exercises have lost somewhat in personal interest because of the radical change which was introduced twenty years ago. Following is the list of the Commencement appointees from '67 to '77, the men whose names are italicised having been excused from speaking:

'67 William M. Brown,
" George E. Church,
" Isaac N. Elwood,
" William J. English,
" Henry N. French,
" George S. Hastings,
" Edward E. Kane,
" Dwight N. Lowell,
" George L. Maris,
" Isaac N. Otis,
" Artemas Richards,
" Edward W. Wetmore,
'68 William K. Anderson,
" Wickliffe W. Belville,
" Francis A. Blackburn,
" Daniel W. Crouse,
" Isaac N. Demmon,
" John C. Freeman,
" Mark W. Harrington,
" George S. Hickey,
" Roselle N. Jenne,
" Edward C. Lovell,
" Albert H. Pattengill,
" Galusha Pennell,
" Edward L. Walter,
'69 W. J. Cocker,
" W. J. Darby,
" F. S. Dewey,
" *F. A. Dudgeon,*
" J. M. Gelston,
" W. J. Gibson,
" F. M. Hamilton,
" W. C. Johns,
" M. B. Kellogg,
" *T. F. Kerr,*
" *Henry Lamm,*
" Charles E. Otis,
'69 T. O. Perry,
" *H. G. Snover,*
" *O. S. Vreeland,*
" *A. E. Wilkinson,*
'70 Marcus Baker,
" *Charles Ballenger,*
" Wooster W. Beman,
" Oscar J. Campbell,
" George T. Campau,
" Thomas C. Christy,
" Edwin Fleming,
" Washington Hyde,
" *John S. Maltman,*
" William L. Penfield,
" Vincent S. Lovell,
" Walter B. Stevens,
" Burrie L. Swift,
'71 Charles E. Gorton,
" *Preston C. Hudson,*
" Richard Hudson, Jr.,
" Harry B. Hutchins,
" *Earl Knight,*
" Edward L. Mark,
" *Joseph A. Mercer,*
" Rufus E. Phinney,
" Edward B. Sumner,
" Robert M. Wright,
'72 Charles G. Bennett,
" Archer H. Brown,
" Walter A. Brooks,
" Henry F. Burton,
" Horatio N. Chute,
" Will J. Herdman,
" Lester McLean,
" Herbert Maguire,
" Barton Smith,
" Madelon L. Stockwell,

'72 Charles K. Turner,
" William T. Underwood,
'73 Sidney C. Eastman,
" Henry W. Gelston,
" Robert S. Gross,
" Albert P. Jacobs,
" Charles B. Keeler,
" Loyal E. Knappen,
" *Sherwood R. Peabody*,
" Marshall K. Ross,
" Volney M. Spalding,
" *Ernest T. Tappey*,
" Charles M. VanCleve,
" William B. Williams,
" Charles L. Wilson,
'74 Frank A. Carle,
" Lyman D. Follett,
" Emma M. Hall,
" Sarah D. Hamlin,
" Frank C. Hayman,
" George H. Jameson,
" Theodore H. Johnston,
" Chester T. Lane,
" Don A. Matthews,
" Lawrence Maxwell, Jr.,
" Charles H. May,
" Henry R. Pattengill,
" Henry W. Rogers,
" Mary D. Sheldon,
" Calvin Thomas,
'75 Olive S. L. Anderson,
" James M. Barrett,
" *Lorenzo Davis, Jr.*,
" Bronson C. Keeler,
" Jerome C. Knowlton,
" Andrew J. McGowan,
" James B. McMahon,
" Leslie C. McPherson,
" Jonathan W. Parker,
" *John S. Stoddart*,
'76 Charles A. Blair,
" Clarence S. Brown,
" Henry M. Campbell,
" Annie W. Ekin,
" Alice E. Freeman,
" James K. Ilsley,
" Howard B. Smith,
" Orlaf Varlo,
" Bryant Walker,
" Willis S. Walker,
'77 George S. Bishop,
" Granville W. Browning,
" *George C. Comstock*,
" John S. Crombie,
" Frank C. Ferguson,
" Ferris S. Fitch, Jr.,
" William J. Gray,
" Lawrence C. Hull,
" Mary O. Marston,
" George N. Orcutt.

Class Day, the most distinctive function of a college class as such, seems to have had its origin in the "Class Day Exercises" held by '62 in its junior year on the evening of March 19, 1861, in the Congregational Church. The entertainment consisted of an address by the President, Albert J. Chapman, a poem by M. L. D'Ooge, a "chronicle" by J. H. Goodsell, an oration by Albert Nye, and a prophecy by J. E. Colby. Class Day proper, however, is supposed to refer particularly to the senior class; and the first celebration of this kind whereof we have record was held by '61 on the Monday before Commencement, when an oration and a poem were publicly delivered in the afternoon, a history and a prophecy being presented at the class supper at Hangsterfer's in the evening. The observance of Class Day by '63 and '64 was very informal, the latter class being satisfied with the formation of a tumulus near the north college from such materials as text-books and geological specimens; but the class of '65 had a very formal celebration on the last day of May, the beginning of senior vacation. The exercises were held in the Presbyterian Church. Professor Boise "presented" the class in a Greek speech, to which President Haven replied in Latin. It is said that of the other exercises the class poem by Gabriel Campbell was particularly worthy of mention. Every subsequent class, with one exception, has carefully celebrated its "Day", the date chosen being, at first, the opening of the senior vacation. When that vacation was abolished, Monday before Commencement was preempted by the graduating class, but when Commencement was moved from Wednesday to Thursday, Tuesday was selected for these exercises. The class of '66 was presented by Professor Frieze, who spoke in Latin, as did also President Haven. Professor Winchell delivered the presentation address for '67. Owing to the absence of President Haven the class of '68 was not presented, but otherwise the customary exercises took place. When the turn of '69 came the presentation was by Professor Evans. That class, like its predecessors, gave its presentation exercises, its oration, and its poem in the forenoon in one of the city churches, but unlike earlier classes it planned to hold its afternoon exercises in the open air. However there was rain, and the class history and prophecy were read in the law-lecture room. Later in the day the class planted a white elm in front of south college, near by its previously-placed memorial, "calico rock". Professor Olney made the presentation speech for the class of '70, and his address was the last of its kind, for when '71 was to be graduated an unpopular professor stood next in the line, and the class would have none of him, nor would any other member of the Faculty so violate inter-professorial courtesy as to accept an invitation over his head. Thus a very interesting custom perished. The class of '70 held afternoon exercises on the campus, an unique feature of the occasion being the presentation, in an address by George T. Campau, of the class memorial, a statue of Benjamin Franklin. This class also added to the usual exercises the presentation to the homeliest of its number by the next homeliest of a leather medal. Prizes were given by '71 on its Class Day to the best (?) ponyist, the best (?) penman, the best (?) whiskered man, the best (?) orator, and the biggest eater. The class of '72 gave as "Rewards of Merit" a "Mean Time Chronometer to "The Coming Man", and a copy

of the treatise "What I know about Farming" to the Representative of the Farmers' club (an association organized for the purpose of inspecting corn juice and malt fluids). Presentations also figured in the Class Day exercises of '77.

At first not much attention was paid to the history read on Class Day, but gradually the historian learned the art of detailing therein exploits which never had been performed, or which had been performed on a scale much humbler than the narrative disclosed. Often also members of the Faculty were insulted. Twice or thrice, particularly in 1871, the authorities manifested a wish to revise the class history before the reading thereof; but this was strenuously resisted. Finally action was taken, and in February, 1878, the Faculty adopted a resolution providing that if any member of a graduating class should thereafter upon Class Day indulge in words or acts regarded by the Faculty as disrespectful to any officer of the University, or deemed of a nature to encourage misdemeanors in other students and to interfere with the good government of the institution, the name of such offender should not be presented for graduation. This decree brought grief to the heart of the historian of '78, for it took away his vocation. If one could not indulge in boastful recitals, if one could not "get even" with professors and instructors who had made college life a bore, why should one set up the pins for election as historian? Efforts were made to do away with Class Day, but other counsels prevailed. In consequence of the indignation of many members of the class against certain class officers who, chosen as "Independents" had joined in forming a new society and had refused to resign, there was no celebration by the class of '80, and consequently there was no oration, history, poem, or prophecy.

In the professional departments, with the exception of the law school, Class Day is not so formal an affair as in the college proper. Formerly the celebration took place in March; but beginning in 1885 June has been the favored month. Of course, the exercises of each department are distinct from those of the other schools.

Nearly all of the important social functions among the students have originated with and have been conducted under the auspices of some one of the academic classes. To '68 belongs the honor of having introduced the Senior Hop. "Friday evening, Nov. 29, 1867", says a college paper of the time, "forty ladies and an equal number of gentlemen assembled by invitation of the Senior class at the Gregory House to trip the light fantastic toe. We congratulate '68 on their (its) success, and we hope that many seniors may be found in coming years to continue the custom thus happily inaugurated". It should be said here that the Gregory House so often named in accounts of social affairs of the sixties and seventies was a hotel long since discontinued but occupying the large brick block at the northwest corner of Main and Huron streets. In speaking of the Hop given by the class of '70, at which twenty-eight couples were present, The Chronicle of November 20, 1869, speaks of the Senior Hop "as one of the established customs of college life" and declares that the success of the class of '70 "should put to flight all scepticism in the matter". A similar party was given by the class of '71 in December, 1870, but for some reason '72 failed to follow suit, and the custom fell through.

The Junior Promenade Concert given by the class of '73 on the evening of the ninth of February, 1872, was the first of the long series of entertainments given by the junior class or by the secret-fraternity men in that class. We are told by the college paper that '73's effort "was a great success", and the same periodical records the gradual development of this function. "The invitations of '73, '74, and '75 had not", says The Chronicle, "the least bit of engraving" (by which was meant illustration, for all the invitations were printed from steel plates), "though each was an improvement on its predecessor". With '76 the place of giving the "Junior Hop" was changed from the hotel to the Armory, and various improvements were introduced. "Sixty couples" we are told, "attended, including many guests from Toledo, Detroit, East Saginaw, and other cities". By '77 and '78 the Junior Hop was brought up to the standard of similar entertainments given by Eastern colleges. When given by '79 this affair was officially styled "Promenade Concert", and the invitations contained illustrations of the college buildings. As the time for the class of '81 to begin preparing for its Junior Hop drew near, a spirit of opposition to the continuance of the function was disclosed; and just before the Thanksgiving recess the class by a large majority voted to abolish the entertainment. In strictness the Hop never had been a class affair, and never could be made such. Nominally carried on under class auspices it never happened that a majority of its participants was drawn from the class. As The Chronicle of December 6, 1879, said "The class has the privilege of taxing themselves (itself) so much each to pay for the invitations, of fretting around a month to make every arrangement complete, and, perhaps, of finally making up a deficit in the finances. . . . As a general thing, probably, not one out of five of the juniors will be found on the floor".

It was however felt that the Junior Hop should continue; and the secret societies—which from the first had really managed

the entertainment,—now came forward to sustain it when abandoned by the juniors as a class Saturday, December 13, delegations from Chi Psi, Alpha Delta Phi, Delta Kappa Epsilon, Sigma Phi, Zeta Psi, and Psi Upsilon met to discuss the advisability of giving a Junior Hop under the auspices of the secret fraternities. It was determined to invite the remaining societies (Beta Theta Pi and Phi Kappa Psi) to join, and after adopting several resolutions the meeting adjourned until Saturday, December 15, when a permanent organization was effected. For many years the eight societies named above, and Delta Tau Delta, (admitted to the league in 1883), conducted the annual ball which had become so strongly entrenched in student esteem.

The first Junior Hop officially conducted by the secret fraternities was given at Hangsterfer's on the evening of January 30, 1880. Engraved invitations illustrated with several misprints had been sent into many peaceful homes in the chief cities of Michigan and of the neighboring states, and were very generally accepted. As for the Hop itself "it was a brilliant affair, and reflected credit upon the ambitious juniors. The hall was handsomely decorated with festoons of evergreens, spreading from the chandeliers to the sides of the hall, and with a liberal display of bunting looped up in graceful folds. The monograms of the societies which united in giving the entertainment were displayed upon the walls, and added materially to the generally good effect of the decorations". Another Hop was given under fraternity management in 1881, and a third in 1882. In 1882–83 Alpha Delta Phi, Psi Upsilon, and Phi Kappa Psi, owing to alleged unfairness in the distribution of the committeeships, and influenced no doubt by the animosities which had arisen in the recent elections of The Chronicle and the Students' Lecture Association, withdrew from the Junior Hop, and that entertainment was given by only five societies, February 3, 1883. Efforts were made in November, 1883, to reconcile the warring factions, and there was a full attendance of delegates from the eight fraternities, together with a representative from Delta Tau Delta seeking admission into the league. Then the Hop committee was organized by the election of a chairman and secretary from the element which had given the last preceding ball, and an adjournment was taken. An unfavorable distribution of the sub-committee honors being foreshadowed, Psi Upsilon at the next meeting of the committee announced its withdrawal, alleging, says The Chronicle, "its superior advantages for giving private parties, and a lack of interest on the part of its members". At the following meeting the resignation was accepted, and Delta Tau Delta was admitted to representation. Then Alpha Delta Phi and Phi Kappa Psi withdrew, the latter giving no reasons, the former expressing itself dissatisfied with the appointments which in the meantime had been made by the chairman. Influenced by the action of the three dissentients Delta Tau Delta soon withdrew, leaving five societies to conduct the festivities. But owing to the deaths of two members and the serious illness of a third member of the fraternity party which was supporting the Hop, the entertainment was omitted for that year. An amicable agreement was effected before another year passed; and on the evening of February 19, 1885, the Junior or Society Hop was given in the skating rink, nine fraternities participating, and everybody being happy. This peaceful state of affairs continued for several years, the annual Hop all the time gaining in importance. In 1888–89 a disagreement arose over the committees, the fraternities which had founded The Argonaut demanding a reapportionment of the honors, and in lieu thereof that the tax should be changed from one per capita to a fixed amount to be paid by each fraternity irrespective of the number of its members. Of course the latter method of taxation is the only just one where each society has one vote and only one vote. At the next meeting of the committee the tax proposition was withdrawn, and the first demand was renewed. This being refused, Alpha Delta Phi, Psi Upsilon, Chi Psi, and Phi Kappa Psi withdrew. However a compromise was effected, and the Hop took place as usual. By a system which assured to each of the constituent members of the society trust proper recognition, affairs were for several years successfully and harmoniously conducted. But opposition to the management by nine fraternities of what was in name at least a class function gradually increased among the independents, and especially among the members af the excluded Greek-letter orders. To the latter—the men of Delta Upsilon, Phi Gamma Delta, Phi Delta Theta, Sigma Alpha Epsilon, and Theta Delta Chi, the unrelenting attitude of the older fraternities was as gall and worm-wood. With the completion of the Waterman Gymnasium, in which building the Junior Hop was held as early as 1893, this annual festival became so important that the non-participating organizations determined at all hazards to gain admission. From the stronger members of the nine the opposition to increasing the number of the elect was somewhat perfunctory, and it was quietly said in the principal chapter houses that two or three of the outside groups were stronger at Ann Arbor and elsewhere than some of the elect; but the weaker societies, realizing the value of the inside seats, obstinately refused to enlarge the train. In 1894–95 President Angell so far yielded to the importunities of the aggrieved orders and to the neutrals whom the latter influenced, that he declined to grant the use of the Gymnasium to the nine fraternities, the ground of refusal being that the organization had not the sanction of the junior class or a majority thereof. This recognition of an officially obsolete class system was not cheerfully acquiesced in by the nine societies, all the members of which united at least outwardly in resisting dictation. They gave up the old name Junior Hop, and adopted for the festivities of 1895 the title "Nineteenth Annual Ball". Why that particular ordinal should have been selected it is hard to say, since the Junior class balls, by whatever name called, began in 1872, while those conducted under the auspices of the fraternities began in 1880. But other than numerical calculations interested the members of the old combination. Their enemies sought to prevent them from obtaining the Gymnsium, and it was only after much discussion that the Regents adopted a resolution authorizing the President and the Secretary to allow the use of the building "to any properly organized body of students at a rental of $100 a night". At the "Nineteenth Annual", so.called, given February 15, 1895, the nine fraternities appeared in full regalia, reinforced by the two dental societies, one of the law societies, and a group of independents, the nine however being the sole managers. Two hundred and fifty couples were present. So successful was the affair that another like it was planned for 1896. Accordingly, under the resolution of the Regents, the Gymnasium was leased for the appointed night, and the rent-money was duly paid; but the opposition, not discouraged by this vested interest, appeared before the Regents and begged them not to allow the use of the building to so proscriptive a body as the nine. They contended that the Annual Ball should not take place in the gymnasium unless it were made a genuine University affair in which there should be no discrimination against any society or body of students; and they showed that although they had been admitted to the floor on payment of a fixed fee they were there snubbed and discriminated against, and were not allowed to put up booths or insignia. In the appeals made to the Regents the sad state of the outside societies was movingly portrayed, while the undemocratic and unfeeling attitude of their oppressors was scathingly condemned. In truth the Regents cared for none of these things; they knew they were legally bound to carry out their lease; but an appeal unto the people had been threatened, and it was feared that appropriations would be withheld. After attempts to effect a compromise between the warring factions had failed, the Regents by a divided vote rescinded their lease, and adopted a resolution which excluded the illiberal nine unless the latter should reform. Undaunted by this rebuff the coalition took back the money it had paid in advance for the Gymnasium, and all of its constituent fraternities save Delta Kappa Epsilon went to Toledo for the "Twentieth Annual". On the other hand the academic fraternities—now reduced to four by the demise of Phi Gamma Delta—which had so long been kept in the anteroom, gave a hop of their own in the Gymnasium. Each of these entertainments was successful if the reports of its partisans are to be accepted.

From what has been said it is plain that the nine fraternities were not broadly liberal in their treatment of younger rivals; nor can the action of the latter in persistently forcing themselves upon those who did not want their company, be approved. After the nine had surrendered the old name they were strictly within their rights, although it is of course true that rights are not always to be insisted upon. Toward the close of 1896 a settlement was effected. All the academic societies and the independents are allowed representation on the committee for the Annual Ball, the general chairmanship going to the fraternities in order of establishment; while the other places on the committee are chosen by lot. This arrangement having been made, all hands united in labor for the Hop of 1897, which occurred on the evening of February nineteenth. Whatever may be said about the present plan it has the advantage of conducing to harmony.

Senior Reception, a social event hardly second in importance to the Junior Hop, was, like the latter, inaugurated by the class of '73. The invitations issued by that class were printed from a steel plate the chief feature of the design being a monogram of the letters "U" and "M", with the class numerals in the centre. A committee appointed by the class president, and consisting of A. G. Bishop, S. T. Douglas, J. R. Goff, R. D. Harrison, V. M. Spalding, F. H. Walker, and W. B. Williams—one member of each of the five secret societies in the class, and two neutrals—managed this very successful affair, which was given in University Hall on the evening of May 27, 1873, the night before Class-Day. Room A, then used by Professor Cocker, was set aside for dancing, and the entire lower floor was thrown open to the guests. Similar receptions were given by '74, '75, and '76. In 1877 the Methodist Conference adopted a resolution protesting against the use of the college buildings for dancing, and the Board of Regents deemed it wise to forbid such use; so the class of '77 put up on the north side of the campus near the present homœopathic college a pavilion in which the afternoon exercises of Class Day, and also the Senior Reception—with abundant dancing—were held. In 1878 and for some years thereafter a pavilion for the use of dancers was erected close to the east entrance to University Hall, and the latter was open to the guests. The Regents in 1882 rescinded their decree against dancing in Room A. By the class of '84 it was resolved not to give a reception with dancing, and as this was the action of a majority of the class, a petition from members to be allowed the use of the halls and grounds of the college for the purposes of a reception was refused by President Angell, he conceiving that he had no right to grant such a privilege to any but the class in its entirety. Consequently the Senior Reception that year was given by those seniors who favored dancing. The invitations were to the St. James Hotel, and later to the skating rink. Since the completion of the Gymnasium the Senior Reception has been held in that building, on the Tuesday evening before Commencement.

In 1886, on the evening of the sixth of November, a "fraternity sophomore hop" was given, and several events of like character have occurred since. At present the sophomore hop is not restricted to members of the societies.

Strictly a class custom was the burning or hanging of Mechanics, Physics, or Mathematics, which certainly began as early as 1860, and which, with variations and interruptions, lasted until 1881. The class of '61 burned Mechanics on the night of February 6, 1860; but '64 put its enemy to death in another way, as appears from the elaborate four-page programme of the obsequies, entitled "Severance of the Mechanical Jugular by the Class of '64. 'Fiat justitia ruat coelum' University of Michigan". That programme contains a "Dirge", an "Opening Hymn", a "Paean of Victory", a "Closing Ode", a "Grand Finale!! The Corpus abducted by the Prince of Medicks", and a "Doxology by the Class". The programme emitted by '65 is entitled: "Suspension of the Physical Corpus! by the Class of '65", and the one which '66 published had on the first page these words: "Corpuscularian Separation of the Mechanical Body of Physics, Through the Instrumentality of Spontaneous Combustion, by the class of '66". Many unique ceremonies accompanied the burning or hanging. Professor Williams, popularly called "Punky", was much averse to the custom, and in 1865 he told the boys they'd "better not do that any more", but '67 burned Physics just the same in 1866, "the examination of witnesses being postponed until after execution, as there is no doubt of the culprit's guilt". Toward the close of Dr. Williams's labors there was little to rejoice at in the finishing of the study of Mechanics, for no one pretended to study the subject; and so the annual burning was dispensed with. But when the class of '73 reached its junior year a new man stood in "Punky's" shoes, and the men who had planned to take their ease remained to work. Consequently the old custom was revived, and the ashes of Ganot's treatise were dispersed to the four winds in the most approved manner. By '74 also the custom was observed. The class of '75 gave an entertainment at Hangsterfer's in which Physics, in its most ludicrous aspects, was portrayed. There was no burning or other ceremony by '76, but the custom cannot be said to have become obsolete until after 1881. The programmes of the executions are an interesting and a very rare part of the memorabilia of student life at Ann Arbor.

PROGRAMME.

IGNOMINIOUS EXECUTION

—OF—

PHYSICA MECHANICA.

In accordance with a judgment rendered by a Military Commission, authorized by President O'Mahony, under a special suspension of the Writ of Habeas Corpus.

CONDUCTED BY THE CLASS OF '67.

"Am I to be physicked and blistered by this vile wretch?"

FEBRUARY 10, 1866

UNIVERSITAS MICHIGANENSIUM.

"Hazing" at Michigan as elsewhere is one of the outgrowths of class feeling. Half a century ago there was little of it, although we are told that occasionally a precocious freshman received by way of admonition a nocturnal application of cold water. With the rapid increase in the number of students which marked the third decade of the University, class spirit waxed fiercer, and sophomoric attentions to freshmen became more varied and more frequent. Three or four years after the close of the Civil War an old soldier, having entered the freshman class, was waited upon by a committee of sophomores who informed him that he was to be "smoked out". He treated his uninvited guests with great politeness, and after closing all the windows seated himself upon the floor. The sophomores smoked, and he smoked. Some of them began to feel the joke had gone far enough, but he thought otherwise. Finally they left, making, as he related, a very disorderly retreat. Not long afterwards another freshman, learning that the tormentors were upon him, stood armed with a full grown baseball bat, behind his door. As the foremost sophomore entered he was received with so tremendous a whack that his comrades withdrew to effect upon him the needed repairs. This failure to appreciate the humor of a college joke was severely criticised by all the sophomores.

Before the building of University Hall four hundred students of the literary department were crowded into the same halls and recitation rooms which preceding classes aggregating fewer than two hundred had filled. Here were occasions and opportunities for class rushes which could not fail to be improved. If sophomores going down stairs were jostled by freshmen going up, a "rush" ensued. Early in October, 1867, there was a spirited fight between '70 and '71, in which a freshman fiercely laid low a professor who was trying to quell the tumult. The *novus homo* remarked "that feller thought he could send me to grass, but he can't do it; I can down him every time". After this a good-natured test of strength and weight took place every year between the newly-fledged sophomores and the entering class. For some time the Faculty interposed no objection to this annual contest. On the other hand, disorder in chapel was regarded as a high breach of discipline; and when the sophomores of '72 in their anxiety to demolish their enemies of '73 hurled at them as they were taking their seats apples and other missiles, the former were compelled by a per capita assessment to pay for the damage inflicted upon the walls, windows, and pictures of the chapel. The annual struggle between the classes soon took the form of a football contest in which the organization and discipline of the sophomores were usually more than a match for the greater numbers of the freshmen. Long after the Rugby rules had been introduced at Ann Arbor the old and simple style of football prevailed so far as this particular game was concerned. All that was necessary was to kick two out of three goals, and as many men as possible were mustered on each side. Of course the game often degenerated into a rush; and it was usually followed—or preceded—by boxing and wrestling. The Chronicle of October 6, 1888, suggested doing away with the annual football rush, but this was not heeded. In the great contest between '92 and '93, when 117 sophomores captained by Van Inwagen met 163 freshmen commanded by Dygert, one of the freshmen had a rib smashed; and this led to the declaration by The U. of M. Daily that the University had finally outgrown this antiquated sport. No more conflicts of the kind have occurred; but in the autumn of 1886 some old-time "rushing" occurred, two freshmen were suspended, and a petition for their reinstatement was denied.

It has been related that the class of '73, in order to secure the return to college of some of its malefactors, was obliged to pledge itself to proper behavior. Accordingly chapel exercises for the first time in years were quiet and orderly at the opening of college in September, 1870. But '73 construed its pledge as requiring the class to maintain good order; and learning that some of the members of '74 were engaged in serenading with horns an objectionable tutor, a select band of sophomores showed the freshmen the error of their ways by "pumping" them, that is, treating their heads to a cold-water bath. This started the ball, and "pumping" thenceforth and for some time was a collegiate exercise much in vogue.

One evening in October, 1872, occurred a lively pumping contest and a moonlight rush between '75 and '76. The former conceived itself to be victorious, and one of its members prepared a neat banner out of the trousers of one of the enemy. Another member attempted to take this ensign into chapel, but one of the professors interfered, and the young man was suspended for one year. All attempts to secure the reinstatement of their classmate proving ineffectual, the men of '75 remained irreconcilable during the rest of their college life.

In the spring of 1874 "hazing" had become so common a

species of amusement that the Faculty determined to put an end to it. Accordingly three members of '76 and three of '77 were suspended for the rest of the college year. This occasioned great indignation, the condemned and their classmates complaining of lack of warning; and papers were drawn up in which the signers—thirty-nine sophomores and forty-five freshmen—declared themselves equally guilty with the six. Before doing this a procession of 150 students from both classes, headed by an omnibus containing the suspended men passed through the streets of an afternoon, stopping before the houses of various professors, cheering those supposed to be favorable, and giving groans to those regarded as hostile to their cause. They also followed one or two professors through the streets, howling and hissing at them. Two days later at a union meeting of the two classes a committee was by unanimous vote instructed to present an apology for the insults offered to the professors, but by a heavy vote the papers were allowed to remain. The Faculty waited one week before taking official action upon the papers; and in the meantime it was intimated that the signatures might be withdrawn. Several names were withdrawn. At its next meeting the Faculty suspended for the rest of the college year the eighty-one students whose names remained. Soon after a committee from the upper classes issued a circular sustaining the sophomores and freshmen, and stating in these words the nature of hazing:

> "As practiced in the University of Michigan hazing is simply an athletic contest between the sophomore and freshman classes, and, like other athletic sports, is participated in with the best of mutual good-feeling. Only hazers are hazed. A principle of hazing here is that those who refrain from it are not molested."

Among the signers of this letter, which was addressed to the friends of the University throughout the State, were Lawrence Maxwell, Jr., recently Solicitor-General of the United States, and Calvin Thomas now of the Faculty of Columbia University.

Kidnapping the toastmaster of the freshmen on the eve of the class supper came into fashion between 1880 and 1890. In May, 1890, the sophomores took the "magister bibendi" of '93 to the little village of Mooreville twelve miles from Ann Arbor. He was rescued by his comrades, and five sophomores were suspended from college for their villainy. As late as 1895 the abduction and mild mistreatment of freshmen by sophomores led to the suspension of the latter. So severe have been the preventive influences of athletic sports and of the gymnasium, that hazing is now almost a lost art. While it lived it gave rise to much harmless fun, but when it died it was not to be regretted.

When the exterior of University Hall was finished certain members of '73 were troubled—as many other students have been since—by the plain and bald appearance of the structure. One evening nine men of the class climbed at dead of night to the top of the dome and nailed to the newly-erected flag-staff a banner twenty feet long upon which appeared an immense rooster, and, in large letters, the words "Junior Brigands". Toward the close of the course a deputation from the same class put a Modoc squaw theretofore used as a tobacco sign, on the pedestal surmounting the dome, just where it was hoped the generosity of some benefactor would place a statue of Michigan. To the wooden Indian they tied four roosters, which crowed unceasingly from the middle of the night until morning, when the janitor gave to them their liberty and to her owners the Indian.

One of the rules of the University punishes concerted absence from any appointed duty by a class. This regulation was suddenly called to the attention of members of '73 and '74, who, on Tuesday, May 23, 1871, had "bolted" their recitations for the purpose of attending the circus. Forty-seven of the sixty-one victims were sophomores, nearly all being members of the Greek section. Their instructor, Acting-Professor Jones, had promised to give them a holiday, but for some reason had refused to give this particular day. He found in his class-room only two students—those two having failed to receive notice of the proposed "bolt"—but the recitation, one in the most difficult part of the Antigone, went on just the same. All the "bolters" were suspended from college until September. The college paper pronounced the punishment too sudden and sweeping. However, "concerted absences" have been rare since the experience of '73; and the members of that turbulent class never think of a circus without recalling their "bolt" and its penalty.

Every class, holds, or is expected to hold, a reunion at Ann Arbor three years after it has left college. Sometimes classmates meet at Ann Arbor or Detroit in the year following their graduation. The second formal reunion generally takes place six years after the departure of the class from college. Another assembly is formed ten years after graduation, and at the close of every later decade. Reunions after fifteen years are not infrequent. The class of '70 has been particularly successful in its gatherings, which have been conducted with a good deal of zeal and ceremony. A class book describing the last preceding reunion, and giving all attainable information concerning the members, follows or should follow every formal post-graduate assembling of a class. The most elaborate of these reports was issued by the class of '70 after the members of that fine delegation had celebrated their vigentennial. Class books have also been printed by '66, '69, '73, and '75, and one is preparing for '68.

VIEW ON THE HURON.

CHAPTER V

TOWN AND GOWN

Ann Arbor is said to have derived its name from an incident which occurred when the adjacent country was first settled. The story runs that two pioneers established themselves and their families one on the east side the other on the west side. As the distance was too great for frequent visits, the wives of the two settlers used to meet in a beautiful grove half way distant from each home. Their husbands called the meeting-place Ann's Arbor, as each of the women was named Ann. In time the meeting place gave its name to a village. According to another account the Indian name of the district was Anaba, which, carelessly pronounced and erroneously written, became the name of the town.

When Ann Arbor was chosen as the site of the University the number of its inhabitants was much less than the present attendance in the halls of our Alma Mater. What was an insignificant village sixty-one years ago has become a beautiful city with handsome public buildings, fine churches, and twelve thousand permanent residents. The environment is the most picturesque in southern Michigan. Most of the city lies upon an elevated plateau all the sides of which descend only to meet ground which rises into the encircling hills.

LIBRARY BUILDING.

Many years ago the presence in Ann Arbor of not a few families of wealth and prominence gave rise to a local society quite distinct from that of which the professors and their wives were the constituents. Deaths and removals have nearly obliterated this peculiar coterie to which many alumni gratefully acknowledge indebtedness; and the town is overshadowed socially and otherwise by the extraordinary growth of the University.

In the present prosaic times the students seldom have with the town-people disputes more serious than are wont to arise over unsettled bills for board, lodging, and laundrying. Of old, things were different. Ann Arbor counted among its people a railroad element and a foreign element; and to neither of these elements were the college boys strictly congenial. Therefore when the student met the "townie" on the latter's ground trouble was likely to result; and it is not to be supposed that the college youth treated too courteously his less fortunate fellow-being. An illustration of this is furnished by the so-called "Dutch War," which arose from the rough treatment accorded one evening in the winter of 1856 to two students who were making themselves unpleasantly conspicuous in Hangsterfer's saloon. The next night they returned with many of their comrades, and the obnoxious proprietor was told he must treat the crowd or suffer dire consequences as to his beer, his head, and his assembled friends. He refusing, the boys raised the battle cry "Revenge or Beer" and made a wild charge. Knives were drawn, clubs were flourished, kegs and barrels were staved in, and much beer was spilled. Finally the Germans fled, hotly pursued past the old Franklin House and out into the suburbs, until the boys were halted by the police. The parley wound up, we are told, with some complimentary remarks from the marshal, and three cheers for college spirit. But hard feeling remained, and one night, after an Alpha Nu "election-spread" at Hangsterfer's, six students ripe for mischief started to attend a Dutch ball which was in progress at Binder's. That they were not invited to attend the entertainment made no difference except in the degree of caution required. Having climbed the high ground behind the house they looked through a window and saw the refreshments spread in a vacant room. Improvising a ladder they crawled through the window, and soon were among the provisions. Elated with success they grew noisy, and the enemy came upon them so quickly as to capture one of their number who had stopped to take a farewell drink. Rushing to the campus his comrades secured reinforcements, and all hurried to the rescue, but Binder insisted upon a ransom of ten dollars. Meanwhile the alarm reached the medical students, and they too hastened to the scene of action. The crowd, grown larger and fiercer, chose a leader, and made a final demand, which was refused, for the surrender of the captive. Three large timbers were procured and used as battering rams. The brick walls began to give way, the girls within screamed, and a huge dog which Binder had sent out was met and killed by another furnished by one of the besiegers. Then a squad of students was detailed to fetch from the campus the muskets with which the boys were wont to drill. This move frightened Binder and he released the prisoner.

The next day six warrants of arrest were sworn out, and officers were sent to apprehend the accused. One of the latter was called upon to recite, but an innocent man rose in his place and went on with the lesson, the professor making no objection. When the class was adjourned an officer in waiting bade the one who had arisen to follow him, which he did, while the real culprit took to the woods. Again and again were the officers foiled. Students exchanged clothes, took breakfast in one place, dinner at another, and supper at a third. Three were concealed in the observatory, and three in a regent's house. Finally the boys devised a scheme to get rid of their troubles. Two students under age were sent to Binder's as decoys, and bought liquor there. The statute prohibiting the sale of intoxicating liquors to minors was invoked against the truculent Teuton, who withdrew his complaints and allowed his warrants to be quashed. This ended the "Dutch War," one of the most stirring episodes in Michigan student life.

Away back in the fifties some of the more reckless students began to devote an occasional evening to tearing up sidewalks and to lifting gates. So much stone flagging has been laid since 1890, and so much more attention has been given to the streets by the authorities, that it is hard for one familiar with the present condition of things to realize what pedestrians used to suffer. In 1882 one of the college papers made a complaint on this score, but matters in earlier years were far worse. Perhaps the extreme of dilapidation was revealed to the student eye when, under the influence of spring sunshine, the rickety planks of Ann Arbor's walks lay bare of snow after the winter of 1869-70. To the class of '73 the opportunity of working a great reform now presented itself; and on Monday evening, April 11, about half of those members whom the semi-annual examinations had spared executed upon aged side-walks a raid unsurpassed in Michigan annals for extent and thoroughness. The consequences were more serious than had been anticipated; warrants of arrest were gotten out, and only with the utmost difficulty, by dodging from one boarding-house to another, and by taking hasty trips to Detroit, did the chief malefactors avoid the minions of the law. It is impossible to tell what would have happened, for the city officials were wild with rage, had not Acting President Frieze, having obtained from the authorities an estimate of the damage caused by the freshmen, paid the amount—$225—out of his own pocket. One of the histories of the University says "the students engaged in the work at once repaid it (the money) to him"; but as a matter of fact the class of '73 raised the money for Dr. Frieze by levying a tax of $2.25 a head upon its members, regardless of whether or not they had been invited to attend the midnight party which brought on so much trouble. Although the tax was cheerfully paid there were those who thought that very bad form had been shown somewhere. At the Exhibition given by the class in May of the same year the glee-club sang an original song entitled "Send Me Some Money From Home", one stanza of which ran:

> "And now we've to pay for the piper
> For dancing on that April night;
> Two hundred and twenty-five dollars—
> Why don't the old gentleman write?"

Not long afterwards The Chronicle innocently inquired whether the money had not been spent for the aldermen's beer instead of for new sidewalks.

Another "fine" time was enjoyed in May, 1881, by a few unior medical students, who paid $150 for sundry street-lamps smashed by them in the course of a nocturnal spree. The college paper heartlessly suggested to the victims that at $10 apiece street-lamps come high.

PROFESSOR FRIEZE.

From 1877 until after 1890 Hallowe'en was an occasion when gates required to be fastened with unusual care, and when walks and signs needed to be watched. On that night in 1883 there was much disturbance; more plank walks were raised than at any time since the outburst of '73; the statue of the late B. Franklin received a coat of paint; and many business signs were removed to places where they could not be discerned. These varieties of lawlessness have now almost disappeared, and certainly are not as frequent as might be expected when the number and age of the students are considered.

A standing aggravation to law-breaking used to be the Ann

Arbor policeman, a queer compound of prejudice, ignorance, and stupidity. In the early years of the "force" indiscriminate threats to shoot students for the offence of gathering in little groups at the down-town street corners, or for singing their college songs, were often made. In October, 1874, two students wrestling after dark on the campus were arrested by the vigilant guardians of the peace. There was a show of resistance, and the next night counter demonstrations were made by the students. The Chronicle with good reason remonstrated against the invasion of the University's grounds by the police. Soon afterwards the latter attacked a group of sophomores, and seizing the smallest of the lot began to drag him to the lock-up. The prisoner, now a representative in Congress from one of the Illinois districts, made a sudden jump, partially freed himself, and being caught by the coat-tails adroitly slipped his arms out of the coat and made good his escape. The astonished officers held up the coat and blandly invited the young fellow to get back into it, but were told where they might go with the garment. They concluded, says The Chronicle, to wait until cooler weather before they hung the coat on its accustomed peg in those warm regions.

Before 1882 the post-office was in a small and inconvenient building the entrance into and the egress from which were by the same narrow door. The carrier-delivery system had not yet been introduced, and the students were accustomed to assemble at the office every evening about the time of the arrival and distribution of the mails from the east and the west. Often there were provoking delays in the delivery, and it could hardly be expected that every one of five hundred or more students would refrain from jostling and pushing, or from raising his voice somewhat higher than the conversational pitch. On the night of the 12th of October, 1877, the freshmen and sophomores came into closer contact at the post-office than the patience of either would allow, and as the office seemed not the best of places for a "rush" they adjourned to the campus. After they had gone the Mayor and his minions came forward and boldly arrested a young fellow who had taken no part in the disturbance. He was released that night on his own recognizance, and was discharged the next morning.

More serious trouble came two years later. From the opening of the fall session of 1879 the policemen took especial satisfaction in making themselves obnoxious to students. A group of twenty-five could not assemble in any place without an officer's making his appearance. Tuesday evening, October 14, the boys on reaching the post-office found at the door policemen who would allow but one student to enter at a time. The passage to the delivery windows was long and narrow, and as the closing hour was early, it became evident that unless the delivery was rapid many would not get their letters that night. Still, the students kept remarkably good order, but finally, incensed by the rough movements and language of the police they broke out into shouts and yells, whereupon several of them were struck and arrested. On the following night a large crowd of students and citizens gathered in the same place. This assemblage was a signal for the ringing of the fire-bell to call out the state militia and also a gang of roughs deputized as special policemen. The former charged with fixed bayonets, wounding a citizen of the town; and the special police, incited, it was said, by an offer from the mayor of two dollars for each arrest, laid hands on every student who could be found, no matter where he was going or what he was doing. Ten or twelve sons of Michigan tax-payers passed the night in the county jail, to be discharged the next morning, none of the officers who made the arrests being on hand to prefer charges. For the disturbances of that term Mayor Smith was chiefly responsible. His action—influenced by hostility to the University—in calling out the militia and in summoning special policemen was both ridiculous and dangerous. Mr. Sessions, the city attorney, who refused to uphold the mayor's course was removed by the city council. Money having been raised, suits for false imprisonment were brought against the city and the Mayor, but on the advice of Judge Cooley and others who feared the consequences to the University of prolonging an unfortunate conflict, the actions were discontinued. In April, 1881, Mayor Smith, to the great delight of the students, failed of re-election.

One afternoon a few months after the post-office incident, fire broke out in a small room adjoining the law-building. The fire company having arrived on the scene too late to be of service in extinguishing the fire, and being angered by the raillery of the students, attacked the latter and were worsted. The Chronicle deprecated the affair, saying that the firemen had reached the fire as soon as they could.

About the middle of January, 1882, a policeman named Porter whose officiousness in quelling serenades had made him decidedly a *persona non grata* to the students, wantonly assaulted some members of the Alpha Delta Phi as they were returning from a supper at Hangsterfer's. For this he was prosecuted, the society courageously standing up for its rights. On the first trial the jury disagreed, although the evidence was clearly in favor of the prosecution; but on the second trial he was found guilty, and was sentenced to pay a fine of six dollars and four dollars costs.

Of all the encounters between town and gown the most serious occurred Wednesday, November 12, 1890. Several days before five undergraduates had been arrested for "rushing" in the post-office, and the student community was in a state of great excitement. Consequently when the sound of rifle-shots was heard on the evening of the day mentioned, many supposed that trouble was at hand. At least four hundred students soon gathered at the place of the firing, which was in front of a house in the most densely populated part of the city. It seems that the marriage of a member of the local militia company was celebrating in the house that night, and that a number of the bridegroom's comrades, being about to attend the ceremonies, fired, before entering the house, several volleys in honor of the occasion. Assembled in front of the house the students gave the University yell, and called for a speech. Some one came out and said to the boys—who had ceased their cries so they could hear—"This is the biggest crowd of ignorant people I ever saw". Of course this did not tend to disperse the crowd, which however was very good-natured and not particularly noisy. Soon the same speaker appeared again, and threateningly ordered the gathering to disperse. In a little while the militia-men filed out, and marched down the street to the intersection of Division and Liberty streets. Here Sergeant Granger, the commander of the detachment, urged his men to resist the students who were following and guying the squad. The so-called soldiers charged, using their muskets as clubs, and chased the unresisting students hither and thither, following them individually. Two or three of the excited militia-men rushed to the side-walk

PHYSICAL LABORATORY.

and ordered I. J. Denison, a member of the freshman class, to "go". He had been standing quietly upon the walk, taking no part in the tumult, and when he asked where he should go, one of the soldiers struck him on the head with the butt end of his musket, and felled him to the ground. Then the students rallied, and having supplied themselves with sticks and stones began to make show of resistance. Some one whose name it is to be hoped will not forever remain unknown to the chroniclers of deeds worthily done by Michigan men, hurled a missile at Granger, hitting the latter in the head, cutting a fearful gash, and completely disabling him. He still urged on the "military", and in a second charge four or five students were slightly injured. Then several policemen appeared on the scene, the soldiers were advised to go down town, Professor Thompson persuaded the boys to proceed to the campus, and comparative quiet reigned. After listening to a short speech in which the Professor thanked them for their self-restraint under difficult circumstances, the students went home, not realizing the extent of the injury to their associate. Young Denison died early the next morning, an artery under the skull having been ruptured. He was of a very quiet disposition, and during the few weeks of his stay in Ann Arbor had greatly endeared himself to his comrades. His parents lived in Toledo. As for Granger, a piece of his skull had to be removed, and he was for some time in a critical condition; but he survived to carry permanently the mark of the avenging stone. At the inquest it was shown that permission to fire had been refused by the mayor, that the discharge of musketry within the city limits was prohibited by the ordinance, and that the students had been guilty of nothing but noise. Eight of the militia were arrested on two counts, murder and manslaughter, but it was impossible to ascertain who dealt the fatal blow. The Governor of the State disbanded the Company for the unsoldierly conduct of its men, and not long afterwards a new military organization composed of some of the best citizens of the town, together with several of the University's professors, was effected. Mayor Manly, fearful of prosecution for the unwarranted arrest of students at the post-office, caused the cases against the boys to be discontinued, they agreeing not to sue him for damages, and he paying the costs.

Another episode of which the sensational press made much to the temporary injury of the University occurred on the evening of March 21, 1891. A member of the junior academic class, H. W.

Booth, was a passenger in one of the cars of the new electric street railway, and having been carried beyond the street at which he wished to alight, he demanded that the car should return. Of course the motor-man refused to put the car back, whereupon an altercation ensued, both men getting out and standing beside the car. Whether apprehensive of attack, or in sheer anger, Booth drew a revolver and shot the motor-man, inflicting a slight wound. Booth was arrested, on the charge of assault with intent to kill, and also of assault with intent to do great bodily injury, but pleading self-defence he escaped conviction. He was however expelled from the University and from his fraternity.

Disputes between students and those good citizens of Ann Arbor who furnish the former with food, lodging, and other necessaries, are not so frequent as the number and the circumstances of the undergraduates would lead one to expect. Occasionally a student or a newly-fledged graduate leaves the city without settling an account which some landlady or shopkeeper has allowed to run too long; but as a rule the college boys pay their bills. Not many years ago two students were sued in trespass by an angry woman whose table they had forsaken, and over whose ground they were wont to pass *en route* to the abode of another provider of meals. Nothing came of the action.

CHAPTER VI

RELIGIOUS SOCIETIES

Although the instruction given by our University is entirely secular, yet the religious needs of the students are served even more amply than in most of the denominational colleges by certain institutions which private liberality has founded and endowed, and which the zeal of the undergraduates has kept in active and beneficial operation. The oldest of these valuable adjuncts to student life and culture, in fact the oldest society of its kind in America, is the Students' Christian Association, itself the successor of an older organization which had been established some years prior to 1857 for the encouragement of foreign missions and for the propagation of information concerning mission work. It confined its efforts chiefly to the taking of a few periodicals, and to the holding of occasional meetings for reading and for the discussion of missionary affairs. Not long after the beginning of the academic year 1857-58, a disposition was manifested to modify the character of this institute. Foremost in the reorganization, which took place in February, 1858, was Adam K. Spence, '58, the first President of the new society, and afterwards President of Fisk University. Henry A. Humphrey, also of '58, identified himself with the movement at the start. Fayette Hurd, '58, Simon C. Guild, '60, Eben L. Little, '61, Byron M. Cutcheon, '61, and R. H. Tripp, '61, were all early and influential members. Charles Kendall Adams, '61, now President of the University of Wisconsin, says that the organization of the Association was very largely due to the powerful Christian influence of the class of

STUDENTS' CHRISTIAN ASSOCIATION BUILDING.

1861. He adds "The nature of the work in those early days was somewhat different from that of similar associations at a later time. The exercises were largely devotional; but at almost every meeting a paper was read on some religious subject believed to be of more or less vital importance to Christian living and working".

A room on the fourth floor of South College, now the south wing of the Main Building, was the meeting-place of the Students' Christian Association until 1864, when room 9, at the right of the north entry of South College was set apart for the use of the society. This continued to be the headquarters until the organization obtained a home of its own. In 1883 the twenty-fifth anniversary was celebrated, and the society became a corporation. As a result of the interest then aroused a building fund was started, and in September, 1883, the lot directly in front of the central entrance to the campus was purchased for $2,500. Work upon the building was begun in April, 1888, the corner-stone was laid May 26 of the same year, and the dedication—deferred until the debt resting upon the edifice had been paid—took place June 21, 1891. Of the total cost of the building, $36,775, the sum of $17,400 was given by Mrs. Helen F. Newberry of Detroit, widow of the late John S. Newberry, '47, in whose honor the structure is named Newberry Hall. With outside dimensions of 62x91 feet, the building is two stories in height above the basement. The material is field-stone, trimmed with Ohio blue stone and "Forest City" brown stone. On the first floor are reception rooms, a library, and three rooms for prayer meetings. The floors are of hard wood. A staircase of oak leads to the upper story, which is mainly devoted to a hall capable of seating 550 persons. There is a large memorial window on one side, and leading out of the hall are two rooms for those who take care of the building.

From the outset the S. C. A., as it is familiarly called, has been an important factor in college life. During the year 1866–67 work was begun by it in the medical and law schools. The society opened its doors to women as soon as they were admitted to the University; but they did not take an active part in its operations until 1874. The successive heads of the University, and many of the leading professors, have been earnest promoters of the Association, attending its meetings, advising its councils, and contributing to its funds. Until 1895 students not members of evangelical churches were not eligible to active membership, though they could be admitted to associate membership; but by a change in the pledge a more liberal rule now prevails. About 3250 members have been enrolled by the Association, and the present number of active members is 675, far more than the entire collegiate attendance upon any of the denominational institutions in the State. Under an arrangement recently made the duties of the officers are divided so that the woman vice-president has entire charge of the work among the women members. The men and women meet together once a month; the other meetings are separate. The Association offers courses in the systematic study of the Bible; assists new students in obtaining rooms and boarding-places; and extends the valuable privileges of its library and reading-rooms to all members and persons introduced by members. In February, 1880, the society began the publication of a periodical called The Monthly Bulletin, which, as the S. C. A. Bulletin, is now issued every week. Another and a very useful publication of this organization is a Students' Hand-Book or manual of information concerning the University, Ann Arbor, and the Association, which is issued annually at the opening of college. Early in March, 1898, this society celebrated its fortieth anniversary. An endowment of $10,000 is now sought, and a large part of that sum has been subscribed. Following is the list of those who have served as presidents of the S. C. A.:

HARRIS HALL (EPISCOPALIAN).

A. K. Spence, '58,
S. C. Guild, '60,
E. L. Little, '61,
H. A. Burt, '62,
J. H. McClure, '63,
W. B. Hendryx, '64,
John Thompson, '65,
J. A. VanFleet, '66,
I. N. Elwood, '67,
J. C. Freeman, '68,
W. C. Darby, '69,
T. C. Christy, '70,
W. B. Millard, '71.
J. F. Dutton, '72,
H. W. Gelston, '73,
D. A. Matthews, '74,
J. W. Parker, '75,
W. J. Warner, '76,
H. C. McDougall, '77,
F. A. Barbour, '78,
J. F. Millspaugh, '79,
T. C. Green, '80,
A. G. Hall, '81,
F. C. Bailey, '82,
A. T. Packard, '83,
W. S. Hough, '84,
F. C. Wagner, '85,
H. J. Powell, '86,

A. J. Covell, '87,
John E. Hodge, '88,
E. C. Goddard, '89,
W. E. Goddard, '90,
W. H. Nichols, '91,
C. P. McAllaster, '92,
F. A. Manny, '93,
A. J. Ladd, '94,
N. A. Gilchrist, '95,
W. M. Mertz, '96,
H. M. Rich, '97,
J. K. Marden, '98 *m*.

Formerly the Students' Christian Association was a member of the Young Men's Christian Association, State and National, but the firm adherence of its leaders to the union of men and women in religious work led to the severance of the connection. In 1895 the society decided not to permit the organization within its membership of the Y. M. C. A. and the Y. W. C. A., and in consequence a college branch of the Y. M. C. A. was founded by students who had been members of the older organization. This new society occupies the Presbyterian hall at the southwest corner of Huron and State streets. Its first presiding officer was F. A. Beach, '95; his successor was G. G. Crozier, '96 *m*; and the present incumbent is C. E. Tompkins, '98.

In the college year 1867–68 students attached to the Protestant Episcopal Church joined in organizing "The St. Andrew's Church Society", a society designed to do for undergraduates of Episcopal affiliations what the S. C. A. seeks to accomplish in a wider field. Among the presidents of this organization were W. J. Stuart, '68, George T. Campau, '70, and Albert P. Jacobs, '73. After 1873 the society became dormant; but when the late Samuel S. Harris was consecrated Bishop of Michigan, he learned about the organization which had existed at Ann Arbor a few years before, and under his advice and direction it was revived in 1885 as "The Hobart Guild". Of his action President Gilman of John Hopkins University has written thus in The North American Review:

> "The Bishop of Michigan, having seen the vigor and prospects of the great foundation at Ann Arbor, has wisely directed his zeal to the building of a great collegiate hall, which shall not be in rivalry with the state university, but in cordial though informal coöperation with it".

Through the zealous labors of Bishop Harris, supplemented by contributions and bequests from pious churchmen and churchwomen, the edifice at the northwest corner of State and Huron was built at an expenditure of $31,000, and was formally dedicated in April, 1887. An endowment of $30,000 has been raised, the income of which is used partly in maintaining the house—now called Harris Hall—and partly in sustaining courses of lectures. The Hobart Guild has a large membership, and the privileges of the

Hall—library, reading-rooms, bowling-alley, lecture-room, etc.,—are fully improved. It may be added here that Bishop Perry of Iowa, following the example set in Michigan, has laid in connection with the Iowa State University a foundation similar to the one at Ann Arbor. Doubtless the chief theological school of the Episcopal Church west of New York will be established before many years upon the basis furnished by Harris Hall and its endowment.

Another religious society affiliated with the University is "The Presbyterian Tappan Hall Association", the objects of which are to bring the Presbyterian students of the University into closer communion with each other, and to increase their influence in advancing the cause of Christianity. Professor Francis W. Kelsey, in papers which have attracted the attention of all thinking Presbyterians throughout the United States, has shown that our undergraduates include more students of Presbyterian connections than are to be found in the aggregate attendance at half a dozen colleges of the denomination named; so that the importance of the work of the Tappan Guild is apparent. In 1888–89 the society came into possession of the lot and building at the southwest corner of State and Huron streets. Early in 1890 Senator James McMillan gave $15,000 for the erection of a building in Huron street, and this gift he supplemented with $5,000 to complete the structure, which was dedicated May 23, 1891. At present the property is used by the Young Men's Christian Association, but efforts are making to secure an endowment and to establish courses of lectures.

SACKETT HALL—TAPPAN HALL.

In 1888 a society which had been formed three years before for the purpose of bringing students into closer relations with the Methodist Episcopal Church, was reorganized as "The Wesleyan Guild of the University of Michigan". Through the liberality of the Hon. Henry M. Loud of Oscoda, who gave $15,000 for the purpose, a course of lectures has been endowed. The property at the southwest corner of Huron and Washington streets has been secured, and it is planned to erect a commodious hall in the near future. As early as 1870 students of the University contributed $500 to aid in paying the debt of the Methodist Church.

A fourth organization, the Foley Guild, which was founded in 1889–90 by the Roman Catholic interest at Ann Arbor, is doing good work among the many students for whom it is designed; and about one year ago a similar society was established under the auspices of the Congregational Church.

It is difficult to exaggerate the importance of these voluntary associations which include in their memberships or spheres of influence the greater part of the student attendance. When provided with chapter houses and adequately endowed, they will accomplish much in a field which the University itself cannot enter directly It may be that before many years have passed the leaders of other religious bodies will realize, as the Episcopalians have realized, the futility of seeking to rival with their little colleges the great institution which the State itself fosters, and, turning those colleges into academies, will establish at Ann Arbor theological schools in which the graduates of the University may be trained for the Christian ministry.

CHAPTER VII

LITERARY SOCIETIES

In each of the older Eastern colleges the undergraduates founded as soon as practicable two literary societies, to which were given Greek-letter names or names compounded of Greek words. Adopting this custom, students of our University organized during the first academic year at Ann Arbor a literary club called the Phi Phi Alpha. This was started June 10, 1842, under the presidency of the late William B. Wesson, '44, of Detroit. To it belonged Collins, Fish, Goodrich, Lawrence, Marsh, and Pray, all of '45. On the 30th of September, 1843, some of its members, including Collins, Fish, and Marsh, joined in forming the Alpha Nu, of which P. W. H. Rawles, '45, was the first presiding officer. The two societies embraced in the early days most of the students in college, and were nearly equal in membership. It is said that they were generally at variance about questions of college import. "The elections of their officers" says a graduate of '48, "were fruitful of bitter contests managed after the most approved methods of the political wire-pullers of the day". For some years the societies were measurably secret, and to reveal their transactions was an offence for which members were tried and punished. This imitation of Princetonian methods did not however last long.

On the 6th of March, 1857, Phi Phi Alpha was deserted by a large number of its men, members of secret fraternities, who, appropriating another hall, founded the Literary Adelphi. From that time Phi Phi Alpha gradually grew weaker until, on the 1st day of November, 1861, it expired, leaving its library and other effects to the Adelphi. Cushman K. Davis, '57, was the first President of the society. Still another literary society, Delta Nu, was founded with a large membership in 1865, but it seems not to have survived more than one year.

The exercises of the literary societies in old as in present times consisted of debates, orations, and papers. We are told that at their meetings all business was transacted with the closest reference to parliamentary law, and that questions of current interest were discussed, and, as far as possible in such forums, settled. Each society supported a monthly serial made up of carefully edited manuscripts upon almost every conceivable topic. These writings were copied into a book "to be read monthly for the edification of the hearers and the glory of the writers." Phi Phi Alpha's paper was called The Castalian, Alpha Nu's The Sibyl, and Adelphi's The Hesperian. Annual debates between chosen members of the Alpha Nu and the Adelphi were collegiate events in the sixties, and in 1868 each society had in its own membership a series of prize contests. In 1885 Alpha Nu and the Jeffersonian (law) Society had a "joint programme". This was regarded as a great innovation.

Up to 1868-69 Alpha Nu and the Literary Adelphi flourished. The former had 113 members—its largest enrolment—in 1865-66, and its rival had seventy-three at that date and eighty in 1867-68. These figures sank in 1880 to thirty-four for the Adelphi and to twenty-seven for Alpha Nu. Toward the close of the sixties the college papers began to complain that little interest was taken in the literary clubs. "The majority of the students" says The Chronicle for September 24, 1870, "never frequent these societies, and never become acquainted with them". The lack of social intercourse in the societies between members of the different classes was also deplored. In May, 1871, the combined membership of the two academic literary organizations was about 140, but of that number barely fifty in both societies could be found at any one meeting, and adjournment for want of a quorum was frequent. Many students were members solely for the purpose of drawing books. Yet partly because of occasional revivals of interest, and partly because of the tendency to keep going when once started, the Alpha Nu and the Adelphi have outlived by nearly thirty years the time set for their demise. The former published in 1870 a catalogue of the 920 volumes then in its library. It had at Commencement in 1876 a reunion of its alumni, almost every class as

ENGINEERING LABORATORY.

far back as '49 being represented. In 1877 this society opened its doors to women, as its rival had done three years before. Each of the literary organizations holds, as it always has held, a room in the college buildings free of rent. In 1896 Alpha Nu's quarters were refurnished at an expense of $200, the proceeds of the sale to the University of its library of 1,000 volumes. Neither of the societies has published a catalogue of its members, and it is probable that a complete catalogue could not now be compiled. Alpha Nu must have admitted at least 1,200 men, and the total membership of the Literary Adelphi is about 200 less.

For the loss of the prestige and influence formerly possessed and exerted by the literary societies blame has been attached to the secret fraternities, the Students' Lecture Association, undergraduate journalism, the Oratorical Association, and the advanced requirements of the college curriculum. Whatever the cause of the decline of interest, it is to be hoped that it will not long continue, and that these ancient organizations will not be allowed to perish.

Among the prominent alumni of Phi Phi Alpha, these may be named: the late Judge Lyman Cochrane, '49; William A. Moore, '50; Henry M. Cheever, '53; Judge James B. Eldredge, '55; Duane Doty, '56; Levi T. Griffin, '57; Professor James C. Watson, '57; Judge Albert H. Horton, '60; and General Isaac H. Elliott, '61. Alpha Nu, of course, has a longer list, and includes such men as the late John S. Newberry, '47; Dr. Edmund Andrews, '49; O. M. Barnes, '50; Lewis R. Fiske, '50; Ashley Pond, '54; William E. Quinby, '58; Judge C. B. Grant, Dr. T. A. McGraw, and Judge A. H. Wilkinson, all of '59; Charles Kendall Adams, Byron M. Cutcheon, and Henry M. Utley, all of '61; Edwin F. Uhl, '62; Ex-Regent Levi L. Barbour, Judge O. W. Coolidge, and Dr. Henry M. Hurd, all of '63; Schuyler Grant, '64; Harry A. Conant, '65; Melvin M. Bigelow, '66; John M. Hinchman, and Professor Newton H. Winchell, both of '66; Professor George L. Maris, '67; Justin R. Whiting, '67; H. H. C. Miller, Edward C. Lovell, and William J. Stuart, all of '68; William A. Butler, Henry A. Chaney, Professor I. N. Demmon, and A. E. Wilkinson, all of '69; H. P. Davock, James D. Hawks, George H. Lothrop, and William C. Maybury, all of '70; Professor Richard Hudson, '71; Dwight C. Rexford, '72; George P. Voorheis, '72; Sidney C. Eastman, Charles B. Keeler, and Professor V. M. Spalding, all of '73; Frederick A. Maynard and Calvin Thomas, both of '74;

Charles H. Aldrich, Judge George S. Hosmer, and Professor J. C. Knowlton, all of '75; Frederick L. Bliss, '77; E. H. Guyer, '77; and Professor G. W. Knight, '78.

Among the alumni of the Literary Adelphi are United States Senator Cushman K. Davis, '57; Jonas H. McGowan, '61; Hoyt Post, '61; Martin L. D'Ooge, '62; Judge Henry H. Swan, '62; Noah W. Cheever, '63; Seth C. Moffatt, '64; Judge E. D. Kinne, '64; Edward E. Kane, '67; Isaac M. Weston, '67; O. H. Dean, Mark W. Harrington, and Edward L. Walter, all of '68; Regent W. J. Cocker, '69; Oscar J. Campbell, '70; Acting-President H. B. Hutchins, '71; F. L. Geddes, J. J. Mapel, and W. T. Underwood, all of '72; Lawrence Maxwell, Jr., '74; and Ben T. Cable, '76.

Besides the regular literary societies there have been many class debating clubs, such as the Homotrapezoi and the Philomathean of the class of '68; the Prescott Club, the Philologoi, the Jay Club and the Panarmonian, of '69; the Aristotelian, the Huron, and the Philozetian of '70; the Excelsior Club, the Tyler Club, the Alpha Club, and the Delta Club of '71; the Frieze Club, the R. T. V. Society, the Spenser Club, and the Sophomore Society ("The Seven"), of '72; the Everett Club, the Haven Club, and the Senior Forum, of '73; the Adams Club and the Morris Club, of '74; the Sumner Debating Club of '75; and the '77 Debating Club.

"The Literary Q. C." a society for women in the literary department was founded November 18, 1872, and existed until 1878. It seems to have been in some respects a secret organization, and its name—supposed to stand for "Quidnunc Combination"—was the theme of much guessing and joking. In The Palladium for 1876-77 is a picture entitled "Q. C.'s Studying Art", which represents six women engaged in a lively and complicated fight with one another. A new literary society for women was started in 1897. It is called Philologia.

Literary associations have thrived in the law school. Soon after the opening of that Department a movement was set on foot to organize a club for practice in oratory and debate. That club is the present venerable and flourishing Webster Literary Society, which received its name on the 21st of October, 1859. Edward P. Clark, of '60, the first President, was killed in the battle of New Orleans, July 15, 1862. An active membership of sixty-six is recorded for the Webster in The Palladium of 1860-61, and the undergraduate roll to-day includes about 150 names. As the Society has had forty-two delegations which have averaged about thirty-five men each, the total membership is in the neighborhood of 1,500. The Webster was incorporated May 1, 1886. Among the distinguished alumni are T. J. Anders, '61, Chief Justice of the Supreme Court of Washington; Dan H. Ball, '61, of the Marquette Bar; the late Isaac Marston, '61, Chief Justice of the Supreme Court of Michigan; John Atkinson, '62, of the Detroit Bar; Edwin W. Keightley, '65, Edward P. Allen, '67, A. J. Holmes, '67, S. R. Peters, '67, Marriott Brosius, '68, W. H. Harries, '68, James Laird, '71, W. C. Maybury, '71, and R. P. Bishop, '72, Representatives in Congress; James L. High, '66; Allen Zollers, '66, of the Supreme Court of Indiana; Don M. Dickinson, '67, formerly Postmaster-General; Regent R. W. Butterfield, '68; Joseph N. Carter, '68, of the Supreme Court of Illinois; Professor M. D. Ewell, '68; LaVega G. Kinne, '68, of the Supreme Court of Iowa; J. V. Quarles, '68, of the Milwaukee Bar; Henry A. Chaney, '71, and Charles K. Latham, '72, of the Detroit Bar; William B. Gilbert, '72, United States Circuit Judge; John C. Shields, '72, late Chief Justice of Arizona; and William R. Day, '73, now Secretary of State.

LEVI L. BARBOUR, '63.

On the 15th of December, 1869, the Webster celebrated the close of its first decade. This society began in 1868 a series of annual public exercises, the usual programme for each entertainment being an oration by one member and a debate between four members, two on a side.

Webster did not long remain without a rival, for the Justinian Society took the field in 1860. It had thirty-three members in 1860–61, forty-four in 1861–62, and forty-two in 1862-63. To it belonged the late Attorney-General and Regent, J. J. VanRiper, '61; Circuit Judge Levi L. Wixson; and William Story, '64, of the Federal District Court. In March, 1864, Justinian's place was taken by the Jeffersonian, which inherited some of the members of the earlier association, and which had for its first chief executive Elijah J. Osborne of '64. J. H. O'Neall, '64, recently a member of the National House of Representatives; James H. Cartwright, '67, now of the Supreme Court of Illinois; Thomas J. Wood, '67, formerly Representative in Congress; John W. McGrath, '68, formerly Chief Justice of Michigan; and J. E. Riddick, '72, of the

Supreme Court of Arkansas, are a few of the many eminent Jeffersonians. The active membership was for a long time constitutionally limited to forty, and during most of its career the society has carried fewer men than the Webster. About 1,100 members have been admitted from the thirty-eight classes, '64 to '01. This society gave its first public exercises in debate and oratory on the evening of St. Valentine's Day, 1872. Not long afterwards it and the Webster began a series of joint annual debates. These two associations have enjoyed a mutually beneficial rivalry for more than a third of a century, and both are very firmly rooted in student esteem. Like the academic literary societies they have not published catalogues of their members; and like those societies they have, so far as is known, neither seals nor other insignia.

A law-school society now extinct was the Douglas, which maintained an active membership of about thirty from 1865 to 1870. The Clay society, organized in 1865, reappeared as the Lincoln in 1866, and by that name survived until 1871. Other societies of law students were the Fletcher, 1868–69; the Independent Society, 1869-70; the Junior Independent Society, which carried a large membership from 1869 to 1873, and of which M. M. Boothman, '71, J. D. White, '72, and T. A. E. Weadock, '73, all representatives in Congress, and T. L. Norval, '71, Chief Justice of Nebraska, were members; the Law Literary Society, 1873–77; and the Omega Club, 1871–72. Numerous "Congresses" and "Moot Courts" have ephemerally flourished in this branch of the University.

Owing to the vastly increased attendance upon the law school in recent years the ancient literary societies have been unable fully to occupy the field; and a new literary society, the Sumner, and four debating societies, the Benton, the Lincoln, the Choate, and the Hamilton, have entered the Department since 1890, and are now flourishing. Of course they are too young to have eminent alumni.

An uninviting field for literary societies is found in the medical school. Here in 1860 was started an organization called "The Serapion Society"; it had forty-two members in 1860–61, rather fewer the following year, and it died in 1862. In 1873–74 we find among the medical students a "Senior Lyceum" and, a few years later, a "Junior Lyceum"; but neither of these is mentioned in The Palladium of 1880–81. In the Homœopathic Medical College a society called the "Hahnemannian" made its appearance about 1880, and is still in existence, being, it is said, very prosperous. It is of a literary-social character, and is represented by chapters in nearly all the Homœopathic colleges.

Deserving rank as a literary society, but doing its work by indirection rather than with the methods of the Alpha Nu, Adelphi, Webster, and Jeffersonian, is the Students' Lecture Association, founded in October, 1854, and incorporated in 1893. It is impossible to overestimate the value to the University of the services of this organization. Not only are the students indebted to it for the opportunity of listening to the chief orators and lecturers of the country, but they also owe to it the supplying of the University Library for many years with magazines and newspapers. Very properly the office of President of the society is regarded as one of the most honorable positions in the gift of the student body. In May, 1881, Frank W. Davenport, a member of Psi Upsilon, and E. E. White, then a "neutral", were rivals for this coveted post, both being members of the coming senior class. In the canvass no unnecessary scruples were allowed to interfere with the prospective success of either candidate, and the zealous friends of one or the other played so strong a game that votes commanded prices unheard of up to that time. When election day arrived the college was excited as never before; ballot followed ballot, neither side obtaining a majority, and a third (but lightly supported) candidate—believed by Davenport's supporters to be in league with the White forces—developing enough strength to prevent a choice. After a session of eight hours the meeting was compelled to adjourn until another Saturday. The schemes laid during the interval, and the inducements held out to wavering electors, are better imagined than described. At half-past ten Saturday morning the voting began, and it lasted until half-past one. The first ballot showed a tie between the two principal candidates, with a few scattering votes. On the second ballot White had a plurality of two, with more scattering votes than before. Then by resolution the voting was limited to the two leading candidates, and Davenport secured a plurality of three. He would have been declared elected, but for the discovery, claimed to have been made then for the first time, of a clause in the Association's fundamental law forbidding the eliminating resolve. On another trial Davenport had a plurality of eight in a total vote much smaller than either of the preceding ballots, but on the fourth ballot his opponent received of the previous "scattering" enough to elect him.

This unprecedentedly determined and bitter struggle for place was marked by incidents which do not lead one to look with much enthusiasm for the advent of the scholar in politics. Some of Davenport's admirers claimed that his election would have been certain but for reports adverse to his good character circulated by unscrupulous adversaries in the feminine part of the electorate. Soon after the election Mr. White appeared as a Sigma Phi, and some claimed that he had been admitted into that fraternity before the election, but had kept the fact secret so as to hold "Independent" votes. But this was denied. The successful candidate when some of his erstwhile supporters suggested he should resign, declined to do so. At the election for the same office held one year later, E. F. Mack, '83, a member of the fraternity to which Davenport belonged, was chosen by a large majority. By a curious turn of student interest The Chronicle in 1884 was called upon to deplore the absence of candidates for and the indifference of electors to the position so vigorously fought for in 1882. In 1891 the constitution of the Association was amended so as to render eligible as members all students purchasing season tickets. Before that time none but academic undergraduates could vote or hold office. Following is the roll as complete as the records furnish, of the Presidents of the S. L. A.:

ANATOMICAL LABORATORY.

Edwin Willits, '55,
S. H. White, '56,
G. M. Landon, '57,
C. A. Thompson, Jr., '60,
J. H. McGowan, '61,
Charles Hurd, '62,
W. S. Harroun, '63,
Schuyler Grant, '64,
W. H. Fifield, '65,
J. E. McKeighan, '66,
T. M. Potter, '67,
E. C. Lovell, '68,
O. S. Vreeland, '69,
Charles Ballenger, '70,
P. A. Randall, '71,
George Colt, Jr., '72,
V. M. Spalding, '73,
T. H. Johnston, '74,
H. C. Ford, '75,
Ben Safley, '76,
G. S. Bishop, '77
H. B. Walmsley, '78,
H. W. Ashley, '79,
I. H. Bullock, '80,
C. W. Sessions, '81,
E. E. White, '82,
E. F. Mack, '83,
W. C. Foote, '84,
R. F. Eldredge, '85,
H. A. Reynolds, '86,

C. Y. Dixon, '87,
C. A. Read, '88,
A. E. Jennings, '89,
E. M. Coolidge, '90,
Thomas Kerl, '91,
P. W. Ross, '92,
W. W. Griffin, '93,
W. W. Wedemeyer, '94,
J. W. Powers, '94,
E. C. Lindley, '95,
E. G. Ryker, '96 *l*,
H. H. Emmons, '97,
F. P. Sadler, '98 *l*.

Another very important organization among the students is the Oratorical Association. In January, 1890, at the instance of Professor Trueblood, a few enthusiastic students met to establish an annual intercollegiate oratorical contest open only to undergraduates. Invitations were sent to Cornell, Northwestern, Oberlin, and Wisconsin. Favorable replies were received from all but Cornell, which university would not join unless allowed to send as its representative a graduate student who had won the prize in oratory in 1889. The remaining colleges formed the Northern Oratorical League, and afterwards admitted the Universities of Iowa and Chicago. The constitution of the League provided for the establishment of associations in each college to form a groundwork, and so the Oratorical Association was organized here with about forty members. This society has prospered, and is the centre of the efforts made to render our University successful in the annual competition with other institutions of learning. Membership is open to all students of the University, but the orators who are to compete in the League are by preliminary contests selected from the collegiate department and from the law school, two seniors, one junior, and one sophomore from the former, and two seniors, one junior, and one freshman from the latter, persons who have taken degrees being barred. Then the eight meet in a final contest, and the winner has the honor of representing Michigan in the League meeting. He who comes out second best is the alternate who takes the place of the winner should the latter be unable to appear in the inter-collegiate contest.

In 1894 the alumni residing in Chicago established a medal and a testimonial of seventy-five dollars to be given annually to the student winning first honor in the University contest. This offer the Oratorical Association has supplemented with a testimonial of fifty dollars for the winning of the second honor. The medal is of bronze, was designed by Louis H. Sullivan, a prominent artist of Chicago, and was executed at the United States mint. Mr. Ferdinand W. Peck, the father of a former student at Ann Arbor, has founded prizes of one hundred dollars and fifty dollars respectively for the winners of the first and second honors in the League.

At the first annual contest of the Northern Oratorical League which was held at Ann Arbor in May, 1891, the first place was taken by A. C. Gormley, '91 *l*, of Michigan. In the second contest, which took place at Evanston, May 7, 1892, Wisconsin won, our representative, Jesse E. Roberts, '92 *l*, standing fourth among the five contestants. Every subsequent contest thus far has been won by Michigan; for this we are indebted to Linley G. Long, '93, Frank P. Sadler, '96, James H. Mays, '95 *l*, Fred L. Ingraham, '96 *l*, Bayard H. Ames, '97, and Charles Simons, '98.

The success of the oratorical contests suggested intercollegiate debates, and on Friday, March 31, 1893, a contest took place at Ann Arbor between three undergraduates of Michigan and a like number of students from the University of Wisconsin, in which the former were successful. Owing to a disagreement as to methods of marking the two universities did not meet again, and arrangements were made with Northwestern University for debates in 1894 and 1895. In both of these Michigan was unsuccessful. In 1896, 1897, and 1898, debating contests were held with the University of Chicago, Michigan winning the first and third, and losing the second. Up to 1896 our representatives in these debates were chosen in a University contest out of eight men who had survived preliminary contests in the two literary and the two law societies. Now the debates are under the control of the Oratorical Association, and nearly one hundred men participate in the preliminaries. In 1896-97 a Central Debating League, composed of Michigan, Chicago, Northwestern, and Wisconsin (Minnesota substituted in 1898), was formed and a plan was arranged by which the universities debate in semi-finals by groups, the winners of the two groups coming together in the final contest.

1893—A. W. Jefferis, '93 *l*,
I. B. Lipson, '93 *l*,
C. T. Purdy, '96,
1894—E. C. Lindley, '95,
E. W. Marlatt, '94 *l*,
J. H. Mays, '95 *l*,
1895—C F. Kimball, '95 *l*,
J. V. Oxtoby, '95,
1895—F. P. Sadler, '96,
1896—P. Y. Albright, '98 *l*,
Edmond Block, '96 *l*,
C. J. Vert, '96 *l*,
1897—F. X. Carmody, '97,
W. M. Chandler, '97 *l*,
J. S. Lathers, '97,
1898—T. A. Berkebile, *p. g.*,
L. C. Whitman, '99 *l*,
D. F. Dillon, '99 *l*,

Following are the names of those who have served as presidents of the Oratorical Association:

1890-91—J. L. Haner, 90, 91 *l*,
1891-92—A. J. Ladd, '94,
1892-93—Milton Johnson, '93 *l*,
1893-94—Gertrude Buck, '94,
1894-85—J. H. Quarles, '96,
1895-96—B F. Deahl, '96 *l*,
1896-97—H. G. Paul, '97,
1897-98—C. F. Kelley, '98 *l*.

CHAPTER VIII

STUDENT PUBLICATIONS

As early as the college year 1843–44 an attempt, necessarily abortive, was made to establish a college paper at Ann Arbor. In July, 1853, the first number—there were but two numbers in all—of The Peninsular Quarterly and University Magazine, was issued in Detroit. This publication, though not peculiarly representative of Michigan, was largely made up of contributions from professors and alumni of our Alma Mater. Postponing mention of the college annuals (which had their origin in a broadside issued in 1856), the original effort of Michigan students in the magazine line was the University Quarterly, which was edited during 1861 by W. E. Ambruster, '62, and E. A. Fraser, '63, on behalf of the Alpha Nu literary society, and by G. A. Marr, '62, and Stephen Powers, '63, for the Literary Adelphi. The University Independent, the first number of which made its appearance in November, 1861, was the outgrowth of the bitter feeling which had arisen between the independents and the members of the secret societies. Four numbers each of forty octavo pages, were printed. In March, 1862, the name was changed to The University Magazine. Only one number appeared under the new title. This was edited by a board composed of two members of each of the four academic classes, and the leading article of the number was entitled "Objections to Secret Societies Supported by the Opinions of Eminent Men." It contained also articles of a non-partisan character, and some college songs.

CIVIL ENGINEERING BUILDING.

Five years passed before another attempt was made to start a magazine. The need of a record of current events in college life was recognized by three members of '68, who on the second day of March, 1867, issued the first number of The University Chronicle, a bi-weekly paper. It was a single sheet folded in eight pages, and was printed three columns to a page. The price of it was ten cents. In June, 1867, the founders turned the paper over to the incoming junior class, which adopted a constitution putting it in the exclusive control of a board of four editors (changed in 1868 to six), equally divided between the independents and the secret-society men, and chosen at the end of each year by the outgoing sophomores from their own number. The paper was a financial success the first year, but in the second year the board was obliged to omit one number at the end of the volume, and in the third year money was lost. It being clear that the students could not or would not support two magazines, a consolidation with the monthly then published by the students was effected in May, 1869, thus creating The Chronicle, which remained for many years the organ of the undergraduates. The editors of The University Chronicle, 1867–69, were these:

Brutus J. Clay, '68,
Charles Quarles, '68,
L. P. Tarlton, Jr., '68,
O. S. Vreeland, '69,
A. E. Wilkinson, '69,
B. A. Crane, '69,
Henry Lamm, '69,
W. C. Johns, '69,
W. J. Cocker, '69,
D. H. Rhodes, '69,
C. S. Carter, '70,
T. C. Christy, '70,
H. P. Davock, '70,
Edwin Fleming, '70,
V. S. Lovell, '70,
R. H. Thayer, '70,
Bernard Moses, '70,
S. R. Winchell, '70.

In June, 1867, a pamplet of forty-four small octavo pages, the first number of The Michigan University Magazine, was issued. The second number appeared in the following October, and these two constituted the first volume, of which there were in all 86 pages. Volume II, 1867–68, contained 402 pages, and the third and last volume had 414 pages. Except during August and September the magazine was issued every month. It was edited by a board of six members chosen from the junior class on the Saturday before Class-Day, and equally divided between neutrals and society-men. The University Chronicle being a record of current events, this magazine was an expression of student thought. As above stated it was merged in The Chronicle in May, 1869. The following students served as editors:

G. E. Church, '67,
I. N. Elwood, '67,
W. J. English, '67,
D. N. Lowell, '67,
I. N. Otis, '67,
J. J. Davis, '68,
I. N. Demmon, '68,
J. C. Freeman, '68,

G. S. Hickey, '68,
E. C. Lovell, '68,
J. C. Magill, '68,
E. L. Walter, '68,
W. J. Cocker, '69,
W. J. Darby, '69,
O. H. Dean, '69,
F. A. Dudgeon, '69,
W. J. Gibson, '69,
T. F. Kerr, '69,
D. H. Rhodes, '69.

Although the meeting which determined to consolidate the monthly and the semi-monthly published by the undergraduates was held May 22, 1869, the first number of the new magazine did not appear until September 25, 1869. Sixteen broad, double-columned pages, the last two of which were devoted to advertisements, formed the initial issue and the normal type of The Chronicle. The first volume contained nineteen numbers and 304 pages. Until 1883, when the opening number of the fifteenth volume appeared in a wrapper illustrated with pictures of the college buildings, the first page of the paper had no protecting cover. This periodical was issued on every alternate Saturday during the college year until 1877, when a weekly issue was begun.

For eighteen years The Chronicle was edited by a board composed of eight students, four of whom—two independents and two secret-society men—were elected by the academic undergraduates from the junior class at the end of the first semester, while four more were chosen from the same class at the close of the college year. Each editor served one year, so that in the first half of the academic year all the editors were seniors, while in the last half the board was made up of four seniors and four juniors. In 1887 the number of editors was increased from eight to twelve, still chosen equally from the independents and the secret societies, and four "department editors" were added.

As conducted by '70, '71, and '72, The Chronicle was the best college paper in the country. Editorials ably written, contributions well selected, and remarkable freedom from typographical errors, made the magazine a model of its kind. Nor was the management of succeeding classes, at least for some years, inferior in skill to that of similar periodicals. But after a time the editing became careless, and misprints increased alarmingly. Thus in the four numbers for January, 1890, the date 1889 appears on the first page after the name of the month.

In 1876 an incorporation under the name of "The Chronicle Association" was effected, and the right of voting for the eight directors—who were *ex-officio* editors—was limited to members of the Association. An annual fee of two dollars, which included a year's subscription, was exacted of each member, and only students in the literary department were held to be eligible to membership. While these provisions were thought to be essential to the welfare of The Chronicle, they led to a division of student support and ultimately to the destruction of the magazine.

By a combination effected in 1880-81 two of the leading secret-societies and several of their allies were practically excluded from representation upon The Chronicle board. When the work of the coalition became apparent, measures were taken by the proscribed societies to secure what had been denied them. That the undivided assistance of all the elements which made up the student body was needed by the magazine was not realized, else a compromise would have been effected. But fraternity interests were involved, and war was inevitable. Pledges from voting members were secured for the nominee who had been selected to represent the "opposition" at the election in May, 1882, and to make matters certain the aggrieved societies paid many subscriptions for their members and other students, thus gaining as they thought additional supporters. All money thus offered was cheerfully accepted, and the new members affixed their names to the constitution presented to them. But at the election the voting list made up by The Chronicle board—which board was wholly in the control of the combination—did not contain the names of the new members nor indeed of others who had long been voters. Whatever was the technical explanation or legal justification of the omissions, it failed to satisfy the opponents of the combination, and a tremendous uproar ensued. Finding himself unable to restore order the managing editor declared the meeting adjourned subject to his call. The "outs" remained, and elected editors, whom of course the editors holding over refused to recognize. Recognition was however extended by the latter to editors chosen at a meeting attended by none but their own faction, and the "ins" celebrated their alleged victory by eating a supper, and

UNIVERSITY HOSPITAL.

by publishing a four-page sheet called The Boomerang. Then a new bi-weekly, The University Argonaut, was started by the dissatisfied element, which was composed of five fraternities. Before this there had been trouble on account of Delta Upsilon, which, not being a secret-society, and not wishing to be ranked with the independents, had ever since 1877 been trying to have the word "fraternities" substituted in the constitution for the term "secret-societies".

As for The Argonaut, it started upon a broader basis than that of its rival. Espousing the cause of the whole University, it allowed the professional schools and the academic under-classmen a share in the control of the paper. At first a semi-monthly sheet of twenty double-column pages, it became in 1884 a weekly containing eight pages of reading matter, three columns to a page. It was conducted with vigor, and succeeded in paying its way, but neither it nor its contemporary was able to reach the high standard set by The Chronicle from 1869 to 1872. Each of the rival papers was controlled by a fraternity faction, although each professed great regard for the independent element. In 1886 one of the smaller societies which had seceded from The Chronicle Association returned to it, and the latter was joined also by the new fraternities that were established from 1885 to 1889. On the other hand four of the non-society editors of The Chronicle resigned from it in 1889 for the purpose of advancing the interests of a new daily paper which the Independent Association proposed to publish, and which appeared in September, 1890. This movement hastened the consolidation—which must otherwise have taken place sooner or later—of the two weekly papers. The Chronicle-Argonaut as the new magazine was named, lasted through the year 1890–91. In October, 1891, the fraternities decided to have a periodical of their own, and leaving The Chronicle-Argonaut to die of inanition they established The Yellow and The Blue, a short-lived weekly paper of which the first number appeared October 24, 1891.

In 1879 the students in the professional departments, holding that their interests had been neglected by The Chronicle, started a paper called The University. Of this the first number was published December 12, 1879. It contained sixteen pages of reading matter, and appeared every other week. The style of the paper was like that of The Chronicle. Two volumes sufficed for this enterprise.

Following is the roll of those who have served as editors of The Chronicle:

Bernard Moses, '70,
W. B. Stevens, '70,
Edwin Fleming, '70,
T. H. Bush, '70,
J. S. Maltman, '70,
S. R. Winchell, '70,
H. C. Granger, '71,
H. B. Hutchins, '71,
E. L. Mark, '71,
R. M. Wright, '71,
Charles Chandler, '71,
J. L. Gillespie, '71,
C. E. Gorton, '71,
Richard Hudson, '71,
W. B. Millard, '71,
H. W. Montrose, '71,
H. G. Prout, '71,
James Christie, '72,
J. J. Mapel, '72,
C. G. Bennett, '72,
C. K. Turner, '72,
A. H. Brown, '72,
W. H. McKee, '72,
C. C. Worthington, '72,
F. L. Geddes, '72,
Hiram Myers, '72,
W. F. Clark, '73,
W. B. Williams, '73,
C. L. Wilson, '73,
W. S. Sheeran, '73,
C. S. Wilson, '73,
G. F. Robison, '73,
C. R. Wells, '73,
Henry Russel, '73,
C. T. Lane, '74,
G. H. Jameson, '74,
T. H. Johnston, '74,
H. R. Pattengill, '74,
Calvin Thomas, '74,
W. H. Wells, '74,
L. B. King, '74,
V. H. Lane, '74,
J. C. Knowlton, '75,
B. C. Burt, '75,
B. C. Keeler, '75,
L. C. McPherson, '75,
Lorenzo Davis, Jr., '75,
C. S. Burch, '75,
J. W. Parker, '75,
J. D. McMahon, '75,
C. A. Blair, '76,
A. L. Daniels, '76,
Ben Safley, '76,
H. M. Campbell, '76,
J. H. Steere, '76,
W. P. Durfee, '76,
E. D. Barry, '76,
R. J. Young, '76,
W. R. Roberts, '77,
F. H. Kimball, '77,
P. T. Cook, '77,
F. L. Bliss, '77,
V. J. Tefft, '77,
W. J. Gray, '77,
M. L. Woolsey, '77,
J. S. Crombie, '77,
F. C. Ferguson, '77,
W. W. Augur, '78,
J. H. Edwards, '78,
Clarence Griggs, '78,
G. H. Harrower, '78,
W. L. Jenks, '78,
H. G. Myers, '78,
S. D. Walling, '78,
J. H. Raymond, '78,
H. B. Walmsley, '78,
F. S. Bell, '79,
J. P. Brown, '79,
W. F. Bryan, '79,
E. A. Christian, '79,
Leroy Halsey, '79,
Newton Macmillan, '79,
F. D. Mead, '79,
C. G. VanWert, '79,
J. L. Ambrose, '80,
A. W. Burnett, '80,
J. M. Brewer, '80,
E. M. Brown, '80.
C. H. Campbell, '80,
J. T. Ewing, '80,
C. L. Dubuar, '80,
N. W. Haire, '80,
P. B. Loomis, Jr., '80,
A. J. Potter, '80,
William Helmle, '80,
F. F. Reed, '80,
Max Zinkheisen, '80,
Willis Boughton, '81,
F. M. Townsend, '81,
C. A. Towne, '81,
H. M. Oren, '81,
G. W. Lilly, '81,
G. B. Daniels, '81,
C. T. Brace, '81,
M. K. Perkins, '81,
W. L. Liggett, '81,
F. H. Goff, '81,
J. E. Beal, '82,
R. T. Gray, '82,
Rufus Waples, Jr., '82,
William Streeter, '82,
F. E. Baker, '82,

H. E. Spalding, '82,
R. G. West, '82,
R. W. Cooley, '82,
C. T. Wilkins, '83,
J. T. Winship, '83,
J. A. McLennan, '83,
L. S. Berry, '83,
Harry McNeal, '83,
Bethune Duffield, '83,
D. G. Taylor, '83,
J. W. Payne, '83,
E. E. Fall, '83,
Elmer Dwiggins, '83,
W. L. McDonald, '83,
J. A. Case, '84,
D. R. Phillips, '84,
J. M. Zane, '84,
C. E. Boyce, 84,
F. A. Giddings, '84,
H. F. Forbes, '84,
E. S. Clarkson, '84,
F. W. Gregory, '84,
G. B. Sheehy, '84,
T. C. Phillips, '85,
Dwight Goss, '85,
D. C. Corbett, '85,
F. W. Job, '85,
R. S. Dawson, '85,
A. C. Robeson, '85,
M. D. Atkins, '86,
J. E. Burchard, '86,
W. W. Campbell, '86,
L. E. Dunham, '86,
W. M. Giller, '86,
E. C. Pitkin, '86,
J. C. Shattuck, '86,
F. W. Stevens, '86,
O. B. Taylor, '86,
T. J. Ballinger, '87,
W. A. Blakely, '87,
G. L. Canfield, '97,
J. D. Hibbard, '87,
T. F. Moran, '87,
A. G. Newcomer, '87,
Benno Rohnert, '87,
F. J. Woolley '87,
G. W. Whyte, '87,
F. R. Belknap, '88 *m*,
G. C. Manly, '87 *l*,
H. L. Barie, '87 *p*,
J. S. Campbell, '87 *h*,
I. P. Eddy, '87 *d*,
H. J. Williams, '88,
J. L. Duffy, '88,
R. D. Lampson, '88,
J. H. Powell, '88,
G. R. Mitchell, '88,
J. B. Burtt, '88,
H. H. Brown, '88,
W. R. Parker, '88,
E. E. Hubbard, '88,
H. K. White, '88,
G. L. Kiefer, '88,
P. M. Hickey, '88,
W. J. Beckley, '89,
James Chalmers, '89,
A. E. Rowley, '89,
Lincoln McMillan, '89,
H. B. Bracewell, '89,
C. S. Hyde, '89,
T. C. Severance, '89,
C. K. Eddy, '89,
J. W. Adams, '89,
E. L. Miller, '90,
J. A. C. Hildner, '90,
J. R. Rogers, '90,
W. F. Hubbard, '90,
W. J. Baldwin, '90,
Pomeroy Ladue, '90,
P. B. Herr, '90,
L. E. Torrey, '90,
G. R. Brandon, '90,
J. D. Armstrong, '89 *l*,
R. P. Lamont, '91,
A. D. Rich, '91,
F. S. Baillie, '91,
Martin McVoy, '91,
H. T. Abbott, '91,
J. E. Haines, '91,
W. H. Turnbull, '91,
E. H. Smith, '91,
R. C. Thayer, '91,
F. G. Cadwell, '91,
L. V. DeFoe, '91,
E. W. Dow, '91,
B. P. Mossman, '91,
P. A. Walling, '90 *l*,
F. M. Phillips, '90 *m*,
C. W. Baker, '90 *p*,
F. S. Henry, '91 *d*,
J. A. VanArsdale, '92,
H. C. Bulkley, '92,
A. C. Lewerenz, '92,
A. H. Covert, '92,
N. D. Kean, '90 *m*,
G. L. Nye, '91 *l*,
L. Y. Baker, '90 *h*,

The roll of the editors of The University Argonaut is as follows:

C. D. Willard, '83,
A. A. Boyer, '83,
W. H. Mace, '83,
F. N. Scott, '84,

F. W. M. Cutcheon, '85,
F. W. Lamey, '83 *l*,
T. A. Noftzger, '83,
H. G. Ohls, '83,
J. C. Gibbs, '83,
A. S. VanValkenburgh, '84,
Hugh Brown, '84,
J. E. Cornell, '84,
W. E. Brownlee, '85,
F. B. Leland, '84 *l*,
C. H. Johnston, '83 *m*,
W. S. Brown, '85 *m*,
H. C. Kasselman, '83 *h*,
N. E. Degen, '86,
E. C. Field, '83 *p*,
W. F. Overholser, '83 *d*,
W. B. Chamberlain, '84,
T. S. Jerome, '84,
E. L. Lockwood, '85,
Woods Hutchinson, '84 *m*,
S. A. Warner, '85 *m*,
J. H. Yoell, '84 *l*,
C. J. Bacher, '84 *l*,
A. G. Hopper, '84 *p*,
P. P. Sanborn, '85 *h*,
L. J. Mitchell, '84 *d*,
J. V. Denney, '85,
A. G. Pitts, '85,
A. H. Williams, '85,
D. H. Browne, '85,
E. A. Clary, '86,
J. O. Reed, '85,
B. W. Schumacher, '85,
J. H. Patterson, '85,
C. E. Chapin, '86,
W. A. McAndrew, '86,
N. D. Corbin, '86,
A. A. Clokey, '88,
F. A. Ainsworth, '86,
S. A. Warner, '85 *m*,
T. A. Boot, '86 *m*,
G. C. Cooke, '85 *l*,
K. S. Searle, '86 *l*,
A. W. Smith, '85 *p*,
H. B. Wilson, '86 *h*,
H. W. Davis, '86 *d*,
H. S. Swift, '86,
F. T. Wright, '86,
Josiah McRoberts, '86,
F. L. Weaver, '86,
W. A. McAndrew, '86,
C. A. Wheeler, '86,
F. J. Baker, '87,
S. A. Moran, '88,
R. C. Bryant, '87,
A. L. Benedict, '87,
M. M. Mann, '88,
C. U. Champion, '88 *l*,
W. H. Allport, '88,
C. E. Norris, '86 *m*,
Charles Dresbach, '86 *l*,
F. W. Stevens, '86,
G. H. Felt, '86 *p*,
R. C. Taylor, '87 *h*,
J. B. Thomas, '87,
R. E. Park, '87,
F. J. Baker, '87,
Moritz Rosenthal, '88,
J. E. Talley, '89,
P. G. Sjoblom, '90,
A. L. Benedict, '87,
P. V. Perry, '88,
C. A. Read, '88,
T. H. Gale, '88,
F. G. Plain, '88,
J. N. McBride, '88,
G. T. Gamble, '89,
H. M. Bates, '90,
F. H. Abbott, '89,
P. R. Whitman, '89,
H. B. Dewey, '90,
L. Z. Caulkin, '90,
A. H. Covert, '92,
L. D. Milliman, '90,
Isabella M. Andrews, '89,
D. C. Worcester, '89,
F. S. Loomis, '89,
Bertha E. Pritchard, '91,
O. R. Hardy, '91,
G. E. McIlwain, '90,
M. G. Paul, '92,
B. P. Bourland, '89,
R. E. Dunbar, '90,
G. H. Snow, '90,
H. V. Winchell, '89,
J. B. Smalley, '91,
Hudson Sheldon, '90,
Caroline C. Penny, '90,
J. K. Freitag, '90,
F. H. Dixon, '91,
F. E. Wood, '92,
L. J. Richardson, '90,
Arthur Frantzen, '92,
J. R. Effinger, Jr., '91,
E. F. Gay, '90,
W. B. Kelly, '91,
Gustav Kleene, '91,
Mary E. Sanborn, '91,
Edith L. Sheffield, '91,
L. G. Whitehead, '93,
Jacob Lowenhaupt, '91,
W. L. Mann, '90,
H. B. Shoemaker, '91,
E. D. Warner, '91,
G. A. Katzenberger, '90 *l*,
Wallace Palmer, '90 *p*,
W. D. Wood, '90 *m*,
F. C. Sizelan, '90 *d*.

Following are the editors of The Chronicle-Argonaut, 1890–91:

J. R. Effinger, Jr., '91,
B. P. Mossman, Jr., '91,
S. M. Trevellick, '91,
H. C. Bulkley, '92,
L. B. Trumbull, '91,
P. W. Ross, '92,
L. V. DeFoe, '91,
G. S. Curtiss, '91,
W. F. Hubbard, '91,
E. V. Robinson, '90,
J. H. Harris, '91,
E. S. Beck, '94,
F. L. Sherwin, '92,
W. H. Butler, '91,
Thomas Kerl, '91,
S. C. Park, '91,
R. E. VanSyckle, '91,
G. P. Cheney, '92.

The editors of The Yellow and The Blue were:

B. F. Hall, Jr., '93,
F. W. Pine, '94,
E. E. Beal, '94,
R. G. Lathrop, '93,
H. F. McGaughey, '93,
J. A. Whitworth, '94,
B. F. Brough, '93 *l*,
W. L. Webster, '93 *d*.

Twenty-one years having passed since a monthly magazine was decided to be impracticable, the class of '91 at the opening of its senior year decided to make another attempt, and that attempt has been successful. The Inlander—for by so peculiar a title was the new monthly christened—is now in its eighth volume. "Its aim is to furnish a medium of expression for the literary life and thought of Michigan University". Originally the magazine was almost square in form—the page being 6⅞ x 8⅝ inches—but now the page is narrower though not longer. The subscription price, originally $1.50 a year, is now only half of that sum, and the price of single copies has been reduced from twenty-five to ten cents. This magazine is published on the fifteenth of each month during the college year. The editors of The Inlander have been:

Volume Seven — Number Four

JANUARY — *MDCCCXCVII*

The Inlander

A Magazine published on the fifteenth of each month during the college year, and devoted to the Literary Interests of the University of Michigan. Established by the Class of '91

Edited and published by a Board of Editors chosen from among the Students of the University of Michigan. Printed at the Inland Press and entered at the post-office at Ann Arbor as second-class mail matter. For sale in the Main Hall and at all newsdealers.

PRICE, TEN CENTS

1890–91—C. B. Warren, '91,
H. B. Shoemaker, '91,
J. A. McLaughlin, '91,
E. H. Smith, '91,
E. D. Warner, '91,
Day Krolik, '91.
1891–92—Wilhelm Miller, '92,
E. O. Holland, '92,
1891–92—P. W. Ross, '92,
W. C. Quarles, '92,
F. L. Sherwin, '92.
1892–93—F. F. Briggs, '93,
H. A. Friedman, '93,
I. C. Belden, '93,
L. A. Strauss, '93.
1893–94—G. W. Harris, '94,

1893–94—F. W. Pine, '94,
C. J. Harmon, '94,
D. F. Lyons, '94,
L. G. Seeley, '94,
S. H. Perry, '94.
1894–95—F. H. Willits, '95,
J. H. Prentiss, '96,
L. A. Pratt, '96,
C. C. Parsons, '96,
Harry Simons, '95.
1895–96—L. A. Pratt, '96,
J. H. Prentiss, '96,
L. C. Walker, '96,
1895–96—J. F. Thomas, '97,
1896–97—H. M. Rich, '97,
W. L. Mack, '97,
K. E. Harriman, '98,
A. H. Zacharias, '98,
H. M. Bowman, '98, '99 *l*.
1897–98—H. M. Bowman, '98, '99 *l*.
H. M. Rich, '97,
Butler Lamb, '98,
S. E. Knappen, '98,
Katherine M. Brown, '98,
T. M. Marshall, '98.

In February, 1892, appeared the first number of a new monthly magazine, The Michigan Law Journal. Four more numbers were issued during that college year; and the publication still continues. Ralph Stone, '92 *l*, H. D. Jewell, '91 *l*, and E. R. Sutton, '91 *l*, were chiefly responsible for the institution of this periodical, and for the conduct of it from 1892 to 1894. The Dental Journal, another monthly still extant, was started by the students of the dental school, May 1, 1892. The Bulletin, the organ of the Students' Christian Association has been mentioned already (page 89).

The Michigan Alumnus, a magazine "published monthly during the college year in the interests of the alumni and old students of the University of Michigan"; made its first appearance in October, 1894. Alvick A. Pearson, '94, was the editor and publisher. The first number was a pamphlet of sixteen pages, without a cover; but covers were provided for subsequent numbers. The final number for the first year appeared in June, having united with itself The Commencement Annual. There were 191 pages in the first volume. One dollar a year was and is the subscription price. During the year 1895–96, the Alumnus continued under the management of Mr. Pearson, but the third volume was edited by Louis A. Pratt, '96, Clifford G. Roe, '99, and Allen P. Cox, '00, with Professor Demmon, '68, Professor Scott, '84, Gertrude Buck, '94, Duane R. Stuart, '96, and George B. Harrison, '97 *l*, as "Department Editors". This was more ambitious than either of the preceding volumes; it contained 292 printed pages, and not a few illustrations. Gradually the magazine fought its way until it secured a fair measure of support. In 1897–98 this periodical became the official paper of the Alumni Association, the secretary of that society, James H. Prentiss, '96, becoming Editor in Chief, with L. A. Pratt, '96, as Managing

Editor, and Professor Scott as University Editor. The Department Editors are Professor Demmon, D. R. Stuart, '96, Jessie S. Gregg, '98, Katherine Reed, '98, and F. S. Simons, '98.

The U. of M. Daily, the origin of which was mentioned in connection with The Chronicle (ante, page 107), first appeared on the morning of September 29, 1890. It was and is a four-page sheet, four columns to a page, much of the space being devoted to advertisements. In the first volume there were 174 issues. The pages are not numbered, so that the volumes cannot be indexed. At first the price was five cents a number, but now it is three cents; and the annual subscription charge is $2.50. While the initial volume was not a financial success, yet the management persevered, and now the paper has an assured footing. Fourteen anti-fraternity men constituted the first editorial board. In 1895–96 a rule giving a few editorships to members of fraternities was adopted. The following have served as editors:

H. M. Butzel, '91,
W. E. Griffin, '91,
M. B. Hammond, '91,
H. D. Jewell, '91 *l*,
W. B. O'Neill, '91 *l*,
H. B. Shoemaker, '91,
C. C. Spencer, '91,
A. W. Tressler, '91,
A. H. Covert, '92,
S. W. Curtiss, '92,
W. B. Dellenback, '92,
R. W. Doughty, '92,
J. G. Erdlitz, '92 *l*,
F. D. Green, '92,
E. O. Holland, '92,
A. W. Jefferis, '92 *l*,
F. J. McElwee, '92,
F. E. Ruggles, '92 *m*,
Ralph Stone, '92 *l*,
E. J. Blair, '93 *l*,
W. E. Bolles, '93,
C. A. Denison, '93,
G. B. Dygert, '93,
W. H. Evans, '93 *l*,
F. E. Janette, '93,
W. E. McEncroe, '93 *l*,
F. A. Manny, '93,
W. P. Parker, '93,
C. W. Southworth, '93,
C. N. Sowers, '93 *m*,
J. G. Spitzer, '93 *l*,
C. K. Stewart, '93 *h*,
L. A. Strauss, '93,
E. K. Towl, '93,
L. G. Whitehead, '93,
Mary E. Alcott, '94,
J. R. Arneill, '94 *m*,
A. S. Bailey, '94 *d*,
Gertrude Buck, '94,
G. L. Chapman, '94,
H. B. Gammon, '94, '98 *m*,
R. F. Hall, '94,
C. G. Jenkins, '94 *h*,
Lucia Kieve, '94,
A. W. Lockton, '94 *l*,
E. L. Martindale, '94 *m*,
E. J. Ottaway, '94,
C. W. Ricketts, '94,
O. E. Scott, '94 *l*,
H. A. Spalding, '94,
J. C. Travis, '94,
Frank Walters, '94 *l*,
W. W. Wedemeyer, '94,
C. F. Weller, '94,
R. O. Austin, '95,
Charles Baird, '95,
C. D. Cary, '95 *l*,
H. A. Dancer, '95,
E. L. Evans, '95 *l*,
C. M. Holt, '95,
J. L. Lorie, '95,
Mattie E. McFarland, '95,
J. S. Pearl, '95 *l*,
W. N. Choate, '96,
Norman Flowers, '96,
L. R. Hamblen, '96 *l*,
H. D. Haskins, '96 *m*,
G. M. Heath, '96 *p*,
C. A. Houghton, '96 *d*,
J. A. Leroy, '96,

E. P. Lyle, '96,
L. A. Pratt, '96,
F. P. Sadler, '96,
A. W. Smith, '96,
Carrie V. Smith, '96,
S. R. Smith, '96 *l*,
W. A. Spill, '96 *l*,
W. W. Thayer, '96 *l*,
L. C. Walker, '96,
Harry Coleman, '97,
G. B. Harrison, '97 *l*,
W. A. Mogk, '97,
Agnes Morley, '97,
A. M. Smith, '97,
S. W. Smith, '97,
E. R. Sunderland, '97,
J. F. Thomas, '97, '00 *l*,
Mary M. Thompson, '97,
Frederick Engelhard, '98,
C. H. Farrell, '98,
J. S. Finley, '98,
F. A. Fucik, '98,
E. L. Geismer, '98 *l*,
O. H. Hans, '98, '00 *l*,
W. W. Hughes, '98,
S. E. Knappen, '98,
F. M Loomis, '98,
W. P. Morill, '98,
C. B. Roe, '98 *m*,
H. B. Skillman, '98 *l*,
J. C. Walsh, '98 *m*,
T. R. Woodrow, '98,
Allan Campbell, '99,
H. H. Corwin, '99,
Louise F. Dodge, '99,
R. C. Faulds, '99 *m*,
~~C. M. Green, '99,~~
P. W. Jones, '99,
Cabot Lull, Jr., '99 *m*,
R. R. Reilly, '99,
Susannah H. Richardson, '99,
G. E. Sherman, '99,
G. R. Sims, '99,
I. A. Campbell, '00,
G. D. Hudnutt, '00,
Butler Lamb, '00,
A. H. McDougall, '01.

Friday, October 13, 1893, saw the first issue of Wrinkle, Michigan's humorous bi-weekly. William E. Bolles and H. H. Smith, both of '95, conceived the idea, and George W. Harris suggested the name. A stock company was formed, under the auspices of which the first number, a twelve-page affair, was issued; and in spite of many discouragements, financial and otherwise, the paper has appeared regularly every two weeks—except in vacation time—since the doubly inauspicious day of its birth. Sixteen pages, including the cover, now make up each regular number, but twenty are assigned to each of the issues representing Thanksgiving, Christmas, Junior Hop, Decoration Day, and Commencement. At the head of the editorial page appears the motto "Enjoy life while you live, for you will be a long time dead". Most of the jokes are new and good, many of the illustrations are excellent, and on the whole Wrinkle may be said to be a very creditable publication. Wagner's cover designs and other illustrative work did much for the magazine during its early years. Following is the roll of editors:

C. K. ADAMS, '61.

W. E. Bolles, '95,
H. H. Smith, '95,
J. L. Lorie, '95,
R. L. Wagner, '95,

H. A. Williams, '94,
G. W. Harris, '94,
H. C. Ryan, '93,
M. W. Campau, '96,
H. R. Kellogg, '95,
Frank Briscoe, '95,
A. M. Smith, '97,
K. E. Harriman, '98,
S. E. Galbraith, '95,
G. R. Barker, '98,
F. H. Petrie, '96,
W. A. Starrett, '97,
E. H. Humphrey, '97,
H. M. Bowman, '98, '99 *l*,
Norman Flowers, '96 *l*,
Edward Ferry, '96 *l*,
J. H. Harris, '98,
J. E. Lawless, '98,
C. B. Parsons, '99,
E. J. Bement, '97,
G. B. Harrison, '97 *l*,
C. M. Green, '99,
Standish Backus, '99,
Lafayette Young, Jr., '00,
F. L. Baxter, '00,
J. S. Symons, '00,
R. C. Woodworth, '00,
G. S. Benson, Jr., '00,
R. R. McGeorge, '99,
H. C. Thurnau, '99,
C. M. Bush, '99 *l*,
F. D. Eaman, '00,
J. A. Bardin, '99 *l*,
F. R. Blair, '01.

Fifty-seven years ago William E. Robinson, a charter-member of Psi Upsilon at Yale, and afterwards a representative in Congress from one of the Brooklyn districts, edited and published The Yale Banner, the prototype of the student annuals now issued at every college of note in America. Yale's example was followed slowly by other institutions. Michigan came into the field earlier than most others, and like all other annuals published before 1860 our first attempt was a newspaper sheet. This was The University Register, an affair of four pages—the page measuring twelve inches by sixteen and three-fourths—and it appeared in June, 1857. John Payne, '58, and Alexander Richard, '58, got up the paper on their own account. In The Register one finds the names of the regents and professors, and of the graduates and students, and also lists of the members of the literary societies and of the secret clubs. Each of the fraternity rolls is accompanied by a cut of the badge. Of the secret societies Chi Psi comes first with twenty-nine alumni and twelve students, while Beta Theta Pi has twenty graduates and twenty-one undergraduates, Alpha Delta Phi forty-one and nineteen respectively, Delta Kappa Epsilon seven and twenty-five, and Delta Phi one alumnus and eleven students. According to The Register the alumni of the literary department numbered 173, and the medical graduates 186. Of the 396 students 234 were academic, 140 medical, and twenty-two chemical. Upon the whole The Register was much like the early sheets printed at Yale, Amherst, Williams, and Kenyon. It was followed by a similar sheet, The Peninsular Phoenix, which Edward W. McGraw, '59, one of the leading members of the Bar of San

Francisco, mentions in an account—written for this book—of the origin of The University Palladium:

"In 1857-58, S. D. Green, now (by catalogue) of Berlin Falls, N. H., then an Alpha Delta Phi of class of '60, and a printer, got up a little ill-looking sheet printed and published by himself, the name of which I have forgotten, devoted to college matters, and containing lists of members of secret societies. In 1859 I thought it disgraceful that the University of Michigan could not show something better in the shape of a society catalogue, and I endeavored to get the secret societies to unite in getting up one. Then secret society feeling ran very high and it was impossible to effect any combination for any purpose. But having started in on the matter, I would not give it up, and published the first and second numbers of The Palladium at my own cost and as a private enterprise. In the first number I paid for all the cuts of the badges that appeared. I furnished cuts only for the societies friendly to Alpha Delta Phi. I don't know how many cuts I did furnish—I think for Alpha Delta Phi, Chi Psi, Beta Theta Pi, and Sigma Phi, possibly Delta Phi also. For the second number I think the other societies furnished their own cuts. It was a lively paper while I ran it, and the fun of it compensated me for the few dollars I lost as publisher. Only two numbers were published under my supervision—alike as to size".

The first number of The Palladium in pamphlet form appeared at the close of the college year 1859-60. It contains twenty-four pages within a cover of white, glazed paper, and carries these words in bronze-gilt within a three-lined border: "The University Palladium. University of Michigan, Commencement day, June 27, 1860. Vol. II No. 2, Published by the Secret Societies. Ann Arbor: Michigan Argus Print. 1860". Then follows a page with this: "Secret Societies. Arranged in the Order of their Establishment". Upon the title page the names of the seven editors appear. The third page and the fourth page are taken up with a preface signed by W. Jesse Buchanan, and toward the bottom of the fourth page are given the names of the members of the "Publishing Committee", Walter McCollum and H. M. Utley. This number of The Palladium was preceded by an earlier sheet in the autumn of 1859. With the fifth page begin the membership lists of the seven secret societies which joined in publishing the book, Chi Psi coming first. Each fraternity has a page by itself, and each is typified by a wood-cut vignette. Chi Psi uses its well-known and effective device, a white cross overlaid with the monogram of the society's letters and surrounded by a circle of light within dark clouds. Beta Theta Pi is characterized by a circle inscribed in a triangle around which are clouds. Alpha Delta Phi and D. K. E. exhibit their coats-of-arms; Delta Phi shows an enlarged badge lying upon a scroll; Sigma Phi presents a fac-simile of its badge, and Zeta Psi employs the monogram and scroll device which has done duty at many other colleges. After the seven fraternities follows a mock society, the Lambda Beta Delta.

Of course The Palladium for 1860 contained the names of the Regents and a roll of the Faculty. Then follow the class lists (class officers not given), the officers and members of the three literary societies, the officers of the Society of the Alumni, College awards (the holders in the class of '63 of the four scholarships in those times awarded to freshmen), the officers of the Students' Lecture Association and of the Students' Christian Association, the names of a musical sextette, eight lines of type with reference to sundry jovial students, and the programme of Commencement Week. That is all.

The Palladium of 1860–61 carries on its cover of glazed white paper the words "University of Michigan" in a curve above the numerals "1860–61", all in blue ink. It bears on its title page the date December, 1860, and contains forty-eight pages. Class officers and class seals are given, there are literary societies in every department, and the number of miscellaneous organizations is greatly increased. In The Palladium of December, 1861, we find a four-page editorial, a memorial on the decease of Phi Phi Alpha, and a list of students in the Army, which list is repeated and enlarged in the issue for 1862–63, and again in the volume for 1863–64. In The Palladium for 1864–65 are two original songs, the results of an offer of a prize of ten dollars; and a well-written article about societies at Harvard appeared in the issue of 1867-68. In later years songs, sketches, poems, and illustrations were numerous.

HOMŒOPATHIC HOSPITAL.

In 1883–84 The Palladium appeared with stiff card-board covers, and since then the intention has been to provide a permanent binding every year. The most unique and at the same time most objectionable covering was the untanned and malodorous leather which enwrapped the annual of '89. This volume, at which much fun was poked, also set the bad example of departing from the established and convenient octavo form; and it was followed by the edition of 1889–90, which was oblong in shape. From 1891 until the close of the series a quarto form was adopted. The price of the publication gradually increased from twenty-five cents in 1860 to thirty-five in 1873, to fifty in the early eighties, and finally to one dollar.

After the thirty-seventh annual volume of The Palladium had appeared the undergraduates wisely decided to combine with it the annual of the Independents and the annual of the senior law-class; but unfortunately they decided to adopt a new title, instead of giving to the consolidated book the name of the oldest of the publications which it displaced. An account of the editorial boards of The Palladium will now be given.

After the issue of June, 1860, this annual continued to be edited by the seven secret societies which had been established in the University prior to 1860. But in 1865 Psi Upsilon, organized by fourteen of the fifteen undergraduate members of Beta Theta Pi, took a place on the board, and the remaining member acted as editor for a chapter consisting solely of himself. To the board for 1864–65 was added a delegate from Alpha Phi, the law-school society. In the following year Beta Theta Pi had an editor for the five initiates of foreign chapters who were at work in the professional schools; and in place of the Alpha Phi editor appeared an envoy from the newly founded Phi Delta Theta. In 1866–67, Beta Theta Pi disappeared, and was not again represented upon the board until 1879. However, the number of editorial chairs which had been nine since the graduation of the class of '64, was preserved, Kappa Phi Lambda being given a seat. The society editorships in 1867–68 were the same as those for the preceding year. Kappa Phi Lambda dropped out in 1868–69, and Phi Delta Theta lost its place in 1869–70. From 1869 to 1872 the secret societies numbered only seven, and there were seven editors each year. Phi Delta Phi, the law-school fraternity, was given room in 1872. No further change occurred until 1875, when the demise of Delta Phi reduced the board to seven. In that year a new society, Delta Tau Delta, was refused representation under a rule which required three years' continuous existence at Ann Arbor as a condition precedent to participation in editorial labors. In 1878–79 Beta Theta Pi was re-admitted, and Phi Kappa Psi was admitted, those societies having complied with the condition already mentioned; but Delta Upsilon, not being a secret society, was not allowed to have an editor. Sigma Chi, established in the law department in 1877, gained representation in 1879–80, and Delta Tau Delta, having succeeded in living for three consecutive years, and having published during its probationary period a little four-page account of itself, was rewarded in 1882–83 by Palladium honors. With the organization of several professional fraternities, to say nothing of sundry sisterhoods, it became evident in 1883 that the editorial board would soon become too large, even with the beneficial three year rule in force, and the constitution of The Palladium was changed so as to confine the management of this annual to the nine collegiate secret fraternities and to such others as should secure unanimous approval. Of course such approval was hard to get, for exclusive association with the old societies was a valuable franchise which the younger members of the nine were not anxious to share with still newer rivals. So from 1884 until after 1892 The Palladium was conducted by nine societies and by nine only. In time other societies so multiplied that threats of a rival annual were heard, and it was decided to let down the bars. For "secret societies" in the fundamental law of The Palladium, and on the title-page of the annual itself, the word "fraternities" was substituted, thus giving Delta Upsilon a chance; and Phi Delta Theta, Phi Gamma Delta, Alpha Tau Omega, Sigma Alpha Epsilon, and Theta Delta Chi, were admitted also. Subsequently the demise of Alpha Tau Omega and Phi Gamma Delta reduced the board to thirteen members. The roll of editors follows:

1858–59—E. W. McGraw, '59,
1859–60—W. N. LaDue, '60,
W. J. Buchanan, '60,
H. M. Utley, '61,
Walter McCollum, '61,
A. C. Jewett, '62,
S. S. Walker, '61,
O. E. Fuller, '60.
1860–61—C. K. Adams, '61,
C. S. Draper, '62,
J. H. Goodsell, '62,
J. S. Lord, '61,
A. C. Jewett, '62,
L. H. Redfield, '63,
S. G. Morse, '61.
1861-62—C. E. Wilbur, '64,
T. H. Hurd, '62,
R. H. Baker, '62,
W. E. Ambruster, '62,
C. B. Wood, '62,
C. W. Noble, '63,
L. S. F. Pilcher, '62.
1862–63—H. M. Hurd, '63,
J. C. Hart, '64,
L. T. Farr, '63,
L. L. Barbour, '63,
H. E. Duncan, '65,
E. D. W. Kinne, '64,
H. L. Wright, '64.
1863–64—W. J. Maynard, '65,
Schuyler Grant, '64,
W. D. Hitchcock, '64,
S. C. Stacy, '64,
W. J. Booth, '64,
O. P. Bills, '65,
B. F. Stage, '66.
1864-65—E. C. Boudinot, '65,
Andrew Wing, '65,
C. M. Goodsell, '65,
S. B. Ladd, '65,
G. W. Crutcher, '66,
G. B. Remick, '66,
G. W. Hunt, '66.
J. B. Root, '65,

1864-65—G. W. Seevers, '65 *l*.
1865-66—J. W. Remington, '66,
W. V. Richards, '67 *l*,
O. P. Dickinson, '66,
J. R. Blish, '66,
Henry Smith, '66,
H. P. Churchill, '67,
L. P. Judson, '67,
A. E. Mudge, '66,
G. C. Harris, '66.
1866-67—T. M. Shaw, '68,
Charles Quarles, '68.
E. W. Wetmore, '67,
E. S Johnston, '68,
H. N. French, '67,
J. M. Darnell, '67,
G. L. Maris, '67,
J. C. Magill, '68,
W. W. Belville, '68.
1867-68—L. P. Tarlton, '68,
R. N. Jenne, '68,
E. C. Burns, '68,
B. J. Clay, '68,
J. M. Stout, '68,
W. K. Anderson, '68,
Galusha Pennell, '68.
J. G. Magill, '68,
O. H. Dean, '68.
1868-69—C. W. Durham, '69,
W. C. Johns, '69,
A. E. Wilkinson, '69,
B. L. C. Lothrop, '69,
W. A. Butler, '69,
E. M. Avery, '71,
M. B. Kellogg, '69,
J. W. Johnson, '70.
1869-70—M. A. A. Meyendorff, '70,
W. R. Day, '70,
H. P. Davock, '70,
E. H. Jones, '72,
C. P. Gilbert, '70,
W. A. Kingsley, 70 *l*,
L. B. Swift, '70.
1870-71—J. L. Gillespie, '71,
C. M. Wilkinson, '71,
A. B. Raymond, '71,
Addison Millard, '73,
H. C. Willcox, '71,
M. W. Latson, '71,
E. J. Knight, '71.
1871-72—W. H. Wells, '73,
D. C. Rexford, '72,
W. H. Hinman, '72,
L. B. Parsons, '72,
C. B. Lothrop, '72,
J. E. Ensign, '74,
W. T. Underwood, '72.
1872-73—S. T. Douglas, '73,
H. O. Perley, '73,
A. G. Bishop, '73,
G. H. Jameson, '74,
F. H. Walker, '73,
J. S. Richardson, '74,
George Rust, '73,
S. E. Kemp, '73 *l*.
1873-74—E. C. Hinman, '74,
C. M. Lungren, '74,
E. W. Withey, '74,
G. H. Jameson, '74,
C. R. Wing, '74,
H. T. Thurber, '74,
C. A. Warren, '75,
L. E. Morris, '74 *l*.
1874-75—A. L. Arey, '75,
E. R. Hutchins, '75,
W. S. Russel, '75,
G. E. Pantlind, '75,
C. O. Ford, '75,
H. C. Ford, '75,
S. W. Smith, '75,
G. E. Putnam, '75 *l*.
1875-76—E. C. Swift, '76,
C. L. Van Pelt, '76,
Bryant Walker, ,76,
A. W. Hard, '76,
B. B. Campbell, '76,
C. W. H. Potter, '76,
J. P. Dunn, Jr., '76 *l*.
1876-77—E. H. Guyer, '77,
W. B. Ferris, ,77,
E. A. Gilbert, '77,
A. W. Hard, '77,
C. A. Bosworth, '77,
V. J. Tefft, '77,
W. S. Judy, '77.
1877-78—W. V. Grove, '78,
T. H. Noble, '78,
Ross Wilkins, '78,
M. B. Allen, '78,
J. H. Black, '78,
D. H. Stringham, '78,
B. F. Bower, '78 *l*.
1878-79—E. A. Christian, '79,
E. C. White, '79,
J. R. Russel, '79,
W. T. Hall, '79,
W. L. Axford, '79,
Oren Dunham, '79,
C. E. Epler, '79 *l*,
W. F. Bryan, '79,
J. W. McKinley, '79.
1879-80—W. W. Hannan, '80,
F. F. Reed, '88,
C. H. Campbell, '80,
R. H. McMurdy, '80,
C. S. Mitchell, '80,
C. C. Whitacre, '80,
A. J. Babcock, '80 *l*,

1879–80—D. A. Garwood, '80.
H. M. Pelham, '81,
M. C. Miller '80 *l*.
1880–81—M. K. Perkins, '81,
E. H. Bowman, '81,
F. C. Mandell, '81,
E. H. Ozmun, '82,
C. T. Brace, '81,
C. H. Johnston, '81,
G. S. Fuller, '81 *l*,
O. F. Hunt, '81,
C. R. Buchanan, '81,
W. B. Stickney, '81 *l*.
1881–82—J. H. Norton, '82,
W. E. Martin, '82,
H. S. Pratt, '82,
F. D. Weeks, '82,
T. W. Sargent, '82,
C. L. Coffin, '82,
J. W. Remick, '82 *l*,
J. H. Grant, '82,
F. G. Coldren, '82,
W. H. Hughes, '82 *l*.
1882–83—H. S. Ames, '83,
J. J. Comstock, '83.
H. A. Mandell, '83,
E. E. White, '83,
L. K. Merrill, '83,
John Morris, Jr., '83,
E. W. Parkhurst, '83 *l*,
Harry McNeal, '83,
J. H. Jennings, '83,
F. M. Gilmore, '83 *l*,
F. A Walker, '83.
1883–84—W. J. Abbott, '84 *l*,
William Savidge, '84,
W. B. Clapp, '84,
Elmer Dwiggins, '8Þ,
H. F. Forbes, '84,
L. B. Hanchett, '84,
W. F. Word, '84,
L. A. Rhoades, '84,
J. L. Callard, '84.
1884–85—D. C. Corbett, '85,
A. H. Williams, '85,
G. B. Sheehy, '85,
Delos Thompson, '85,
T. J. Ballinger, '87,
R. F. Eldredge, '85,
T. C. Phillips, '85,
J. V. Denney, '85,
A. G. Pitts, '85.
1885–86—R. H. Hunt, '86,
A. F. McEwan,
L. E. Dunham, '86,
F. W. Job, '87,
E. C. Pitkin, '86,
F. B. Wixson, '86,
H. G. Hetzler, '86,
1885–86—F. B. Hollenbeck, '86,
E F. Saunders, '86.
1886–87—W. A. Blakeley, '87,
J. E. Carpenter, '87,
G. L. Canfield, '87,
J. D. Hibbard, '87,
M. W. Mills,
J. E. Ball, '87,
W. T. Smith, '87,
Joseph Halsted, '87,
G. L. Kiefer, '87.
1887–88—A. B. Clark, '88,
M. M. Mann, '88,
L. K. Comstock, '88,
G. R. Mitchell, '88,
G. J. Waggoner, '88,
T. H. Gale, '88,
D. K. Cochrane, '88,
F. C. Plain, '88,
F. D. McDonell, '88.
1888–89—G. B. Hayes, '89,
B. P. Bourland, '89,
H. W. Douglas, '89,
C. E. Rockwood, '89,
W. J. Beckley, '89,
O. F. Schmid, '89,
A. E. Rowley, '89,
H. T. Bannon, '89,
C. K. Eddy, '89.
1889–90—J. W. Anderson, '90,
H. M. Bates, '90,
J. R. Angell, '90,
O. C. Smith, '90,
H. R. Seager, '90,
W. B. Ramsay, '90,
R. K. Reilly, '90,
G. M. Ford, '90,
J. R. Kempf, '90.
1890–91—H. T. Abbott, '92,
J. M. Crosby, '91,
H. B. McGraw, '91.
T. H. Hinchman, Jr., '91,
R. C. Thayer, '91,
F. R. Ashley, '91,
P. E. Stillman, '91,
J. R. Effinger, Jr.,
W. J. Hinkson, '91.
1891–92—W. W. Cheney, '92,
D. W. McMorran, '92,
H. C. Bulkley, '92,
Fitzhugh Burns, '92,
F. L. Sherwin, '92,
W. R. Murray, '92,
H. W. Hawkins, '92,
F. C. Smith, '92,
A. C. Lewerenz, '91.
1892–93—G. McA. Tyng, '93,
F. P. Graves, '93,
R. G. Lathrop, '93,

1892–93—E. C. Peters, '93,
C. W. Stratton, '92,
E. D. Babst, '93,
Frank Rich, '93,
J. J. Morsman, '93,
I. W. Durfee, '93,
F. W. Callam, '92 *l*,
A. W. Hookway, '93,
A. A. Pearson, '94,
W. J. Fisher, '93,
A. J. Tuttle, '92,
H. F. McGaughey, '93.

1893–94—J. F. Breakey, '94 *m*,
G. J. Cadwell, '94,
T. P. Bradfield, '94,
Goldwin Starrett, '94,
Frank W. Pine, '94,
R. E. Jones, '94,
L. J. Wentworth, '94,
C. W. Sencenbaugh, '94,
B. F. Hall, '94,
C. R. Rose, '94,
Fred Waterhouse, '94,
J. A. Whitworth, '94,
H. I. VanTuyl, '94,
L. B. Lindsay, '94 *l*,
R. C. Whitman, '94.

1894–95—J. H. Dunbar, '95,
N. T. Bourland, '95,
A. C. Bloomfield, '95,
Jerome Ingersoll, '95,
B. F. McLouth, '95,
E. C. Weeks, '95,
O. L. Spaulding, Jr., '95,
C. H. Morse, Jr., '95,
G. R. Slater, '95,
F. B. Richardson, '95,
H. D. Mills, '95,
C. W. Foster, '95,
G. C. Keech, '95,
Frank Briscoe, '95.

1895–96—W. J. Cahill, '96,
F. H. Petrie, '96,
Kirke Lathrop, '96,
M. W. Campau, '96,
L. C. Whitman, '96,
F. W. B. Coleman, '96,
W. H. Thorp, '96,
J. H. Prentiss, '96,
G. F. Greenleaf, Jr., '96,
M. B. Hoyt, '96,
G. K. McMullen, '96,
J. D. Kennedy, '96 *l*,
L. A. Kreis, '96.

In 1865–66 those students who were opposed to secret societies began the publication of The University Castalia. From the preface of the first number of this annual the following is taken:

"In the introduction of a new University publication, a plain exposition of the cause is required, which we hope fairly and candidly to make. In 1845 the first Secret Society was established in the University. At that time, and once afterwards, the Faculty, or part of it, took strong grounds against them. The natural result of course followed. All high-spirited young men, and those who disliked the charge of toadyism, flew to the 'Secret Societies'. It only confirmed the truth, that even a poor barren principle, irritated by the hard hand of authority, gains a false glow which attracts votaries. 'Secret Societies,' therefore, until within a few years, have held undisputed control. The few who did not belong either from want of means or talent (though generally the former), were as badly persecuted as the twelve fishermen who left their nets, and were called 'scum', 'paupers', 'poor-house pets', and other pleasing titles. But at length there came those into the University who were willing to bear ridicule, if they could glorify principle. Such men always command respect finally, and are magnets. In 1863 they held the balance of power. The 'Secret Societies' splitting into two parties, the no longer 'scum', but courted and respected independent party, formed a coalition upon equal terms, for two years. Respectability and power always win followers: and hence last year they quietly but decidedly resumed the aggressive, and swept the field in the college elections, forgetting not mercy. What our strength is now the Castalia shows as well as the Palladium. Our statements are not made in the spirit of boasting, although when we recall the taunts and jeers of former years we can hardly refrain. We simply state facts however."

The Castalia for 1865–66 contained fifty-two pages within covers of blue paper. There were five issues in all, with 288 pages.

Except for the omission of the devices and membership lists of the secret societies, and for the inclusion of arguments against such societies, the contents of The Castalia were substantially the same as those of the other annual. Whatever was said in opposition to secretism was couched in dignified language, and was clearly and forcibly expressed. With the era of good feeling inaugurated in 1869, and with the graduation, in the classes of '68, '69, and '70, of the leading opponents of the secret-society system, it became doubtful whether an annual like The Castalia could be sustained; so the number issued in 1870 was the last of the set.

The following were the editors and publishers from 1865 to 1870:

1865-66—J. E. McKeigan, '66,
P. B. Lightner, '67,
N. P. Garrettson, '68,
C. S. Fraser, '66,
Joseph H. Reid, '67,
F. M. Smith, '68.
1866-67—W. J. English, '67,
E. E. Kane, '67,
I. N. Demmon, '68,
E. C. Lovell, '68,
Charles Woodworth, '69,
H. A. Chaney, '69,
J. A. Rollins, '67,
1867-68—J. B. Steere, '68,
T. C. Reynolds, '68,
H. A. Chaney, '69,
N. L. Guthrie, '69,
V. S. Lovell, '70,
G. E. Dawson, '70,
L. A. Foster, '71,
D. W. Crouse, '68,
Samuel Hayes, '69,
1867-68—E. E. Darrow, '70,
1868-69—James DuShane, '69,
O. S. Vreeland, '69,
Charles Ballenger, '70,
C. M. Wells, '70,
P. C. Hudson, '71,
P. A. Randall, '71,
L. H. Jennings, '72,
H. A. Chaney, '69,
W. B. Stevens, '70,
H. L. Gleason, '71,
O. D. McArdle, '72.
1869-70—C. S. Carter, '70,
Charles Ballenger, '70,
Charles Chandler, '71,
G. E. Dawson, '70,
W. B. Millard, '71,
W. A. Brooks, '72,
J. H. Emery, '73,
Roland Williams, '72,
D. H. Roe, '73.

In November, 1889, the anti-society interest determined to publish an annual. For reasons by no means obvious the name chosen for this new enterprise was The Castalian, and the first number, which appeared in March, 1890, was called Volume V. Except in the college year 1892-93, when the cuts intended for the book were destroyed by fire, The Castalian was issued every year until 1896-97. By that time the unwisdom of having more than one annual had become so obvious that a combination was effected, as has been told in connection with the account of The Palladium. The six numbers of The Castalian were among the most creditable of our undergraduate publications. They contained literary matter that was interesting and valuable, and they were finely illustrated. Of argument against fraternities they attempted nothing. Following are the editors of The Castalian:

1889-90—E. L. Miller, '90,
R. E. Dunbar, '90,
Loretta Crissman, '90,
H. B. Dewey, '90,
J. K. Freitag, '90,
J. A. C. Hildner, '90,
W. F. Hubbard, '90,
Ruth A. Willoughby, '90.
1890-91—W. E. Healy, '91,
Hudson Sheldon, '91,
Marguerite B. Cook, '91,
Clara M. Meiser, '91,
Mary E. Butler, '91,
Sallie A. Szold, '91,
H. B. Shoemaker, '91,
M. B. Hammond, '91,
D. P. Shuler, '91,
W. B. Kelly, '91,
R. P. Lamont, '91,
1891-92—Carl Schlenker, '92,
J. N. Hatch, '92,
W. A. Cutler, '92,
E. L. Allor, '92,
W. H. Dorrance, Jr., '92.
R. W. Doughty, '92,
H. D. Haskins, '92,
Hugo Pam, '92,
Helen A. Atkins, '92,
Alice E. Hatch, '92,
Julia Herrick, '92,
Ada Thomas, '92.
1893-94—E. J. Ottaway, '94,
S. H. Perry, '94,
D. B. Luten, '94,
1893-94—Richard Quinn, '94,
Marion Patton, '94,
F. A. Sager, '94,
H. H. Eymer, '94,
W. W. Wedemeyer, '94,
H. A. Spalding, '94,
D. F. Lyons, '94,
Irene Stewart, '94,
Marion Strong, '94,
Jeanette E. Caldwell, '94,
H. A. Williams, '94.
1894-95—H. R. Kellogg, '95,
S. B. Shiley, '95,
C. H. Duncan, '95,
F. D. Adams, '95,
H. A. Dancer, '95,
Alice Biester, '95,
R. O. Austin, '95,
H. W. Wyckoff, '95,
P. W. Dykema, '95,
Edmond Block, '95,
Nellie J. Malarkey, '95,
Pearl L. Colby, '95,
Ann L. Richards, '95,
Lucia Kieve, '95.
1895-96—L. A. Woodard, '96,
F. R. Cutcheon, '96,
Annie L. Bacorn, '96,
C. A. Manning, '96,
W. H. Thompson, '96,
G. T. Lamont, '96,
Ada M. Cartwright, '96,
Charlotte E. Pickett, '96,
Ada Stewart, '96.

In 1873, Charles O. Tattershall, '75 *l*, and John E. Weaver, '75 *m*, "having seen and felt that the interests of the Law and Medical Departments demanded something more than the pages of The Palladium permitted, and knowing that the only way to accomplish the ends desired was to publish an independent pamphlet devoted exclusively to those departments", put forth The Sapphire, a pamphlet of seventy octavo pages bound in covers of blue paper. This was styled "Vol. 1, No. 1", but there were no more volumes or numbers. The publication was in the interest of the short-lived Phi Chi fraternity. Besides giving a good representation of the departmental clubs and other organizations, it attacked with great ferocity Phi Delta Phi and Zeta Psi, which societies had been instrumental in excluding Phi Chi from The Palladium. The book contains seventeen cuts which must be seen to be appreciated.

In 1893 the senior class of the Law Department resolved to imitate its name-sake of the college by issuing an annual. This was called To Wit:, and it appeared in the spring of 1894. It was an exceedingly neat volume of 238 octavo pages bound in cloth-boards. Among the principal features of the book were a carefully annotated roll of the 289 members of the class, full accounts of the different fraternities, literary societies, club courts, and other organizations of the law school, portraits and sketches of the members of the Faculty, and a list of "Representative Alumni". The editors were the following:

C. A. Denison, '94 *l*,
E. D. Babst, '94 *l*,
O. E. Scott, '94 *l*,
B. F. Wollman, '94 *l*,
F. C. Kuhn, '94 *l*,
E. W. Sims, '94 *l*,
G. W. Fuller, '94 *l*,
C. A. Park, '94 *l*,
Eugene Batavia, '94 *l*,
H. C. Walters, '94 *l*.

In 1895 and again in 1896 the senior law class published an annual, but the name adopted in each year was Res Gestae. Both books were very creditable. The editorial boards were:

1894–95—D. F. Lyons, '95 *l*,
J. W. Bingham, '95 *l*,
W. M. Wheeler, '95 *l*,
W. O. McNary, '95 *l*,
S. C. Hubbell, '95 *l*,
W. A. Keerns, '95 *l*,
C. B. Henderson, '95 *l*,
W. W. Wedemeyer, '95 *l*,
H. G. Hadden, '95 *l*,
Lucien Gray, '95 *l*,
J. V. Rosencranse, '95 *l*,
T. F. Doyle, '95 *l*.

1895–96—H. R. Marlatt, '96 *l*,
E. S. Ferry, '96 *l*,
C. S. Turnbaugh, '96 *l*,
R. J. Covert, '96 l,
J. T. Harrington, '96 *l*,
D. B. Cheever, '96 *l*,
H. Y. Saint, '96 *l*,
E. L. Norris, '96 *l*,
H. W. Conner, '96 *l*,
M. R. Sturtevant, '96 *l*,
H. W. Barnes, '96 *l*,
C. P. Lund, '96 *l*.

The Michiganensian, a consolidation of The Palladium, The Castalian, and the Res Gestae, is put forth once a year by the senior literary, law, and engineering classes. The first volume, issued in April, 1897, is in octavo form, and contains 400 pages. It has many excellent illustrations drawn by Standish Backus, '98. May 3, 1898, the second volume, a profusely illustrated quarto, appeared. In neither of these books are the pages numbered, so that indexes and also tables of contents are lacking. Following is the roll of editors, the first name for each year being that of the managing editor, while the second is that of the business manager:

1896–97—S. W. Smith, '97,
E. H. Humphrey, '97,
H. M. Rich, '97,
Katharyne G. Slenau, '97,

1896–97—Jennie P. White, '97,
A. H. Stoneman, '97,
R. R. Wiley, '97,
R. G. George, '97 *l*,

1896–97—C. H. Stearns, '97 *l*,
G. C. Bagley, '97 *l*,
C. L. Moore, '97 *l*,
J. R. Crouse, '97.
1897–98—T. R. Woodrow, '98,
E. L. Geismer, '98 *l*,
F. S. Simons, '98,
M. W. Turner, '98,

1897–98—Eva J. Hill, '98,
Louise P. Weinmann, '98,
Robert Steck, '98,
B. C. Dickinson, '98,
J. H. Harris, '98,
J. Q. Adams, '98 *l*,
S. B. Haskin, '98 *l*,
W. E. Stowe, '98 *l*.

To the academic class of '69 we are indebted for a magazine which has become one of the institutions of the University, and which is now the oldest of all the student publications at Ann Arbor. March 9, 1867, the first number of The Oracle, an eight-page sheet measuring eight by ten inches, made its appearance as the annual representative of the sophomore class. Butler, Chaney, Kerr, Waterloo, and Wilkinson, all prominent men of '69, were the editors. By the class of '70 the paper was enlarged to sixteen pages. Under the auspices of '75 a pamphlet of fifty pages, bearing the seal of the class on its paper cover, was issued. The sophomores of '82 decided not to publish this annual, "thus saving themselves", said The Chronicle, "considerable trouble, and conferring an appreciated blessing on mankind". But the action of '82 has not been imitated by any later class, so that The Oracle of '01 is the forty-second of the series. Recent issues contain about 100 pages with illustrations. The reading matter relates to the sophomore class and its organizations, and includes short stories, bits of verse, and "grinds".

ACTING-PRESIDENT HUTCHINS, '71.

At first consisting of five men, the editing board of The Oracle now includes twice that number. Society interests are involved in the selection of editors for this as for every other student publication. When the class of '95 met to elect a board, a resolution that there should be ten editors, five from the societies and five from the neutrals, one of each class to be a woman, was adopted. Then a member of one of the nine so-called Palladium fraternities named four candidates as "nominees of a fraternity caucus". To the surprise and grief of the Palladium combination, four representatives of the societies not included in the Palladium group were nominated and elected. In consequence The Oracle for 1895 was "boycotted" by two of the larger

Palladium fraternities, and the sales were not so large as they would have been under other circumstances. Following is the roll of the editors of The Oracle:

W. S. Waterloo, '69,
W. A. Butler, Jr., '69,
H. A. Chaney, '69,
T. F. Kerr, '69,
A. E. Wilkinson, '69,
G. E. Dawson, '70,
G. T. Campau, '70,
C. S. Carter, '70,
T. C. Christy, '70,
G. C. Wattles, '70,
E. E. Darrow, '70,
V. S. Lovell, '70,
Frank Emerick, '70,
E. M. Avery, '71,
H. L. Gleason, '71,
E. L. Marks, '71,
R. E. Phinney, '71,
C. A. Rust, '71,
R. M. Wright, '71,
George Colt, Jr., '72,
W. H. McKee, '72,
C. K. Turner, '72,
O. D. McCardle, '72,
J. J. Mapel, '72,
M. M. Ward, '72,
V. M. Spalding, '73,
R. S. Gross, '73,
S. R. Peabody, '73,
M. T. Keenan, '73,
J. H. Emery, '73,
C. L. Doolittle, '73,
P. B. Gorman, '74,
F. A. Maynard, '74,
J. C. Knowlton, '74,
T. H. Johnston, '74,
D. A. Matthews, '74,
J. D. Warner, '74,
W. T. Belfield, '75,
W. G. Doty, '75,
Lorenzo Davis, Jr., '75,
E. H. Smith, '75,
W. H. Potter, '75,
F. A. Platt, '75,
Emma S. Stockbridge, '76,
Louisa M. Reed, '76,
A. C. Stevens, '76,
H. M. Campbell, '76,
C. W. Wooldridge, '76,
C. A. Marshall, '76,
J. C. Floyd, '76,
G. A. Cady, '77,
W. J. Gray, '77,
Octavia W. Bates, '77,
W. R. Roberts, '77,
Sarah George, '77,
G. N. Orcutt, '77,
L. S. Smith, '77,
William Carpenter, '77,
G. H. Harrower, '78,
G. F. Foster, '78,
H. B. Walmsley, '78,
Annie S. Peck, '78,
Cora I. Townsend, '78,
S. D. Walling, '78,
George W. Knight, '78,
A. C. Angell, '78,
F. S. Bell, '79,
J. P. Brown, '79,
T. C. Green, '79,
H. W. Ashley, '79,
F. D. Mead, '79,
Newton McMillan, '79,
R. T. Chandlee, '79,
W. F. Bryan, '79,
David Felmley, '80,
P. B. Loomis, Jr., '80,
C. C. Whitacre, '80,
C. S. Mitchell, '80,
A. B. Pond, '80,
F. F. Reed, '80,
B. S. Waite, '80,
J. H. Willard, '80,
E. H. Bowman, '81,
G. H. Fletcher, '81,
H. H. Kingsley, '81,
H. M. Pelham, '81,
F. C. Robbins, '81,
C. T. Thompson, '81,
C. A. Towne, '81,
J. D. Wilson, '81,
F. J. Jennison, '83,
J. T. Winship, '83,
John Morris, Jr., '83,
C. T. Wilkins, '83,
T. W. Peers, '83,
F. A. Walker, '83,
H. E. Tinsman, '83,
C. D. Willard, '83,
Hugh Brown, '84,
W. B. Chamberlain, '84,
D. U. Fairbanks, '84,
A. E. Miller, '84,
Edmond Palmer, '84,
F. N. Scott, '84,
F. C. Wagner, '84,
A. H. Williams, '84,
J. W. Maish, '84,
L. M. Dennis, '85,

F. F. Bumps, '85,
F. K. Ferguson, '85,
W. J. Gregory, '85,
A. G. Pitts, '85,
R. S. Dawson, '85,
Ellis Goddard, '85,
R. C. Peters, '85,
J. E. Burchard, '86,
E. F. Demmon, '86,
W. A. McAndrew, '86,
A. F. McEwan, '86,
O. B. Taylor, '86,
G. W. Whyte, '86,
F. T. Wright, '86,
Sarah E. Satterthwaite, '96,
Eliza P. Underwood, '86,
J. E. Duffy, '87,
F. E. Beeman, '87,
J. W. Case, '87,
J. D. Hibbard, '87,
E. A. Hoover, '87,
Charles Hudson, '87,
A. J. Covell, '87,
J. B. Thomas, Jr., '87,
L. G. Townsend, '87,
Moritz Rosenthal, '88,
G. L. Bolen, '88,
F. S. Arnett, '88,
L. K. Comstock, '88,
F. W. Hawks, '88,
D. E. Heineman, '88,
M. M. Mann, '88,
J. C. McNaughton, '88,
Honta B. Smalley, '88,
Elsie Jones, '88,
W. W. Parfet, '89,
W. R. Antisdel, '89,
C. S. Hyde, '89,
D. B. Gann, '89,
A. E. Jennings, '89,
W. S. Holden, '89,
F. B. Spaulding, '89,
H. C. St. Clair, '89,
Clarissa S. Bigelow, '89,
Lillie E. Rosewarne, '90,
L. J. Richardson, '90,
E. L. Miller, '90,
Faith Helmer, '90,
L. E. Torrey, '90,
E. F. Gay, '90,
E. B Conrad, '90,
W. D. Ball, '90,
E. M. Coolidge, '90,
Alice H. Damon, '90,
G. H. Snow, '90,
P. E. Stillman, '91,
Bertha E. Pritchard, '91,
R. C. Thayer, '91,
A. S. Butler, '91,
Jacob Lowenhaupt, '91,
R. T. Holland, '91,
Eda M. Clark, '91,
L. L. Munn, Jr., '91,
T. H. Walker, '91,
W. J. L. Lyster, '92,
H. C. Bulkley, '92,
May Carpenter. '92,
Fitzhugh Burns, '92,
A. C. Gormley, '92,
C. P. McAllaster, '92,
Wilhelm Miller, '92,
A. C. Rogers, '92,
S. M. Trevellick, '92,
Lulu B. Southmayd, '92,
H. A Friedman, '92,
W. J. Currer, '93,
Margaret M. Cahill, '93,
F. H. Smith, '93,
W. P. Parker, '93,
F. E. Janette, '93,
S. S. Harris, '93,
H. H. Denham, '93,
W. B. Ward, '94,
D. F. Lyons, '94,
Mabel E. Holmes, '94,
Florence E. Wolfenden, '94,
W. B. Canfield, '94,
C. W. Sencenbaugh, '94,
H. H. Sharpless, '94,
R. V. Friedman, '94,
D. B. Luten, '94,
W. E. Bolles, '95,
H. H. Smith, '95,
Myra M. Post, '95,
Isabel A. Ballou, '95,
H. M. Cox, '95,
C. W. Foster, '95,
M. W. Neal, '95,
C. E. Wakefield, '95,
F. H. Willits, '95,
H. B. Hoyt, '95,
L. A. Pratt, '96,
J. H. Prentiss, '96,
Florence R. Jones, '96,
Norman Flowers, '96,
S. H. Woodard, '96,
E. R. Harrington, '96,
Maud I. Cooley, '96,
J. H. Deitz, '96,
J. Earl Brown, '96,
A. K. R. Hutchinson, '97,
E. H. Humphrey, '97,
R. C. Whitman, '97,
W. E. Taylor, '97,
H. C. Jackson, '97,
R. L. Dean, '97,
E. P. Lamont, '97,
C. O. Cook, '97,

Belle L. Otis, '97,
Stella Westcott, '97,
G. C. Shirts, '98,
R. E. Wisner, '98,
Hellen E. Ramsdell, '98,
Winifred Beman, '98,
S. B. Coolidge, '98,
Harry Helfman, '98,
C. H. Farrell, '98,
H. P. Treadway, '98,
D. H. Trowbridge, '98,
B. C. Dickinson, '98,
M. B. Beattie, '99,
Allan Campbell, '99,
C. E. Cartwright, '99,
E. A. Davis, '99,
Emilie A. Flintermann, '99,
H. T. Griswold, '99,
C. B. Hole, '99,
Mary H. S. Hudson, '99,
J. B. Pell, '99,
G. R. Sims, '99,
C. W. Whitney, '99,
I. A. Campbell, '00,
R. C. Woodworth, '00,
Ada M. Safford, '00,
Anna Daley, '00,
E. S. Corwin, '00,
F. D. Eaman, '00,
J. J. Walser. '00,
B. O. Greening, '00,
S. P. Cobb, '00,
J. B. Wood, '00.

In June, 1881, The Commencement Annual, containing in two numbers, each a large single sheet, the addresses and other literary exercises of Commencement week, was issued by a few students. Similar numbers were emitted in June, 1882, and in 1883 this annual was issued in pamphlet form. The publication is now merged in The Michigan Alumnus.

In 1882–83 the feminine contingent of the junior class published The Amulet, a pamphlet resembling The Oracle and designed to defend the interests of the women students. The editors of this annual—which has not had a successor—were Mary Case, Isabella H. Hull, Jane Emerson, and Mary G. Taylor.

Another annual, The Technic, was started in 1884–85 by the students in engineering. It was—and still is—issued in pamphlet form; and it is devoted to the technical problems which interest civil engineers.

CHAPTER IX

STUDENT MUSIC

In American colleges the singing of distinctively student songs is a custom of somewhat recent origin. Not many of the college songs—except those of German parentage—were composed before 1850, although two or three of the fraternities have songs written a few years earlier. The first printed collection of secret-society songs appeared in 1849, and the first book of Yale songs carries the date 1853. To German universities we owe the music of "Integer Vitae," and both the words and the music of "Lauriger Horatius."

One may trace in the annuals and other publications the gradual introduction of college singing into Michigan. The Palladium for December, 1860, says: "Of all features in college life which fix imperishable associations and bind indissolubly the heart of friend to friend, we hail the advent of none with more unqualified gratification than that of college songs". The same paper adds: "Although their adoption and use has not as yet become entirely general, yet we predict for them universal favor:—and we trust that the cordiality with which they shall be welcomed may in some measure atone for their tardy appearance among us". In The University Magazine for February, 1862, appears not merely a class ode for '62, but also "Ann Arbor Litoria", a song which enjoyed great popularity until the allusions in it became obscure, and of which the first stanza and the chorus read thus:

Ann Arbor is a jolly home;
  Sweedle inktum bum.
We love it still where e'er we roam;
  Sweedle inktum bum.
The very songs we used to sing,
  Sweedle inktum hi ru sa,
In memory's echoes long shall ring,
  Sweedle inktum bum.

CHORUS.—Litoria, litoria,
  Sweedle inktum hi ru sa,
  Litoria, litoria,
  Sweedle inktum bum.

The Palladium for 1863–64 said that the University should be able to boast of songs peculiarly its own. "We have", wrote the editors, "many songs, and good ones too, but they are all transformations from those of other colleges"; and the hope was expressed that a precedent would be established in the next number of the annual. Accordingly the editors for 1864–65 offered a prize of ten dollars for the best original song. President Haven and Professors Frieze and Evans passed upon the production offered; and they selected as of equal merit two songs, one by Arthur H. Snow, '65, for the air of the "Marseillaise", and the other by James K. Blish, '66. The former used to be sung at all the great festivals of the University, nor have we any other song that takes its place. It is in four stanzas and begins with these lines:

Come, jolly boys, and lift your voices,
Ring out, ring out, one hearty song;
Praise her in whom each son rejoices,
And let the notes be loud and long.
'Tis Alma Mater wakes the spirit,
And prompts the strain of harmony—
Oh, sing to her triumphantly!
The glorious theme—do ye not hear it?

The chorus is:

Hurrah! Hurrah! ye sons
By Alma Mater blest!
All hail! All hail! her honored name,
The pride of all the West!

The other prize-song of 1865 is entitled our college home, and is—or was—sung to the same tune as "Upidee". It has four stanzas, which follow:

Come, throw your busy cares away,
And join us in our cheerful lay;
With many voices we'll prolong
The accents of our fav'rite song—
Of Upidee, etc.

Our University for fun,
She wins the love of every son,
And while our joyful hearts beat high,
We'll send our chorus to the sky—
Of Upidee, etc.

The poorest lad within the land
Receives the favors of her hand,
And those who come unto her door,
Will sing her praises evermore—
In Upidee, etc.

The memories that linger here,
Shall ever live, our souls to cheer;
The very stars will brighter shine,
When linked with thoughts of thee and thine—
In Upidee, etc.

Another song by Blish of '66 is "Quodlibet," sung to the tune of "The Captain with his Whiskers." It was a great favorite thirty years ago, and appeared first in The Palladium for 1865–66. The opening verses of it are these:

'Tis September's golden month, when the opening is at hand,
That we watch the trains and registers, to see the Freshmen land.
There is stumpy Fresh and seedy Fresh, and Freshies short and tall,
The Freshman with the goggles, and the Fresh who wears a shawl.
Some are hopeful, some despondent, and a very knowing one
Asks you if it is a fact that the Prex now weighs a ton.
Oh, they all are model boys, study hard the whole day long,
Always go to chapel regular, and sing this little song;
"Oh, that will be joyful,
Joyful, joyful,
Oh, that will be joyful,
When young men sin no more."

Richard S. Dewey, '69, won the prize offered by the Palladium Board of 1868–69, his effort being in four stanzas entitled "Let Every Student Fill his Bowl." The air is that of "Come, Landlord, Fill Your Flowing Bowl." This was one of the popular songs of the sixties and seventies. The first stanza and the chorus run thus:

Ann Arbor is the jolliest town
This side the broad Atlantic,
And holds enough fine-looking youths
To drive the girls all frantic.
Freshmen so verdant—green,
Soph'mores of pompous mien,
Juniors, for fun so keen,
And seniors so pedantic.

CHORUS—Let every student fill his bowl
With something not too strong, sir,
And pledge our Alma Mater's health,
And join this jovial song, sir.
Ann Arbor is the place, you know,
To which our warmest feelings flow,
We'll love it still where'er we go
And fate shall life prolong, sir.

An attempt to collect and publish the college and class songs of Michigan has not been made. Several of the verses sung in earlier days at Ann Arbor are included in Waite's Carmina Collegensia which was published in 1869; and individual classes, for example '73 and '75, have put in print collections of their favorite songs. In 1889 appeared a pamphlet entitled Songs of the Yellow and Blue, the words by Charles M. Gayley, '78, and Fred N. Scott, '84, the music by Professor A. A. Stanley. A second edition containing twenty songs was issued in March, 1890. First in the book, and unquestionably the most popular of all the songs of the University, is "The Yellow and Blue," which is sung to the air of Balfe's famous "Pirate's Chorus." The words of it are these:

DENTAL BUILDING, 1877–91.

Sing to the colors that float in the light;
    Hurrah for the Yellow and Blue!
Yellow the stars as they ride thro' the night,
    And reel in a rollicking crew;
Yellow the fields where ripens the grain,
And mellow the moon on the harvest wain;
        Hail!
Hail to the colors that float in the light;
Hurrah for the Yellow and Blue!

Blue are the billows that bow to the sun
    When yellow-robed morning is due;
Blue are the curtains that evening has spun,
    The slumbers of Phœbus to woo;
Blue are the blossoms to memory dear,
And blue is the sapphire, and gleams like a tear;—
        Hail!
Hail to the ribbons that nature has spun;
Hurrah for the Yellow and Blue!

Here's to the college whose colors we wear;
    Here's to the hearts that are true!
Here's to the maid of the golden hair,
    And eyes that are brimming with blue!
Garlands of blue-bells and maize interwine;
And hearts that are true and voices combine;—
        Hail!
Hail to the college whose colors we wear;
Hurrah for the Yellow and Blue!

The college cheer—modified to suit the metre—finds place in the song "Rah! Rah." There is also a "Cigarette Song," and the alumni have a special hymn "The Star of Other Days."

One of the best songs in this collection is "Alma Mater Mine," by Fred N. Scott. The first stanza runs thus:

Thy voice is in the ears of men,
Thy finger points the way
To where the tender flush of dawn
Foretells the coming day.
Oh, guide them through the darkness, thou,
Nor hide thy face benign—
The light of sunrise on thy brow,
O Alma Mater mine!

Some of these songs, for example "The Answer," "Witchery," "Morning Song," "Evening Song," and "Romeo and Juliet" are subject to the criticism that they are not college songs, for they have nothing to do with college life or college matters. However the delicious absurdity of "Romeo and Juliet" almost justifies the inclusion of that song. "Elixir Juventatis" by Professor Scott is a drinking song at which the "prohibition" element need not take offence. The opening stanza of it runs thus:

A health! clink! clink! and now we drink
No juice of grape or grain,
But we sip forsooth, the wine of youth
That leaps from heart to brain;
We're young! We're young! let every tongue
Intone the choral hymn,
While memory swings her silent wings
Above each beaded brim.

Gayley's well known song "Birds of a Feather" begins with the following lines:

O whiles we tell of rushes
O whiles we sing and sup,—
And sip the wine that flushes,
In Hebe's amber cup,
And toast the maid that blushes
And smiles, and then looks up,
And toast the maid that blushes,
And smiles, and then looks up!

The chorus is:

In sad or singing weather,
In hours of gloom or glee;
Birds of a feather
We haunt the same old tree,—
And sing, sing together,
O Michigan, of thee!

"Ann Arbor" a song in the air of "Die Wacht am Rhein," has two stanzas, of which the first reads:

Ann Arbor, 'tis of thee we sing,
From thee our choicest blessings spring;
Accept the tribute of our song,
O Alma Mater, wise and strong.
We love thy classic shades and shrines,
We love thy murm'ring elms and pines;
Where'er our future homes shall be,
Our hearts, our hopes are all with thee.

One more of this collection should be mentioned here. This is the song "Goddess of the Inland Seas" by Gayley. The first of the four stanzas has these verses:

Sing no more the fair Aegean,
  Where the floating Cyclads shine,
Nor the honey'd slopes Hyblaean,
  Nor the blue Sicilian brine,
Sing no storied realms of morning
  Rob'd in twilight memories,—
Sing the land beyond adorning,
  With her zone of inland seas.

Of the music which accompanies the Songs of the Yellow and Blue it is enough to say that it was composed or arranged by Professor Stanley. The collection as a whole is easily superior to the song-book of any other college; and were four of the irrelevant songs omitted from it and six of the older Michigan odes added to it, we should have an admirable collection. One of the results of the excellent songs written by Professors Gayley and Scott was a revival in college singing at Ann Arbor. A class formed in 1889 for practicing the songs profited by the instruction of Professor Stanley during that and the following year.

It must not be supposed that all the songs of Michigan are included in the general book of college hymns or in the collection which has received particular mention in these pages. Scattered throughout The Palladium and The Castalian are many excellent verses, adapted for popular airs. Among these is the song "Universitas Michiganensium," which appeared in The Castalian for 1892. Frank W. Howe, '92, is the author, and the tune for which it is intended is "Maryland, My Maryland." Following is the first stanza:

Thy call has brought us to thy side,
    Michigan, our Michigan.
We take the charge with loyal pride,
    Michigan, our Michigan.

We gladly pledge our vows with thee
Beneath the shadowing oak and pine
That guard the glory of our shrine,
Michigan, our Michigan.

In The Palladium for 1859–60 mention is made of a musical organization called "Les Sans Souci", composed of E. D. Fiske, '60, Leader and Violin; E. N. Wilcox, '60, Violin; C. E. McAlester, '61, Flute; E. D. Nichols, '61, Flute; Frederick Arn, '61, Guitar; W. J. Buchanan, '60, Guitar; and Caleb Parkinson, '60, Violincello. An "Amateur Musical Club" composed of nine members, and an "University Choir" of four persons, are catalogued in The Palladium for 1860–61. In the following year the "University Choir" had eight members, and the class of '64 is credited with a "Sophomore Glee Club" composed of J. H. Kidd, F. A. Buhl, William Brewster, and J. D. Town. The Palladium for 1862–63 mentions not any musical clubs; but the same annual in 1863–64 tells of a "Junior Glee Club" with five members, and of an organization called the "Sophomore Aeolians". Names now well known figure in these societies. In 1864–65 the "Junior Glee Club" adding a member, became the "Senior Glee Club". Also in the class of '65 existed the "Cremona Club" which furnished instrumental music. Twelve members of '68 in their sophomore year constituted the "Beethoven Society" which was devoted both to vocal and to instrumental music. For the year 1866–67 there is no record of any musical club save only the "Arion" a vocal quartette composed of R. S. Dewey, '69, F. A. Dudgeon, '69, F. M. Smith, '68, and E. A. Kilbourne, '68 *m*.

DENTAL BUILDING.

Three musical associations flourished in 1867–68. These were the "Amphionic" with seven members, the "Quintette Club" of the class of '70, and the famous "Minstrels" of '69, J. E. Hinman, Samuel Hayes, Jr., A. M. Hurty, W. C. Johns, and W. A. Butler, Jr. In 1868–69 three of the secret societies, Alpha Delta

Phi, Delta Kappa Epsilon, and Psi Upsilon, had serenading clubs, each composed of eight members. These fraternity clubs, with additions from other societies, were maintained, nominally at least, for many years.

In 1867-68 the "University Glee Club" was organized. The members of it were S. R. Winchell, O. J. Campbell, J. A. Baldwin, V. S. Lovell, T. H. Bush, J. S. Maltman, and Edwin Fleming, all of '70, and W. J. Herdman of '72. This club in 1868-69 had seven members, all of the class of '70, viz., J. A. Blackburn, T. H. Bush, O. J. Campbell, G. E. Dawson, Edwin Fleming, V. S. Lovell, and J. S. Maltman. To it belongs the credit of starting a new order of things at Ann Arbor, and of elevating and popularizing college songs. In senior year the club gave a series of concerts in different cities of the state, beginning at Jackson on Friday, February 4. More than one hundred students formed an excursion party to attend the debut of the club, and we are informed that the pleasure of the trip was enhanced by special railroad accommodations and fine weather. In reporting the concert The Jackson Citizen said:

> "The Concert of the Glee Club of the University of Michigan, last night, was a splendid musical treat. The members composing it have fine natural voices, in the main, which they have well cultivated. That the large audience before them was pleased was testified by repeated applause".

The club gave in all twenty-six concerts with very satisfactory results. Everywhere it met good audiences, and everywhere the alumni were enthusiastic and hospitable. By wearing University caps the glee club gave to some persons the impression that they were members of a fire-company, while others took them to be Arabs travelling with Forepaugh's circus.

Through the indirect influence of '70's glee club a "College Choir" was formed in 1869 which led acceptably the devotional singing at chapel services. In 1870-71 the University glee club was made up of juniors, and there was a sophomore club with ten members. Then came a year of stagnation; the University glee club became dormant; and The Chronicle, after noticing the entire absence of musical organizations, declared that society singing and the "distressing pæan of '73" were the only choruses heard. In accordance with a suggestion of the college paper a glee club was formed in every class, and the societies and classes vied with each other in practicing college songs. The University Sodality, devoted to instrumental music, was organized in 1874, and in 1875 the University Glee Club was revived. The college year 1876–77 was characterized by a renewal of interest in college singing; meetings for practice were held frequently; and the Glee Club made a successful tour, visiting Detroit, Jackson, and Eaton Rapids. After 1878 the Club again became dormant.

In 1878–79 the only musical association composed wholly of students was the "University Orchestra", at the head of which was L. J. Locy, '78. Five years later Harold Wilson, '82, '86 *h*, had charge of the society. In 1884–85 it gave place to the "Chequamegon Orchestra", which continued to exist until the formation in November, 1895, of the "University Band", now a flourishing and useful organization.

The University Glee Club was revived—this time effectually—in 1884, and since that year it has been one of the most important of our student societies. It is supplemented by the University Banjo Club, formed in 1889–90, and by the University Mandolin Club, organized in 1895–96. From 1883 to 1891 the Ladies' Amphion Club was one of the musical organizations of Michigan. For six years each of the freshman classes has maintained a glee club and a banjo club. The University Glee Club in 1890, accompanied by the University Banjo Club, visited several Michigan cities and also Chicago, Madison, Minneapolis, and St. Paul, giving concerts which were very favorably received. In 1891–92 the annual tour of the Glee and Banjo Clubs included St. Louis, Kansas City, and Omaha, and in 1896 the combined organization travelled as far west as Salt Lake City. The members of the Glee Club from the final revival in 1884 have been the following:

H. S. Ames, '85 *l*,
J. V. Denney, '83,
L. H. Dennis, '85,
S. F. Hawley, '85,
A. H. Williams, '85,
A. A. Boyer, '86 *m*,
Harold Wilson, '86 *h*,
M. H. Clark, '87,
J. D. Hibbard, '87,
S. B. Hodge, '87,
S. K. Pittman, '87,
J. B. Thomas, Jr., '87,
E. S. Upson, '87, *p*,
J. N. Blair, '88,
J. E. Carpenter, '88,
R. G. Cole, '88,
S. H. Crowl, '88,
D. E. Ewald, '88,
J. E. Hodge, '88,
C. H. Perry, '88.
R. S. Smith, '88,
G. J. Waggoner, '88,
F. D. Wiseman, '88 *p*,
J. E. Boyer, '89,
H. F. Briggs, '89 *d*,
W. H. Dodge, '89 *m*,
W. C. Elliott, '89 *m*,
W. W. Harris, '89.
C. A. Howell, '89,
E. L. McAllaster, '89,
C. P. Taylor, '89,
H. V. Winchell, '89,
C. T. Alexander, '90,
J. E. Ball, '90 *l*,
F. W. Crane, '90,
H. P. Geisler, '90 *l*,
B. L. Green, '90,
P. B. Herr, 90,
C. E. Martzloff, '90 *p*,
H. F. Pennington, Jr., '90 *l*,

O. C. Smith, '90,
A. J. Vantine, '90,
J. O. Ballard, '91 *m*,
A. M. Cross, '91 *l*,
J. A. Jameson, Jr., '91,
J. L. Mitchell, '91 *l*,
William Wilhartz, '91,
W. W. Morrison, *p. g.*,
Eleazer Darrow, '92,
E. H. Harriman, '92,
H. M. Joy, '92 *m*,
J. B. Miller, '92,
W. B. Rogers, '92,
E. B. Spalding, '92 *d*,
R. F. Thompson, '92 *l*,
W. E. Walter, '92,
E. H. Cheney, '93,
R. G. George, '93,
E. C. Peters, '93,
H. A. Leese, '93 *l*,
H. V. Richardson, '93,
W. L. Webster, '93 *d*,
D. R. Barlow, '94 *l*,
E. N. Bullock, '94,
Archibald Cattell, Jr., '94 *l*,
H. B. Gammon, '94,
W. W. Pepple, '94 *l*,
J. A. Pratt, '94 *m*,
A. J. Purdy, '94,
W. W. Woodbury, '94 *l*,
H. F. Worden, '94,
W. H. Andrews, '95,
J. E. Bland, '95,
Frank Briscoe, '95,
R. W. Dunn, '95.
H. I. Dunton, '95,
R. F. Flintermann, '95,
G. A. McCollum, '95,
L. S. McCreary, '95,
B. F. McLouth, '95,
G. D. Price, '95,
J. Reynolds, '95,
W. A. Spitzley, '95,
J. A. Stevens, '95,
J. B. Archer, '96,
Howard Bement, '96,
H. E. Bodman, '96,
A. G. Cummer, '96,
J. C. Davies, '96,
D. M. Ferry, Jr., '96,
C. F. Fitch, '96,
B. A. Gage, '96,
K. R. Miner, '96,
W. G. Povey, '96,
C. H. Snyder, '96,
Boone Gross, '97,
W. E. Janes, '97.
A. E. Maas, '97,
C. E. Mead, '97,
H. S. Snyder, '97,
R. H. Sutphen, '97.
E. F. Berger, '98 *l*,
C. J. Dovel, '98,
H. T. Harrison, '98,
C. E. Pease, '98,
C. D. Terrell, '98,
H. P. Treadway, '98,
H. B. Wetmore, '98,
T. R. Woodrow, 98,
E. C. Worden, '98,
A. H. Fiebach, '99,
P. R. Furlong, '99 *d*,
W. G. Law, '99 *d*,
W. M. McKee, '99,
S. I. Motter, '99 *l*,
W. C. Smith '99 *l*,
L. D. Verdier, '99,
H. S. Pingree, Jr., '00,
J. S. Symons, '00,
W. W. Talman, '00,
J. E. Watson, '00 *l*,
A. M. Webster, '00 *m*,
W. R. Wood, '00,
C. W. Aird, '01,
H. W. Hayes, '01.

The University Banjo Club has had these members:

P. R. Gray, '90,
O. C. Smith, '90,
F. R. Ashley, '91,
J. O. Ballard, '91 *m*,
J. A. Jameson, Jr., '91,
B. E. Page, '91,
H. W. Booth, '92,
J. E. Ferris, '92,
J. B. Miller, '92,
A. D. Rathbone, Jr., '92,
G. C. Prentis, '92,
W. B. Rogers, '92,
E. L. Sanderson, '92,
H. E. Sauer, '92,
H. F. VanDeventer, '92,
C. C. Warden, '92,
H. P. Dodge, '93,
E. C. Peters, '93,
J. R. Sutton, '93,
R. F. Hall, '94,
Roger Sherman, '94,
Goldwin Starrett, '94,
J. B. Taylor, '94,
Adolph Tyroler, '94,
H. F. Worden, '94,
R. R. Case, '95,

B. S. Colburn, '95,
C. H. Conrad, '95,
R. F. Flintermann, '95,
A. H. Hunt, '95,
C. H. Morse, Jr., '95,
R. F. Hall, *p. g.*,
H. S. Barton, '96,
H. E. Bodman, '96,
R. D. Ewing, '96,
H. P. Hart, '96,
F. E. Miller, '96,
J. S. Pratt, '96,
W. W. Thayer, '96 *l*,
H. W. Cummings, '97,
F. S. Gerrish, '97,
A. F. Maitland, '97,
W. B. Rich, '97,
W. A. Starrett, '97,
A. H. Stoneman, '97,
R. S. Cummings, '98,
J. R. Davis, '98 *d*,
W. J. O'Brien, '98,
R. F. Palmer, '98,
H. W. Standart, '98,
C. F. Steinbauer, '98 *d*,
R. B. Upham, '98 *l*,
A. R. Wren, '98,
C. C. Adams, '99,
E. B. Adams, '99 *l*,
W. C. Boynton, '99,
W. C. Cooper, '99,
H. A. Fenton, '99 *l*,
H. T. Griswold, '99,
E. B. Jones, '99,
Paul Oliver, '99,
D. H. Wagar, '99 *l*,
C. E. Wehrle, '99 *h*,
A. B. Groesbeck, '00,
J. H. Thompson, '00,
P. B. Pendill, '01,
A. M. Rust, '01.

The membership of the University Mandolin Club follows:

C. H. Morse, Jr., '95,
R. D. Ewing, '96,
G. A. Geist, '96 *m*,
L. R. Hamblen, '96 *l*,
E. M. Holland, '96,
J. J. Lasalle, '96 *m*,
W. W. Thayer, '96 *l*,
H. A. Cole, '97,
A. H. Stoneman, '97,
G. E. Ball, '98 *l*,
J. C. Blair, '98,
R. S. Cummings, '98,
J. R. Davis, '98 *d*,
C. E. Groesbeck, '98,
Allan Loomis, '98,
W. J. O'Brien, '98,
H. W. Standart, '98,
C. F. Steinbauer, '98 *d*,
W. C. Boynton, '99,
W. L. Cooper, '99,
H. A. Fenton, '99 *l*,
H. T. Griswold, '99,
F. R. Hoover, '99,
E. B. Jones, '99,
J. T. Mountain, '99,
Paul Oliver, '99,
W. J. Stone, '99,
C. E. Wehrle, '99 *h*,
A. B. Groesbeck, '00,
A. W. Norton, '00,
M. H. O'Brien, '01,
P. B. Pendill, '01.

Since the year 1881 the University has maintained a chair of music, and has offered a varied and comprehensive curriculum in the theory and history of music. It also lends its support to the University School of Music, an institution with which it is sympathetically though not organically connected, Francis W. Kelsey, of the University Faculty, being the President of the corporation by which the school is governed, and Albert A. Stanley, the Professor of Music in the University, being the Director of the School. In 1893 an auxiliary corporation erected the building in Maynard street now occupied by the School of Music. Identified both with the School and with the University are the University Musical Society and the Choral Union, affiliated organizations which have existed since 1879–80, and which gave their first public rehearsal on the evening of May 4, 1880. It was through the efforts of the Musical Society, seconded by Professor Kelsey, by Mr. Charles Buncher of Detroit, and by other friends of the University, that the great Columbian Organ was secured for University Hall four years ago. In May, 1894, the Choral Union having become so strong that it was able to perform by itself the great oratorios, a musical festival was held in the great hall of the University. Annually repeated with constantly increasing success, the May festival at Ann Arbor has come to be regarded as the chief musical event of the year in this part of the country. Besides the festival the Musical Society gives every year through the Choral Union a series of grand concerts.

CHAPTER X

SPORTS AND GAMES

In the days before the Civil War desultory games of football, baseball, and cricket, for which there had not been any regular practice, constituted the "athletics" of Michigan students. In *The Palladium* for 1860–61 we find the first mention, so far as the undergraduate press is concerned, of this now absorbing department of college life. By page 46 of the publication above mentioned the "Pioneer Cricket Club" of the class of '64 is credited with eight officers and twenty-five members, Frank Todd being the President. In 1861–62 this organization continued to thrive; F. A. Buhl was President, and Schuyler Grant, J. C. Hart, and Q. A. Thomas were the "Ground Committee". In 1864–65 was formed the "University Cricket Club", with P. Baldy Lightner, '67, as President, Melville M. Bigelow, '66, now eminent as a law-writer, as Treasurer, Dwight N. Lowell, '67, as Secretary, and H. W. Stevens, '66, as Captain of the first eleven. At the request of this organization the Regents appropriated fifty dollars to prepare playing grounds, which were fitted out not far from the Laboratory. The same club flourished in 1866–67 with fifty-four active members, with the same President as before, and with Edward L. Walter, '68, as Secretary, E. E. Kane, '67, as Treasurer, and F. M. Smith, '68, as Captain of the first eleven. Joshua W. Waterman (long afterwards the founder of our Gymnasium) repeatedly visited Ann Arbor for the purpose of encouraging this sport; but *The University Chronicle* of October 12, 1867, noted that the Cricket Club had become disorganized, and that the students had been "rifled of all ambition or stir in that direction". The game was supplanted by baseball and football, although there was a revival of it in April, 1872, when a new club was formed with S. T. Douglas, '73, as President, and with a first eleven composed of S. T. Douglas, '73, W. H. Wells, '74, St. H. C. Parker, '74, F. A. Maynard, '74, Wayne Hayman, '73, L. B. King, '74, E. F. Laible, '75, H. A. Thayer, '74, C. R. Wells, '74, G. S. Cook, '73 *p*, and F. W. Fletcher, '75. This club played and won two match games with the club organized at Lodi, and lost a game to the Peninsular Club of Detroit. There was another brief revival in 1881–82, but evidently the game is too much of an exotic to take firm hold here.

Baseball was formally introduced among our students in the spring of 1863 by John M. Hinchman, '66, of Detroit, who had been a member of the Detroit Club. Oscar P. Bills and E. C. Page, both of '65, laid out a diamond in the northeast part of the campus, and three years later the Regents appropriated one hundred dollars for the improvement of the grounds. The batter faced the medical building, and many long drives were made in the direction of that seat of learning. Of course the game differed considerably from that now played: the pitcher was restricted to an underhand delivery; the catch of a foul bound made an "out"; strikes were not called on the batter; bases were not given on "balls"; and owing to the straight-arm pitching the batting was much heavier and the scores far larger than now.

TAPPAN HALL.

In the spring of 1864 a meeting of the students was held, and the organization of the first "University Baseball Club" was effected, J. M. Hinchman being elected President, S. B. Ladd, '65, Vice-President, E. C. Page, '65, Secretary, E. L. Grant, '66, Treasurer, and W. J. Maynard, O. P. Bills, and H. E. Burt, all of '65, directors. These officers chose the following first nine:

J. M. Hinchman, '66, c.,
E. L. Grant, '66, p.,
E. C. Page, '65, 1,
J. P. Nixon, '65, 2,
F. J. Simmons, '66, 3,
O. P. Bills, '65, s.,
C. M. Goodsell, '65, l.,
W. J. Maynard, '65, m.,
C. S. Fraser, '66, r.

Hinchman was chosen captain of the team. The members of the nine had no uniforms, and paid their own expenses. There was no charge for admisson to the match games. Scores of the games played in 1864 have not been preserved, but it is known that the nine was successful; and there was great enthusiasm. A class nine, the first of its kind, was formed that year by the freshmen of '67, and it played games with nines from Dexter, Lodi, the Ann Arbor High School, and the Normal School.

The University nine for 1864–5 was the same as for the preceding year, except that W. J. Cocker, '69, took the place of F. J. Simmons, '66, at third base. Hinchman was re-elected captain, and the team had match games with Jackson, Ypsilanti, Dexter, and Lodi, all but the last named being defeated. In the autumn of 1865 E. L. Grant, '66, became captain, Hinchman having left college. In the spring of 1866 the organization of the University Club was enlarged so as to include the professional departments, and two teams were selected, which played regularly together, and from which the first nine of the University was chosen. This was made up thus:

F. A. C. Macmanus, '67, *l*, c.,
W. J. Cocker, '69, p.,
J. C. Bigger, '68, *l*, 1,
L. O. Goddard, '67, 2,
Samuel Hayes, '69, 3,
Galusha Pennell, '68, s.,
A. H. Pattengill, '68, l.,
E. W. Gale, '68, m.,
A. E. Wilkinson, '69, r.,
J. M. Stout, '68, sub.

During 1866 games were played with nines representing Ann Arbor, Jackson, and the Union School of Ypsilanti, in all of which the University was successful, the scores being 33 to 11, and 19 to 5, with Ann Arbor, and 61 to 41 with Jackson. Both '68 and '69 had class nines that year.

In 1867 the newly established University Chronicle urged the team to go into training in order to win the championship of Michigan, and it invited larger subscriptions from the students for the purpose of helping the nine. Early in the spring the men were put in training by daily practice on the campus. Every afternoon the University team met one of the class nines. On the fourth of May uniforms of white, the first ordered for a Michigan nine, were received. After defeating nines from Ann Arbor, Ypsilanti, and Jackson, by scores of 30 to 26, 42 to 12, and 43 to 15, the nine made arrangements for meeting the Detroit Club, the champions of Michigan. Seventy students accompanied the team to Detroit for the purpose of witnessing the first game, which was played on June 15. It is said that on their way to the grounds the boys were met by an old baseball enthusiast who asked them with whom they were going to play. "The Detroit Club", they answered. "What", he rejoined, "not the Detroit first nine"? Receiving the assurance that such was the fact, he turned and looked the speaker full in the face, and after a moment's silence, gravely remarked, "Well, boys, you'll be sick enough before night". Michigan won by a score of 70 to 18, the Detroit players being able to do little with Blackburn, the University pitcher. The game lasted three and one-half hours, and among its features were six home runs, four by Dawson, Michigan's catcher. Ten "missed flies", four of which were credited to Michigan, show that the fielding game was hardly up to present standards. On their return to Ann Arbor the victorious team was welcomed by a great crowd of students.

About this time *The Yale Courant* asked why Michigan University could not send a baseball nine to play at the approaching Harvard and Yale Regatta; but the early closing of our college year, and the distance, were insurmountable obstacles.

The nine for the spring of 1867 was formed thus:

G. E. Dawson, '69, c.,	A. H. Pattengill, '68, l.,
J. A. Blackburn, '70, p.,	Samuel Hayes, '69, m.,
W. J. Cocker, '69, 1,	W. A. Butler, Jr., '69, r.,
A. E. Wilkinson, '69, 2 & p.,	W. H. Boardman, '69, sub.,
E. W. Gale, '68, 3,	W. C. Maybury, '70, sub..
E. F. Cooley, '70, s.,	Robert McCart, '67 *l*, sub.

In the return game (played October 17) with Detroit, the University men, owing to over-confidence, were defeated by a score of 36 to 20. As the final game, scheduled for November 2, was not played, the championship for that year was not decided. *The University Chronicle* declared that Blackburn as a pitcher had not his superior in the state or in the Northwest; and no doubt this was true. The same paper also expressed regret that there was not some college near, where our nine could go to play, and from which visits could be received.

In April, 1868, Samuel Hayes, '69, was chosen captain of the first nine, and W. C. Maybury, '70, was selected to lead the second. The two teams practiced regularly, and on May 30 the long postponed final game with Detroit was played. In the eleventh inning Michigan made two runs, winning by a score of 26 to 24. "Never", said *The University Chronicle*, "has a more closely contested game been played in the West. Never did men feel happier than the University men after the game". Another game between the same clubs took place at Ann Arbor, June 4, and the University was again successful, the score being 26 to 18. The nine for this year was the following:

G. E. Dawson, '69, c.,	E. F. Cooley, '70, s.,
J. A. Blackburn, '70, p.,	F. A. Crittenden, '71, l.,
W. J. Cocker, '69, 1,	Samuel Hayes, '69, m.,
A. E. Wilkinson, '69, 2,	C. C. Smith, '71, r.
G. H Lothrop, '70, 3,	

The same team was selected for 1869, but owing to the disbandment of the Detroit Club and to the unwillingness of other neighboring clubs to meet the renowned representatives of Michigan, no games were arranged. Class games were frequent that year and the next. The nine for 1870 consisted of the following undergraduates:

A. G. Bishop, '73, c..
A. G. Tyng, '73, p.,
C. C. Smith, 71, 1,
Morris Starne, '70 *l*, 2,
R. D. Harrison, '73, 3,
E. F. Cooley, '70, s.,
B. W. Smith, '71, l.,
J. A. Fulton, '71, m.,
C. H. Coldren, '72, r.

This nine played only one game, defeating the Ann Arbor Club on April 11. In the autumn of 1870 a class league was formed, and '73 came out victorious. There was however a decided lack of interest in baseball, owing to the introduction of football, a game in which more of the students could take part.

April 25, 1871, the University Baseball Club was reorganized, J. A. Fulton, '71, being chosen President, and J. A. Mercer, '71, captain of the first nine. The team selected was this:

H. A. Thayer, '74, c.,
Wayne Hayman, '73, p.,
G. E. Hall, '74, 1,
W. S. Sheeran, '73, 2,
J. A. Mercer, '71, 3,
W. H. Wells, '74, s.,
F. A. Maynard, '74, l.,
R. D. Harrison, '73, m.,
C. H. Dane, '73, r.,
C. B. Keeler, '73, sub.,
W. R. Clark, '74, sub.

For at least one thing this team was remarkable: all of its members with but one exception, were underclassmen. Both '73 and '74 contained excellent baseball material, while '71 and '72, particularly the latter, were very deficient in this respect. Although the nine for 1871 was strong, a schedule of games could not be arranged, and the record for that year is limited to the annual game between the freshmen and the sophomores, in which the latter were victorious by a score of 74 to 19. A team to represent the University was not selected in 1872, although many students took part in "scrub" games. Doubtless the attention given to football and to the revived game of cricket caused a temporary slackening of interest in baseball, but the chief difficulty, a difficulty which continued for long, was the absence of strong teams with which to play. In 1873 the regular nine was reorganized so as to present these names:

F. E. Bliss, '73, c.,
F. N. Wood, '75, p.,
G. E. Hall, '74, 1,
W. L. Sheeran, '73, 2,
W. M. Safford, '75, 3,
W. H. Wells, '74, s.,
F. A. Maynard, '74, l.,
E. D. Root, '75, m.,
Wayne Hayman, '73, r.

October 11, 1873, the Mutuals of Jackson were defeated at Ann Arbor by a team composed chiefly of juniors and freshmen, the score being 19 to 9; and on October 25 the freshmen defeated the sophomores by a score of 60 to 43. The team for 1874, as selected by Captain G. L. Winslow, was as follows:

G. L. Winslow, '77, c.,
W. R. Roberts, '77, p.,
P. R. Wilson, '75, 1,
F. K. Stearns, '77, 2,
G. H. Abbott, '75, 3,
A. J. Stellwagen, '75, s.,
W. F. Baxter, '77, l.,
E. D. Root, '75, m.,
F. R. Buell, '76, r.

Of the games played by this nine the only one of which record remains was with Ypsilanti; and was a victory for Michigan. The deciding contest of a series of games between the seniors and juniors was gained by the seniors, May 23, by a score of 13 to 9; and the annual sophomore-freshman game was won by the freshmen, October 3, 1874, by the score of 34 to 21. In the spring of 1875 the team was organized with E. D. Root, '75, as captain, and was formed thus:

G. L. Winslow, '75, c.,
G. H. Abbott, '75, p.,
C. S. Burch, '75, 1,
F. K. Stearns, '77, 2,
O. W. Ferdon, '77, 3,
W. R. Roberts, '77, s.,
O. P. Shepardson, '75, l.,
E. D. Root, '75, m.,
W. C. Johnson, '78, r.

The games played in 1875 were with the Mutuals of Jackson, May 18, 5 to 7; Ætnas of Detroit, May 29, 15 to 10, and June 5, 6 to 7; and Unas of Kalamazoo, October 22, 5 to 2. Owing to the abolishment of "straight-arm" pitching, and the calling of strikes on batsmen, the number of runs per game now began to fall off considerably. Stearns, the fine second baseman of the 1875 team, afterwards became President of the Detroit Baseball Club, which under his guidance won the championship in the National League.

In the spring of 1876 the following nine was selected:

F. E. Bliss, '79 *l*, c.,
J. S. Ayres, '77, p.,
C. L. VanPelt, '76, 1,
W. R. Roberts, '77, 2,
O. W. Ferdon, '77, s.,
W. C. Johnson, '78, s. s.,
W. W. Augur, '78, l.,
E. S. Siebert, '76 *l*, m.,
W. H. Murphy, '79, r.

The schedule for 1876 was greatly abbreviated by the refusal of the Faculty to permit the team to play games out of town; for it was impossible to induce clubs to visit Ann Arbor when return games were prohibited. In consequence of this ruling a projected tour fell through in 1877, and with it the home games which had been arranged. A nine containing only a few of the regular players was defeated, May 26, 1877, by the Mutuals of Jackson, 12 to 10; and a hurriedly picked team was defeated in October by the strong nine of the Memphis (Tenn.) Club. The Michigan team for 1877 was:

G. J. Lonstorf, '80, c.,	O. W. Ferdon, '77, 3,
G. P. Castle, '77, c.,	W. R. Roberts, '77, s.,
W. C. Johnson, '78, p.,	W. W. Hannan, '80, l.,
W. W. Augur, '78, 1,	W. M. Thompson, '80, m.,
A. S. Deacon, '80, 2,	W. H. Rand, '77 *h*, r.

The first game played in 1878 was at Ann Arbor, May 11, when the club from Three Rivers was defeated by a score of 31 to 1. The team for the year was as follows:

F. E. Bliss, '79 *l*, c.,	W. C. Johnson, '78, s.,
R. H. McMurdy, '80, p.,	W. W. Augur, '78, l.,
W. M. Thompson, '80, 1,	O. W. Ferdon, '77, m.,
W. W. Hannan, '80, 2,	H. S. Richards, '80 *p*, r.
E. L. Webster, 80, 3,	

Early in the spring of 1879 two teams selected by the baseball committee of the Athletic Association began practice on the campus. A game played by the nine with Detroit's new professional team at Detroit, May 17, resulted in a defeat for Michigan, 2 to 22. Six days later a nine from the Tecumseh Club was defeated at Ann Arbor, 27 to 7, and in the return game, played on Decoration Day, Michigan won, 14 to 3. A second contest with the Detroit professionals, at Ann Arbor, resulted in favor of the latter, 17 to 7.

DON M. DICKINSON, '67 *l*

In the autumn of 1879 the game between the sophomores and freshmen was won by the former, 11 to 3, the sophomore battery, Davenport and Hodges, being very effective. Hodges was made captain of the University nine in 1880, and the team was constituted thus:

C. H. Hodges, '82, c.,	D. F. Kendall, '80, s.,
F. W. Davenport, '82, p.,	M. P. French, '82, l.,
W. M. Thompson, '80, 1,	F. F. Reed, '80, m.,
J. F. Gallaher, '82, 2,	A. H. Brown, Jr., '83, r.
W. W. Hannan, '80, 3,	

The nine just named was remiss in practice, and was twice defeated by the Tecumseh Club, 4 to 1, and 15 to 3. In the following year more attention was paid to practice. F. W. Davenport was chosen captain of the nine, which made a creditable showing in two games with the strong professional team of Detroit, twice defeated the cadets of Orchard Lake, lost a game to the Cass Club of Detroit by the score of 5 to 0, and won a victory over Dexter, 40 to 17. The nine was made up in the following manner:

G. B. Daniels, '81, c.,
F. W. Davenport, '82, p.,
G. A. Derby, '83, 1,
J. F. Gallaher, '82, 2,
A. H. Brown, '83, 3,
W. M. Thompson, '81, s.,
M. P. French, '82, l.,
E. P. Hathaway, '82, m.,
Harry Bitner, '84, r.

In the winter of 1881–82 an intercollegiate baseball league composed of Michigan, Wisconsin, Northwestern and Racine, was formed. In anticipation of the approaching season a gymnasium was fitted up in a large room over one of the hardware stores in town, and there the baseball men practiced steadily. In April preliminary games were played with the Fort Wayne team of Detroit, 23 to 0, the League Club of Detroit, 4 to 14, and the Cass Club, 6 to 5. About the first of May new suits, of gray with blue trimmings, and with "U. of M." in blue on the breast, arrived for the players. A nine was now selected for the league series, as follows:

M. F. Walker, '84 *l*, c.,
A. T. Packard, '83, p. & 3,
T. P. Antle, '84 *m*, p.,
F. W. Davenport, '82, 1,
R. M. Dott, '84, 2,
J. H. Rollins, '82 *l*, 3,
A. S. Harvey, '84 *h*, s.,
C. G. Allmendinger, '85, l.,
Walter Davis, '85, m.,
J. F. Gallaher, '82, r.

Of this team Harvey was chosen captain. The Cass Club was defeated at Ann Arbor, May 6, by a score of 20 to 14. The Chronicle of May 13, 1882, said "At no time in the last eight years has there been shown so much interest in baseball as during the present season". On the 20th of May the first of the league games was played at Ann Arbor with the Wisconsin team, and was won by our men, 20 to 8. Packard, the Michigan pitcher, struck out eleven men, and Davenport's first base play was excellent. May 26 the team started on its Western tour, in the course of which it defeated Racine 12 to 2 and 11 to 10, Wisconsin 16 to 6, and Northwestern 20 to 3. As Northwestern forfeited its second game, the end of the league season left Michigan the champion, with six victories and no defeats. Other games played before college closed were these: Michigan against Fort Wayne, 6 to 2; Michigan against Cass, 10 to 18 and 22 to 6. Because of a lack of money it became necessary to abandon the proposed Eastern trip in which Michigan as the winner of the Western collegiate championship would have met the Eastern champions.

In March, 1882, Michigan withdrew from the Western Colle-

11

giate League because satisfactory arrangements could not be made for the expenses of our team on its Western tour. The season of 1883 began April 21, with a game against a picked nine, which Michigan won by a score of 9 to 8. Then the University defeated Adrian College, April 28, and a few days later was beaten at Ann Arbor by the Detroit League team, 17 to 5. May 19 the Jackson Mutuals were defeated 20 to 2. The professional team of Toledo was beaten at Ann Arbor, June 2, by a score of 14 to 11, and one week afterwards the strong professional nine of Port Huron played on the fair grounds at Ann Arbor, winning against the University by the narrow margin of 2 to 0. In the return game at Port Huron our nine was defeated 22 to 0. The team in 1883 was as follows:

H. E. Montgomery, '86, c.,
A. T. Packard, '83, p.,
C. H. Blackburn, '83 *h*, 1,
Charles Hueber, '84 *p*, 2,
W. W. Walker, '84 *h*, 3,
C. G. Allmendinger, '85, s.,
W. D. Condon, '86 *p*, l.,
A. E. Miller, '83, m,
Lincoln MacMillan, '89, r.

In 1884 the baseball interest withdrew from the Athletic Association and formed an association of its own, choosing H. F. Forbes, '84, as President, and Don C. Corbett, '85, as manager of the team. The following were the players selected for the nine:

C. C. Smith, '86, c.,
W. R. Payne, '87, c.,
J. D. Hibbard, '87, p.,
C. G. Allmendinger, '85, 1,
C. B. Weatherwax, '87, 2,
W. W. Walker, '84 *h*, 3,
Lincoln MacMillan, '89, s.,
W. D. Condon, '86 *p*, l.,
F. R. Carson, '84 *d*, m.,
E. C. Best, '88, m.,
I. M. Long, '89, r.

During the season of 1884 ten games were played with Plymouth, St. Louis Reserves, Cass, Orchard Lake, Detroit Amateurs, Ypsilanti Crescents, and the Agricultural College, in eight of which Michigan was victorious. One of the games was a tie, and one was a defeat. The University made 89 runs to 54 scored by its opponents, and the base hits were 90 and 59 respectively. The fielding average of Michigan was .837. Condon made not a single error during the season. Carson led the batting with the high average of .353, but he played in only four games. Condon with an average of .261 surpassed all others who played throughout the series.

Early in the spring of 1885 the rink was secured for practice, and new uniforms of crimson and gray were obtained. The following games were played before Commencement: Michigan against Jackson, 16 to 13; against Plymouth, 10 to 5; against Cass,

4 to 11. The batting average of the team was .214, and the team was made up thus:

C. C. Smith, '86, c.,	C. T. Miller, '88, s.,
J. D. Hibbard, '87, p.,	W. D. Condon, '86 *p*, l.,
F. W. Mehlhop, '88, 1,	C. G. Allmendinger, '85, m.,
F. D. McDonell, '88, 2,	E. C. Best, '88, m.,
Lincoln MacMillan, '89, 3,	L. S. Bigelow, '86 *l*, r. & c.

John D. Hibbard, '87, who had been captain in 1885, was re-elected in 1886, and his team played seven games, defeating the Detroit Hiawathas, 15 to 10, the Detroit Amateurs, 7 to 4, Orchard Lake, 14 to 1 and 13 to 8, and Oberlin, 9 to 7, and losing to the Maple Leaf Club of Guelph, 3 to 13, and to the Cass Club of Detroit, 9 to 13. The fielding average of the team was .826, the batting average .271. McDonell had a batting average of .333 for seven games. The team was constituted as follows:

C. C. Smith, 86, c.,	W. B. Carpenter, '89, s.,
J. D. Hibbard, '87, p.,	W. D. Condon, 86 *p*, l.,
F. W. Mehlhop, '88, 1,	A. D. Welton, '88, m.,
F. D. McDonell, '88, 2,	R. M. Lee, '86 *l*, r.,
H. S. Bush, '88, 3,	J. M. Jaycox, '87, r.
C. T. Miller, '88, s.,	

In the opening game of 1887 the University was defeated at Lansing by the Agricultural College, 9 to 8. May 7, the Detroit Amateurs were beaten in a close game on the campus, 4 to 3. Oberlin was defeated on its own grounds, May 14, by a score of 8 to 7. One week later the Cass team, assisted by several of the Detroit League team, won at Ann Arbor a heavy-hitting game with the score of 18 to 11. In later games the University defeated the Detroit Athletics, 11 to 6, and was defeated by the Hiawathas, 10 to 11, and by the Agricultural College, 9 to 11. The defeats experienced by our team were chiefly due to catcher Miller's having been hurt early in the season. No one else could successfully hold the swift pitching of MacMillan and Hibbard. The fielding average of the team was .869, and the batting was .315. MacMillan's high batting average of .552 for six games led the team. It has been declared that Hibbard, MacMillan, Miller, and McDonnell were four of the best players ever in the University. The team as a whole was as follows:

C. T. Miller, '88, c.,	W. B. Carpenter, '89, s.,
J. D. Hibbard, '87, p. & l.,	W. H. Booth, '90, l.,
T. L. Wilkinson, '90, 1,	C. F. Lawson, '88 *p*, m.,
F. D. McDonnell, '88, 2,	W. C. Malley, '89 *l*, m.,
Lincoln MacMillan, '89, 3 & p.,	J. M. Jaycox, '87, r.
W. H. Muir, '88, 3,	

As in 1887 the rink was secured for preliminary practice early in 1888. The team selected was composed of the following players:

W. H. Booth, '91 *d*, c. & m.,
G. P. Codd, '91, p.,
F. D. McDonell, '88, 1,
Lincoln MacMillan, '89, 2,
W. H. Muir, '88, 3,
J. T. Scott, '91, s.,
J. R. Sapp, '88 *l*, s.,
W. S. McArthur, '89, l.,
J. J. Marker, '90 *m*, m. & c.,
T. N. Jayne, '90, m.,
A. D. Rich, '90, r.,
T. L. Wilkinson, '90, r.

Beginning with a victory of 5 to 4 at Orchard Lake, April 28, 1888, the University nine played the following games: D. A. C., 5 to 11, 15 to 10, and 9 to 2; Hiawatha, 3 to 3 in twelve innings; Cass, 3 to 9, 9 to 8, and 10 to 7; Jackson, 1 to 9; Agricultural College, 15 to 5, making six victories, three defeats, and one tie. That year's work was memorable for the batting of McDonell and MacMillan, whose averages for nine and eight games respectively were .448 and .406. As for the team as a whole, it was better in fielding than in batting, the average for the former being .908, an exceptionally high figure, while the batting average was only .211. Of the work of the team for 1888 The Chronicle of October 27, 1888, said:

"All friends of the University will be glad to learn of the wonderful success of the University Baseball Association for the season. After defeating some of the leading teams in the state, and securing victories over others that for years held the palm, our team withdrew at the end of the season with an unprecedented and remarkably brilliant record. But this was not all: the financial success was equally remarkable. The team was fitted out with elegant new suits, and everything else was obtained to put the nine in first class shape, and after this, and after all the other incidental expenses have been met, there is still a surplus of $50 in the treasury".

The rink could not be secured for baseball practice in 1889, and as the team had lost three excellent players the prospects for success were not bright. A team was selected as follows:

W. H. Booth, '91 *d*, c.,
C. S. McIndoe, '89 *d*. c.,
G. P. Codd, '91, p.,
A. D. Rich, '91, 1,
P. R. Gray, '91, 2,
J. H. Todd, '90, 3,
E. R. Lewis, '91, s.,
T. L. Wilkinson, '90, l.,
G. W. Denney, '91, l.,
T. N. Jayne, '90, m.,
J. J. Marker, '90 *m*, r.

The nine for 1889 was at the outset defeated by the Kalamazoo professionals, 3 to 8, and by the D. A. C., 7 to 15. Then came victories over the M. A. A., 12 to 4, the Owashtanongs of Grand Rapids, 25 to 1, and the Agricultural College, 18 to 5. But the return game with the Agricultural College resulted in a defeat, 10 to 12. June 24 our team beat the Cass Club 10 to 9. The batting average of the team for 1889 was .328, Jayne's individual average for six games being .532, and Wilkinson's being .424. The fielding average of the team was .846.

Early in 1890 an Eastern trip in which a defeat could be administered to Cornell was planned, and an unusually large number of candidates for the team appeared at the rink, which had been rented for preliminary practice. The team for the season was the following:

W. H. Booth, '91 *d*, c.,
G. P. Codd, '91, p.,
A. D. Rich, '91, 1,
P. R. Gray, '90, 2,
J. H. Todd, '90, 3,
August Bauer, '91 *l*, s.,
T. L. Wilkinson, '90, l.,
J. J. Marker, '90 *m*, m.,
L. I. Abbott, '91 *l*, r.,
E. R. Lewis, '91, sub.

In the first regular game of the season of 1890, which was played with the Detroit League Club, the latter won by a score of 10 to 1. On the third of May the M. A. A. team was beaten at Ann Arbor, 15 to 2. On the fourteenth of May the team started on the first Eastern trip ever undertaken by a Michigan nine, and stopping at Detroit it defeated the D. A. C., 6 to 5. At Ithaca, May 16, a close and exciting game was played with Cornell, Michigan winning, 2 to 1. Over-confidence the next day lost the game played with Colgate University, in which the score was 7 to 10. Later games that season were as follows: Oberlin, 7 to 6, 11 to 13, 8 to 5; D. A. C., 19 to 6; Agricultural College, 19 to 5; Cass, 7 to 3. The record for the year was eight victories and three defeats. The fielding average was .911, the batting .264. Abbott led the batting with an average of .389 for six games. To the remarkable pitching of Codd much of the success of that year, as of the preceding season, was due.

In 1890–91 the management of all athletic sports was entrusted to one association. An Eastern trip with games against Harvard and Yale was arranged early in the winter, and much enthusiasm was aroused, seventy-five candidates for the team handing in their names. From the first of February every candidate was pledged to keep up strict training. Daily practice was had in the rink until the weather permitted the use of the campus, after which a class team was pitted every afternoon against the University nine. Peter Conway, the famous pitcher of the National League, was secured as a coach for the team, which, when selected, was as follows:

Joseph Walsh, c.,
G. P. Codd, '91, p.,
T. E. Robinson, '92 *p*, p.,
A. H. Seymour, '92 *l*, p.,
A. D. Rich, '91, 1,
J. H. Kelley, '91 *l*, 2,
W. W. Pearson, '93 *m*, 3,
S. C. Spitzer, '94, s.,
T. L. Wilkinson, '90, l.,
W. H. Booth, '91 *d*, m.,
L. I. Abbott, '91 *l*, r & c.

The season of 1891 began with victories over the Agricultural College, 10 to 0 and 26 to 4, and Oberlin, 25 to 0. On the 9th of May 1,200 students went to Detroit in a special train to see the University defeat Cornell 8 to 6. One week later Northwestern was beaten 15 to 3. May 22 the team departed upon its visit to the Eastern colleges. Hamilton was easily defeated, 18 to 3, but the University of Vermont, which had hired a non-student pitcher for the game, won a victory from us with a score of 2 to 6, our team securing but two hits from the opposing pitcher. The game at New Haven on the 26th of May was also a defeat for us, but it was almost as good as a victory. Yale made only three hits off Codd, not having been held to that number by any other pitcher during the season; and the two runs made by our opponents resulted from passed balls on a slippery ground. Michigan although making six hits secured no runs. A close game at Brown was lost by us, 2 to 5. Our nine then defeated Wesleyan, 6 to 3, Trinity 20 to 3, and Harvard 4 to 3, so that the result of the expedition was four victories and three defeats. On this trip Michigan made 52 runs, 63 hits, and 24 errors against 25 runs, 38 hits, and 32 errors made by its opponents.

After the return of the team the D. A. C. was defeated, 11 to 1, and the M. A. A. lost a game to us during Commencement week. During the year fourteen games were played, of which all but three were won. Again Codd's fine pitching was largely responsible for the success of the team, but the heavy batting of Wilkinson, Robinson, Pearson, Codd, Kelley, and Spitzer, and the fine fielding of the team at critical times, contributed to the gratifying results of the season. The batting average of the team was .309, Wilkinson's individual average for the thirteen games played by him being .405, while Robinson for five games had an average of .458. The fielding average of first baseman Rich in 12 games was .953, and Abbott as right field and catcher had an average of .970.

In 1892 Conway was again secured as coach; T. E. Robinson, '92 *p*, was captain; and the team was made up thus:

F. E. Bowerman, '93 *p*, c. & m.,
Frank Crawford, '93 *l*, c. & l.,
T. E. Robinson, '92 *p*, p. & r.,
G. P. Codd, '93 *l*, p. & r.,
A. H. Seymour, '92 *l*, p. & l.,
A. W. Jefferis, '93 *l*, 1,
E. F. Spurney, '93 *l*, 2,
W. W. Pearson, '93 *m*, 3,
S. C. Spitzer, '94, s.,
C. B. Smeltzer, '94, l. & c.,
E. C. Shields, '94, m.

Worth W. Pepple, '95, played six games as third baseman, and W. J. Harness, '94, pitched two games for the team. Codd played in seven games only, and Smeltzer in eight.

About the middle of April the team began a two weeks' tour during which Albion was beaten 18 to 3, Wisconsin 7 to 4, Beloit 13 to 1, Illinois 18 to 0, Northwestern 14 to 4, and Olivet 15 to 0. Michigan however, was defeated by Notre Dame, 4 to 6. Two games were then played at Ann Arbor with the D. A. C., one of which was a tie, 4 to 4, while the other was a defeat, 1 to 2. Likewise at Ann Arbor were played games with Albion and Northwestern, both victories, 13 to 2 and 15 to 0. During a second Eastern trip Yale was beaten 3 to 2, Lafayette 6 to 0, Lehigh 12 to 4; but Michigan was defeated by Pennsylvania, 2 to 5, by Princeton, 9 to 4, by Harvard 4 to 2, and by Toronto 5 to 4. A game with Brown was ended by Michigan's withdrawing from the field because of unfair umpiring, when the score was 2 to 1 against Brown. In the autumn of 1892 the University was defeated by the D. A. C., 4 to 11, on the grounds of the former. Of the twenty games played in 1892 Michigan won eleven and lost seven. Our team made 161 runs against 67 scored by our opponents. Of the sixteen games played to a finish with other colleges we gained eleven and lost five, two of the latter by a single run and two by two runs. Spitzer and Bowerman led the batting with averages of .315 and .305 respectively, and Crawford as catcher and left field had the high average of .976 in seventeen games, while Jefferis played nineteen games at first base with a fielding average of .974. Spitzer played nineteen games as short-stop with only five errors, and had a fielding average of .934.

HOMŒOPATHIC MEDICAL COLLEGE.

During the season of 1893 Frank Crawford, '93 *l*, had the captaincy of the baseball team, the manager being H. G. Cleaveland, '93 *l*. The nine was as follows:

Frank Crawford, '93 *l*, c.,
H. B. Krogman, '94, p.,
A. W. Jefferis, '93 *l*, 1,
E. F. Spurney, '93 *l*, 2,
W. W. Pearson, '93 *m*, 3,
S. C. Spitzer, '94, s.,
G. F. Rich, '93 *l*, l.,
E. C. Shields, '94, m.,
C. B. Smeltzer, '94, r.

The substitutes were C. C. MacPherran, '95, R. E. Russell, '96,

T. P. Griffin, '93 *l*, and M. A. Banks, '95 *d*. Eighteen games were played during the three months of the season; of these Michigan won fourteen. Of the sixteen games played with other colleges our University won thirteen, being defeated twice by Cornell and once by Minnesota. The club went to Ithaca for a game with Cornell, but proceeded no further East. The teams of Illinois, Northwestern, and Wisconsin, lost two games apiece to us, and Albion, Kentucky, Centre, Purdue, Denison, Minnesota, and Iowa, each lost one game. Of the two games played with the D. A. C., one was gained, the other was lost. Michigan scored 211 runs as against 103 made by opposing teams. The team as a whole was not as strong as that of 1893, its greatest weaknesses being in the pitcher's box and at the bat. During the second game with Cornell, which was played at Detroit, May 30, the bases were twice filled by Michigan with nobody or only one out; but the single hit needed to win the game was not forthcoming, and Cornell won 6 to 5.

For 1894 George J. Cadwell, '94, was manager, and E. C. Shields was captain. The team was constituted thus:

C. B. Smeltzer, '94, c.,
J. W. Hollister, '95 *l*, p.,
H. B. Krogman, '94, p.,
Ray Hart, '95 *l*, 1,
W. D. McKenzie, '96, 1,
S. C. Spitzer, '94, 2,
R. E. Russell, '96, 2,
E. V. Deans, '96 *d*, 3,
W. W. Pepple, '95, s.,
James Baird, '96, s.,
W. W. Waterman, '97, l.,
E. C. Shields, '94, m.,
L. J. Wentworth, '94, r.

During the season of 1894 nineteen games were played, Michigan winning eleven. The team easily defeated the nines of the Ohio, Illinois, and Wisconsin colleges—although Oberlin beat it—but venturing in Eastern territory it met with an unbroken series of rebuffs from Vermont, Dartmouth, Harvard, Princeton, and Cornell. After returning home the club recovered from its temporary demoralization, and by the close score of 3 to 2 defeated on Decoration Day at Detroit the nine of the new University of Chicago, an institution which is now our chief competitor in baseball.

In 1895 E. C. Weeks, '95, acted as manager of baseball affairs, and E. C. Shields, '96 *l*, was the captain of the team, which was made up as follows:

W. F. Holmes, '96 *h*, c.,
J. C. Condon, '96, c.,
F. J. Sexton, '98 *m*, p.,
C. F. Watkins, '96 *p*, p. & r.,
W. D. McKenzie, '96, 1,
J. A. Bloomingston, '96 *l*, 2,
E. V. Deans, '96 *d*, 3,
R. E. Russell, '96, s.,
W. W. Waterman, '97, l.,
E. C. Shields, '96 *l*, m.

This team, which was one of the strongest we have had, defeated with little trouble most of the Western college nines which it played, but of the Eastern teams it met Cornell only. The latter was successful in a 2 to 1 game at Ithaca, but was defeated May 30, at Detroit, by the score of 11 to 0. Chicago beat Michigan 13 to 1 in Chicago, but lost the return game at Ann Arbor, 6 to 4.

For 1896 the veteran player, E. C. Shields, was manager, and W. F. Holmes was captain. As for the team, it contained the following undergraduates:

W. F. Holmes, '96 *h*, c.,
J. C. Condon, '96, c.,
A. H. Kinmond, '98 *d*, c.,
C. F. Watkins, '96 *p*, p.,
G. A. Miller, '98, p.,
W. D. Scott, '98 *l*, p.,
W. D. McKenzie, '96, 1,
J. A. Bloomingston, '96 *l*, 2,
E. V. Deans, '96 *d*, 3,
D. J. Lowney, '99 *m*, s.,
J. W. Hollister, '96 *l*, l.,
E. C. Shields, '96 *l*, m.,
D. C. McKinney, '98 *d*, r.

That year no games were played with Eastern teams except with Toronto, which was beaten 13 to 8. There were twenty-two contests, Michigan winning seventeen, losing four, and tying one, and scoring 248 times while its opponents scored 124. The colleges defeated were Albion, Ohio State (twice), Wittenberg, Indiana, Illinois (twice), Oberlin (twice), Wisconsin (twice), and Toronto. A series of five games was played with Chicago, and after each team had won two games the final contest was awaited with great eagerness. Just before it was played the management learned that two of the Michigan men had recently played under assumed names on a professional team. The Board of Control immediately debarred the offenders from further contests, and by this and a previous ruling three of the best men were taken from the team. Consequently the final game with Chicago was lost. No other college defeated Michigan in 1896.

The manager for 1897 was A. L. C. Atkinson, '98 *l*; Guy A. Miller, '98, was captain; and the team—necessarily composed chiefly of new players—was as follows:

G. W. Lunn, '99, c.,
H. S. McGee, '00, c.,
G. A. Miller, '98, p.,
T. M. Sawyer, '98, p.,
F. C. Condon, '99, 1,
C. F. Heard, '98 *m*, 2,
E. L. Cooley, '99, 2,
W. E. Sullivan, '98 *p*, 3,
Francis McMurray, '99 *m*, s.,
W. F. Wolf, '99 *l*, s.,
O. A. Ludlow, '98 *l*, l.,
J. R. Sheean, '98, m.,
J. E. Butler, '98, r.

From this new and inexperienced team little was expected; yet it made a creditable showing. It was defeated by the Detroit

League nine, 0 to 6; by Wittenberg, (which, though a college team, included six professionals), 7 to 17; by Notre Dame, 3 to 18; by Cornell, 2 to 14 and 1 to 6; by Wisconsin, 5 to 15 and 14 to 15; by Illinois, 0 to 3; and by Chicago, 3 to 5, 1 to 4, and 3 to 24. It defeated Chicago 5 to 3, Ohio State 11 to 4, and the Detroit Athletic Club 13 to 9.

In the spring of 1898 a series of games with Chicago, Northwestern, and Illinois was commenced. Thus far Michigan has won three of four games played with Chicago, one of three with Illinois, and both of the two played with Northwestern. A. H. Keith, '98, is the manager of baseball interests for 1898, and J. E. Butler is captain of the Michigan team, which is constituted as follows:

G. W. Lunn, '99, c.,
A. Thompson, '99 *d*, c. & r.,
G. A. Miller, '98, p.,
H. E. Lehr, '98 *d*, p.,
F. C. Condon, '99, 1,
E. L. Cooley, '99, 2,
W. F. Wolf, '99 *l*, 3,
F. L. Gilbert, '01, s.,
D. M. Matteson, '00 *d*, s. & l.,
Edwin McGinnis, '00, m.,
M. L. Davies, '00, l.,
J. E. Butler, '98, r.

Baseball is with us an exceedingly popular sport. Probably three hundred different students play it every spring. All of the literary classes, and many of the classes in the professional departments are represented by nines, which not only play against the University team, but engage in league contests with one another. Eleven years ago the leading secret societies formed a baseball league and fought for the fraternity championship, a "spread" paid for by the defeated nines being the reward of success. By a rule recently adopted a member of the University team is prohibited from playing on a class or fraternity nine, as an injury received in an unimportant game might cause the loss of an intercollegiate match.

In the autumn of 1866 the sophomores purchased a football, and the college paper declared that every afternoon excited "sixty-nine" men could be seen in their shirt sleeves running after the ball "with zeal so unremitting that had it been turned in the direction of learning it could not have failed to have placed them at the head of whatever profession they might have chosen". One year later the sport was said to have gone "to a grave too cold by far". In 1869–70 the game was revived, and the first football match of which record remains was played April 23, 1870, between the freshmen and sophomores ('73 and '72). "Football", said The Chronicle, "is a new institution on the campus, and bids fair to be popular, at least on cool days"; and the same paper commended the game as affording "exercise to the whole body of students at a comparatively trifling expense". Of course football in 1870 differed much from the sport of to-day. It was entirely a kicking game, and was played with many men—usually thirty—on a side. Winning consisted in sending the ball over the enemy's line a majority of a previously agreed number of times. Matches between the classes were the chief games during the early years of football at Ann Arbor. The class of '73 defeated '72, and twice defeated '74.

In 1872 the football organization consisted of the captains of the four class teams, W. S. Sheeran, '73, Calvin Thomas, '74, E. D. Root, '75, and E. C. Fox, '76. October 11, 1873, a football association was formed, and it was decided to challenge Cornell to play a match game in Cleveland, thirty on a side. But the Cornell Faculty refused to grant leave of absence to the students who had been selected to meet our men. The names of our thirty appear in The Palladium for 1873–4, on page 73. In 1874 and 1875 the sophomores defeated their freshman foes at football by scores of 7 to 0 and 5 to 0. September 30, 1876, the forty-two sophomores who appeared on the field were defeated by eighty-two freshmen; but the result was reversed when thirty picked members of each class met. As a rule the numbers engaged in class contests, even as late as 1889–90, were not limited.

Michigan was the pioneer in modern football in the West. Charles M. Gayley, '78, now Professor of English Literature in the University of California, introduced the Rugby game here in 1876. The following team, with Roberts, '77, as captain, was chosen:

W. R. Roberts, '77,
E. J. Snover, '87,
B. H. Colby, '77,
A. C. Angell, '78,
D. N. DeTar, '78,
W. C. Johnson, '78,
Evart VanPelt, '78,
I. K. Pond, '79,
C. J. Reynick, '79,
T. E. Walbridge, '77 *m*,
Ernest Copeland, '78 *m*.

In the spring of 1877 the Rugby rules were printed in The Chronicle, and in the autumn of that year another team was selected with Edwards, '79, as captain:

A. C. Angell, '78,
D. N. DeTar, '78,
W. C. Johnson, '78,
J. A. Beaumont, '79,
R. T. Edwards, '79,
C. S. Henning, '79,
I. K. Pond, '79,
A. S. Dean, '80,
J. A. Green, '80,
F. G. Allen, 81,
Everett Marshall, '81.

In December, 1878, the Athletic Association elected two football elevens, from which a team to represent the University was taken as soon as sufficient practice had been had. On the 30th of May the first football game played by a Michigan team under the new rules, and the first football game ever played by us with an outside team, took place at the White Stocking Park, Chicago, between our eleven and a delegation from Racine College, in the presence of about 500 Racine students and Michigan graduates. Michigan was represented by the following team:

RUSHERS.

D. N. DeTar, '80 *m*,	W. W. Hannan, '80,
John Chase, '79, '81 *m*,	F. F. Reid, '80,
I. K. Pond, '79,	R. G. DePuy, '79, '81 *h*.,
J. A. Green, '80,	T. R. Edwards, '79.

HALF-BACKS.

C. H. Campbell, '80,	E. H. Barmore, '82.

GOAL-KEEPER.

C. S. Mitchell, '80.

A. S. Pettit, '79, was substitute. Collins H. Johnston, '81, was one of the regular team, but could not go to Chicago. The game, according to The Chronicle, was "the finest game of football ever played this side of the Rocky Mountains." It began at 4:15 P. M., Racine making the opening kick. In the first inning Pond secured a touch-down for Michigan, and in the second DeTar kicked a goal. Racine could only make a safety touch-down. Telegraphic minutes of the game were posted upon a blackboard which the Steward of the University had caused to be placed under one of the trees near the medical building, and "when the last despatch was bulletined those who were present manifested their feelings in the usual student manner." That evening the winners were properly welcomed at the Michigan Alumni banquet held in the Palmer House, Chicago.

THE GYMNASIUM.

Our football team in the autumn of 1879 was the same as the one which had played at Chicago, except that C. H. Johnston, '81, and F. G. Allen, '81, replaced Campbell and Pond. A game was arranged with the University of Toronto, and of it The Chronicle gave this account:

"The first day of this month the 9 A. M. Kalamazoo Accommodation pulled out from our station with four cars cosily filled with students bound for Detroit to see the match at football between the Toronto eleven and our own team. The day was clear and bright, though a little cold, which seemed to stir the blood of the boys, causing them to open their mouths and pour forth their joy, like tuneful owl-eagles. All the college songs were sung and resung. . . . . Toronto took the wind, giving our boys the kick-off, and from the time De Tar sent the ball flying toward their goal to the close of the game our team had the advantage, except once or twice, and then only for a few minutes. Why this was it is hard to say, for Toronto played a strong game, and in almost every individual point excelled. It was a particularly close and exciting game. The excitement was especially intense when during the last few minutes of the game the ball was kept within a few feet of the Toronto line, our boys trying to force it through or get a drop for goal. Then the crowd seemed determined to take a part in the play. But no goal was made, and when time was called it all went up in a long, hearty cheer for Toronto and Ann Arbor. Our boys seemed satisfied not to have lost, and well they may, considering their youth in Rugby, and the high standing of the Toronto among Canadian teams."

In this game the Toronto men showed superior running ability. De Puy and Hannan made fine runs for Michigan. Neither side scored a goal or a touch-down, although several times our men had the ball within a few feet of the goal line. The Athletic Association lost $150 on the game; but this did not lessen football enthusiasm. Said The Chronicle of February 28, 1880: "The students of Ann Arbor need no argument to convince them that Rugby is the better game".

Another contest between Toronto and Michigan took place November 6, 1880, on the Toronto Lacrosse Club's grounds. The following was the make-up of our team, John Chase, '81 *m*, being captain:

FORWARDS.

John Chase, '81 *m*, R. G. De Puy, '81 *h*,
F. G. Allen, '81, W. H. Graham, '82,
W. S. Horton, '82 *l*, W. B. Calvert, '82 *h*,
C. H. Johnston, '81.

QUARTER-BACK.

E. H. Barmore, '82.

HALF-BACKS.

R. W. Brown, '81, R. M. Dott, '85.

FULL-BACK.

E. P. Hathaway, '82.

De Puy was injured during the game, and F. B. Wormwood, '83, took his place. Michigan won, making two touch-downs and a goal, while Toronto failed to score.

The failure of our football management to arrange a game with Racine College led The Chronicle to express the hope that there would be enough interest manifested in athletics that spring "to enable us to attain that consummation, so long sought and 'devoutly to be wished for', a game with some of the Eastern colleges;" and in the autumn of 1881 the following team was sent East to play with the chief elevens of that region:

FORWARDS.

John Ayres, '80, C. M. Wilson, '83 *l*,
P. G. DeW. Woodruff, '81 *l*, Harry Bitner, '84,
F. M. Townsend, '81, T. W. Gilmore, '84.

QUARTER-BACK.

W. S. Horton, '82 *l*.

HALF-BACKS.

R. M. Dott, '85, R. G. De Puy, '81 *h*,
F. B. Wormwood, '83.

FULL-BACK.

W. J. Olcott, '83.

SUBSTITUTES.

H. S. Mahon, '82, W. O. De Puy, '83 *a*.

Michigan was beaten by Harvard 4 to 0, by Yale 11 to 0, and by Princeton 13 to 4.

During the college year 1882–83 football at Ann Arbor was dormant. A challenge sent to an association in Detroit was not accepted, and only practice games were played. In 1883 a number of students joined in forming the Rugby Association, which was incorporated in May, 1886. In November, 1883, a second Eastern tour was made, the team selected being as follows:

FORWARDS.

E. E. Beach, '84, H. J. Killilea, '85 *l*,
Harry Bitner, '84, H. P. Borden, '84 *l*,
H. G. Prettyman, '85, R. M. Dott, '84 *l*.

QUARTER-BACK.

T. H. McNeil, '85.

HALF-BACKS.

R. G. Gemmell, '84, A. I. Moore, '84 *m*.

THREE-QUARTER-BACK.

W. J. Olcott, '83.

FULL-BACK.

T. W. Gilmore, '84.

SUBSTITUTES.

R. W. Beach, '86, H. S. Mahon, '84 *l*,
E. W. Wright, '84 *l*.

Prettyman was manager and Olcott was captain of this team, which was beaten by Yale 46 to 0, by Harvard 3 to 0, and by

Wesleyan 14 to 6, but which defeated Stevens Institute 5 to 1. From these games it was seen that Michigan could not compete with the Eastern colleges until the opportunities for practice in the West became greater. The Rugby team for the autumn of 1884 was made up of the following students:

RUSHERS.

E. L. Dorn, '86, H. J. Killilea, '85 *l*,
E. E. Beach, '84, H. G. Brock, '85,
H. G. Prettyman, '85, Dwight Goss, '86 *l*,
G. C. Schemm, '85.

QUARTER-BACK.

T. H. McNeil, '85.

HALF-BACKS.

W. J. Olcott, '84 *g*, W. J. Duff, '85 *m*.

THREE-QUARTER-BACK,

J. M. Jaycox, '87.

GOAL-KEEPER.

E. F. Duffy, '84 *l*.

This team, after defeating Albion College by the score of 18 to 0, played at Ann Arbor a brilliant game with Chicago, in which the latter club was beaten, 10 to 18. In the Chicago game Duffy played instead of Brock, and Olcott and Jaycox were the half-backs. In April, 1885, the Rugby Association became a member of the Intercollegiate Athletic Association.

Early in the autumn of 1885 the University team and the Windsor Club played at Windsor, Ontario, a game according to the old Rugby rules, Michigan winning, 10 to 0. A return game resulted in our favor, 30 to 0. Thanksgiving Day our eleven met the Peninsular team of Detroit, and defeated it 42 to 0. That year J. R. McCammon, '87, was manager, and H. G. Prettyman, '87 *m*, was captain of the team, which was constituted thus:

FORWARDS.

F. G. Higgins, '86 *l*, R. W. Beach, '86,
W. M. Morrow, '90, C. N. Banks, '87 *l*,
H. G. Prettyman, '87 *m*, J. L. Skinner, '87,
F. F. Bumps, '87.

QUARTER-BACK.

T. H. McNeil, '85.

HALF-BACKS.

J. M. Jaycox, '87, J. E. Duffy, '89.

GOAL-KEEPER.

J. L. Duffy, '88.

SUBSTITUTES.

C. D. A. Wright, '87 *m*, L. F. Gottschalk, '88,
H. G. Hetzler, '86.

The first football game of the season of 1886 was played with Albion College, October 16, and resulted in an easy victory for Michigan, the score being 50 to 0. In the return game, October 30, Michigan won, 24 to 0. The team for the year was as follows:

FORWARDS.

H. G. Prettyman, '87 *m*, George Higgins,
F. F. Bumps, '87, C. D. A. Wright, '87 *m*,
F. G. Higgins, '86 *l*, A. C. Kiskadden, '89.
C. N. Banks, '87 *l*.

QUARTER-BACK.

W. M. Morrow, '90.

HALF-BACKS.

J. M. Jaycox, '87, J. E. Duffy, '89.

GOAL-KEEPER.

J. L. Duffy, '88.

SUBSTITUTES.

W. W. Harless, '90, W. R. Trowbridge, '89 *m*,
W. C. Malley, '90 *l*.

On the 12th of November, 1887, our team defeated, by 30 to 0, the Albion College eleven. Soon afterwards Michigan defeated Notre Dame 8 to 0, and, at Chicago, the strong team of the Harvard School. In April, 1888, our team again defeated Notre Dame, the score being 26 to 6. The football representatives of Michigan for 1887–88 were the following, John L. Duffy, '88, being their captain:

RUSHERS.

W. W. Harless, '90, J. H. Duffie, '88 *l*,
E. M. Sprague, '88, G. H. Wood, '89 *l*,
Fred Townsend, '88 *l*, Lincoln MacMillan, '89,
J. T. Scott, '91, G. W. De Haven, '90.

QUARTER-BACK.

R. T. Farrand, '90.

HALF-BACKS.

J. E. Duffy, '89, E. W. MacPherran, '89.

FULL-BACK.

J. L. Duffy, '88.

SUBSTITUTES.

R. S. Babcock, '89, Mulford Wade, '90,
Leverge Knapp, '88.

Thanksgiving Day, 1888, the Rugby team played at Chicago the University team of that city, composed largely of graduates who, while students, had belonged to their respective college teams. A cup valued at $300 had been offered to the team which should be the winner for two successive years. The game was attended by a great number of persons, among whom were more than two hundred Michigan students. Chicago won by the score of 26 to 4.

The weakness of Michigan's rush line was largely responsible for our defeat. Michigan's team was as follows:

RUSHERS.

H. G. Prettyman, '87 *m*, W. C. Malley, '90 *l*,
R. W. Beach, '89 *l*, S. S. Bradley, '91,
James Van Inwagen, '92, N. C. Paine, '92.

QUARTER-BACK.

F. L. Smith, '90.

HALF-BACKS.

E. W. MacPherran, '90, J. E. Duffy, '90.

FULL-BACK.

Lincoln MacMillan, '89.

SUBSTITUTES.

W. D. Ball, '90, E. P. Coman, '90 *l*,
E. P. de Pont, '94.

In the autumn of 1889 Albion College was beaten at Ann Arbor, 33 to 4; Cornell gave Michigan a severe defeat at Buffalo, the score being 56 to 0; and the Chicago graduates won their second game from our team, 20 to 0. The following constituted our eleven for that year, E. W. MacPherran being captain:

RUSHERS.

S. C. Glidden, '93, W. C. Malley, '90 *l*,
David Trainer, Jr., '90, B. J. Boutwell, '90 *l*,
G. M. Hull, '90 *m*, H. G. Prettyman,
Benton Strait, '91 *l*.

QUARTER-BACK.

H. T. Abbott, '91 *l*.

HALF-BACKS.

J. E. Duffy, '90, E. W. MacPherran, '90,

FULL-BACK.

James Van Inwagen, '92.

SUBSTITUTES.

H. F. VanDeventer, '92, F. L. Smith, '90,
J. R. Sutton, '90 *l*, W. D. Ball, '90,
H. S. Haines, '91 *l*.

In 1890 Michigan defeated Albion 56 to 10 and 16 to 0, the D. A. C. 18 to 0, and Purdue 34 to 6, but was beaten 20 to 5 by Cornell at Detroit, November 15. That year there was no game with the Chicago graduates. The regular team, of which W. C. Malley, '90 *l*, was captain, was as follows:

ENDS.

T. L. McKean, Roger Sherman, '94.

TACKLES.

David Trainer, Jr., H. G. Prettyman,
W. C. Malley, '90 *l*, W. W. Harless, '90.

GUARD.

Clark Sutherland, '91 *m.*

CENTRE.

T. L. Chadbourne, Jr., '94.

QUARTER-BACK.

G. S. Holden, '91.

HALF-BACKS.

L. C. Grosh, '94, J. E. Duffy, 92 *l.*

FULL-BACK.

G. H. Jewett, '94 *m.*

In the autumn of 1891 Frank Crawford, Yale '91, was secured to coach the team, which was greatly in need of efficient training. Of the games played that season Michigan won three and lost five. Olivet was defeated 18 to 6, Oberlin 26 to 6, and Butler 42 to 6. Our eleven was beaten by Cornell 12 to 58, and, in a game at Chicago, 0 to 10. A team from Cleveland won a game from us by the score of 8 to 4, and the Chicago graduates, with the aid of extremely unfair umpiring, laid us low 20 to 0. At the very opening of the season Albion took a game from Michigan, 10 to 4. The team that year was composed of the following men:

ENDS.

R. W. E. Hayes, '95, C. W. Southworth, '93.

TACKLES.

H. J. Mowrey, '93 *l*, W. W. Pearson, '93 *m.*

GUARDS.

E. D. Wickes, '93, Virgil Tupper, '95.

CENTRE.

A. W. Jefferis, '93 *l.*

QUARTER-BACK.

Roger Sherman, '94.

HALF-BACKS.

James VanInwagen, '93 *l*, C. F. Rittenger, '93 *l.*

FULL-BACK.

G. B. Dygert, '93.

Twelve games, seven of which were won by Michigan, were played during the season of 1892. The opponents and the scores were the following: Michigan Athletic Association, 74 to 0 and 68 to 0; Wisconsin, 10 to 6; Minnesota, 6 to 16; De Pauw, 18 to 0; Purdue, 0 to 24; Northwestern, 8 to 10; Albion, 60 to 8; Cornell, 0 to 44 and 10 to 30; Chicago, 18 to 10; Oberlin, 26 to 24. In the game with Purdue four of our men were disabled, and the game had to be called because we had not a fourth substitute. W. E. Griffin, '93 *l*, was the football manager for 1892, and Frank

E. Barbour, Yale '91, did the coaching. Dygert, '93, was the captain of the team, which was made up thus:

ENDS.

Paul Woodworth, '94 *l*, R. W. E. Hayes, '95.

TACKLES.

Frank Decke, '93, W. W. Griffin, '96.

GUARDS.

Virgil Tupper, '95, C. L. Thomas, '95.

CENTRES.

C. T. Griffin, F. F. Harding, '96.

QUARTER-BACK.

E. L. Sanderson, '93.

HALF-BACKS.

L. C. Grosh, '94, G. H. Jewett, '94 *m*.

FULL-BACK.

G. B. Dygert, '93.

In the autumn of 1893 Barbour again coached the team. Charles Baird, '95, was manager, and George B. Dygert was captain. Ten games were played with outside teams, as follows: Detroit Athletic Club, 6 to 0 and 26 to 0; Chicago, 6 to 10 and 28 to 10; Minnesota, 20 to 34; Wisconsin, 18 to 34; Purdue, 46 to 8; De Pauw, 34 to 0; Northwestern, 72 to 6; Kansas, 22 to 0. Of the ten contests Michigan lost three. There were scored 272 points for Michigan, 102 for opposing teams. The team for the year was made up thus:

ENDS.

R. W. E. Hayes, '95, G. H. Ferbert, '97,
H. M. Senter, '96, Roger Sherman, '94.

TACKLES.

W. W. Griffin, '96, W. I. Aldrich, '96,
G. R. F. Villa, '96 *l*, J. L. D. Morrison, '94 *l*.

CENTRES.

C. H. Smith, C. T. Griffin.

QUARTER-BACKS.

James Baird, '96, G. F. Greenleaf, '97.

HALF-BACKS.

R. S. Freund, '96, L. C. Grosh, '96 *m*,
L. P. Paul, '94 *l*, J. W. Hollister, '95 *l*,
A. C. Bartels, '95 *l*, H. B. Leonard, '95.

FULL-BACKS.

H. L. Dyer, '95 *l*, G. B. Dygert, '95 *l*.

During the season of 1894 the football team had the advantage of excellent training. W. L. McCauley, Princeton '94, was the coach, James Baird, '96, was the captain of the team, and Charles Baird, '95, was the manager. Games were played with the following teams and resulted in the following scores: Orchard Lake, 12 to 12 and 40 to 6; Albion, 26 to 0; Olivet, 48 to 0; Adrian, 46 to 0; Case School, 18 to 8; Cornell, 0 to 22 and 12 to 4; Kansas,

22 to 10; Oberlin, 14 to 6; Chicago, 4 to 6. Eight games were won, two were lost, and one contest was tied. Captain Baird was badly hurt in one of the Orchard Lake games, and hardly recovered in time to take part in the last three meets. The game in which Michigan defeated Cornell—played at Detroit, November 24—was the first victory gained by us over the Ithacans. Following are the men who played in 1894:

ENDS.

H. M. Senter, '96, R. W. E. Hayes, '95.
G. D. Price, '95,

TACKLES.

H. G. Hadden, '95 *l*, J. G. Yont, '96 *l*,
G. R. F. Villa, '96 *l*, F. B. Reynolds, '95 *l*.

GUARDS.

F. W. Henninger, '97, D. B. Ninde, '95 *l*,
B. M. Carr, '97 *m*, W. S. Rundell, '95 *l*.

CENTRE.

C. H. Smith.

QUARTER-BACKS.

James Baird, '96, G. F. Greenleaf, '97.

HALF-BACKS.

G. H. Ferbert, '97, H. B. Leonard, '95,
H. L. Dyer, '95 *l*, J. B. Freund, '97,
J. DeF. Richards, '98, J. A. LeRoy, '96,
G. B. Dygert, '96 *l*.

FULL-BACK.

J. A. Bloomingston, '96 *l*.

The season of 1895 was one of the most satisfactory in the annals of Michigan football. W. L. McCauley, '98 *m*, continued to coach the team, which was captained by F. W. Henninger, '97. The manager was Baird, '95. After an unbroken series of victories (over Orchard Lake, 34 to 0; Detroit Athletic Club, 42 to 0; Adelbert, 64 to 0; Lake Forest, 40 to 0; and Oberlin, 42 to 0), the eleven played Harvard, on the grounds of the latter, and suffered defeat by the honorable score of 0 to 4. Then followed three successes: Purdue, 12 to 10; Minnesota, 20 to 0; and Chicago, 12 to 0. The total score of points was 266 for, and 14 against, Michigan. Our team contained the following players:

ENDS.

H. M. Senter, '96, G. F. Greenleaf, '97,
J. H. Farnham, '97 *e*.

TACKLES.

G. R. F. Villa, '96 *l*, F. W. Henninger, '97 *e*,

GUARDS.

J. H. Hooper, '99, F. M. Hall, '96 *l*.

CENTRES.

B. M. Carr, '97 *m*, Edwin Denby, '96.

QUARTER-BACKS.

James Baird, '96, J. DeF. Richards, '98,
W. R. Morley, '99 *e*.

HALF-BACKS.

G. H. Ferbert, '97, W. H. Holmes, '96 *h*,
J. W. Hollister, '95 *l*.

FULL-BACK.

J. A. Bloomingston, '96 *l*.

Aspirants for football honors were more numerous in 1896 than ever before. Four elevens appeared on the practice-field, and the range of selection was wide. For that year the coaches were W. L. McCauley, '98 *m*, and W. D. Ward, a Princeton graduate who had entered the medical school. After winning nine games, in which only four points were scored against the team, our eleven was defeated by Chicago, in the finishing contest of the season, by a single point. The schedule was as follows: Michigan Military Academy, 18 to 0; Grand Rapids, 44 to 0; College of Physicians and Surgeons, 28 to 0; Lake Forest, 66 to 0; Purdue, 16 to 0; Lehigh, 40 to 0; Minnesota, 6 to 4; Oberlin, 10 to 0; Wittenberg, 28 to 0; Chicago, 6 to 7. Michigan's total score was 262 to 11. The captain of the team was J. R. Hogg, '99 *l*, and the following players took part in the games:

ENDS.

H. M. Senter, '98 *m*, T. L. Farnham, '97 *e*,
G. F. Greenleaf, '97, Loomis Hutchinson, '97 *e*.

TACKLES.

G. R. F. Villa, '96 *l*., F. W. Henninger, '97 *e*.

GUARDS.

B. M. Carr, '97 *m*, J. W. F. Bennett, '98 *e*,
F. L. Baker, '98 *e*.

CENTRE.

J. D. Wombacher, '97.

QUARTER-BACKS.

T. J. Drumheller, '97 *l*, J. DeF. Richards, '98,
Howard Felver, '98 *e*.

HALF-BACKS.

G. H. Ferbert, '97, H. S. Pingree, Jr., '00,
W. H. Caley, '99 *l*.

FULL-BACKS.

J. R. Hogg, '99 *l*, I. M. Duffy, '98 *d*.

In 1897 it became necessary to construct a football eleven almost wholly of new material. Fifty students subjected themselves to training, and a band of coachers from the alumni—such men as J. E. Duffy, '90, W. C. Malley, '90 *l*, James Baird, '96, and G. H. Ferbert, T. L. Farnham, and F. W. Henninger, all of '97.

—assisted in the development of the team. New features adopted that year were the training quarters, an alumni game, and a system of home "coaching". Victories were secured over the State Normal School, 24 to 0; Ohio State, 36 to 0; Oberlin, 16 to 6; Purdue, 34 to 4; Minnesota, 14 to 0; and Wittenberg, 32 to 0. The Michigan team was tied, 0 to 0, by Ohio Wesleyan, and was defeated, in the last game of the season, by Chicago, 21 to 12. Ward Hughes, '98, was the football manager in 1897, and J. R. Hogg, '99 *l*, was the captain of the team, which was organized thus:

ENDS.

J. W. F. Bennett, '98 *e*, N. B. Ayres, '99,
C. T. Teetzel, '00 *l*.

TACKLES.

W. B. Steckle, '01 *m*, R. S. Lockwood, '01,
W. P. Baker, '98, C. F. Juttner, '00 *l*,

GUARDS.

M. B. Snow, '99, W. H. Caley, '99 *l*,
J. E. Egan, '99 *l*, H. E. Lehr, '98 *d*.

CENTRE.

W. R. Cunningham, '99 *m*.

QUARTER-BACKS.

Howard Felver, '98, J. DeF. Richards, '98.

HALF-BACKS.

J. R. Hogg, '99 *l*, H. S. Pingree, Jr., '00,
G. D. Stewart, '01, C. A. Barabee, '01.

FULL-BACKS.

F. C. Hannan, '98, L. J. Keena, '01.

For the season of 1898 J. W. F. Bennett, '98 *e*, has been chosen captain and H. T. Heald, '98, is football manager.

During the past few years football has been rapidly increasing in popularity at Ann Arbor. Every autumn more than two hundred men are candidates either for the University team or for some of the class elevens. Last fall all the classes in the literary department, and also the law class of '98 and the medical class of '00, were represented by teams.

The history of boating in our University covers the period from 1873 to 1878, when the country was interested in the great regattas of the Eastern colleges. The advocates of this sport aroused such enthusiasm among the students that an association was formed, boats were purchased, and the limited facilities of the Huron River were enjoyed to the utmost. Professor Tyler was reported to have said that the water facilities at Ann Arbor are as good as those at Oxford or Cambridge, but a series of conscientious trials proved that the Huron is better adapted to canoes than to shells. A picture in *The Palladium* of 1877 shows the difficulties under which the oarsmen labored. An attempt to deepen the river with one of the two shells owned by the students was a disastrous failure; the boat had to be sold to pay the expense of repairing it; and in 1878 shell-racing at Michigan became a thing of the past. In the fall of 1896 interest in boating revived, and at the present time canoeing on the river is one of the favorite recreations of the undergraduates.

As far back as 1881–82 the sport of lawn-tennis was mentioned in the college annual. *The Chronicle* in 1883 noted a large increase in the number of players, and on the 5th day of November in that year an association to take charge of the interests of the game was formed. In the spring of 1884 a vacant space in the southwest corner of the campus, and room for one court in the southeast corner, were set apart for the use of the association. The sport, though enjoyed by many students, has not with us been carried to the degree of excellence attained at certain other colleges. The following undergraduates have won the University championships in tennis singles:

L. M. Dennis, '85,
Charles McClellan, '86,
C. T. Miller, '88,
J. R. Angell, '90,
B. E. Page, '91,
V. M. Elting, '92 *l*,
L. H. Paddock, '93 *l*,
W. D. McKenzie, '96,
W. D. Herrick, '98,
C. W. Seabury, '98.

The championships in doubles have been won by the following:

E. O. Grosvenor, '85,
S. F. Hawley, '85,
J. C. Hamill, '85 *l*,
J. M. Jaycox, '87,
W. H. Muir, '88,
T. H. Gale, '88,
C. T. Miller, '88,
J. R. Angell, '90,
G. P. Codd, '91,
B. E. Page, '91,
T. N. Jayne, '90,
W. F. Slocum, '92,
A. S. Brown, '93 *l*,
R. M. Shaw, '92 *l*,
L. H. Paddock, '93 *l*,
H. P. Dodge, '93,
H. W. Suydam, '94,
H. E. Chickering, '94,
W. D. McKenzie, '96,
C. W. Seabury, '98,
W. D. Herrick, '98,
L. M. Harvey, '98,
R. S. Danforth, '98,
Butler Lamb, '00.

In 1893 Lewis H. Paddock, '93 *l*, won the Northwestern T. A. A. championship in singles, and he and H. W. Suydam, '94, won that year the championship in doubles.

It is hardly practicable to present a complete and at the same time an interesting history of field and track sports at Michigan. On the Monday before Commencement in 1876 an "Athletic Tournament" was held on the Fair Grounds under the auspices of the Boating Association. According to the college paper of the day the affair was a success; sundry records made elsewhere were beaten; and the sum of $100 was netted for the Boat Club. The chief honors were carried off by J. H. Fiske, W. R. Roberts, E. J. Snover, and J. E. Turtle, all of '77, and by R. W. Corwin, '78 *m*, and W. S. Jenkins, '78. The first "Field Day," so-called, at Michigan, was held June 23, 1879, and was an athletic as well as a financial success. Many of the events were captured by W. W. Hannan and W. M. Thompson, both of '80, the former winning the 100 yards' dash, the 220 yards' dash, and the baseball throw, while the latter won the ten-mile walk and the fencing contest. I. K. Pond, '79, won the standing long-jump. All of the records made that day have been broken, and need not be repeated here. May 15, 1880, an "Athletic Tournament" was held, and there was another Field-Day, June 29, 1880. In 1881 two Field-Days, the one in the spring, the other in the autumn, were held. After a time the Baseball Association took charge of the first, and the Rugby Association managed the second field meeting.

POWER HOUSE.

In 1885, on account of F. N. Bonine, '86 *m*, a fast "sprinter," Michigan secured a membership in the Intercollegiate Athletic Association, and he won the 100 yards' dash at New York. Several times in recent years our University has had representatives at intercollegiate meetings in the East.

For lack of systematic management interest in track and field sports waned after 1886 until 1888, when the presence in Ann Arbor of several amateur athletes from Detroit brought about a revival. Again there was a period of repose, but interest was aroused once more by the organization of the Northwestern Intercollegiate Athletic Association, composed of Michigan, Northwestern, Wisconsin, and Minnesota Universities. At the Field Day of this combination, held in Chicago, June 4, 1893, Michigan made 52 points, Wisconsin 45, and Northwestern 15. The honors for Michigan were won by A. M. Ashley, '93 *l*, I. C. Belden, '93,

G. L. Reed, '94 *l*, G. H. Chapman, '96, and W. F. Geary, '96.

When the spring of 1894 arrived the Northwestern Athletic Association was a thing of the past. In its stead an arrangement for holding Western intercollegiate games at Chicago was made, but Michigan decided to ignore the western contests, and to send to the American Intercollegiate contests at New York any men who qualified. This determination excited so much unfavorable comment that it was reversed, and entries were sent to Chicago only ten days before the games. The result was disastrous, Michigan's representatives scoring only five points and coming out sixth in a series of contests in which eleven colleges took part. Illinois scored 37, Wisconsin 22, Iowa State 16, Chicago 10, and Iowa College 10.

From 1879 to 1883 considerable interest was manifested in fencing, and spasmodic revivals of that sport have occurred in recent years. Of course there have been walking clubs, bicycle clubs, hunting clubs, and fishing clubs, but interest in these has been neither wide-spread nor permanent. The chief outdoor games among us are and probably always will be baseball, football, and tennis.

Organization has been found to be as necessary in the matter of sports and games as in other departments of college life. Some mention of baseball and football clubs has been made in the preceding pages; but a fuller account will now be attempted.

From 1872 until 1878 the interests of baseball were in the hands of a general organization at first called informally the "Baseball Clubs", but named in 1876 the Baseball Association. This gave way in 1878-79 to the Athletic Association. Upon the demise of the latter it was revived; and it was continued until the formation of a new Athletic Association in 1890. The Presidents were these:

1872-73, C. B. Keeler, '73,
1873-75, E. D. Root, '75,
1875-76, F. E. Bliss, '73, '79 *l*,
1876-77, E. J. Snover, '77,
1877-78, W. C. Johnson, '78,
1883-85, H. F. Forbes, '84,
1885-86, D. C. Corbett, '85,
1886-88, P. R. B. dePont,
1888-89, F. W. Hawks, '89,
1889-90, C. A. Higley, '90 *l*.

As early as 1873-74 an association to manage football affairs was formed. This was maintained with little or no interruption until 1878, when a general "Athletic Association" was established. The Presidents of the old organization were:

1873-74, C. J. Thomas, '74,
1874-75, G. E. Pantlind, '75,
1876-78, D. N. DeTar, '78,
1878-79, F. S. Bell, '79.

In 1884 it was thought that football interests had been neglected by the Athletic Association, and so the "Rugby Association" was formed, which in 1890 was merged in the present Athletic Association. The Presidents of the Rugby were:

1883–84, T. W. Gilmore, '94,
1884–85, E. A. Rosenthal, '85 *l*,
1885–86, E. L. Dorn, '86,
1886–87, F. F. Bumps, '87.
1887–88, J. L. Duffy, '88,
1888–89, J. E. Duffy, '90,
1889–90, T. H. Hinchman, Jr., '91.

An institution called the "University Athletic Club" was formed in 1874 for the purpose of encouraging boxing and other gymnastic exercises. As it had nothing to do with baseball or football, its scope was much less extensive than its title suggests. Albert L. Arey, '75, was the first President, and his successor was F. L. Sizer, '78.

October 26, 1878, the Football Association was reorganized as the "Athletic Association of the University". A few months later the new society became incorporated, and by one of its articles a trust fund to be known as the "Gymnasium Fund" was established, with President Angell, Judge Cooley, Professor Tyler, and two others as trustees. Augmented by subscriptions, by the receipts from entertainments and by the contributed earnings of various student enterprises, the fund gradually increased to more than $6,000, and was used, thirteen years after its foundation, in equipping the Waterman Gymnasium.

For a time the new Athletic Association flourished. In 1881 a memorable contest took place over the presidency of it, and according to the college paper the votes of impecunious members found a ready market at prices ranging from one to three dollars, while the friends of the candidates readily paid the back dues of old members and the entrance fees of new men in order to secure votes. Two years later the offices sought the men, and in 1884 the association collapsed "the victim of the football and baseball teams which it sought to control". In 1890 all the athletic interests of the University were wisely, and, it is hoped, permanently, reunited in one management, the "University of Michigan Athletic Association", by which a new and carefully-drawn constitution was adopted. Following is the list of Presidents from 1879 to 1884, and since 1890:

1879–80, C. S. Mitchell, '80,
1880–81, F. G. Allen, '81,
1881–82, H. S. Mahon, '82,
1882–83, A. T. Packard, '83,
1883–84, S. F. Hawley, '85,
1890–91, H. G. Field, '91,
1891–92, S. C. Spitzer, '94,
1892–94, E. C. Shields, '94,
1895–96, J. H. Prentiss, '96,
1897–98, J. DeF. Richards, '98,
1898–99, H. I. Weinstein, '99.

The University Boating Association did not get fairly under way until 1875, and its Presidents were:

Ben T. Cable, '76,
H. C. Moore, '77,
C. E. Beecher, '78.

A separate association was maintained by tennis players until the formation, in 1890, of the general Athletic Association. The Presidents and their respective terms have been as follows:

1883-84, J. L. Hamill, '85 *l*.
1884-85, H. B. Wilson, '86 *h*,
1885-87, S. K. Pittman, '87,
1887-88, W. H. Muir, '88,
1888-89, C. P. Taylor, '89,
1889-90, J. R. Angell, '90.

For all of their regular athletic exercises except tennis the students now use the ten-acre tract on the west side of South State street, half a mile from the campus, bought by the Regents in 1890. The price paid was $3,000, and the sum of $4,500 was expended in fitting up the grounds, which could not be used until the spring of 1892. The batting of balls on the campus is now prohibited. For tennis, fine courts have been laid in the campus, south of the Gymnasium. With the acquisition of the State street grounds, and with the opening of the Gymnasium, a new era in Michigan "athletics" began, although it is as yet too early to realize fully the benefits which are certain to result from these privileges.

Since 1893 athletic sports among the students of Michigan have been subject to the supervision of a Board of Control composed of five professors or instructors selected by the University Senate, and of four undergraduates chosen by the Athletic Association. There is also an Advisory Board made up of professors and graduates.

In-door amusements have not received the attention given to field sports. The Palladium for 1860-61 mentions the "University Chess Club", fourteen members, Ira Olds, '62, President, and the "Lloyd Chess Club", of which Frederick Arn, '61, was President, and which had thirteen members. Then in 1861-62, there was the "Paulsen Chess Club", composed of sixteen men, with J. E. Eastman, '62, for President. The class of '68 supported in its senior year, perhaps earlier, a chess club with ten members. Nothing more is recorded of chess until 1877-78, when we read about the "University Chess Club", whereof C. C. Whitacre, '80, was President, and to which twenty-five men paid dues. Of a chess club which flourished with thirty-five members in 1885-87, C. P. Beckwith, '87, was the presiding officer.

Two years ago a club for the playing of chess was formed, and of it Allan Campbell, '99, and R. B. Griffith, '00 *m*, have been the Presidents.

Whist clubs at Ann Arbor have been numerous. Of them may be mentioned the "Whist Club" of 1872–73, the "University Whist Club" of 1876–76, the "Odd Trick Whist Club" (law department) of 1878–79, and the present "Whist Club", formed in 1897, of which Butler Lamb, '00, is the President. It is possible that other games of cards have had their devotees among us, but records of them have not been preserved.

In 1860–61 there was a "Shakespearian Club" of which W. S. Harroun, '63, was the President. It had thirteen members. A "Shakespeare Club" flourished with thirteen members in 1872–73, and another "Shakesperian Club" existed in 1878–79. More enduring and more successful than any of the foregoing was the "Dramatic Club" which lived from 1886 to 1890. Of it F. W. Mehlhop, '88, was the President during the first year, and after that C. T. Alexander, '90, had charge. This organization presented very successfully several plays in public. What may have been a continuation of the same club existed in 1890–91 with A. C. Lewerenz, '91, as President. "The U. of M. Comedy Club", now one of the most notable of our student organizations, was formed in 1894. From the start E. P. dePont, '94, has been the stage-manager. In 1896–97, A. M. Smith, '97, was the President, and T. J. Weadock, '98 *l*, is now the official head of the club.

CHAPTER XI

ACADEMIC FRATERNITIES

For the origin of the Greek-letter fraternity system at Michigan and elsewhere one must look to the venerable Phi Beta Kappa, founded one hundred and twenty-two years ago by undergraduates of the old Virginian and Episcopalian College of William and Mary. It used to be said that this Society was a branch of the Bavarian Illuminati, but nothing in the records or in the conduct of the order warrants the statement. On the other hand one of the founders declared that Phi Beta was instituted to "rivalise" an earlier society, the name of which, long since forgotten, was expressed by Latin initials. In this connection it is worth while to note that Phi Beta Kappa also bore a Latin name, the Roman letters "S. P." on the reverse of its badge standing for "Societas Philosophica". Doubtless the founders of the original Greek-letter society had recourse to the Hellenic tongue that they might go their rivals one better.

ORIGINAL BADGE OF PHI BETA KAPPA.

It was on the 5th day of December, 1776, that John Heath, Thomas Smith, Richard Booker, Armisted Smith, and John Jones, inspired, as their record runs, "by a happy spirit and resolution of attaining the important ends of Society", resolved to establish a Greek-letter fraternity. To their numbers were soon added Daniel Fitzhugh, John Stuart, Theodore Fitzhugh, aud John Starke; and on the 5th of January, 1777, the members took and instituted the following oath which, but slightly modified, was afterwards transmitted to the Northern branches:

"I, A. B., do swear on the Holy Evangelists of Almighty God, or otherwise, as calling the Divine Being to attest this my oath, declaring that I will, with all my possible efforts, endeavor to prove true, just and deeply attached to this, our growing fraternity, in keeping, holding, and preserving all secrets that pertain to my duty and for the promotion and advancement of its internal welfare."

Originally the order was an undergraduate literary and social fraternity. There were meetings weekly or fortnightly, with declamations, essays, and debates. Those who failed to fill an appointment to literary duty were heavily fined. That the social side of college life might not be neglected, every anniversary of the foundation was celebrated by a feast in the Apollo Hall of the old Raleigh Tavern at Williamstown. The records tell us of "a very elegant entertainment" given to the Society, at the Raleigh, April 19, 1779, by Mr. Bowdoin, who was about to depart for Europe. After many toasts suitable to the occasion, the evening was spent by the members in a manner which indicated the highest esteem for their departed friend, mixed with sorrow for his intended absence, and joy for his future prospects in life".

Membership was confined at first to collegians who had "arrived at the age of sixteen", but two years after the foundation of the fraternity this rule was abrogated, evidently in favor of young officers of the patriot army stationed in the vicinity. Not much later Captain John Marshall, afterwards Chief Justice of the United States, was admitted. The report, long current, that Thomas Jefferson was one of the founders, and that he imported the society from France, was as baseless as the alleged German origin of the order. William Short, afterwards distinguished as a diplomat, was the last surviving founder of Phi Beta Kappa.

In 1879 it was determined to issue charters to members applying for them, giving authority to establish branches—"meetings" they were called—in other cities and towns of Virginia. The new branches were named in the order of the Greek alphabet, and had a distinct relation to the mother "Alpha" at William and Mary. Whether these chapters, five in number, were actually established, we do not know. It seems, however, that the "Beta" was really organized at Hampden-Sidney. If in fact instituted none of them survived the parent chapter.

December 5, 1780, Elisha Parmele, sometime an undergraduate at Yale, and a graduate of Harvard in the class of 1778, having become a member of Phi Beta Kappa during a term of teaching at Williamstown (probably as a tutor in the college), was granted a charter for the establishment of an "Epsilon" at Harvard; and four days later a charter for a "Zeta" at Yale was also granted to him. However, the charters, when prepared, designated the new "meetings" as the Alpha of Massachusetts Bay, and the Alpha of Connecticut. The first of these documents began in these words:

"The members of the Phi Beta Kappa of William and Mary College, Virginia, to their well and truly beloved brother, Elisha Parmele, greeting:—

"Whereas it is repugnant to the liberal principles of Societies that they be confined to any particular place, men, or description of men; and (whereas it is expedient) that the same should be extended to the wise and virtuous of every degree and of whatever country,—

"We the members and Brothers of the ΦBK, an Institution founded on literary principles, being willing and desirous to propagate the same, have at the instance and petition of our good brother, Elisha Parmele, of the University of Cambridge, in the State of Massachusetts Bay, and from the confidence we repose in the Integrity, Discretion, and good Conduct of our said Brother, unanimously agreed and resolved to give and delegate, and we do therefore by these our present letters of Party Charter give and delegate by unanimous consent to you the said Elisha Parmele the following rights, privileges, authority, and power, that is to say,—

"1st. That at the University of Cambridge to establish a Fraternity of the ΦBK to consist of not less than three Persons of Honor, Probity, and good demeanor, which shall be denominated the Αλφα of Massachusetts Bay, and as soon as such number of those shall be chosen you shall proceed to hold a meeting to be called your Foundation Meeting, and appoint your officers agreeably to Law.

2dly. That the form of Initiation and oath of Secrecy shall be, as well in the first, as in every other instance, those prescribed by Law, and none other".

The charter continues in ten articles. Like it was the one for the *Αλφα* of Connecticut, and like it also, *mutatis mutandis*, were all the other early charters. But for these instruments confided to Parmele Phi Beta Kappa must have perished; for soon after they were granted the approaching tide of war caused the death of the Alpha of Virginia. During the year 1780 the attendance at the meetings of the society greatly decreased, as many of the students had entered the army or for other reasons had left college. On the fourth anniversary, December 5, 1780, only five members assembled at the Raleigh. A month later these five met to provide for the preservation of their records; they decided to make the College Steward the depository of them "to remain with him until the desirable Event of the Society its Resurrection", and further stating that they made the deposit "in the sure and certain hope that the fraternity will one day rise (in) life everlasting and glory immortal". The seal was taken by Archibald Stuart, the Vice-President, and after his death it was found in a secret drawer in his house, in 1832. The records were discovered in 1849, and through William Short (then living in Philadelphia), steps were taken which resulted in the reorganization of the parent Alpha in 1855. But the Civil War again killed the chapter. By the estab-

SEAL OF COLLEGE OF WILLIAM AND MARY.

lishment, ten years ago, in connection with the ancient foundation at Williamstown, of the State Normal College of Virginia, the perpetuity of William and Mary has been assured; and in the year 1895 Phi Beta Kappa for the third time was organized at Williamtown.

In 1781, Mr. Parmele, armed with the charters which have been mentioned, and with the "Code of Laws" of the parent chapter, proceeded to fulfil the obligations imposed upon him. In April he initiated at Goshen, Connecticut,—his birthplace—Ezra Stiles, Jr., Samuel Newell, Reuben Parmelie, and Linde Lorde, five students of Yale, who in the following November admitted at New Haven a number of "Bachelor seniors and juniors". Proceeding to Cambridge this connecting link between the dead and the living Phi Beta Kappa, between the South and the North, agreed with four members of the Harvard class of '82 to receive them into the fraternity. Their foundation meeting seems to have been in July, 1781, and their first regular meeting was held September 5, following, when five more men of '82 were chosen "to be sounded for admission in Phi Beta Kappa".

As the mother Alpha was dead, and as Mr. Parmele had passed away soon after he organized the two New England Alphas, the latter were left to provide for the extension and perpetuity of the order. In each charter there was a provision investing the chapter with the privilege of establishing other branches in the state, and provision was made for correspondence between the different "meetings" on matters pertaining to the general interests of the fraternity. Under these provisions arose a custom, which prevailed for a hundred years, whereby each Alpha was allowed to charter new branches in its own state, the consent of all the Alphas being, however, required before a college in a new state could receive a charter.

In 1787 the two Alphas united in awarding a charter to Aaron Kinsman, a Dartmouth senior, who, with four of his classmates, founded a chapter at his college on the 20th of August. Three years later a charter was refused to Brown University because that institution had admitted as "Sophimores" persons who would not rank as freshmen at Cambridge.

For nearly thirty years the fraternity was composed of the Alphas of Connecticut, Massachusetts, and New Hampshire. The three chapters were senior societies of a literary and social kind. Meetings for literary work were held quite regularly, and every Commencement there was a reunion. The connection between the Alphas was slight, and the inter-chapter correspondence, somewhat forced at the best, flagged after 1789.

In 1817, the established policy of non-extension was set aside in favor of Union College. By the concurring resolves of the Alphas of Connecticut, Massachusetts, and New Hampshire, the charter of the Alpha of New York was granted, May 1, to Chancellor Kent and two others, thus permitting the organization of a branch which, besides becoming the mother of seven chapters, really is entitled to the credit of suggesting the present Greek-letter fraternities; for the oldest of the latter was instituted at Union eight years after the establishment there of Phi Beta Kappa. In 1825 a branch of Phi Beta was started at Bowdoin, and in 1830 Brown was added to the roll. Not until 1845, when Trinity and Wesleyan received charters, did other admissions occur.

SEAL OF PHI BETA KAPPA AT YALE.

Toward the close of the first third of the present century the order was confronted with a grave crisis. As early as 1789 at Harvard the society narrowly escaped investigation for tending "to make a discrimination among the students"; and at Yale undergraduate jealousy led to the rifling of the chapter's archives. Both at Harvard and at Dartmouth the charter provisions in regard to secrecy caused trouble at an early date. In 1826 the New Hampshire Alpha abolished the obligation concerning secrecy—save as to the symbols on the medal. Five years later the Harvard Chapter was subjected to an anti-secret crusade led by John Quincy Adams, and was involved in the general agitation against all secret societies which resulted from the "Morgan mystery". About this time Avery Allyn, himself a member of Phi Beta Kappa, published the "Ritual of Freemasonry", in which appears a "Key to the Phi Beta Kappa". For this perjury he assigns the secret nature of the fraternity and its "infidel motto". He declares that the society, like Freemasonry, is of foreign manufacture, and discloses both the motto (*Φιλοσοφία Βίου Κυβερνήτης*) and its meaning (Philosophy, Guide of Life). "Philosophy", he says, "has been the watchword of infidels in every age". Admitting that the members as far as he knows are "all highminded and honorable, employing their talents for the public good in the various departments of civil and religious society, he demands that the order abandon its "secrecies" and "assume an American name", or disband. Bowing to the storm the Alpha of Massachusetts gave up its secrets. The Alphas at Yale, Union, Bowdoin, and Brown held the fort bravely, and for many years continued to style themselves secret societies. Even as late as 1870–71 the society annual at Brown ridiculed members of the anti-secret fraternity for joining this "secret" association. A few years ago the Senate of Phi Beta Kappa declared secrecy to be unnecessary, and recent charters impose no obligation of that sort.

With secrecy departed all the charm and nearly all the prestige of the order. Excepting perhaps for a brief period at Yale the Northern Phi Beta Kappa never was a fraternity in the old Virginian or in the modern sense; and gradually the society became an honorary organization with an "active" membership composed of about one-third of each senior class elected according to scholarship as indicated by the books of the Faculty. In most colleges elections are conferred at the close of junior year, and often there is a second "drawing" in senior year. One-fourth is now the usual proportion selected, and at Yale and Harvard the total number chosen from each class is less than one-sixth. For many years chapter meetings nearly everywhere have been confined to those held for the election of members, and to the annual reunion at Commencement.

SEAL OF HARVARD UNIVERSITY.

Although long before the close of the first half of the present century Phi Beta Kappa had become a scheme for indicating and rewarding scholastic attainments, the various Alphas continued to grant charters in their respective states, or to combine in placing chapters in states not before entered. Thus the Alpha of Ohio was instituted at Western Reserve in 1847, the Alpha of Vermont at the University of Vermont in 1848, and the Alpha of Alabama at the State University in 1850. Amherst received a charter in 1853, Kenyon in 1858, New York University in 1858, Marietta in 1860, Williams in 1864, the Free Academy (now the College of the City of New York) in 1867, Middlebury College in 1868,

Rutgers and Columbia in 1869, Hamilton in 1870, Hobart in 1871, Colgate in 1878, and Cornell in 1883.

At the annual meeting of the Alpha of Massachusetts in 1880, a committee of five members, of which the Rev. Edward Everett Hale was chairman, was appointed to arrange for a convention of all the chapters of Phi Beta Kappa to be held in Cambridge the day after Commencement in 1881, in commemoration of the centennial of the Harvard Chapter. Invitations requesting each chapter to send five delegates to the convention were issued by this committee. The convention assembled June 30, 1881, twelve chapters being represented by twenty-nine delegates. By a series of preliminary steps, the first of which were taken at this conclave, a constitution has been adopted for "The United Chapters of Phi Beta Kappa", and a National Council, or governing body, consisting of twenty Senators and of three delegates from each chapter, has been provided for. Every third year a meeting of the Council is held, and ten new senators are elected to succeed ten whose terms have expired. In the interval between the meetings of the Council the Senate acts for the United Chapters. The first triennial session was held in 1883. All of the existing chapters of Phi Beta Kappa have acceded to the new constitution; and the society, while incapable of an active undergraduate life, seems to be assured of a dignified and useful existence as a graduate institution.

Under the new regime chapters have been instituted at Dickinson, Lehigh, and Rochester, in 1887; at DePauw, in 1889; at Kansas, Northwestern, and Lafayette, in 1890; at Tufts and Minnesota, in 1892; at Pennsylvania, in 1893; at Colby, Syracuse, Swarthmore, Johns Hopkins, Iowa, and Nebraska, in 1895. The total number of living chapters is forty. Formerly there were chapters in the Universities of Alabama and Mississippi, but they are now extinct. As for the number of members, dead or living, it is about 19,000. Many of the chapters have printed their respective rolls, but a general catalogue has not been issued.

The original badge of Phi Beta Kappa was a square silver medal engraved on one side with an index hand, three stars, and the Greek initials of the society's motto, while on the reverse are the letters S. P., and the date December 5, 1776. This badge was worn suspended on a cord by an eyelet attached to the middle of one of the sides. At the North the medal was for a time worn suspended by a pink or blue ribbon, and afterwards the badge became a gold key with an oblong shape instead of a square. The number of stars varies somewhat in the different chapters.

Nearly fifty years ago a movement to organize a chapter of Phi Beta Kappa at Michigan was set on foot, but the absence of a marking system and the indifference or hostility of the Faculty defeated the project. It is to be regretted that there exists among us no society instituted for the purpose of high scholarship in classical studies; and perhaps the obstacles in the way of founding such a society are not insurmountable.

KEY OF PHI BETA KAPPA.

As has been related, a chapter of Phi Beta Kappa was organized at Union College in 1817. This branch of the old Virginian order never had more than an honorary existence, although membership in it, as in the three other Northern branches, was valued as evidence of high scholarship. A few years after the institution of the chapter a company of about sixty students for out-door exercise and military drill was formed in the college. Upon the graduation, in 1825, of Captain Edward Bayard, so warm a conflict for the command ensued that it was deemed advisable to divide the company. A reaction of feeling led to indifference; the military fever had run its course; and, to use the words of a founder of the oldest of the present Greek-letter societies, "there was left only an aching void, waiting to be filled by an inspiration of genius from some quarter, which was not long in coming". About the middle of November, 1825, certain members of the military company mentioned, including two of its chief officers, determined to organize a new secret society for literary and social purposes; and, November 26, Messrs. Hunter, Jackson, and Hun, of the senior class, formally initiated two of their classmates, Young and Knox, after which action the name of Kappa Alpha was formally adopted. Early in the following month seven more members of '26 were initiated into the new order.

On the 4th day of March, 1827, the fraternity of Sigma Phi was founded at Union by members of the class of '27, some of whom had belonged to the same military company in which were the originators of Kappa Alpha. Then came Delta Phi, organized in November, 1827, by nine men of '28. Psi Upsilon, also of Union College, was founded by seven undergraduates in November, 1833. In the meantime Sigma Phi had started a branch at Hamilton College, which may be said to have suggested—or hastened—the foundation of Alpha Delta Phi in the same college in January, 1832. Kappa Alpha placed a chapter in Williams College in 1833, and was followed there by Sigma Phi a year later. A third branch of Sigma Phi, organized in 1835 in New York University, found itself preceded there by Alpha Delta Phi, which, having placed a chapter at Miami University in 1834, had, one year later, entered New York. A third chapter of Kappa Alpha, the one at Hobart, was not organized until 1844, in which year Delta Kappa Epsilon was founded at Yale. Before that date both Alpha Delta Phi and Psi Upsilon had become widely extended fraternities, the former having formed a roll of twelve chapters, eight of which were alive at the close of 1843, while Psi Upsilon at the opening of 1844 had ten branches, all in active operation.

In 1839 Beta Theta Pi, the oldest of the societies of Western origin, was founded at Miami University, having been suggested by the five-year old chapter of Alpha Delta Phi in the same institution. Chi Psi was organized at Union in 1841; and Theta Delta Chi, instituted in 1847, completes the roll of the fraternities now existing which trace their origin to the ancient college in Schenectady. Earlier in 1847, possibly in 1846, Zeta Psi arose in New York University, where it had for rivals Alpha Delta Phi, Sigma Phi, Psi Upsilon, and Delta Phi. The last named fraternity was slower than most of its rivals in extending its boundaries, for its chapters organized before 1844 were only four in number, viz., Union, Brown, New York, and Columbia. At the last-named college, and at the same time at New York University, Delta Psi, the ninth in age of the ten Eastern fraternities, was founded in 1847. Chi Psi, starting at Union in 1841, and D. K. E. at Yale in 1844, were extended very rapidly, as also were Zeta Psi and Theta Delta Chi. Delta Upsi-

BADGE OF KAPPA ALPHA.

lon, the non-secret fraternity, took a Greek name in 1857–58, having previously existed as the "Anti-Secret Confederation", of which the oldest branch was founded in 1834, at Williams College.

As has been said, Beta Theta Pi was the earliest fraternity of Western origin. Phi Gamma Delta, founded in 1848, at what was really a Western institution, Jefferson College in Western Pennsylvania, was the second. Phi Delta Theta arose in Miami University in 1848, and there also Sigma Chi was organized seven years later. In the meantime a fraternity called Phi Kappa Sigma had been started in the University of Pennsylvania, and Phi Kappa Psi, now a widely-extended order, was instituted at Jefferson College early in 1852. Another society, which, until recently, was chiefly confined to the Western states, is Delta Tau Delta, founded in 1859 at Bethany College, West Virginia. All of these societies have branches in the Eastern, many of them in the Southern states.

In 1854 a fraternity called Chi Phi was organized in the College of New Jersey, now styled Princeton University. An attempt has been made to connect this society with an organization said to have existed in 1824 at Princeton, and to have been known as *Χριστοῦ Φιλοί.* Even if such a society really existed in 1824 no actual connection between it and the later Chi Phi has been shown or even claimed, nor is the name of any member of the earlier organization known. In view of these facts the claim of Chi Phi to seniority in age among the existing Greek-letter fraternities has not been allowed except within the limits of that order. The society as it exists at present is a combination of three distinct fraternities, and has branches in widely separated states.

In 1856, at the University of Alabama, was founded the earliest of the present Greek-letter Southern fraternities. It had a somewhat rapid extension before the Civil War, and since then has spread into all parts of the country. Other fraternities of Southern origin are the Alpha Tau Omega and the Kappa Alpha, both founded in 1865, the Kappa Sigma, formed in 1867, the Pi Kappa Alpha organized in 1868, and the Sigma Nu, started in 1869.

Besides the twenty-five fraternities already mentioned there have been many others which have died or which have been merged in some of the existing societies. None of these was important, although some of them had individual chapters that were locally strong. There have also been many local societies, that is, organizations confined to a single college. Most of them have perished or have been absorbed by the intercollegiate fraternities, but some still flourish. Among the latter are the I. K. A. of Trinity, the Lambda Iota and Delta Psi of Vermont, the Phi Nu Theta of Wesleyan, the Kappa Kappa Kappa of Dartmouth, and the Berzelius and the Book and Snake of the Yale Scientific School.

It is usual to divide the collegiate fraternities into classes, according to the geographical distribution of their chapters. Except in the chronological sense this arrangement is somewhat misleading, for most of the Western and two or three of the Southern fraternities now have chapters in New England and New York. As a rule the Eastern societies, though older than the others, have shorter chapter rolls; and they have extended themselves very cautiously in the West, and almost not at all in the South. Kappa Alpha, the oldest of all the fraternities, has also the fewest chapters, having had only eight in all, of which six survive. Sigma Phi has had ten chapters, of which two are dead. Delta Phi has had sixteen in all, twelve of which remain. Delta Psi has granted nineteen charters, and now has eight branches. Of the twenty-two chapters instituted by Psi Upsilon, twenty-one are living. Chi Psi retains eighteen of a list of twenty-eight branches. Alpha Delta Phi now has twenty-three active chapters, the total number of its charters thus far being thirty-one. Of the thirty-one branches started by Zeta Psi, twenty remain. Theta Delta Chi has instituted thirty-nine chapters and holds twenty-one, while D. K. E., the largest of all the Eastern fraternities, flourishes in thirty-five of the forty-eight colleges which it has entered. Many of the fraternities of Western or Southern origin surpass even Delta Kappa Epsilon in the number of their chapters, Phi Delta Theta having had eighty-six branches of which sixty-three survive, while Sigma Alpha Epsilon has had eighty-six in all, and has preserved fifty-five. Of the eighty-one chapters instituted by Beta Theta Pi sixty-two are in active operation. Sigma Chi has entered seventy-two different colleges and now has fifty branches. Of Phi Gamma Delta's seventy-two chapters, forty-five survive. Delta Tau Delta has been less fortunate, having preserved only thirty-eight of its sixty-seven charges. Phi Kappa Psi has granted fifty-seven charters, thirty-nine of which are held at the colleges for which they were issued. Delta Upsilon, the non-secret fraternity, has thirty-one living and only five inactive chapters.

SEAL OF YALE COLLEGE.

Kappa Alpha has fewer members than any of its younger rivals, having initiated only 1,360 men. Sigma Phi has 2,100, Delta Phi 3,000, Delta Psi 3,000, Chi Psi 3,800, Theta Deta Chi 3,900, Zeta Psi 4,500, Delta Upsilon 6,500, Alpha Delta Phi 7,800, Psi Upsilon 8,800, and D. K. E., the largest of the Eastern fraternities, 13,000. Of the other fraternities, Beta Theta Pi and Phi Delta Theta have about 9,600 apiece, while Phi Kappa Psi has 7,300, Phi Gamma Delta 6,100, Sigma Chi 6,000, Delta Tau Delta 5,700, and Sigma Alpha Epsilon 5,000.

From insignificant groups of students the older Greek-letter orders have developed into select and powerful organizations which hand down their traditions from generation to generation, and which include in their ranks most of the eminent college graduates of the past sixty years. Half a century ago nearly all of the college presidents of the country were unfriendly to the secret orders; today the presidents of Harvard, Yale, Dartmouth, Amherst, Trinity, Vermont, Columbia, Union, Hamilton, Rochester, Rutgers, Pennsylvania, Johns Hopkins, Michigan, Wisconsin, Minnesota, California, and other prominent institutions, are men who during college life wore the badges of secret orders.

The first catalogue printed by any of the modern Greek-letter societies was issued by Sigma Phi in 1832. Kappa Alpha first published the roll of its members in 1835. Alpha Delta Phi, the first fraternity to secure a long list of chapters, issued a catalogue in 1837. Four years later appeared the first roll of Psi Upsilon. Delta Kappa Epsilon's earliest catalogue came out in 1851. Sigma Phi was the first society to print a geographical arrangement of its membership, and Psi Upsilon was the first to publish lists showing which of its mem bers were sons or brothers of other members; features which are included in all recent catalogues. The first catalogue illustrated with elaborate biographical data was emitted by Psi Upsilon nineteen years ago. This example has been admirably followed by Alpha Delta Phi, Chi Psi, D. K. E., Sigma Phi, Kappa Alpha, Delta Upsilon, Phi Delta Theta, Sigma Chi, Phi Kappa Psi, and Beta Theta Pi. Nearly fifty years ago Psi Upsilon issued the first song-book, and Alpha Delta Phi followed suit in 1851.

ORIGINAL BADGE OF PSI UPSILON.

The first chapter-house acquired by a Greek-letter fraternity—if we except the log-cabin of Chi Psi at Michigan—was the building purchased by Sigma Phi at Williams College in 1857. Other buildings built or purchased at early dates were the lodge of D. K. E. at Yale, built in 1861, and the house of Kappa Kappa Kappa at Dartmouth, bought in 1862. Psi Upsilon, which has the largest number of buildings, viz., fifteen, built its first lodge in 1870 at Yale. The eight living branches of Delta Psi are all provided with buildings, and so are all but one of the eight chapters of Sigma Phi. Delta Kappa Epsilon has many chapter-houses and lodges, as also has Alpha Delta Phi. The finest society lodge is the one recently purchased by Chi Psi at Cornell, which originally cost $150,000. Among other valuable structures owned by the fraternities are the marble house of Alpha Delta Phi at Amherst, the Pompeiian brick and stone residence of Psi Upsilon at Wesleyan, the chapter-house of Zeta Psi at Cornell, the stone dormitory and lodge of Delta Psi in New Haven, and the mansion of Sigma Phi at Williams.

In 1844–45, when Michigan was about to graduate its first class, and when the initial steps to establish fraternities at Ann Arbor were taking, only eight intercollegiate Greek-letter orders were in existence. These were Kappa Alpha, Sigma Phi, Delta Phi, Alpha Delta Phi, Psi Upsilon, Chi Psi, and Delta Kappa Epsilon, all Eastern societies, and Beta Theta Pi, a Western fraternity. In 1844 the Alpha Alpha, a local society, was formed at Ann Arbor for the purpose of securing a charter from Alpha Delta Phi; and in 1845 organizations preliminary to Chi Psi and Beta Theta Pi were formed. Chi Psi claims to have installed its chapter early in the autumn of 1845; Beta Theta Pi was started in November, 1845, and Alpha Delta Phi was not instituted until Commencement in 1846. All three had men in the class of '45. Chi Psi and Beta Theta Pi for many years claimed priority, but the former is conceded to have made its public appearance first. The establishment of these secret orders led to a long and bitter conflict with the Faculty.

In 1840, before any student had been matriculated, a code of by-laws for the government of the prospective undergraduates was prepared. Rule 20 of this code was as follows:

> "No student shall be or become a member of any Society connected with the University or consisting of students, which has not first submitted its constitution to the Faculty and received their approbation."

Professor Williams, the author of the code, afterward declared that Rule 20 was designed as a check on the too numerous multiplication of literary societies or debating clubs. It was, however, used as a weapon by the Faculty in the struggle between the latter and the secret societies.

Soon after its organization the chapter of Chi Psi had built for itself a log cabin in the depths of what was then known as the Black Forest, extending far east of the campus. The site of this prototype of the scores of chapter houses now owned by the Greek-letter fraternities was in the neighborhood of the present Forest Hill Cemetery. The building was of roughly-hewn oak logs. Its dimensions were twenty-four by twenty feet. At one end was a huge fireplace.

LODGE OF CHI PSI (1846).

In the summer of 1846, while some nocturnal depredations and certain unofficial ringings at midnight of the chapel bell were undergoing inquiry by the Faculty, some of the students were traced by one of the professors to the log cabin of Chi Psi; and being questioned they refused to tell what had occurred within, saying that they were pledged to secrecy. They, however, frankly informed him that the building was their society lodge, and they explained to him the nature of the Greek-letter societies, suggesting their affiliations with similar organizations in other colleges, and intimating that they were too strong to be dealt with harshly. When he attempted to enter—as he conceived himself entitled to do under a rule then in force that students' rooms should at all times be accessible to the officers—he was firmly repulsed. All of which was duly reported to the Faculty. Just before Commencement a member of Alpha Delta Phi who had been graduated elsewhere called upon the Faculty and asked that the organization of a chapter in the University might be permitted, offering to exhibit so much of the constitution as he had authority to reveal. Busied with a meeting of the Regents and with preparations for Commencement, the Faculty promised future attention to the matter, whereupon the new society was organized immediately.

Aware that three secret societies, including a majority of the students, were in active operation in defiance of Rule 20, the Faculty decided not to proceed to extreme measures, but to secure the ultimate extinction of the obnoxious orders. This was to be accomplished by requiring the members of the societies to promise not to initiate any more men, and by exacting of all candidates for matriculation a pledge not to join societies not approved by the Faculty. Alpha Delta Phi however, claiming that it existed if not with the approval at least by sufferance of the Faculty, initiated new matriculates. This the professors learned in March, 1847, and after suspensions and readmissions the new initiates were obliged to withdraw from the society, and the original members, to save themselves from expulsion, were compelled to sign a stringent pledge. In November, 1847, Alpha Delta Phi offered a second time to submit its constitution to the Faculty, but was informed that the latter body "had no authority to legalize them as a society in the University of Michigan". Therefore the students contended that if the Faculty could not legalize the society it could not forbid it; and as a further precaution the chapter changed its style and address. In July, 1848, Beta Theta Pi sought recognition, and was informed that it came "under the prohibition of the law".

Toward the close of the college year 1847–48 the Faculty sent letters to the Presidents of several Eastern colleges asking opinions concerning the desirability and feasibility of suppressing the Greek-letter societies. The answers, condensed, amounted to this: "desirable but impracticable". President Woolsey of Yale thought the influence of the societies to be "either not good or questionable". He also declared "It is doubtful whether a college government can suppress such societies, so long as some cause or other in the feelings or fashions of college keeps them up". Chancellor Frelinghuysen of New York University said: "We believe them (secret societies) to be of no use, and often of great injury". He intimated, however, that so many of the lawyers and other literary graduates belonged to them that suppression would be difficult. President Hitchcock of Amherst wrote that the society system was a "giant evil, which, in secret, is blasting the hopes of many parents", but he thought that to suppress the societies "would not

SEAL OF UNION COLLEGE.

be to kill them but to put them more out of sight and make them more objectionable".

These replies, together with a report from the Faculty, were placed before the Regents, who by a tie vote rejected a resolution favorable to the societies. With but slight check the initiation of new students went on, a fact which, though suspected, was not positively known to the authorities until, in 1849, a professor found on the campus a copy—evidently intended to be sent abroad—of the recently issued catalogue of the University, in which, printed on a loose leaf, were the names of eleven undergraduate Chi Psis, among them several new students. The eleven, when questioned, admitted that the names were on the paper by their consent. At the same time Alpha Delta Phi furnished the Faculty with a list of its men. The defence in each case was substantially that the society was no longer styled a chapter in the University but in Ann Arbor, that the members did not meet on University premises, and that as persons not connected with any college had been admitted to membership, the society could not be regarded as "consisting of students". Overruling this plea, the Faculty announced to the members of Alpha Delta Phi and Chi Psi that their connection with the University would cease at the opening of the next term, unless they renounced their affiliations. Seven men ostensibly withdrew from their societies, and the rest were expelled. The members of Beta Theta Pi were not dismissed until September, 1850, they having made the plea that their constitution was not signed. Many of the expelled students went to Union, others were graduated at Rochester, some returned to Ann Arbor, and some never finished their college courses. Among the men permanently lost to Michigan were not a few who have gained distinction in professional or business careers.

Appealed to by the expelled undergraduates the Regents asked the Faculty the reason of the expulsion of so many students. The reply, as has been well said, "is notable because of its lack of calm dispassionate argument, and because of the abundance of indefinite unsupported statements". It recites that the "whole history of these societies is a detail of obliquities", that "these extended affiliations are a great irresponsible authority", that "they are exclusive and oligarchic", that their meetings "are liable to become, and often are, lawless and convivial", that they are "a great and unnecessary expense to the poor student who joins them," that "the regular literary societies are neglected", and that "these societies are the permanent sources of mutual intrigues and jealousies". The Regents, by a committee, declared that they felt bound to consider the statements of the Faculty as true, and sustained the latter. Both reports were submitted to the Legislature.

In the meantime the matter had been taken up by the newspapers and Greek-letter society graduates who had been in other colleges and had settled in Michigan, began to attack the Faculty. The members of the Masonic body and of other secret orders regarded the movement as a revival of the anti-secret agitation of 1827, and were indignant. In Ann Arbor the following notice was printed and circulated:

ATTENTION!

INDIGNATION MEETING!

The citizens of Ann Arbor are requested to meet at the Court House this evening, at 6 o'clock, to take into consideration the conduct of the FACULTY of the University of Michigan in *expelling* all the students belonging to secret societies!

MANY CITIZENS.

DECEMBER 20, 1849.

The meeting which was very largely attended, adopted vigorous resolutions which vouched for the high character of the expelled students, and declared that in the college secret societies "confidence was engendered, honor cultivated, the intellect expanded, truth enjoined, and virtue and morality taught". A complete change of the Faculty, and another method of choosing the Regents, were recommended.

BADGE OF A. D. PHI.

The students who had withdrawn (?) from their societies—four Alpha Delts and three Chi Psis—memorialized the Legislature in a long paper, wherein they sought to show the falsity of the charges of the Faculty; and also to the capital went a memorial signed by fifteen "neutral" students, in which the Faculty was upheld and action by the Legislature deprecated.

A bill was introduced in the Senate providing that the Regents should be elected by the people instead of being nominated by the Governor. Although probably unconstitutional, it was strenuously resisted by the friends of the Faculty and Regents. As soon as it had accomplished its purpose in drawing the fire of the enemy, it was laid aside. What it sought to do was done by the act which provided for the calling of a Constitutional Convention. That body placed in the organic law of the state the provision for which the proposed statute was drawn; and even before the new Constitution went into effect the authorities of the University were compelled to yield to the pressure of public opinion. In October, 1850, the Faculty granted, one by one, the applications of the three societies for legal admission, sundry conditions being imposed which never were performed and which all parties concerned knew never would be performed. Alpha Delta Phi and Beta Theta Pi exhibited their constitutions (?), but Chi Psi made only a "substantial exhibition of the system of fundamental rules". Thus ended the Society War, and with it passed from our University boarding-school methods of government. The new board of Regents repealed the obnoxious Twentieth Rule. One of the historians of the University seeks to palliate the action of the Faculty, and another chronicler avers that both sides emerged from the contest with garments somewhat torn; but the truth is that the college boys were justified in opposing with technicalities the technical construction of an unreasonable rule, and that the expulsions were both unjust and unwise. Before the members of the Faculty proceeded to extreme measures they were warned by the authorities of other colleges that attempts at suppression had proved fruitless elsewhere. The continuance of the conflict after 1849, in the face of public opinion, and when the Regents themselves were divided, was simply fatuous.

The history of the fraternities in Michigan during the past forty-eight years is not eventful. Chi Psi and Alpha Delta Phi have lived uninterruptedly. Beta Theta Pi became dormant in 1850 soon after it had received permission to exist. It was revived in 1854, and flourished until 1864. Then it was suspended until late in 1875. In 1855 Delta Kappa Epsilon and Delta Phi, both Eastern fraternities, placed chapters here. Sigma Phi, also an Eastern order, prevented by the Society War from granting a charter to Michigan students in 1848–49, organized a branch at Ann Arbor early in 1858, and in June of the same year a strong chapter of the Eastern Zeta Psi was established. From 1858 to 1860 the secret societies, seven in number, and including nearly two-thirds of the students, exerted a controlling influence in undergraduate affairs. But in 1861 the fraternities

ORIGINAL BADGE OF D. K. E.

began to cut down their memberships; a strong feeling of opposition to secret orders, which had for some time been marked in Eastern colleges, showed itself in Michigan; and the societies, divided into two factions, one of which looked to the neutrals for support, were no longer able to control college politics. A powerful "Independent" organization was formed in 1865-66, which lasted until 1870.

In 1864 Psi Upsilon, an Eastern fraternity which, ten years before, had refused to place a chapter in this Western institution, granted a charter to fourteen of the fifteen undergraduates of Beta Theta Pi, which thereafter became dormant. Thus seven of the ten Eastern societies were represented here, a fact significantly indicative of the esteem in which Michigan was held by the chief institutions of the country. Nowhere else west of New York were more than four of the Eastern fraternities to be found at that early day. Somewhat later in 1864–65 appeared Kappa Phi Lambda and Phi Delta Theta. The former lapsed in the autumn of 1868; and as the latter became dormant in 1869, the seven Eastern fraternities were left in full control, thus distinguishing Michigan from all other Western universities and colleges except Kenyon.

TEMPLE OF D. K. E.

An attempt in 1870–71 to start a branch of Delta Tau Delta, then an exclusively Western organization, was not successful. It was renewed in 1874, but the chapter became inactive in the autumn of 1876. Meanwhile a branch of Sigma Chi, also of Western origin, was formed, and lived for a few months in 1874. Soon after the opening of the college year 1875–76 Delta Phi died. Beta Theta Pi was permanently revived late in 1875, and in the spring of 1876 the anti-secret fraternity, Delta Upsilon, now simply non-secret, gained a foothold at Ann Arbor. In December, 1876, Phi Kappa Psi, a fraternity of Pennsylvanian birth, but largely represented in the West and South, instituted a chapter here. A few months later Sigma Chi returned to the University as a law-school society. In 1878 D. K. E. built the first permanent society lodge at Ann Arbor. This was followed by the erection, in 1879–80, of the chapter-house of Psi Upsilon. Delta Tau Delta reappeared in 1880, and two years afterwards short-lived branches of Chi Phi and Phi Alpha were organized. The attendance of the Western societies was swelled by Phi Gamma Delta in 1885, and by the revival of Phi Delta Theta in 1887.

Toward the close of 1888 a Southern fraternity, the Alpha Tau Omega, began a brief career in Ann Arbor, and early in 1889 came Sigma Alpha Epsilon, also of Southern origin. December 13, 1889, a charge of Theta Delta Chi, an Eastern fraternity, made its appearance here, thus raising to fifteen the number of fraternities in the collegiate department. This multiplication of societies did not, however, keep pace with the increase in the number of students; and now began a campaign against the fraternities which was based, not upon objections to secrecy, but rather upon the natural desire of active spirits among the non-society men to share in the offices and editorships. Having a large majority in every class, the neutrals elected to office none but men of their own kind. Holden of '89 was the last senior class president chosen from the ranks of the fraternities. With great difficulty, and only after bolting a regular election, did the societies succeed in saving from the wreck of their former power the freshman toastmastership, which is now regarded as a fraternity perquisite. As for the editorships of the undergraduate publications, the "Independent" leaders, necessarily excluded from The Palladium, started The Castalian in 1889, and, having withdrawn from the Chronicle, they established The U. of M. Daily in 1891. The editorships of the Oracle are still divided among the society men and the neutrals, and a similar arrangement governs The Michiganensian.

ORIGINAL BADGE OF THETA DELTA CHI.

It was announced positively in December, 1892, that the dormant branch of Delta Phi would soon be revived with twenty charter members; but that ancient fraternity wisely decided that the ground was already fully occupied. Alpha Tau Omega returned its charter in 1894, and about one year later internal disagreements led to similar action on the part of Phi Gamma Delta. In 1894–95 an energetic effort to secure a charter of Kappa Alpha was made by a group of undergraduate petitioners, assisted by a member who had come here from another college. It is understood that the society named decided that it would be impossible in these later years to build up at Michigan a chapter equal to the long-established branches of other fraternities. Toward the close of 1896 the Sigma Chi revealed itself as a regular society in the literary department, three years having passed since its disappearance from the law school. A separate account of each fraternity that has had a chapter in the collegiate department will now be attempted.[1] The order adopted will be that of actual public appearance in the University.

Chi Psi.—This order was founded at Union College, May 20, 1841, by ten students, among whom was the ill-fated Philip Spencer. Twenty-eight chapters—called by the society "Alphas"—have been established, the college roll, with the dates of institution, of suspension, and of revival, being as follows: Union, 1841–76, 1892; Williams, 1842–72, 1874; Middlebury, 1843; Wesleyan, 1844–63, 1876; Bowdoin, 1844–69; Hamilton, 1845; Michigan, 1845; Columbia, 1846–58, 1882–83; Princeton, 1851–57; North Carolina, 1855–61; College of the City of New York, 1857–72; Furman, 1858–61, 1866; South Carolina, 1858–61, 1867–74, 1883–97; Mississippi, 1858–61, 1865–92; Virginia, 1860–61, 1868–70; Brown, 1860–71; Amherst, 1864; Cornell, 1869–70, 1885; Wofford, 1869; Minnesota, 1874; Wisconsin, 1878; Rutgers, 1879; Stephens Institute, 1883; Rochester, 1884–89; Georgia, 1890; Lehigh, 1894; Leland Stanford, Jr., 1895; and California, 1895. There are eighteen active and ten inactive branches. Buildings are owned by the "Alphas" at Williams, Hamilton, Michigan, Amherst, Cornell, Minnesota, South Carolina, Wisconsin, and Rutgers. Purple and gold are the colors. Among the 3,800 members of Chi Psi

BADGE OF CHI PSI.

[1] In the pages that follow certain points should be noted. In the first place, the State universities are mentioned by the names of the states only; where a college bears the name of a state the word college will be appended. Secondly: the degrees appended to members' names in the fraternity lists are those and those only which were actually conferred by our Alma Mater, in course, at the dates indicated by the numerals of the classes in which the members were enrolled; the primary purpose being not to furnish a list of degrees, but to indicate what members finished undergraduate courses in the literary department. Thus, all secondary, honorary, and *nunc pro tunc* degrees, and degrees taken at other colleges, are excluded. The attempt has been made, however, where a member has left the literary department without a degree, and has been graduated here in law or medicine, to mention the professional degree taken. Thirdly: Sigma Chi, though a law-school fraternity during the greater part of its career, has been included in the literary fraternities because it began in the literary department and now exists there. Fourthly: pictures of chapter houses rented but not owned are not included.

the following from institutions other than Michigan may be named: Chief-Justice Fuller of the Federal Supreme Court; William Le B. Putnam, late Federal Circuit Judge; Judges Bradshaw, Earl, and Hand of the New York Court of Appeals; Chief-Justice Sanderson of California; the well-known College Presidents Brainerd of Middlebury, Fulton of Mississippi, Peck of the Rennselaer Polytechnic, Appleton of Swarthmore, Kendrick of Shurtleff, and Cochran of the Brooklyn Polytechnic; Professor Henry A. Frink of Amherst; the Rev. Drs. Charles S. Robinson of New York, and Stephen H. Tyng, Jr., of Paris; the authors Willis J. Abbott, Waldo S. Pratt, and Clinton Scollard; Speaker Thomas B. Reed of the Federal House of Representatives, and Charles H. Allen, Horatio C. Burchard, Horace Davis, Thomas A. D. Fessenden, J. V. L. Findlay, Charles W. Gillet, J. N. Hungerford, David R. Paige, William H. Perry, John W. Seymour, T. R. Stockdale, and Harry White, members of the House; Ex-Governor John W. Stewart of Vermont; John C. Sheppard, formerly Governor of South Carolina; Major-General Francis Fessenden; Major-General Henry E. Davies; Brigadier-General James C. Duane; and William Astor, Elbridge T. Gerry, Frederic D. Tappan, and Dr. J. H. Douglas, of New York.

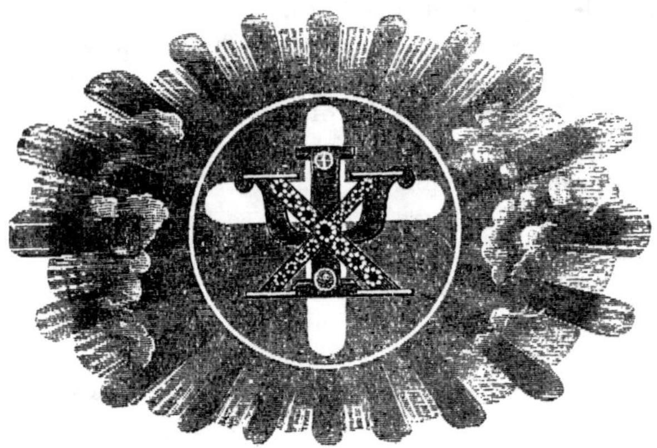

VIGNETTE OF CHI PSI.

Writing in 1887, the late Charles W. Noble, '46, thus described the birth of Chi Psi at Ann Arbor:

"The idea of forming an Alpha of the Chi Psi Fraternity, at the University of Michigan, originated with William Howard Wait, who was a member of the class of 1848. He corresponded chiefly with Cornelius Lansing Seymour, of Hamilton, now deceased, whose residence was then at Cleveland, Ohio. This correspondence resulted in the organization of Epsilon, by Josiah A. Priest, then of Hamilton College, but since a Presbyterian clergyman of repute, well known through his foreign letters to the *New York Observer*. Wait had consulted a good deal with me about petitioning for an Alpha of the Chi Psi; and it was substantially formed before the other students of the University thought of applying elsewhere. At least such were the appearances and our belief. We certainly had the best fellows, the pick of them all . . . . . . Those, only, who have been students in institutions where fraternities did not then exist, can understand the excitement attending our establishment. It was, surely, an event in the history of the University, when Priest came from Hamilton to light our altar fires. He was dignified and agreeable, and well suited to the occasion. All of the original thirteen were initiated the same day . . . . . I was the first, and was put through privately by Mr. Priest; the others the same evening at the room we had hired in the Exchange Hotel. Great was the surprise among the other students when we "Swung out". It hastened the work of the other societies, then in embryo. During my day, we continued to meet at the old Exchange, in rooms which we hired, as occasion demanded. We observed the greatest secrecy, as soon as we came to know that the faculty were opposed to us, and were seeking occasion to quarrel with us. I am glad to say that for the last thirty years or more, their course has changed, and that now some honored professors are reckoned as members of the secret societies."

Chi Psi's early days at Ann Arbor are memorable not merely for the contest successfully carried on by the chapter with the Faculty, but for a romantic excursion taken to Brazil and Spain in 1848–49 by six of its members, Whiting and Witherell of '48, and James, Kellogg, Palmer, and Tillson, of '49. Forty-one years afterwards Palmer returned to Spain as the Envoy Extraordinary and Minister Plenipotentiary of the United States.

In its later years this branch of Chi Psi suffered somewhat from the lack of a chapter house, which was supplied in the summer of 1897 by the purchase for $12,000 of the fine residence of Regent Whitman, 1007 East Huron street. Among the 292 members of the chapter are Thomas B. Cumming, '45, afterwards Acting Governor of Nebraska; the late Merchant H. Goodrich, '45, of Ann Arbor; the late Lyman D. Norris, '45, of Grand Rapids; the late William W. Phelps, '46, formerly Representative in Congress; Thomas W. Palmer, '49, Ex-U. S. Senator, and Minister to Spain; Dr. Moses Gunn; Darius J. Davison, '54, of Detroit, Clerk of the Federal District Court; J. Sterling Morton, '54, late Secretary of Agriculture; the late Dr. Henry F. Lyster, '58, of Detroit; Ex-Circuit Judge and City Counsellor John J. Speed, '58, of Detroit; General Elon J. Farnsworth, '60, deceased; Albert H. Horton '60, Chief Justice of the Kansas Supreme Court; Elliott T.

CHI PSI LODGE.

Slocum, '60; General Henry M. Duffield, '61, D. Farrand Henry, '61, Joseph C. Hart, '64, Ex-Postmaster-General Don M. Dickinson, '67 *l*, Ford DeC. Hinchman, '69, Samuel T. Douglas, '73, William H. Wells, '74, Edward A. Gott, '76, and W. W. Hannan, '80, all of Detroit; and Charles Fox, '75, and E. Crofton Fox, '75, both of Grand Rapids. The chapter includes not a few of the prominent athletes of Michigan: such baseball players as W. J. Maynard of '65, Wayne Hayman of '73, W. H. Wells of '74, W. W. Hannan of '80, and C. B. Weatherwax of '87, and, among football players, W. W. Hannan of '80, James E. Duffy of '92 *l*, H. T. Abbott of '91, L. C. Grosh of '94, Virgil Tupper, '94, and I. M. Duffy, '98 *d*. Very prominent among the editors of student publications is H. M. Bowman, '98. Following is the entire roll of the members of Alpha Epsilon of Phi Psi:

'45 *Thomas B. Cumming, A. B.,
" *Merchant H. Goodrich, A. B.,
" *Lyman D. Norris,
'46 *Henry D. Goodrich,
" *Charles W. Noble, A. B.,
" *W. Walbridge Perry, A. B.,
" *William W. Phelps, A. B.,
" *Homer P. Schoff, A. B.,
'47 *Edmund P. Christian, A. B.,
" Seneca Ewer, A. B.,
" *John B. Myers,
" *Philander C. Safford, A. B.,
'48 Edward F. Burdick,
" *Peter E. Latimer, A. B.,
" Joseph R. Smith, A. B.,
" *William H. Wait, A. B.,
" *William P. C. Whiting,
" *James B. Witherell, A. B.,
'49 *George B. Alcott,
" *Douglas Gibson, A. B.,
" *David E. James,
" *George P. Kellogg,
" *Aaron B. Levisee,
" Thomas W. Palmer,
" *Stephen Tillson, A. B.,
'50 David Bacon,
" George L. Lee, A. B.,
'51 Samuel J. Agnew,
" Edwin C. Becker,
" A. Atwood Brooks,
" Richard H. Frost,
— *Moses Gunn, M. D.,
" Thomas H. Hartwell, A. B.,
" *Hervey B. Nichols,
" *George W. Perry, A. B.,
" *Daniel C. Towner,
" *George L. Trask,
" John A. Wheeler, M. D., '52,
'52 *m* Frederick C. Castelhun, M. D.,
" *Louis Davenport,
" *m* *Morse K. Taylor, M. D.,
" *DeGarmo J. Whiting,
'53 *m* *Ira H. Bartholomew, M. D.,
" Gibson P. Brown,
" William E. Cheever, A. B.,
" *Waldo C. Daniels, A. B.,
" *Leopold Lathrop,
" *Mortimer Thompson,
" *Charles E. Winans,
'54 *m* Boliver Barnum, M. D.,
" H. Deming Bartholomew, A.B.,
" Harrison W. Bassett, A. B.,
" James R. Cook, A. B.,
" Darius J. Davison, A. B.,
" Samuel P. Duffield, A. B.,
" Robert C. Grier, A. B.,
" J. Sterling Morton,
" *Mathaniel Pitcher, A. B.,
" *Lyman Richardson, A. B.,
'55 Galucia C. Gibbs, A. B.,
" *James M. Shanklin,
" *Enos T. Throop,
'56 O. Newberry Chaffee, A. B.,
" *Alvin S. Higgins, A. B.,
'57 Rollin C. Dart,
" *Lycurgus H. Irwin, A. B.,
" Gilbert R. Lyon, A. B.,
" *Hobart Miller, A. B.,
" Jerome W. Turner,
'58 *Hamilton J. Dennis, A. B.,
" Foster Ely,
" Alfred J. Goss,
" *Henry F. Lyster, A. B.,
" *Otis H. McOmber, A. B.,
" Lyster M. O'Brien, A. B.,
" Frank M. Speed,

'58 John J. Speed,
'59 Alfred H. Castle, A. B.,
" *Elon J. Farnsworth,
" William H. Haight, B. S.,
" *Robert B. Maclin,
" *George S. McReynolds,
" Julian E. Winder, A. B.,
'60 *Lewis F. Booth, B. S.,
" John H. Conrad, A. B.,
" *Elbert N. Donaldson,
" Henry M. Duffield,
" *Elon J. Farnsworth,
" Albert H. Horton,
" Wiilam N. Ladue, A. B.,
" *William J. Stephens.
" *Charles A. Thompson, A. B.,
" *Charles F. Trowbridge, A. B ,
'61 *m* William W. Bailey, M. D.,
" Henry Fenton,
" D. Farrand Henry,
" *Charles T. Scammon,
'62 Samuel Davison,
" *William L. Irwin,
" Joseph T. Sanger,
" R. Trumbull Sill,
" Elliott T. Slocum,
'63 Walter M. Burroughs,
" *Charles S. Draper, A. B.,
'64 Joseph C. Hart, A. B.,
" Franklin J. Thwing,
" *Clarence E. Wilbur, A. B.,
'65 *William J. Maynard, A. B.,
" *Anderson Wing,
" *Charles I. Witherell, LL. B.,
'66 Charles D. Barney,
" *George L. Barney,
" John W. Remington, C. E.,
'67 *l* Don M. Dickinson, LL. B,,
" William R. Graham,
" Frederick H. Kent,
" William S. Stanton,
" Pliny H. VanBuren, LL. B. '70,
" Stanley B. Watrous,
" Montgomery S. Woodruff, A. B.,
'68 *Richard D. Craig,
" *m* *Daniel A. Gray,
" William S. MacHarg, M. E.,
" Anthony S. Montgomery, A. B.,
" *William S. Palmer, LL. B. '67,
" Theodore M. Shaw,
" Llewellyn P. Tarlton, Jr., B. S.,
'69 *Roscoe W. Beaman,
" Ford DeC. Hinchman,
" *l* Henry McKey, LL. B.,
'70 William W. Douglas,
" Michael A. A. Meyendorff, C. E.,
'71 Caleb W. Durham,
" *J. Lathrop Gillespie, Ph. B.,
" Alfred B. Sager, LL. B.,
'71 Stephen H. Tyng, LL. B.,
'72 Frank H. Holbrook,
" *Charles S. Hunt,
" *Peter J. Starr,
" Frederick VonSchrader,
" Junius B. Walker,
" Charles A. Whittier,
" Joseph B. Whittier,
'73 Thompson Burnam,
" Samuel T. Douglas, Ph. B.,
" Wayne Hayman, A. B.,
" Charles R. Wells, A. B.,
'74 George F. Ambrose,
" *p* George C. Henry, Ph. C.,
" *Charles C. Hibbard, B. S.,
" Edward C. Hinman, B. S.,
" *l* *George McConnell,
" *Harry St. C. Parker,
" William H. Wells, A. B.,
'75 George L. Arey, C. E.,
" Charles Fox, A. B.,
" E. Crofton Fox,
" Henry D. Turney,
'76 Edward A. Gott, Ph. B.,
" Edward C. Swift, Ph. B.,
" *Lincoln D. Wright,
'77 Wayne Choate,
" Edward H. Guyer, A. B.,
" Oliver Johnson,
" Lyndon S. Smith, A. B.,
'78 *l* William L. Bassett, LL. B.,
" Llewellyn H. Davis,
" *p* William D. Eaton,
" J. Dick DuShane, C. E.,
" William V. Grove, C. E.,
" *p* Theodore F. Meyer, Ph. C.,
" James C. Munson,
'79 Edmund A. Christian, A. B.,
" Henry C. Clements,
" *p* Henry J. Meyer,
" John C. Quintus, M. E.,
'80 Josiah L. Ambrose, Ph. B.,
" *p* Arthur H. Gongar,
" George M. Gillette,
" William W. Hannan, A. B.,
" Fred A. Patrick,
" Max Zinkheisen, A. B.,
'81 *l* *William F. Goodpaster,
" *m* Edward W. Lee, M. D.,
" *l* George W. Middleton,
" Moss K. Perkins, A. B.,
" Henry H. Treadway,
" Frank A. Wadleigh,
'82 William L. Clements, B. S.,
" *p* George E. Dean, Ph. C.,
" George N. Holland,
" Jesse A. Icenhour,
" William R. Johnson,
" Howard H. Kimball,

'82 James H. Norton, B. L.,
" Frederick A. Robinson, A. B.,
" George B. Whitney,
'83 Henry S. Ames, A. B.,
" Charles G. Chaddock, M. D., '85,
" Arthur D. Eddy,
" Frederick W. Jones,
" Theodore H. Lasley, A. B.,
" Alfred B. Schanz,
" *l* Charles M. Sherman, LL. B.,
'84 Willis J. Abbott, LL. B.,
" *l* George F. Brownell,
" Frederick A. Giddings,
'85 Don C. Corbett, Ph. B.,
" Charles H. Hills,
" George F. Lewis.
" Edward C. Miller
" Henry G. Withrow,
'86 *l* Archibald M. Blakeley,
" Herbert G. Finch,
" William M. Lasley,
" Rolla E. Roe,
" *p* Mason S. Thomson, Ph. C.,
'87 William A. Blakeley,
" *l* Edwin W. Christy,
" Lewis C. Hunt,
" Robert H. Hunt,
" *l* J. Bowman Sweitzer, LL. B.,
" Clyde B. Weatherwax,
" *Charles D. Wiley,
" *p* Harry G. Wiley, Ph. C.,
'88 *m* Henry S. Bartholemew,
" Lester E. Campbell,
" *l* A. Braden Clark, LL. B.,
" Charles E. Roehl, B. S.,
" Harry J. Williams, B. S.,
'89 *l* James D. Armstrong, LL. B.,
" Malcolm Gunn,
" *d* George B. Hayes, D. D. S.,
" Frederick A. Joss,
'90 *l* John W. Anderson, LL. B.,
" *l* Frank N. Crosby,
" *m* Conway A. Frost,
" Charles A. Otis,
'91 Howard T. Abbott, LL. B.,
" John W. Baker,
" Albert F. Storke,
'92 *l* Jean LaR. Burnett, LL. B.,
" *h* William W. Cheney, M. D.,
'92 Edward W. Cressey,
" *l* James E. Duffy, LL. B.,
" Frederick C. Struve,
'93 John L. Duffy,
" Frank L. Evans,
" Daniel W. Hand,
" Harold M. Joss,
" William Metcalf, Jr.,
" Dwight C. Morgan,
" Henry E. Sauer,
" George M. Tyng,
'94 James F. Breakey, M. D.,
" William H. Decker,
" Lawrence C. Grosh, M. D. '96,
" Virgil C. Tupper,
" *l* Bartlett Wiley, LL. B.,
'95 Raynor K. Anderson,
" *l* Harry I Dunton,
" R. Prosper Gustin, B. S.,
" Horace Tupper, Jr., LL. B.,
'96 Glenn H. Meeker,
'97 Z. Kent Graham,
" Herman Hegeler,
" C. Edward Mead,
" *m* Wallace Pyle.
" *m* John B. Thielen, M. D.
" George T. White,
'98 Harold M. Bowman,
" Walter J. Cahill,
" John S. Cash,
" *d* Ignatius M. Duffy,
" *l* Craig C. Miller,
" Charles F. Rathfon,
" *e* Charles S. Snyder,
" Thomas J. Weadock,
'99 *l* James A. Bardin,
" *l* Chester L. Benedict,
" Ralph R. Bowdle,
" *l* Hazlett N. Clark,
" *l* Edward H. Fairburn,
" *l* Frank A. Fairburn,
" *l* Frank W. Shepherd,
'00 Vernon E. Bush,
" Lafayette Young, Jr.,
'01 Harry E. Baker,
" Herman T. Bowman,
" George G. Damon,
" John B. Herff,
" Stillman S. Meservey,

In addition to the roll of Alpha Epsilon, Chi Psi has had at Ann Arbor the following students:

'65 *l* E. A. Sturtevant, LL. B.,
'66 *m* Henry S. Jordan,
'76 *l* John E. More, LL. B.,
'77 *m* Frederic E. Barrows,
'78 *l* William L. Bassett.
'83 *l* George S. Grimes, LL. B.,
'84 *l* Richard H. Johnson, LL. B.,
" *l* Frederick Reynolds, LL. B.

Beta Theta Pi was founded early in July, 1839, at Miami University, Oxford, Ohio, by John R. Knox of '39, and Samuel T. Marshall of '40. Eighty-one different institutions have been entered by the fraternity, of which sixty-two—the following—still shelter the society: Miami, Western Reserve, Ohio, Washington and Jefferson, Harvard, DePauw, Indiana, Michigan, Wabash, Centre, Brown, Hampden-Sidney, North Carolina, Ohio Wesleyan, Hanover, Cumberland, Knox, Virginia, Davidson, Beloit, Bethany, Iowa, Wittenberg, Westminster, Iowa Wesleyan, Chicago, Denison, Wooster, Kansas, Wisconsin, Northwestern, Dickinson, Boston, Johns Hopkins, California, Kenyon, Mississippi, Rutgers, Cornell, Stevens Institute, St. Lawrence, Maine, Pennsylvania, Colgate, Union, Columbia, Amherst, Vanderbilt, Texas, Ohio State, Nebraska, Pennsylvania State, Denver, Syracuse, Dartmouth, Minnesota, Missouri, Cincinnati, Wesleyan, Lehigh, Yale, and Leland Stanford, Jr. Until the year 1879 this order was almost exclusively confined to Southern and Western colleges; but since that time many branches have been started in Eastern institutions. However, the bulk of the membership is to be found in the middle West. Buildings are owned by the society at Amherst, Michigan, DePauw, California, Colgate, Pennsylvania State, Denison, Wesleyan, St. Lawrence, and Leland Stanford, Jr., ten in all. Pink and blue are the fraternity colors, and the rose is the fraternity flower. Among the 9,600 members the following—initiated at other colleges than Michigan, and during college life—may be named: Presidents Cyrus Nutt and W. M. Daily of Indiana University, John Bascom of Wisconsin, William T. Reid of California, S. S. Laws and M. M. Fisher of Missouri, William H. Scott of Ohio State, A. D. Hepburn of Miami, Charles N. Sims of Syracuse, William C. Young and Ormand Beatty of Centre College, and J.H.Raymond, of West Virginia. Professors John S. Newberry and James W. Burgess of Columbia; the Episcopalian Bishops Jackson and Sessums, and the Methodist Bishops Joyce and Cranston; Justices Harlan, Matthews, and Woods, of the Federal Supreme Court; United States Circuit Judges Lurton and Grosscup; Justice A. P. Carpenter of the Supreme Court of Vermont, and Justices Ulysses Mercur and J. P. Sterrett of that of Pennsylvania; United States Senators Newton Booth, B. Gratz Brown, M. S. Latham, J. E. McDonald, J. W. McDill, O. P. Morton, M. S. Quay, D. W. Voorhees, J. L. Rawlins, and Boies

BADGE OF BETA THETA PI.

Penrose; Representatives in Congress J. M. Allen, Robert R. Hitt, and W. M. Springer; U. S. Ministers Will Cumback, W. T. Coggesball, Rufus Magee, A. G. Porter, and E. H. Ferrell; John W. Noble, Ex-Secretary of the Interior; and Governors C. H. Hardin and T. T. Crittenden of Missouri, George Hoadley of Ohio, James A. Beaver of Pennsylvania, and John Y. Brown of Kentucky.

Instituted November 13, 1845, by B. F. Millard of the Western Reserve Chapter, the Lambda (Michigan) Chapter of Beta Theta Pi became inactive in 1850. It was revived in 1854, and was suspended again in 1864. October 28, 1875, it was reorganized through the efforts of A. N. Grant, Asbury '74. In 1890 the society at Ann Arbor purchased the property 604 South State street, having previously occupied a rented house. Among the many prominent graduates of the Chapter are George L. Becker, '46, the late John S. Newberry, '47, Levi T. Griffin, '57, Henry A. Reeves, '52, and John J. Lentz, '82, Representatives in Congress; the late James M. Walker, '46, of the Chicago Bar, formerly President of the C. B. & Q. R. Co.; the Rev. Nathaniel West, D. D., '46, of Syracuse; Sidney D. Miller, '48, of the Detroit Bar; the late Charles Beckwith, '49, Judge of the Buffalo Superior Court; the late Lyman Cochrane, '49, Judge of the Superior Court of Detroit; Judge Barzillai Gray, '49, of Leavenworth, Kansas; O. M. Barnes, '50, of Lansing, Mich.; William A. Moore, '50, of the Detroit Bar; the late Andrew J. Poppleton, '51, of the Omaha Bar; Arthur D. Rich, '51, of the Chicago Bar; Alfred Cowles, '54, of The Chicago Tribune; Duane Doty, '56, former Superintendent of Public Instruction, Chicago; the late General William W. Wheeler, '56, of Chicago; the late Professor

VIGNETTE OF BETA THETA PI (1859).

James C. Watson, '57; General Frank Askew, '58; E. Bruce Chandler, '58, the well-known electrician; Colonel Arthur T. Wilcox, '59; Professor DeVolson Wood, '59, of Stevens Institute; General Isaac H. Elliott, '61; Professor Volney G. Barbour, '64, of the University of Vermont; Professor Willis Boughton, '81, of Ohio University; O. F. Hunt, '81, of the Detroit Bar; and Junius E. Beal, '82, of Ann Arbor. In college athletics these members have been prominent: in baseball, W. R. Payne,'87, T. N. Jayne of '90, A. D. Rich, of '91, and L. J. Wentworth, '94; in football, H. G. Hetzler of '86, R. S. Babcock of '89, and G. S. Holden of '91; and in tennis, T. N. Jayne of '90 and W. F. Slocum of '92. Excluding ninety-two initiates of other chapters who, by reason of their attendance upon the professional schools have had a brief connection with the Lambda Chapter, the members of the latter number 289. The roll is as follows:

BETA THETA PI CHAPTER HOUSE.

'45	Paul W. H. Rawls, A. B.,
'46	George L. Becker, A. B.,
"	*James M. Walker, A. B.,
"	Nathaniel West, A. B.,
'47	*Daniel B. Brown, A. B.,
"	*John S. Newberry, A. B.,
"	*Franklin L. Parker, A. B.,
'48	Sidney D. Miller, A. B.,
"	Wyllis C. Ransom, A. B.,
'49	*Charles Beckwith, A. B.,
"	*Thomas S. Blackmar, A. B.,
"	*Lyman Cochrane, A. B.,
"	Barzillai Gray, A. B.,
"	*Dean O. Tiffany,
'50	Edward Bacon, A. B.,
"	Orlando M. Barnes, A. B.,
"	Samuel Harper, A. B.,
"	William A. Moore, A. B.,
"	*Henry H. Powers, A. B.,
"	*Charles J. Wood, A. B.,
'51	Edmund Hewitt,
"	*Andrew J. Poppleton,
"	Arthur D. Rich, A. B.,
"	*O. Hoyt Seymour,
'51	*L. Chapin Taylor,
—	Edmund H. Williams,
'52	William K. Gibson,
"	*James K. Knight,
"	Henry A. Reeves,
"	*Byron Smith,
'54	*Henry Barnes,
"	*Alfred Cowles,
'55	Byron B. Northrop, A. B.,
"	*Emanuel Schmid, A. B.,
"	Charles Toll, A. B.,
'56	Duane Doty, A. B.,
"	Isaac C. Elston,
"	*William W. Wheeler, A. B.,
'57	Henry W. Beeson, B. S.,
"	*Anson Brunson, A. B.,
"	Levi T. Griffin, A. B.,
"	*James C. Watson, A. B.,
'58	Frank Askew, B. S.,
"	Edward B. Chandler, A. B.,
"	*Augustus E. Chesnut,
"	Daniel A. Collins,
"	*Thomas G. Gavin, A. B.,
"	Daniel Kloss, A. B.,

'58 Christopher W. Mykrantz, A. B.,
" Abram Neff, A. B.,
" Browse T. Prentis, A. B.,
" *Oscar F. Price, A. B.,
" George W. Wall, A. B.,
'59 David M. Johnson, B. S.,
" *Eber G. Owen,
" *Bushrod F. Rice, A. B.,
" *James Wallace,
" Arthur T. Wilcox, A. B.,
" *DeVolson Wood, M. S.,
— *James W. Larimore,
'60 *W. Jesse Buchanan, A. B.,
" Godfrey E. Knight, B. S.,
" Edward M. Mason, A. B.,
" *l* *Charles K. Robinson, LL. B.,
" Cyrus B. Thomas, A. B.,
" *A. Edwards Welch,
" *Edgar N. Wilcox, B. S.,
'61 Samuel M. Billings, A. B.,
" S. Porter Brockway,
" *W. Wirt Dedrick, A. B.,
" Isaac H. Elliott, A. B.,
" Elijah J. Hills,
" Charles E. McAlester, B. S.,
" *l* Cyrus D. Roys, LL. B.,
" *Thomas B. Weir, A. B.,
'62 Thomas M. Baxter, B. S.,
" *James W. Bingham,
" *Theodore H. Hurd, A. B.,
" *Henry A. Latson, A. B.,
" *Albert Nye,
" *Ira Olds,
" William V. Richards, A. B.,
" William S. Thomas,
'63 *George S. Decker,
" Clark Gray,
" *Edward A. Hyde,
'64 Volney G. Barbour,
" John W. Barnhart,
" William A. Ewing, A. B.,
" Dwight J. Harris, M. D.,
'65 *Edward C. Boudinot,
" Benjamin F. Paddock,
" John L. Turrel, LL. B., '64,
'66 Edmund Adams,
'67 Clement J. Whipple,
'79 Hubert W. Brown, A. B.,
" William F. Bryan, A. B.,
" Lucius L. Van Slyke, A. B.,
'80 Earl B. Coe, LL. B.,
" Charles A. Fyke,
" John J. Shields,
'81 Fremont C. Blandin,
" Willis Boughton, A. B.,
" T. Bertrand Bronson, A. B.,
" Don A. Garwood, A. B.,
" Ormond F. Hunt, A B.,
" Charles A. McMurray,
'81 John M. C. Smith,
" William T. Whedon, Ph. B.,
— Franklin M. Rule,
'82 Junius E. Beal, Ph. B.,
" William C. Bell,
" William B. Cady, Ph. B.,
" Willard E. Chandler, A. B.,
" John J. C. Davis,
" John H. Grant, A. B.,
" George E. Herrick,
" John J. Lentz, A. B.,
" Daniel E. Osborne, Ph. C., '79,
" Frank Quinby,
" *p* Robert B. Ransom, Ph. C.,
" Almon N. Taylor
" Francis L. York, A. B.,
'83 *Dan Carpenter,
" Arthur M. Gibson,
" Harry McNeil, B. L.,
" Henry E. Moseley,
" David T. Wilcox,
'84 James A. Case, A. B.,
" Charles H. Dennison,
" Charles H. J. Douglas,
" Elbert L. Johnson, Ph. B.,
" Charles S. Powell, A. M.,
'85 Fred R. Babcock,
" David K. Cochrane,
" Carril M. Coe,
" Horace S. Fiske, A. M.,
" Thomas C. Phillips, B. S.,
" Allen S. Whitney, A. B.,
" William F. Word, A. B.,
'86 Charles L. Andrews, A. B.,
" Wilber J. Gregory, A. B.,
" *William W. Harris,
" Howard G. Hetzler, B. S.,
" George L. Price, A. B.,
" Dwight H. Ramsdell,
" Frederick W. Stevens, B. S.,
'87 John H. Cotteral,
" William C. Harris, LL. B., '91,
" Denver J. Mackey,
" George C. Manly, A. M.,
" Claire A. Orr, A. B.,
" John H. Patterson,
" Jesse C. Shattuck, Ph. B.,
" Frederic D. Sherman, A. B.,
" W. Teis Smith, A. B.,
" Franklin L. Velde, A. B.,
'88 David K. Cochrane, Ph. B.,
" Clarence L. Dobyns,
" Fred J. Hodges,
" Ray D. Lampson, Ph. B.,
" Jed H. Lee, B. L.,
" Louis B. Lee,
" Sterling Parks, A. B.,
" Fred W. Ramsdell,
" Victor M. Tuthill,

'88 George W. Whyte, B. S.,
" William E. Wood,
'89 Robert S. Babcock,
" L. Roscoe Doud,
" *m* J. J. Goodyear,
" Daniel P. Grant,
" Julian D. Harmon, A. B.,
" John B. Leonard,
" Julian Millard,
" Arthur E. Rowley, Ph. B.,
" Fred B. Spaulding, A. B.,
'90 Frederick M. Clarke,
" Trafford N. Jayne,
" Robert K. Reilly, Ph. B.,
" *Fred R. Romer,
" Nathan P. Wood, B. L.,
'91 Charles E. Babcock, LL. B.,
" Albert S. Brown, A. B.,
" Earl W. Dow, A. B.,
" Emerson A. Fletcher,
" George S. Holden, A. B.,
" Liberty D. Holden,
" *Albert D. Rich, Ph. B.,
" James R. Robertson,
" Paul E. Stillman, A. B.
" Edgar M. Thorp, Ph. B.,
" William H. Turnbull, A. B.,
" Edward M. Wilson,
'92 Albert S. Brown,
" Horace W. Hawkins, B. S.,
" Robert H. McCrea,
" Richard S. Parmly,
" Ralph M. Shaw, LL. B.,
" Walter F. Slocum, Ph. B.,
" Edwin M. Smith, B. S.,
" William C. Tichenor, A.B.,
" George M. Wisner, B. S.,
'93 Edward S. Beck, A. B.,
" James O. Bennett,
" *William S. Cheever, B. L.,
" Harrison P. Crego, A. B.,
" *l* Griffith O. Ellis, LL. B.,
" John S. W. Holloway, LL. B.,
" *Richard S. Parmly,
" Samuel P. Parmly, Jr ,
" Byron C. Porter,
" Robert Redfield,
" Frank Rich, M. D.,
" Edwin W. Sparks,
'94 *l* Daniel R. Barlow,
" Elmer E. Beal,
" James S. Henton, LL. B., '93,
" D. Conrad Smith, Jr., A. B.,
" Lloyd J. Wentworth, B. L.,
" Earl F. Wilson, B. L.,
'95 Howard O. Bliven,
" Robert W. Dunn, LL. B.,
" Harry A. Engman, Jr.,
" Eugene H. Garnett, B. L.,
" Fred King,
" Robert W. Manly, LL. B., '96,
'95 Earl Munson,
" Oliver L. Spaulding, Jr., A. B.,
" George R. Taylor,
'96 Charles G. Cook, A. B.,
" Charles P. Davis, B. L.,
" Sheridan W. Ehrman, B. L.,
" Adelbert H. Finney, Ph. B.,
" Henry B. Otis, B S.,
" Edwin R. Parker,
" Frank C. Penoyar,
" Ben C. Rich, B. S.,
" Walter H. Thorp, Ph. B.,
'97 Samuel H. Dowden, Ph. B.,
'97 Albert H. Finney,
" Boone Gross,
" William B. Guitteau,
" Richard W. Hawkins,
" Richard G Kirchner,
" Lester E. Maher,
" John M. Parker,
" William B. Rich, Ph. B.,
" John C. Spaulding, A. B.,
" Wesley E. Taylor, B. S.,
'98 William T. Beck,
" Harry N. Campbell,
" George M. Chandler,
" Charles J. Dovel,
" Glenn S. Harrington,
" Henry F. Hawkins,
" Clifton R. Norton,
" John M. Parker,
" Charles G. White,
" Ralph E. Wisner,
" Thomas R. Woodrow,
'99 Henry P. Dowling,
" Daniel I. Elder,
" Gwynn Garnett, Jr.,
" Harold T. Griswold,
" Joseph G. Hamblen, Jr.,
" Harry R. Hurlbut,
" James L. Kocher,
" Spencer B. Moseley,
" Lewis S. Ramsdell,
" Guy E. Stirling,
" David M. Tracy,
" Harry S. Vernon,
'00 Guy B. Cady,
" Herman W. Hippen,
" Frank H. Lamb,
" Robert E. Peacock,
" Alonzo H. Raymond,
" Ralph H. Van Cleve,
" Victor C. Vaughan, Jr.,
'01 Benjamin W. Batchelder,
" Sheldon L. Dickinson,
" Robert M. Hall,
" Howard W. Hayes,
" Edward L. Jones,
" Bryant E. Vail,
" Oliver S. White.

The following list includes those Beta Theta Pi men of other chapters than the Lambda who have studied law, medicine, pharmacy, or dentistry at Ann Arbor.

'57 *m* *Dwight Sayles, M. D.,
'65 *l* William Cessna,
'67 *l* John D. Alexander,
" *l* John A. Keller, Jr.,
" *l* Ben Sheeks,
" *l* John H. Shepherd,
'75 *l* David W. Cooper, LL. B.,
" *l* Horace L. Smith, LL. B.,
" *l* William R. Taggart, LL. B.,
'76 *l* Amandus N. Grant, LL. B.,
" *l* William E. Jones, LL. B.,
'77 *l* Reid Carpenter,
" *l* Frank Taggart,
" *l* John W. Yerkes, LL. B.,
'78 *l* John S. Marques,
" *l* Charles W. Smith, LL. B.,
" *l* Henry S. Tremper, LL. B.,
'80 *l* Charles S. Finch, LL. B.,
'81 *l* Frederick P. Leonard, LL. B.,
'82 *p* Charles C. Cook,
" *m* Frank T. Smith, M. D.,
" *m* William T. Wright, M. D.,
'83 *l* Edward A. Benson,
" *l* Francis J. Cheek, LL. B.,
" *l* Alfred C. Downs,
" *l* William L. January, LL. B.,
" *m* John J. Sturgus,
'84 *m* Joseph W. Cooper,
" *l* *Walter A. White, LL. B.,
'85 *l* Charles H. Forbes,
" *p* Charles E. Parker, Ph. C.,
'86 *l* James G. Smith, LL. B.,
'87 *l* Edward V. Bope,
" *l* James W. Brannum LL. B.,
" *l* Webster W. Davis, LL. B.,
" *m* George A. Hare, M. D.,
" *l* Ellsworth E. Otis, LL. B.,
" *l* George B. Watson, LL B.,
'88 *l* John L. Benedict, LL. B.,
'89 *l* George H. Billman,
" *l* Thomas S. Dunlap,
" *l* Robert L. Simpson, LL. B.,
'90 *l* Daniel W. Crockett, LL. B.,
" *l* Brode B. Davis, LL. B.,
" *m* Emmett A. Hall, M. D.,
" *m* John D. Hare, M. D.,
'90 *m* George W. Ingham, M. D.,
" *m* Asbury N. Loper, M. D.,
" *l* Edward F. McCausland, LL. B.,
" *d* John H. Waterhouse, DD. S.,
" *l* Archie E. Watson, LL. B.,
'91 *l* William D. Cochran, LL. B.,
" *l* Edward C. Gordon,
" *m* Harry E. Greene, M. D.,
" *m* Thomas ap R. Jones, M. D.,
" *m* Donald Macrea, Jr., M. D.,
" *l* Norman A. Phillips, LL. B.,
" *l* Ralph Platt, LL. B.,
" *l* Robert W. Wilde, LL. B.,
'92 *l* Patrick A. Berry, LL. B.,
" *m* Brown Pusey,
'93 *d* Charles A. Church, D.D. S.,
" *l* John W. Clark, LL. B.,
" *m* Clifford R. Hervey, M. D.,
" *l* Harry A. Reese, LL. B.,
" *l* Purcell Rowe, LL. B.,
'94 *l* Alfred F. Bissell, LL. B.,
" *l* Charles W. Burdick, LL. B.,
" *l* Frank W. Marsh, LL. B.,
" *l* William G. Ramsey, LL. B.,
" *l* Raymond G. Scott, LL. B.,
" *l* Elliot Spaulding, LL. B.,
" *l* John G. Stone, LL. B.,
'95 *l* Charles S. McDowell, LL. B.,
" *l* Gilmore D. Price, LL. B.,
'96 *l* James R. Skillman, LL. B.,
" *l* Henry G. Stalder, LL. B.,
" *l* William E. Watt,
'97 *l* Maxwell W. Babb, LL. B.,
" *l* Boyard T. Riley, LL. B.,
'98 *l* Edwin R. Sheetz,
" *d* Thomas B. VanHorne,
'99 *l* Harry W. Robinson,
" *l* Robert Upham,
'00 *d* Herbert S. Allyn,
" *m* Emil F. Baur,
" *l* Burnell Colson,
" *m* Charles H. Mulroney,
" *l* Edward C. Mulroney,
" *m* James R. Richards,
" *l* McLane Tilton, Jr.,
" *l* David H. Thomas.

Alpha Delta Phi.—To Samuel Eells, the valedictorian of the class of '32 at Hamilton College, and to his four associates, is due the foundation of Alpha Delta Phi. Thirty-one colleges have been entered by this fraternity, which to-day has twenty-three active chapters. Following is the entire roll: Hamilton, 1832;

Miami, 1835–73; New York University, 1835-39; Columbia, 1836–41, 1881; Yale, 1836–72, 1888; Amherst, 1836; Brown, 1836–41, 1850; Harvard, 1837–65, 1879; Cincinnati Law School, 1838–40; Hobart, 1840–76; Western Reserve, 1841; Bowdoin, 1841; Dartmouth, 1846; Michigan, 1846; Madison, 1849–51; Alabama, 1850–57; Rochester, 1851; Williams, 1851; College of the City of New York, 1855; Wesleyan, 1856; Kenyon, 1858; Cum-berland, 1858–61; Union, 1859; Princeton, 1865–65; Cornell, 1869; Trinity, 1877; Johns Hopkins, 1889; Minnesota, 1892; Toronto, 1893; Chicago, 1896; and McGill (Montreal), 1897. Chapter halls or houses, some of them very costly, are owned by the branches at Hamilton, Yale, Amherst, Dartmouth, Michigan, Rochester, Williams, Wesleyan, Cornell, Trinity, and Union. Green and white are the colors of the order. Alpha Delta Phi has had branches in the South, and has at the present day five Western branches; nevertheless it is a distinctively Eastern society. The bulk of the membership is to be found in New England and New York, although many alumni reside in Pennsylvania, Ohio, Michigan, Illinois, Wisconsin, and Minnesota. About 7,800 men have been admitted. Postponing for a moment Michigan names, the following may be mentioned as illustrative of the catalogue of Alpha Delta Phi: Senators of the United States, William B. Allison, P. W. Hitchcock, G. E. Pugh, and Watson C. Squire; Foreign Ministers, John Jay, Edward F. Noyes, Horace Maynard, George V. N. Lothrop, James O. Putnam, and John M. Read; Ex-Governors, Chamberlain of Maine, Dennison of Ohio, Harrison and Hubbard of Connecticut, and Willard of Indiana; Theodore Roosevelt, recently Assistant Secretary of the Navy; Justices Blatchford, Shiras, and Brown, of the Federal Supreme Court; the Federal Circuit Judges Shipman and Wallace; Chief Justices Peters of Maine, and Ross of Vermont; James C. Carter, Joseph H. Choate, and Clarence S. Seward, of the New York Bar; the authors, James Russell Lowell, Edward Everett Hale, Charles Francis Adams, Jr., Donald G. Mitchell, George F. Parkman, Moses Coit Tyler, and Alfred B. Street; Presidents Eliot of Harvard, Dwight of Yale, Gilman of Johns Hopkins, Gates of Amherst, Raymond of Union, and Harris of Maine; the late Henry S. Frieze, formerly Acting-President of our University; the Protestant Episcopal Bishops, Brewer of Montana, Brooks of Massachusetts, Coxe of Western New York, Harris of Michigan, Huntington of Central New

BADGE OF A. D. PHI.

York, Johnson of Southern California, Lyman of North Carolina, Watson of East Carolina, Welles of Wisconsin, and Whitehead of Pittsburg.

Having as its germ Alpha Alpha, a local society, organized in 1844, the Peninsular Chapter of Alpha Delta Phi was instituted on the afternoon of Commencement Day, August 5, 1846, when eight members of the classes from '45 to '48 were initiated by Henry A. Swift, Western Reserve '42, and by the Rev. Robert R. Kellogg, N. Y. U. '35. Attacked in its early years by the Faculty, the Chapter was reduced in 1849–50 to three men; but ultimately it triumphed, and since 1850 it has enjoyed uninterrupted prosperity. Initiations have been made in every one of the fifty-seven classes matriculated at Ann Arbor.

VIGNETTE OF A. D. PHI.

During the college year 1875–76 Alpha Delta Phi formerly inaugurated the chapter house system at Ann Arbor by occupying the octagonal structure in North University Avenue. The stone chapter house, 556 South State Street, was begun by the society in 1883, and was finished in the following year. In order to hold the title a corporation called "The Peninsular Society," and composed of prominent alumni, had been affected.

Among the honorary members of Alpha Delta Phi at Ann Arbor are Judge Thomas M. Cooley, the late Regent E. C. Walker, the late Judge C. I. Walker, and John M. B. Sill, recently Minister to Corea. The roll of those who have been students at Ann Arbor includes the following: A. J. Welch, '46, formerly a senator of the United States; Dr. Edmund Andrews, '49, and Dr. Homer A. Johnson, '49, both of the Chicago Medical College; Ex-Lieutenant Governor Dwight May, '49; Ex-President Lewis R. Fiske, '50, of Albion College; Professor Robert C. Kedzie, '51 *m*, of the Agricultural College; Byron G. Stout, '51, formerly speaker of the Michigan House; Rev. Tillman C. Trowbridge, '52, the well known missionary; Jay A. Hubbell, '53, formerly Representative in Congress; Edwin Willits, '55, late Commissioner of Agriculture; Professor John E. Clark, '56, of Yale College; the Rev. Moses

Coit Tyler, '56, now of Cornell's Faculty; William E. Quinby, '58, of the Detroit Free Press, recently Minister to Holland; Dr. T. A. McGraw, '59, of Detroit; Byron M. Cutcheon, '61, recently Representative in Congress; Hoyt Post, '61, of the Detroit Bar; Henry M. Utley, '61, City Librarian of Detroit; Albert H. Wilkinson, '61, of Detroit, formerly Probate Judge; James H. Goodsell, '62, and Charles M. Goodsell, '65, of the (New York) Daily Graphic; Edwin F. Uhl, '62, recently Ambassador to Germany; the late James M. Wilkinson, '64, State Treasurer of Michigan; Professor Gabriel Campbell, '65, of Dartmouth College; Joseph V. Quarles, '66, and Charles Quarles, '68, of the Milwaukee Bar; Professor John C. Freeman, '68, of Wisconsin; Albert H. Pattengill, '68, Professor of Greek at Michigan; Regent W. J. Cocker, '69; William R. Day, '70, Federal Secretary of State; Harry B. Hutchins, '71, Acting-President of our University; Edgar M. Cooley, '72, of the Bay City Bar; Frederick L. Geddes, of the Bar of Toledo; Dr. William J. Herdman, '72, of the Medical Faculty at Ann Arbor; Edward W. Pendleton, '72, of the Detroit Bar; Judson G. Pattengill, '73, Principal of the Ann Arbor High School; William B. Williams, '73, of the Bar of Lapeer; Henry Wade Rogers, '74, President of Northwestern University; Frank F. Reed, '80, of the Law School Faculty; Andrew C. McLaughlin, '82, Professor of American History at Michigan; State Senator William Savidge, '84; and Frank W. M. Cutcheon, '85, of the St. Paul Bar.

CHAPTER HOUSE OF ALPHA DELTA PHI.

The chapter has been represented in the University baseball nines by C. M. Goodsell, '65, E. L. Grant, '66, F. J. Simmons, '66, A. H. Pattengill, '68, W. J. Cocker, '69, F. A. Buell, '76, C. L. Van Pelt, '76, O. W. Ferdon, '77, F. K. Stearns, '77, W. C. Johnson, '78, F. F. Reed, '80, G. B. Daniels, '81, and T. L. Wilkinson, '91. With the football teams have played the following:

W. C. Johnson, '78, Evert Van Pelt, '78, F. F. Reed, '80, W. H. Graham, '82, F. F. Bumps, '87, Muir B. Snow, '99, and H. S Pingree, Jr., '00. The well-known tennis players E. O. Grosvenor, '85, and S. F. Hawley, '85, were also members of this society.

The roll of the Peninsular Chapter of Alpha Delta Phi includes ten honorary members who never were matriculated in the University. Their names are: Witter J. Baxter, Thomas M. Cooley, D. Bethune Duffield, Joseph Estabrook, Clark T. Hinman, Jacob Houghton, Elijah H. Pilcher, John M. B. Sill, Charles I. Walker, and Edward C. Walker. All are dead save Judge Cooley, Mr. Houghton, and Professor Sill. Following is the list of the 413 collegiate members:

'45 *Charles A. Clark, A. B.,
" Edmund Fish, A. B.,
" *Fletcher O. Marsh, A. B.,
'46 George P. Androus, A. B.,
" *James S. Mitchell, A. B.,
" Winfield Smith, A. B.,
" *Adonijah S. Welch, A. B.,
" *James O. Whittemore, A. B.,
'47 *Samuel S. Hall, A. B.,
" Theodoric R. Palmer, A. B.,
'48 Alfred DuBois, A. B.,
" *James A. Duncan, A. B.,
" *Wells R. Marsh, A. B.,
'49 Edmund Andrews, A. B.,
" *Park S. Donelson, A. B.,
" *William J. Goodwin, A. B.,
" *John B. Hutchins,
" *Hosmer A. Johnson, A. B.,
" *Calvin S. Kingsley, A. B.,
" Dwight May, A. B.,
" *George P. Tindall, A. B.,
'50 Lewis R. Fiske, A. B.,
" *James W. Tindall,
'51 Joseph W. Bancroft, A. B.,
" *Chauncey M. Cady, A. B.,
" Elias Cooley,
" *m* Robert C. Kedzie, M. D.,
" *Byron G. Stout, A. B.,
'52 James H. Bates,
" *Sidney A. Bean, A. B.,
" *Walker L. Bean, A. B.,
" *Charles W. Becker,
" Alfred G. Otis, A. B.,
" Sylvenus A. Taft,
" *m* Martyn Taylor, M. D.,
" *Tillman C. Trowbridge, A. B.,
'53 *John F. Becker, A. B.,
" *Benjamin E. Hart,
" *Danforth A. Hart,
" Jay A. Hubbell, A. B.,
Charles W. Tozer,
'54 *Arthur Blackwood,
" *France Chandler, A. B.,
" *William Chandler, A. B.,
" Edward P. Evans, A. B.,
" Henry Strong,
" Daniel L. Wood, A. B.,
'55 James B. Eldredge, A. B.,
" *Charles Hewitt, A. B.,
" *Edwin Willits, A. B.,
'56 Datus C. Brooks, A. B.,
" John E. Clark, A. B.,
" *Mason Gibbs, A. B.,
" *Milton W. Reynolds, A. B.,
" Moses Coit Tyler,
'57 Lewis W. James, A. B.,
" George McQ. Landon, A. B.,
" John Richards, A. B.,
" Edwin B. Wight, A. B.,
'58 John Graves, A. B.,
" *John W. Horner, A. B.,
" Walcott H. Littlejohn,
" Charles R. Miller, B. S.,
" Robert S. Moore, A. B.,
" William E. Quinby, A. B.,
" James W. Stark, A. B.,
" Fitch R. Williams, A. B.,
'59 James R. Cary, A. B.,
" *Charles B. Hankinson, B. S.,
" Rodney J. Hathaway, A. B.,
" Solomon C. Martin,
" Edward W. McGraw, A. B.,
" Theodore A McGraw, A. B.,
" Ephraim A. Otis,
" Orrin Parsons, A. B.,
" Albert H. Wilkinson, A. B.,
'60 Stuart Carkener,
" Silas W. Dunning, A. B.,
" George H. Gould,
" *Sullivan D. Green,
" *Allen W. H. Zacharias, A. B.,
'61 William H. Barnum,

" *Goodwin S. Beaver, A. B,
" Benjamin F. Blair, A. B.,
" *Allen J. Curtis, A. M.,
" Byron M. Cutcheon, A. B.,
" Charles H. Denison, A. B.,
" Edward S. Jackson, A. B.,
" Henry B. Landon, A. B.,
" Henry D. Merrill,
" Erasmus D. Nichols,
" Hoyt Post, A. B.,
" James A. Post, B. S.,
" *Charles H. Stocking, A. B.,
" Henry M. Utley, A. B.,
'62 Rienzi H. Baker, A. B.,
" Hiram A. Burt, A. B.,
" Charles Chandler, A. B.,
" Edward G. Clark,
" Edward A. Fay, A. B.,
" *Harmon D. Follett, A. B.,
" James H. Goodsell,
" Charles M. Hunt,
" David B. Sturges,
" Edwin F. Uhl, A. B.,
'63 James C. Ambrose, A. B.,
" Lincoln T. Farr, A. B.,
" William S. Harroun, A. B.,
" Frank Hendricks,
" Stephen Powers, A. B.,
" *George Sherman,
" *Edward R. Slawson, A. B.,
" Casper E. Yost, LL. B.,
'64 George S. Albee, A. B.,
" Levant W. Barnhart,
" William D. Hitchcock, A, B.,
" James H. Kidd,
" *William C. Moore,
" Henry K. Rowley,
" Henry D. Smith,
" John D. Town,
" *James M. Wilkinson,
'65 Henry R. Austin,
" Gabriel Campbell, A. B.,
" Charles A. Dudley, A. B.,
" *Charles M. Goodsell, A. B.,
" George W. Harmon,
" *Samuel R. McLean,
" *Delos Phillips, A. B.,
" *Alfred N. Smith,
" Samuel Vincent,
" *Charles G. Williams,
'66 Fred W. Becker, A. B.,
" *Eleazer Darrow. A. B.,
" Oliver P. Dickinson, A. B.,
" Emory L. Grant, A. B.,
" James T. Larmonth,
" Joseph V. Quarles, A. B.,
" Edgar Rexford, A. B.,
" Frederick J. Simmons,
" William W. Washburn, A. B.,
'66 George S. White, A. B.
'67 *Moses T. DeWitt,
" George F. Edwards,
" *Schuyler H. Williams,
" George B. Woodman,
'68 *James H. Chapin, A. B.,
" Henry R. Durkee, M. E.,
" John C. Freeman, A. B.,
" *Roselle N. Jenne, A. B,
" *Henry W. Lord, A. B.,
" Frank H. Lyman, B. S.,
" Albert H. Pattengill, A. B.,
" Charles Quarles,
'69 William J. Cocker, A. B.,
" William C. Johns, B. S.,
" Edwin Taylor,
" Stanley Waterloo,
" *William H. Wells,
'70 Oscar J. Campbell, A. B.,
" William R. Day, B. S.,
" Robert N. Fearon, A. B.,
" Edwin Fleming, A. B.,
" Owen E. LeFevre, Ph. B,
" John S. Maltman, B. S.,
" Alfred Noble, C. E.,
" Rufus H. Thayer, A. B.,
" James F. Tweedy, A. B.,
'71 Frank A. Crittenden,
" Frank B. Gilbert,
" Giles J. Holbrook,
" Harry B. Hutchins, Ph. B.,
" *Henry W. Montrose, A. B.,
" Isaac H. Pedrick,
" Horace Phillips, A. B.,
" *Rufus E. Phinney, A. B.,
" Frederick J. Picard,
" James A. S. Warden, A. B.,
" Charles M. Wilkinson, B. S.,
'72 Edgar A. Cooley, A. B.,
" Frederick L. Geddes, A. B.,
" William J. Herdman, Ph. B.,
" Joseph M. McGrath, A. B.,
" Samuel G. Milner, A. B.,
" Edward W. Pendleton, A. B.,
" Dwight C. Rexford, A. B.,
" *Charles K. Turner, Ph. B.,
" George P. Voorheis, A. B.,
'73 Horace G. Burt,
" Henry R. Cocker, B. S.,
" *Edwin J. Ferdon, C. E.,
" Rufus Fleming, LL. B.,
" E. Durfee Galloway, Ph. B.,
" Charles B. Keeler, Ph. B.,
" Charles E. King, A. B.,
" Judson G. Pattengill, A. B.,
" Harry O. Perley, A. B.,
" William B. Williams, A. B.,
" Charles S. Wilson, A. B.,
'74 *Louis R. Fiske, Jr.,

'74 *Lyman D. Follett, A. B.,
" Charles M. Lungren, C. E.,
" Don Alonzo Matthews, A. B.,
" Henry W. Rogers, A. B.,
" Wilbert W. Smith, B. S.,
" James D. Warner, Ph. B.,
'75 Charles A. Clark,
" *J. Clement Eaton, C. E.,
" Eugene R. Hutchins, Ph. B.,
" Edwin T. Laible,
" Horace A. J. Upham, A. B.,
'76 Edmund D. Barry, A. B.,
" Charles A. Blair, A. B.,
" Clarence S. Brown, A. B.,
" Frederick R. Buell,
" Fred L. Forman, Ph. B.,
" James K. Ilsley, A. B.,
" John H. Reynolds, A. B.,
" Albert C. Stevens,
" Charles Van Pelt, A. B.,
'77 William Carpenter, Ph. B.,
" *Odgen W. Ferdon, Ph. B.,
" *William B. Ferris, B. S.,
" Carlton C. Frederick, B. S.,
" Thomas M. Hunter,
" Ortive E. Latham, Ph. B.,
" Milo Lewis, Ph. B.,
" *James A. Stacy,
" Frederick K. Stearns,
" Abram M. Stephenson,
'78 William H. Butts, A. B.,
" William C. Johnson, Ph. B.,
" Harry P. Myrick, A. B.,
" Thomas H. Noble,
" Evert VanPelt, C. E.,
'79 Josiah Bond, Jr.,
" James P. Brown, Ph. B.,
" Cornelius Van C. Ganson,
" Frank D. Mead, A. B.,
" Mark Norris, Ph. B.,
" John H. Tweedy, Jr.,
" William D. Washburn, A. B.,
" Enoch C. White, A. B.,
'80 Richard B. Bancroft,
" *Frederick C. Myrick,
" Frank F. Reed, A. B.,
" John H. Willard, Ph. B.,
'81 Frank P. Boughton, A. B.,
" *Edward H. Bowman, A. B.,
" George B. Daniels, A. B.,
" Duane E. Fox, A. B.,
" Charles W. Goodrich, A. B.,
" Schuyler C. Graves, M. D.,
" Adolph B. Mason,
" Frank C. Robbins,
" Frank T. Terry, A. B.,
'82 William H. Graham, A. B.,
" *Charles Edward Ilsley,
" William H. McEwan, B. S.,
'82 Andrew C. McLaughlin, A. B.,
" William E. Martin, Ph. B.,
" Charles W. Tinsman, A. B.,
'83 Willard I. Brigham,
" John U. Comstock, A. B.,
" Ralph Gray, A. B.,
" Norman D. Hinsdale, A. B.,
" Reinhardt Rahr,
" Homer E. Tinsman, A. B.,
'84 Charles E Ferguson,
" Thomas S. Jerome, Ph. B.,
" William Savidge, A. B.,
'85 Frank W. M. Cutcheon,
" Ebenezer O. Grosvenor, A. B.,
" Samuel F. Hawley, Ph. B.,
" George E. Slocum,
" Harry B. Wheelock,
" Arthur H. Williams, A. B.,
'86 Cyrus B. Lewis, Jr.,
" Alexander F. McEwan, B. L.,
" Albert W. Middleton,
" Henry E. Montgomery,
'87 Frank F. Bumps, Ph. B.,
" Dwight Cutler, Jr.,
" William E. Danforth,
" William G. Latimer,
" Arthur L. Lewis,
" William Mitchell,
" Larmon G. Townsend,
" *Thomas L. Van Deventer,
'88 Joseph E. Carpenter,
" Andrew A. Clokey,
" Samuel H. Crowl,
" John N. Derby,
" Daniel E. Ewald, A. B.,
" Luther S. Harvey,
" Fenton R. McCreery,
" Morgan McM. Mann, Ph. B.,
" Charles P. Wheeler,
" Herbert U. Williams,
'89 Benjamin P. Bourland, A. B ,
" Robert H. Day,
" George T. Gamble,
" Francis G. Howard,
" John A. Nichols,
" William W. Perfet,
" James E. Talley, A. B.,
" Jesse S. Thornham,
" Henry M. Young,
'90 Harry M. Bates, Ph. B.,
" Charles B. Garrison, A. B.,
" Edwin F. Gay, A. B.,
" William W. Griffin,
" William P. Harris, B. L.
" Walter L. Mann, Ph. B.,
" Horace Van Deventer, Ph. B.,
'91 James M. Crosby, B. S.,
" Robert S. Donaldson,
" Chancey R. Lamb,

'91 Thomas A. McGraw,
" Loyal L. Munn, Jr., A. B.,
" Herbert S. Smith, A. B.,
" Thomas L. Wilkinson, B. S.,
'92 Lewis C. Carson, A. B.,
" Eleazer Darrow, B. S.,
" John K. Earp,
" Garrett E. Lamb,
" Stanley D. McGraw,
" David W. McMorran, B. S.,
" Frederick S. Porter, A. B.,
" George C. Rew, B. S.,
" Ashley C. Rogers,
" Richard R. Smith,
" Hugh F. Van Deventer, B. S.,
" Carl C. Warden, Ph. B.,
'93 James E. Ferris, Ph. B.,
" Ransom G. George, A. B.,
" Frank P. Graves, A. B.,
" Samuel S. Harris, A. B.,
" James S. Holland, A. B.,
" Thomas B. Holland,
" George E. Howes,
" John C. Loomis,
" Charles D. Matteson,
" Dan Quirk, Jr. Ph. B.,
'94 George J. Cadwell, Ph. B.,
" Benjamin C. Robinson,
" Robert C. Stevens, A. B.,
" William B. Ward, A. B.,
" Frederick D. Wilkerson, A. B.,
" Harry F. Worden,
'95 William H. Andrews, B. S.,
" Norman T. Bourland, B. L.,
" Philip D. Bourland, B. S.,
" Charles H. Conrad, B. L.,
" Mac Dowell Graves,
" David Lefavour, B. S.,
" William H. Perkins,
" Henry H. Smith, A. B.,
" Stewart E. White, Ph. B.,
'96 Henry S. Barton,
" Horatio S. Goodell,
" Harry G. Nichols,
" Frank H. Petrie, A. B.,
" John B. Tillotson,
" Christopher Van Deventer,
" Fayette F. Van Deventer,
'96 Francis H. Wessels, A. B.,
'97 Robert C. Bourland, A. B.,
" Freeman Field, LL. B.,
" Evans Holbrook,
" Charles J. Phinney,
" Arthur M. Smith, Ph. B.,
" Ralph C. Taggart, Ph. B.,
'98 Benjamin C. Cocker,
" Charles C. Green,
" Clarence E. Groesbeck,
" Julian H. Harris,
" Harry P. Herdman,
" Ernest G. Hildner,
" George C. Shirts,
" George A. Woodruff,
" Eugene C. Worden,
" Orestes H. Wright,
'99 Roswell F. Bishop,
" Ferry K. Heath,
" Eugene B. Jones,
" Benjamin B. Metheany,
" George E. Sherman,
" Frederick H. Skinner,
" Harry A. Smith,
" Muir B. Snow,
" Willard J. Stone,
" Daniel J. Wessels,
" Charles H. Wright,
'00 Fred L. Baxter,
" Austin George, Jr.,
" Arthur B. Groesbeck,
" Frank A. Hatch,
" James S. Hodges,
" Robert C. McKeighan,
" Hazen S. Pingree, Jr.,
" James S. Symons,
" Roy C. Woodworth,
'01 Schuyler B. Eddy,
" Claude L. Lockwood,
" Richard R. Metheany,
" Giles B. Nichols,
" Donald C. Osborn,
" George E. Sudlow,
" James M. Taggart,
" George G. Whitcomb,
" Harrison G. Williams,
" William K. Williams.

The following members of Alpha Delta Phi initiated at other institutions, and not permanently carried upon the rolls of the Peninsular Chapter, have attended the University:

'62 *m* Henry T. Antis,
" *m* Elwood P. Haines,
" *m* Augustus C. VanDuyn, M. D.,
'64 *m* Charles E. Poe,
" *m* Alphonso D. Rockwell,
'65 *m* Charles G. Clark,
'66 *m* William H. Sanborn,
" *l* John R. Vance,
" *l* *Henry R. Waterson,
'67 *m* Archibald S. Dunlap, M. D.,

'68 *l* Alexander D. Anderson, LL. B.,
'69 *l* James R. Willard,
'70 *m* Sidney Crawford,
" *l* *Frank L. Skeels,
'70 *l* *Isaac W. Wood, LL. B.,
'71 *l* Andrew J. Mack,
" *l* *Willard H. Perley, LL. B.,
" *m* Edwin E. Smith,
" *l* Edward T. Waite, LL. B.,
'74 *l* Arthur D. Dean,
" *l* M. Bronson Earnheart, LL. B.,
'75 *l* James O. Jeffreys,
'78 *l* Frederick P. Wilcox, LL. B.,
'79 *m* Lorin Hall,
'82 *m* Lewis R. Dawson, M. D.,
" *m* Harold Gifford, M. D.,
" *l* Sheldon Parks, LL. B.,
'86 *l* George L. Munn, LL. B.,
'88 *l* David B. Day, LL. B.,
'90 *p* Richard F. Van Heusen,
'00 *l* Guy A. Andrews,
" *l* Carl B. Ford.

Delta Kappa Epsilon.—This fraternity was founded at Yale, June 22, 1844, by fifteen membes of the class of '46. Forty-eight chapters, of which thirty-five are now in active operation, have been formed, the entire roll of colleges being as follows: Yale, 1844; Bowdoin, 1844; Colby, 1845; Princeton, 1845–46, 1852–57; Amherst, 1846; University of Nashville, 1847–50, 1855–61; Alabama, 1847–56, 1885; Mississippi, 1850–61, 1865; Brown, 1850; North Carolina, 1850–61, 1887; Harvard, 1851–57, 1860–91; Miami, 1852–73, 1889; South Carolina, 1852–61; Kenyon, 1852; Oakland College, 1852–61; Virginia, 1852–61, 1865; Dartmouth, 1853; Kentucky Military Institute, 1854–61; Middlebury, 1854; Michigan, 1855; Williams, 1855; Lafayette, 1855; Hamilton, 1856; Colgate, 1856; College of City of New York, 1856; Rochester, 1856; Union, 1856–69; Cumberland, 1857–62, 1866–74; Centenary (La.), 1858–62; Washington and Jefferson, 1858–62; Union University (Tenn.), 1861–62; Rutgers, 1861; Troy University, 1861–62; De Pauw, 1866; Wesleyan, 1867; Washington and Lee, 1867–78; Rensselaer Polytechnic, 1867; Western Reserve, 1868; Cornell, 1870; Chicago, 1870–85, 1893; Syracuse, 1871; Columbia, 1874; California, 1876; Trinity, 1879; Central University (Ky.), 1885, Vanderbilt, 1889; Minnesota, 1889; Massachusetts Institute of Technology, 1889. Buildings are owned by the society at Yale, Amherst, North Carolina, Kenyon, Dartmouth, Michigan, Williams, Hamilton, Colgate, Rochester, Rutgers, Wesleyan, and Cornell. Crimson, blue, and gold are the colors. Prominent among the 13,000 members of D. K. E. are these: college presidents, William P. Johnston of Tulane University, Cyrus Northrop of Minnesota, Martin Kellogg of California, George E. Mac Lean of Nebraska, Albion W. Small and Nathaniel Butler of Colby, and the late Francis A. Walker of the Massachusetts Institute of Technology; authors, Julian Hawthorne, Charlton T. Lewis, Rob-

BADGE OF D.K.E.

ert Grant, Theodore Winthrop, John Bach McMaster, Justin Winsor, Edward Bellamy, William L. Alden, William T. Harris, and T. R. Lounsbury; publishers, Henry Holt and A. C. McClurg; United States Senators, Brice, Butler, Dubois, Gibson, Grover, Lodge, Patton, and Washburn; the late Governor William E. Russell, of Massachusetts; Ex-Governors McCreary of Kentucky and Plaisted of Maine; Whitelaw Reid, formerly Minister to France; Stewart L. Woodford, Ambassador to France; John D. Long, the present Secretary of the Navy, and Ex-Secretary Hilary A. Herbert; Theodore Roosevelt, recently Assistant Secretary of the Navy; Wayne McVeagh, formerly Attorney General; Charles S. Fairchild, once Secretary of the Treasury; Ex-Postmaster General Bissell; Bishops Lawrence of Massachusetts, Robertson of Missouri, White of Indiana, Dudley of Kentucky, Vincent of Southern Ohio, Peterkin of West Virginia, and Elliott of Western Texas. In all of the large Northern cities the D. K. E. is represented by many alumni, and unlike most other fraternities of Northern origin it has a Southern wing of great strength.

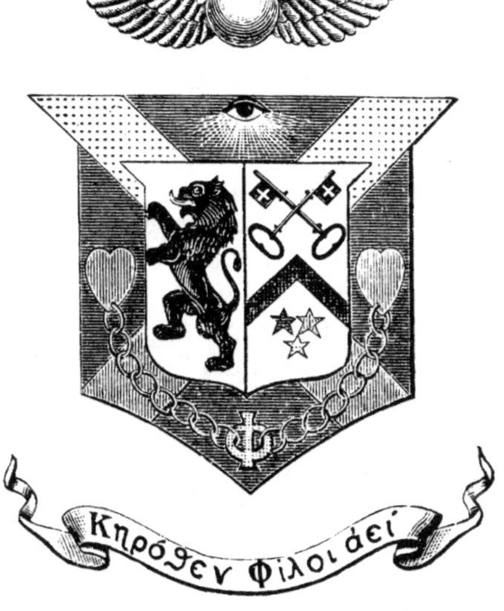

ARMS OF DELTA KAPPA EPSILON.

Omicron, the Michigan branch of Delta Kappa Epsilon, was instituted February 24, 1855, with seven juniors as charter members. The chapter has flourished from the outset. In 1872 an incorporation under the title "The Omicron Literary Association" was effected. Six years later the closed temple owned by the society in Williams street was built and dedicated, and at Commencement in 1889 the chapter house of rough-hewn boulder stone, 81 South State street, was formally opened. The lot on which the house stands is 100 by 120 feet. Among the alumni are ex-Circuit Judge W. D. Williams, '57, of Ontonagon; Ozora P. Stearns, '58, of

Duluth, Minn., formerly U. S. Senator; Professor Bradley M. Thompson, '58, of the Michigan Law School; Raymond C. Davis, '59, Librarian of our University; Claudius B. Grant, '59, of the Supreme Court of Michigan; the late Professor Elisha Jones, '59, of the University; Augustus H. Pettibone, '59, Representative in Congress; Edward H. Butler, '61, of Detroit, formerly State Treasurer; Jacob L. Greene, '61, of Hartford; the late Walter S. Perry, '61, Superintendent of Schools, of Ann Arbor; George P. Sanford, '62, of the Lansing Journal; Regent Levi L. Barbour, '63, of Detroit; the late Seth C. Moffat, '64, Representative in Congress; Newton H. Winchell, '66, Professor of Geology in the University of Minnesota; Charles F. Brush, '69, the inventor of the Brush Electric Light; Harlow P. Davock, '70, of the Detroit Bar; James D. Hawks, '70; Ex-Representative in Congress William C. Maybury, '70, now Mayor of Detroit; U. S. Circuit Court Clerk Walter S. Harsha, '71; DeWitt H. Taylor, '71, Henry Russel, '73, Bryant Walker, '76, Henry M. Campbell, '76, W. J. Gray, '77, and Alexis C. Angell, '78, all of the Detroit Bar; Hamilton Dey, '72, banker, of Detroit; Dr. Ernest T. Tappey, '73, of Detroit; Attorney-General F. A. Maynard, '74, of Grand Rapids; Professor A. V. E. Young, '75, of Northwestern University; John H. Avery, '77 *p*, of Detroit; Professor George H. Harrower, '78, of the Agricultural College; and Professor James R. Angell, '90, of the University of Chicago.

CHAPTER HOUSE OF DELTA KAPPA EPSILON.

Delta Kappa Epsilon claims the following members of the University baseball nines, 1864–98: A. E. Wilkinson, '69, W. C. Maybury, '70, A. G. Bishop, '73, F. A. Maynard, '74, H. A. Thayer, '74, G. H. Abbott, '75, C. S. Burch, '75, P. R. Wilson, '75, W. F. Baxter, '77, W. W. Augur, '78, W. H. Murphy, '79, A. S. Deacon, '80, C. H. Hodges, '82, J. M. Jaycox, '87, W. H. Muir, '88, G. P. Codd, '91, J. C. Condon, '96, J. W. Hollister, '96 *l*, W. W. Waterman, '97, and F. C. Condon, '99. In the football teams the following members have played: A. C. Angell, '78, C. H. Campbell, '80, J. M. Jaycox, '87, W. R. Trowbridge, '89 *m*, W. D. Ball,

'90, R. S. Freund, '96, and J. S. Freund, '97. Of the tennis champions D. K. E. includes in its ranks J. M. Jaycox, '87, W. H. Muir, '88, J. R. Angell, '90, and G. P. Codd, '91.

T. C. Abbott, formerly President of the Agricultural College; the late Professor James R. Boise; J. A. Corbin, of Pontiac; John M. Gregory, of the U. S. Civil Service; Uriah B. Lawton; the poet Bayard Taylor; and the late Professor Alexander Winchell, are ranked as honorary members of the Omicron of D. K. E. The roll, in addition to the seven just mentioned, is as follows:

'56 Lemon Barnes, A. B.,
" *Henry C. Champion, A. B.,
" *James P. Jones, A. B.,
" Marcus A. O. Packard, A. B.,
" Frederic Rowe, A. B.,
" John Q. A. Sessions, A. B.,
" *Lyman A. Soule, A. B.,
'57 William M. Hill, A. B.,
" *Davis H. Taylor, A. B.,
" Edward G. Thurber, A. B.,
" *Zelotes Truesdell, B. S.,
" *William D. Williams, B. S.,
'58 George A. Armstrong,
" William Ball,
" *Luther Beckwith, B. S.,
" *George W. Benedict,
" *Oliver C. Comstock,
" Wesley A. Green, A. B.,
" Ruel M. Johnson, B. S.,
" *Ozora P. Stearns, B. S.,
" Bradley M. Thompson, B. S.,
'59 Augustus A. Chapin, A. B.,
" Raymond C. Davis,
" *George A. Flanders, A. B.,
" Claudius B. Grant, A. B.,
" *Elisha Jones, A. B.,
" Charles B. Lamborn, A. B.,
" Augustus H. Pettibone, A. B.,
" *Charles F. Taylor,
'60 Almon L. Aldrich, B. S.,
" *Augustus W. Chapman, A. B.,
" *Edwin D. Fiske, A. B.,
" *Simeon C. Guilde, A. B.,
" Charles H. McCreery, A. B.,
" Luther Mendenhall, A. B.,
" S. G. Ward,
'61 *Orville S. Abbott, B. S.,
" *Frederick Arn, B. S.,
" Edward H. Butler,
" *William Gillette, B. S.,
" Jacob L. Greene,
" Charles D. Gregory, A. B.,
" John C. Johnson, B. S.,
" John Smith Lloyd, A. B.,
" *Samuel R. B. Lord, A. B.,
'61 *Walter McCollum, A. B.,
" *Henry O. Newcomb, A. B.,
" *Walter S. Perry, A. B.,
" *George P. Sanford, B. S.,
" Edward Searing, A. B.,
" *Eli L. Starr,
" Roswell B. Taylor, B. S.,
" Robert H. Tripp, A. B.,
'62 William W. E. Armbruster, B. S.,
" *John E. Colby, A. B.,
" *Marvin A. Gaylord, A. B.,
" Henry W. Hayward,
" Samuel Howard, A. B.,
" *William E. Nelson, A. B.,
" *Samuel E. Perry, A. B.
" *Moses K. Rosebrugh, A. B.,
" Charles P. Silkman,
" James I. Van Keuren, A. B.,
" *Aaron A. Watkins, A. B.,
'63 Levi L. Barbour, A. B.,
" *John B. Beane,
" Ansel B. Denton,
" *George F. Fish, A. B.,
" Edward P. Kibbee,
" *Ezra D. Lay, Jr., A. B.,
" *Lyford Peavey,
" Edward N. Skinner,
" *Theophilus B. Smyth, B. S.,
" *Henry H. Winn,
'64 *William S. Brewster, A. B.,
" Gordon Y. Gray, LL. B.,
" *Horace V. Knight,
" Herbert A. Lee, A. B.,
" *Seth C. Moffat, LL. B. '63,
" Charles S. Newton,
" *Scovel C. Stacy, A. B.,
" Frank A. Todd,
'65 Horace E. Burt,
" Albert A. Day,
" George L. Graves,
" Sandford B. Ladd, A. B.,
" *Homer C. Powers, B. S.,
" Arthur H. Snow, A. B.,
" *Louis Stoskopf,
" *Francis G. Woodruff,

'66 Sidney Beckwith, A. B.,
" James K. Blish, A. B.,
" William E. Butler,
" Luther Conant,
" Edward S. Elmer, A. B.,
" *Edwin D. Kelley, A. B.,
" Charles D. Martin,
" Lewis E. Prindle,
" Charles A. Sanford, A. B.,
" *James M. Scott, A. B.,
" Newton H. Winchell, A. B.,
'67 William M. Dwight,
" *Isaac N. Elwood, A. B.,
" *George A. Foster, A. B.,
" William S. Roberts, Jr.,
" Leander A. Sheetz,
" Amos Wakelin,
" Edward W. Wetmore, A. B.,
'68 Edward C. Burns, C. E.,
" Lewis W. Hallock,
" Edward L. Hessenmueller, A. B.,
" George S. Hickey, A. B.,
" William E. Lown,
'69 Charles F. Brush, M. E.,
" Egbert J. Mapes,
" Lucian Swift, Jr., M. E.,
" *John Whiting, C. E.,
" Alfred E. Wilkinson, A. B.,
'70 John A. Baldwin, A. B.,
" Darius Boughton, M. D.,
" *Thomas H. Bush, A. B.,
" *George T. Campau, A. B.,
" Harlow P. Davock, A. B.,
" James D. Hawks,
" Edward P. King,
" William C. Maybury, LL. B. '70,
" William L. Oge,
" Frederick Perkins,
" Robertson Winchell, A. B.,
'71 Theodore A. Felch, Ph. B.,
" Walter S. Harsha, A. B.,
" Alexander B. Raymond, C. E.,
" Edward B. Sumner, B. S.,
" DeWitt H. Taylor, LL. B.,
" Floyd Baker Wilson, A. B.,
'72 Frank D. Andrus, A. B.,
" Alexander M. Campau, Jr.,
" Hamilton Dey, Ph. B.,
" William H. Hinman, B. S.,
" *Joseph C. Jones, A. B.,
" James H. Maguire, A. B.,
" William H. McKee, A. B.,
" *Addison Moffat, A. B.,
" William S. Scovill,
" Theodore B. Wilson, A. B.
'73 William Benson, A. B.,
" Arthur G. Bishop, B. S.,
" *Sherwood R. Peabody, A. B.,
" Henry Russel, A. B.,
'73 Ernest T. Tappey, A. B.,
" *Edward E. Thayer, A. B.,
" Charles McA. Winchell, C. E.,
" Edward W. Wood, A. B.,
'74 *p* Charles M. Crofoot,
" James H. Glover, Ph. B.,
" Louis B. King, Ph. B.,
" Fred A. Maynard, A. B.,
" Herbert A. Thayer, A. B,
" Charles H. Walker,
" *Edward W. Withey, A. B.,
'75 *George H. Abbott, Ph. B.,
" Henry G. Allen,
" Frank W. Ball, Ph. B.,
" Charles S. Burch, A. B.,
" *Montgomery T. Campau,
" Franklin N. Fish,
" Frank W. Fletcher, Ph. B.,
" William F. Gelston, A. B.,
" Orlo Phelps,
" Walter S. Russel, C. E.,
" Percy R. Wilson, Ph. B.,
" Abram V. E. Young, Ph. B.,
'76 Henry M. Campbell, Ph. B.,
" Charles D. Cone,
" Frank L. Felch, A. B.,
" Howard B. Smith, A. B.,
" Louis C. Stanley, A. B.,
" Bryant Walker, A. B.,
" Robert J. Young, A. B.,
'77 *p* John H. Avery,
" Witter F. Baxter,
" Edward A. Gilbert, A. B.,
" William J. Gray, A. B.,
'78 Alexis C. Angell, A. B.,
" Walter W. Augur, A. B.,
" Walter H. Cheever,
" George F. Foster,
" George H. Harrower, A. B.,
" Henry W. Judd, M. E.,
" William V. Moore, A. B.,
" James T. Shaw, A. B.,
" Sidney B. Wight, M. E.,
" Ross Wilkins, Ph. B.,
'79 Henry W. Ashley, A. B.,
" Rathbun Fuller,
" *p* William S. McCay,
" *William B. Morris,
" William H. Murphy,
" John R. Russel, A. B.,
'80 John Biddle,
" Charles H. Campbell, Ph. B.,
" Andrew S. Deacon,
" Samuel E. Wheat,
'81 Samuel Chandler, A. B.,
" Allan M. Fletcher,
" Wetmore Hunt, Ph. B.,
" Charles H. Kumler, A. B.,
" George A. Lederle, C. E.,

" Frank C. Mandell, A. B.,
" Delos L. Parker. Ph. B.,
" Charles A. Reed, A. B.,
" Charles T. Thompson, LL. B. '80,
" Louis D. Wight, B. L.,
" Frederick B. Wood, LL. B.,
'82 Edward McE. Benson,
" Benjamin P. Brodie, A. B.,
" Malcolm W. Edgar, B. S.,
" Robert T. Gray, Ph. B.,
" Charles H. Hodges,
" Henry S. Pratt, A. B.,
" Frederick W. Whiting, Ph. B.,
" George Wiley,
'83 Charles H. Black, A. B.,
" Bethune Duffield, A. B.,
" Henry A. Mandell, Ph. B.,
" Edwin L. Strong,
" William G. Webster,
" Charles T. Wilkins, Ph. B.,
'84 Charles S. Ashley, A. B.,
" *Florence L. Beeson,
" Willard M. Clapp,
" Harold O. Crane,
" Frank S. Parker, LL. B. '87,
'85 Preston S. Fancher,
" Charles L. Greene,
" Leonard F. Hatch,
" George B. Sheehy, A. B.,
'86 John E. Burchard,
" Louis E. Dunham, A. B.,
" Charles S. Young,
'87 James F. Blaine,
" George A. Burden,
" George L. Canfield,
" George P. Cary, Ph. B.,
" John W. Case,
" Charles H. Cooley, A. B.,
" Rufus N. Crossman,
" Frederich W. Hodges, B. S.,
" John McI. Jaycox, B. S.,
" Samuel K. Pittman, Ph. B.,
" William R. Trowbridge,
'88 Louis K. Comstock, Ph. B.,
" Henry H. Cushing,
" George W. Kimball,
" William H. Muir, B. S,
" Walter R. Parker, B. S.,
" William M. Strong,
" Herbert J. Stull, A. B.,
'89 William H. Day,
" *Arthur S. Hebard,
" William C. Hebard,
" Otho S. Stull, B. S.,
'90 James R. Angell, A. B.,
" William D. Ball, B. S.,
" Arthur H. Bannon, Ph. B.,
" Frederick B. Close,
" *Frederick W. Crane,
'90 Henry W. Douglas, B. S.,
" Frederick T. Ducharme,
" *m* Harvey McC. Haseltine,
" Frank A. Roda,
" John R. Rogers, B. S.,
" Henry P. Strong,
" Charles S. Withey
'91 George P. Codd, A. B.,
" Thomas B. Cooley, A. B.,
" Roger W. Griswold,
" Franklin S. Hutchinson,
" Harrison B. McGraw, A. B.,
" Frederick S. Richmond, B. S.,
" *Edward H. Smith, Ph. B.,
" John McD. Stull,
'92 Paul F. Bagley,
" Harry C. Bulkley, A. B.,
" Levi D. Johnson,
" William J. LeH. Lyster, Ph. B.,
" John B. Miller,
" Harry T. Smith, A. B.,
'93 Frank R. Gilchrist, B. S.,
" Rufus G. Lathrop, A. B.,
" Walter O. Smith,
" William S. Whiting,
" Lawrence J. Whittemore,
" Edwin C. Wilkinson, Ph. B.,
'94 Thomas P. Bradfield, Ph. B.,
" William B. Canfield, Ph. B.,
" Alfred B. Connable, B. L.,
" *Vincent R. Dwyer,
" Alfred H. Hunt, A. B.,
" David K. Paige,
'95 Arthur C. Bloomfield, A. B.,
" Henry L. L. H. Lyster, A. B.,
" Harry M. Mason,
" Samuel Medbury,
" James O. Murfin, B. L.,
" George R. Russel, A. B.,
'96 John C. Condon, B. S.,
" Dexter M. Ferry, Jr.,
" Raynor S. Freund,
" Stuart E. Galbraith, B. L.,
" Edmund R. Harrington,
" Kirke Lathrop, B. L.,
" George A. Marston,
" Elijah W. Meddaugh,
" Frank E. Miller,
" Harry G. Nicol,
" Albert W. Russel,
'97 Dudley P. Bounell,
" Jed B. Freund,
" Herbert A. Gallup,
" John H. Howard,
" Theodore C. Lyster, Ph. B.,
" W. Howard O'Brien, B. S.,
" W. Whitney Waterman,
'98 Charles B. Davis,
" Walter H. Jennings,

'98 Edward L. Moseley,
" Orville W. Prescott,
" Walter H. Shelby,
" Angus Smith,
" Harold B. Wetmore,
'99 Irving M. Bean,
" John C. Bradfield,
" Frank C. Condon,
" Ernest F. Harrington,
" Frederick A. Leas,
" Harry B. Potter,
" Robert B. Potter,
" Rodolphe R. Reilly,
'99 Julian H. Thomson,
'00 George S. Benson, Jr.,
" Ralph E. Gilchrist,
" Frederick H. Green,
" Arthur W. Plum,
'01 William Cowie,
" Woolsey W. Hunt,
" Charles G. Lathrop,
" Thomas L. B. Lyster,
" Charles I. Marston,
" William R. Nellegar,
" Forris DeA. Stevens,
" Charles MacM. Wetmore.

The following members of D. K. E., initiates of other chapters, and students in the professional schools of our University, are not included in the official list of the Omicron Chapter:

'57 *m* James B. Ford, M. D.,
'63 *l* *Samuel B. Spear,
'65 *m* Charles W. Milliken, M. D.,
'66 *l* Frank Evans,
" *l* De Witt C. Marsten,
" *l* James W. Owens,
" *m* Philip C. Porter,
" *l* Nelson L. Rood, LL. B.,
'67 *l* Calvin S. Brice,
" *l* George P. Davis, LL. B.,
" *l* John J. Davis,
" *l* Le Roy Parker,
" *m* John B. Tyler, M. D.,
'68 *m* Frank H. Carson,
'69 *m* Alfred H. Champlin, M. D.,
'70 *l* Walter J. Collins,
" *l* James F. Elliott,
" *l* John N. Irwin,
" *l* John N. Wyman,
'71 *l* *Edward Egbert, LL. B.,
" *l* James E. Riddick, LL. B.,
" *l* John T. Stringer, LL. B.,
'72 *l* William R. Smith, LL. B.,
'73 *l* George W. Cass, LL. B.,
'74 *l* Howard E. Henderson,
" *ph* Finley B. Pugh, Ph. C.,
" *l* Eberle D. Smith,
" *l* Edwin F. Sweet, LL. B.,
" *l* *Thomas A. Taylor, LL. B.,
" *Robert E. Williams, C. E.,
'75 *m* George G. Baker, M. D.,
'76 *l* *Charles A. Kebler, LL. B.,
" *l* Charles L. Lewis,
" *l* John R. Ranney, LL. B.,
" *m* John E. Weaver,
'77 *m* Walter Schell,
" *l* *Willis E. Walker,
'78 *l* Charles E. Hale, LL. B.,
'78 *m* Olin Kinne, M. D.,
" *m* George H. Littlefield, M. D.,
'79 *p* Charles W. Koons, Ph. C.,
'80 *m* Frederick Baker, M. D.,
" *l* Henry McFarland,
" *l* Elroy D. Sherman, LL. B.,
" *l* Thomas M. Sloan, LL. B.,
" *h* Ashley J. Williams,
'81 *l* George W. Benham, LL. B.,
" George F. Kenaston, A. M.,
" *m* John G. Kennan, M. D.,
" *l* Edgar H. Loyhed, LL. B.,
" *l* Thomas B. Marston,
'83 *l* Edward W. Peterson, LL. B.,
" *l* Orson H. Brooke,
'84 *l* Lincoln Brooke,
'87 *m* Leonard F. Hatch, M. D.,
" *l* Charles Reed, LL. B.,
" *l* James N. Saunders, LL. B.,
'88 *g* Sedgwick Mather.
'90 *h* Leigh Y. Baker, M. D.,
'91 *l* George S. Johnson, LL. B.,
'92 *l* Victor M. Elting, LL. B.,
" *l* Charles S. Witbeck,
" *l* Haynie R. Pearson,
'94 *m* William S. Hubbard,
" *l* Lindsay Russell, Jr., LL. B.,
" *ag* Hinckley Smith,
" *l* Luther O. Wadleigh, LL. B.
'96 *l* John W. Hollister, LL. B.,
" *l* Wallace H. Prescott,
" *m* J. W. Van Dusen, M. D.,
" *l* Frederick W. Winkler,
'98 *m* Thomas S. Burr,
" *m* Jesse K. Marden,
" *l* Rufus P. Ranney,
'99 *e* Cary D. Terrell,

Delta Phi, the third in age of the Greek-letter fraternities, was founded at Union College, November 18, 1827, by nine members of the class of '28. Sixteen chapters lettered successively from Alpha to Pi, have been established at Union, Brown, New York, Columbia, Rutgers, Harvard, Pennsylvania, Princeton, Michigan, North Carolina, Rensselaer Polytechnic, Colgate, Lehigh, Johns Hopkins, Sheffield (Yale) Scientific School, and Cornell, those at Princeton, Michigan, North Carolina, and Colgate, being at present inactive. Of the 3,000 members the following may be named: Garret A. Hobart, Vice-President of the United States; William H. Seward; Ex-Governor William Gaston of Massachusetts; General Adin B. Underwood of Boston; the Rev. T. Stafford Drowne of Long Island; United States Senator Christopher Magee; the late Hon. Samuel S. Cox; Ex-Chancellor Howard Crosby of New York; Ex-Presidents Rankin of Hobart and Totten of Trinity; Professor R. Ogden Doremus; Professor Cornelius R. Agnew of Columbia; the late Bishop W. E. Armitage; Sanford R. Gifford, the artist; and Ex-Governor George C. Ludlow of New Jersey. White, blue, and white are the colors. The chapters at Columbia, Rutgers, and Yale, own buildings. Iota, the Michigan branch, was instituted late in 1855 with eight charter members, chiefly from the classes of '58 and '59. George N. Brady of Detroit, was one of the founders. In 1856 D. O. Farrand, subsequently distinguished as a surgeon in Detroit, and Cushman K. Davis, now United States Sena-

BADGE OF DELTA PHI.

ARMS OF DELTA PHI.

tor from Minnesota, were initiated. Other good men were added to the roll, but the society never became as strong in Michigan as it is in other institutions, and in the autumn of 1875, after a chequered life of twenty years, the Iota, discouraged by the graduation of the strongest class it had ever secured, returned its charter. Three of the five academic undergraduates joined other societies, and one abjured college fraternities altogether. In 1892 the fraternity contemplated a revival, and a number of men stood ready to take the charter, but the ground had been occupied by younger organizations. The chapter was represented upon the baseball nine of the University by J. C. Bigger, '68 *l*, and F. N. Wood, '75. Following are the names of the 104 men carried on the chapter's roll:

'56 *Dwight D. Stebbins, A. B.,
— George N. Brady,
'57 Cushman K. Davis, A. B.,
" *D. Osbourn Farrand,
" Charles M. McDonald,
" *George M. Waldron,
" *m* *Allen M. Walton,
'58 *Adolphus G. Armington,
" *George M. Chester,
" *m* Albert M. Helmer, M. D.,
" *Myron E. N. Howell, B. S.
" *m* Thomas Lothrop, M. D.,
" James P. Mosher,
" *Judd M. Mott, A. B,
'59 *James A. Brown, M. D. '63,
" Alvin J. Cole,
" *m* John V. Cowles,
" Clayton J. Croft,
" George E. Cuming, B. S.,
" Robert E. Frazer, B. S.,
" Robert Heath,
" *James Kingsley, LL. B. '63,
" S. Thomas Moore,
" *l* Gerritt S. Van Valkenburgh,
'60 Henry S. Noble,
" Barry Taylor,
" *John M. Wirts, LL. B.,
'61 John K. Cravens,
" *l* William A. Martin, LL. B.,
" Hugh M. Murphy,
'62 Edward B. Darlington,
" *Lewis Drake,
" A. Theodore Dudley,
" *Aaron C. Jewett, A. B.,
" George Kingsley, LL. B.,
" *Joseph McConnell,
" Charles T. Parks,
" Daniel D. Thurber,
" Charles B. Wood, A. B.,
'63 *l* *Ferdinand A. Ashley,
" Nelson Booth,
" James H. Fairchild, LL. B.,
" *William R. Hosmer,
" *Franklin Johnson,
" *l* William H. Thurber,
" Edward R. Wilcox,
'64 James F. Benedict,
" William J. Booth, B. S.,
" William D. Morton,
" *S. Frank Walker, B. S.,
'65 Henry E. Duncan,
" *Gove Porter,
" *l* George M. Walker, LL. B.
'66 Gabriel W. Crutcher,
" William C. Frew, B. S.,
" *Levy M. Hathaway,
" Henry Smith, A. B.,
'67 *Joseph S. Eaves,
" *H. Clay Gould,
" *l* Harrison Hume, LL. B.,
" Henry P. Rodgers,
" *l* Levi D. Vincent,
'68 Brutus J. Clay, M. E.,
" George C. Fry, A. B.,
" Edgar S. Johnston, C. E.,
" *l* William J. Patterson,
'69 John C. Bigger, LL. B. '68,
" William Borden,
" Adam H. Heldenbrand,
" *m* James G. Hunt,
" Benjamin L. C. Lothrop, A. B.,
" *l* Thomas E. Turner, LL. B.,
'70 Henry B. Farwell,
" Walter E. Johnson,
" *p* Albert Taylor,
'71 John J. Aiken,
" J. Frank Brooks,
" Belno A. Brown,

'71 *l* Lewis L. Kettle,
" William O. Snyder,
" *m* William M. Walker,
'72 Frank C. Duncan,
" *l* Frank M. Hoyt,
" Edward H. Jones,
" Lewis B. Parsons,
'73 *Samuel P. Barstow,
" Addison Millard,
" Joseph Painter, Jr.,
" Frank W. Rorke,
'74 *George H. Jameson, A. B.,
" *l* Stewart Clark,
'75 Fred G. Bulkley,
" Bartolo D'Aubigné,
" Walter J. Heyser, B. S.,
" Charles V. Hicks,
" Arthur D. Lathrop,
" Leslie C. McPherson, A. B.,
" *George E. Pantlind, C. E.,
" *l* Benjamin F. Webster,
" Frank N. Wood,
'76 Harness R. Qninn,
" Frederick G. Waite,
'77 *George K. Brown,
" George H. Lathrop.

Josiah Medbury, '78 *m*, was a member of Delta Phi at Brown University before coming to Ann Arbor.

Sigma Phi, the second in age of the intercollegiate fraternities, was founded at Union College, March 4, 1827, by four students. A branch at Hamilton was formed in 1831; another was instituted at Williams in 1834; a fourth chapter existed in the New York University 1835–48; a fifth chapter was established at Hobart in 1840; a sixth, at the University of Vermont in 1845; a seventh lived at Princeton, 1853–60; and later branches have been instituted at Michigan (1858), Lehigh (1887), and Cornell (1890). Seven of the eight chapters now living own houses. Light-blue and white are the colors. The fraternity is exclusively Eastern in traditions and sentiment. There have been in all about 2,100 members, among whom may be named the late Charles J. Folger, Secretary of the U. S. Treasury; John J. Knox, former Controller of the Treasury; John Bigelow, Ex-Minister to France; Major-General Daniel Butterfield, of New York; U. S. Senators J. J. Ingalls and Theodore Otis; John Cochrane and Charles B. Sedgwick, Representatives in Congress; Ex-Governors Hartranft of Pennsylvania, Hoffman of New York, and Walker of Virginia; George F. Comstock member of the New York Court of Appeals; Elihu Root of the New York Bar; Dr. Lewis A. Sayre of New York City; the late Thomas S. Preston, Vicar-General of New York; Bishop George Worthington of Kansas; Bishop Lemuel H. Wells of Spokane; Bishop Charles E. Cheney, of the Reformed Episcopal Church; the late Rev. Henry M. Field of The New York Evangelist; Anson Judd Upson, Chancellor of the University of New York; Presidents Buckham of Vermont University, Stryker of Hamilton, and Hastings of Union Theological Seminary; Ex-

BADGE OF SIGMA PHI.

Presidents Andrews of Marietta, Le Conte of California, Eaton of Madison, Sterling of Kenyon, and White of Cornell; Professors Oren Root of Hamilton, William D. Whitney of Yale, Asahel C. Kendrick of Rochester, and Charles S. Denison of Michigan.

In 1849 steps were taken under the direction of the Hon. Edward L. Fuller, Union '30, and of other Sigma Phi graduates, to organize a chapter in Michigan. Eight men were selected from the classes of '49, '50, and '51, for a petitioning club, and four others from '52 stood as conditional petitioners. But the Society War necessitated the withdrawal of the petition; and not until 1858 was the Alpha of Michigan—which owed its origin largely to Professor Andrew D. White—instituted. Only one of the first petitioners has been received into the chapter. An incorporation under the laws of the State has been effected, and the society owns a chapter house and lodge delightfully located on a spur of the bluffs overlooking the valley of the Huron. The property was bought for $5,000 from Professor Tyler in March, 1882. Among the alumni of the Alpha of Michigan are the late Theodore R. Chase, '49, of Detroit; the late Richard Beardsley, '59, Consul General at Cairo; Ex-Regent Samuel S. Walker, '61, Judge Conway W. Noble, '63, of Cleveland; Colonel Henry C. Christiancy, '63; Circuit Judge Edward DeW. Kinne, '64, of Ann Arbor; Henry A. Conant, '65, former Secretary of State of Michigan; John M. Hinchman,'66, and George B. Remick,'66, both of Detroit; John F. Lawrence, '66, of Ann Arbor; Ex-Circuit Judge Herman W. Stevens, '66, of Port Huron; Dr. Richard S. Dewey, '68, author of the "Prize College Song", 1869; William A. Butler, '69, of Detroit; William A. Childs, '69, of New York City; Charles P. Gilbert, '70, the late George H. Lothrop, '70, General Henry B. Lothrop, '77,

ARMS OF SIGMA PHI.

CHAPTER HOUSE OF SIGMA PHI.

Alfred E. Brush, '73, Franklin H. Walker, '73, James V. D. Willcox, '75, and Harrie R. Newberry, '78, all of Detroit; Eugene F. Cooley, '70, of Lansing; Henry G. Prout, '75, formerly Governor-General of the Soudan; Charles R. Wing, '74, of Monroe; George S. Willits, '78, and Robert H. McMurdy, '80, of the Chicago Bar; Edward H. Ozmun, '82, of the St. Paul Bar; and Professor Mortimer E. Cooley of the University.

The following members of Sigma Phi have been members of the Michigan baseball nines: O. P. Bills, '65, J. M. Hinchman, '66, W. H. Boardman, '68, W. A. Butler, '69, E. F. Cooley, '70, G. H. Lothrop, '70, R. H. McMurdy, '80, L. S. Bigelow, '86, J. D. Hibbard, '87, Lincoln MacMillan, '90, and E. L. Cooley, '99. In the football teams of the University Sigma Phi has been represented by F. G. Allen, '81, E. P. Hathaway, '82, N. C. Paine, '92, E. D. Wickes, '93, Roger Sherman, '94, H. Mortimer Senter, '96, J. DeF. Richards, '98, and Leo J. Keena, '01.

Following is the roll of the Michigan Alpha of Sigma Phi:

'49 *Theodore R. Chase, A. B.,
'58 *John Q. A. Fritchey, A. B.,
" *John W. Paine, B. S.,
" *Charles S. Patterson, B. S.,
" Alexander Richard, B. S.,
" *Samuel E. Smith, B. S.,
'59 *Richard Beardsley, B. S.,
" *Judson C. Lowell, A. B.,
" *Richard C. Sabin, A. B.,
'60 Charles D. Lyon,
'61 William E. Crumme,
" Archibald B. Darrah,
" William Farnsworth,
" Cholwell Knox, LL. B.,
" Samuel S. Walker, B. S.,
— *m* *Fred C. Hober,
'62 Hiram R. Johnson,
" Charles H. Lewis, A. B.,
" *William F. Rogers,
" William J. Stackhouse,
'63 Henry C. Christiancy,
" John B. Davenport,
" William C. Green,
" Conway W. Noble, A. B.,
" Charles H. Palmer, B. S.,
" *Lewis H. Redfield,
" Rollin P. Saxe,
" Uriah L. Sayrs,
'64 *Frederick A. Buhl,
" Edward DeW. Kinne, A. B.,
" Edward C. Page,
" *l* Emory D. Potter Jr., LL. B.,
" *Jesse P. Winegar,
'65 Lamont C. Bidwell,
" Oscar P. Bills, A. B.,
" James C. Christiancy,
" Henry A. Conant,
" James C. Darragh,
" *Mills H. Landon,
" *William S. Oliver,
" Rufus J. Palen.
" *Ossian R. Ross,
'66 *Theodore R. Adams,
" John M. Hinchman,
" John F. Lawrence, A. B.,
" George B. Remick, A. B.,
" William A. Rogers,
" Herman W. Stevens, A. B.,
" Edward C. Stoddard, LL. B.,
" William B. Thompson, LL. B.
" Charles W. Wright,
'67 Henry P. Churchill, A. B.,
" Horton H. Drury, A. B.,
" Henry N. French, A. B.,
" Charles G. Hickox,
" Dwight N. Lowell, A. B.,
" *George L. Philips,
" Charles H. Starkweather,
'68 William H. Boardman, A. B.,
" Richard S. Dewey, M. D.,
" *Clarence N. Howell, A. B.,
" Isaiah G. Lewis,
" Fillmore M. Smith, M. E.,
" Joseph M. Stoutt, A. B.,
" William A. Butler, B. S.,
" William A. Childs,

'69 *Frederick A. Dudgeon, A. B.,
" William W. Lockwood,
'70 Eugene F. Cooley, A. B.,
" *William T. Emerson, B. S.,
" Charles P. Gilbert, C. E.,
" *George H. Lothrop,
— *m* *Edwin A. Kilbourne,
'71 *George T. Fox, A. B.,
" Charles O. McEntee,
" Charles M. MacLaren,
" Frank M. Millard,
" Henry G. Prout, C. E.,
" *Frank Remick,
" *Harry C. Willcox, B. S.,
'72 *Charles B. Lothrop, A. B.,
" William A. Warner,
'73 Alfred E. Brush, Ph. B.,
" *Eliot H. Brush, Ph. B.,
" *William H. Fox, A. B.,
" William J. Head, C. E.,
" Charles A. Philips,
" Clarence M. Stevens, C. E.,
" Franklin H. Walker, B. S.,
'74 Franklin S. Goodrich,
" Henry B. Goodrich,
" Henry B. Jackson, C. E.,
" Austin W. Mitchell,
" *James F. Potter, B. S.,
" Charles R. Wing, Ph. B.,
'75 Henry D. Bates, C. E.,
" Charles O. Ford,
" James V. D. Willcox,
'76 *Peter E. DeMille,
'77 Stanley C. Bagg,
" Albert W. Hard, Ph. B.,
" Henry B. Lothrop,
'78 *Marion B. Allen, Ph. B.,
" Charles M. Cooley, Ph. B.,
" Clarence Griggs, A. B.,
" Harrie R. Newberry,
" Frank L. Sizer, C. E.,
" George S. Willits, A. B.,
'79 Fred K. Fernald,
" *l* William T. Hall, LL. B.,
" *p* John P. Kelly, Ph. C., M. D.,
" *p* John F. Wallach,
'80 Edwin L. Chapman,
" Robert McMurdy, LL. B.,
" William W. Nash,
" Frank W. Loveland,
'81 Frank G. Allen, A. B.,
" George L. Little,
" *Harry C. Richardson, A. B.,
'82 James S. Collins, A. B.,
" Roger W. Cooley, B. L.,
" Elnathan P. Hathaway,
" William L. Loveland, B. L.,
" *William H. Mitchell, A. B.,
" Percy A. Lane,
'82 Edward H. Ozmun, LL. B.,
" Francis D. Weeks, A. B.,
" *p* William H. White, Ph. C.,
'83 *l* Thomas J. Lynch, LL. B.,
" Willis C. Marsh,
" Edwin E. White, A. M.,
'84 William P. Cantwell, Jr.,
" Elmer Dwiggins, B. L.,
" Frank A. Ross, Ph. B.,
'85 Theodore R. Chapin,
— Mortimer E. Cooley,
" *Frank K. Ferguson,
" Fred W. Job, Ph. B.,
" *m* Charles F. Pettibone, M. D.,
" Delos Thompson, B. L.,
'86 *l* Lewis S. Bigelow,
" *Frank L. Ilgenfritz,
'87 *Charles L. Carter,
" John D. Hibbard, B. S.,
" Charles R. White,
'88 Donnell Davenport,
" George R. Mitchell, A. B.,
'89 Lewis W. Parker, B. L.,
" Everett C. Rockwood, Ph. B.,
" Frank C. Smith, B. S.,
" Charles P. Taylor, Ph. B.,
" Orlando B. Willcox, LL. B.,
'90 Lincoln MacMillan,
" Oliver C. Smith,
" *m* Edgar T. Stephenson, M. D.,
'91 *m* Charles C. Burnett,
" Louis V. DeFoe, B. L.,
" Theodore H. Hinchman, A. B.,
" John A. Jameson, Jr., A. B.,
" Herbert O. Statler, M. D.,
" Lucius E. Torrey,
" John A. Van Ardsdale, A. B.,
'92 Fitzhugh Burns, A. B.,
" Charles A. Howell, B. S.,
" John R. Marfield,
" Nathan C. Paine,
" Alfred D. Rathbone, Jr., A. B.,
" Charles M. Willcox,
'93 Samuel D. Kinne, LL. B.,
" Frank W. McKee,
" Earle C. Peters, Ph. B.,
" Edward D. Wickes, B. S.,
'94 James Blair, B. S.,
" Guy S. Crane,
" Robert F. Hall, A. B.,
" *W. Sheridan Mason,
" Roger Sherman, A. B.,
" Goldwin Starrett, B. S.,
'95 Ford A. Hinchman,
" Jerome Ingersoll,
" Lewis S. McCreary,
" Charles C. Parker, LL. B.,
" Robert L. Wagner,
'96 *l* Sheldon C. Burr,

'96 Melancthon W. Campau,
" Henry P. Hart,
" John H. Porter,
" Royal G. Remick,
" H. Mortimer Senter,
'97 Alexander M. Campau,
" William A. Starrett,
'98 William J. O'Brien,
" J. DeForest Richards,
" Henry W. Standart,
'99 Cuthbert C. Adams,
" Alexander Boyd,
" Walter C. Boynton,
" Frederic V. Carpenter,
" *l* Henry T. Clark, Jr.,
" William M. McKee,
'98 Ralph H. Page,
'99 James J. Parker,
" James B. Pell,
" Duane H. Wager,
'00 Alaton L. C. Atkinson,
" Edgar L. Cooley,
" *l* George von Nieda,
" Ralph L. Roys,
" Lloyd M. Shepard,
" William W. Talman,
'01 Frank R. Blair,
" Leo J. Keena,
" Willing D. Kirk,
" C. Richard Lockwood,
" M. Hubert O'Brien,
" Edwin Porter.

The following members of Sigma Phi, initiated at other colleges, have studied law or medicine in the University:

'58 *m* Horace M. Darling, M. D.,
" *l* Edwin C. Luce, LL. B.,
'66 *l* George P. Bradstreet,
'91 *l* Arthur M. Willcox,
'95 *l* Frank Garrett, LL. B.,

Zeta Psi, the seventh secret society to enter Michigan, was founded in 1846 by John B. Yates Sommers, John M. Skillman, and William H. Dayton, all of New York '49. Following are the colleges of the active and inactive branches: New York University, 1846; Williams, 1848–53, 1881; Rutgers, 1848; Princeton, 1850–78; Pennsylvania, 1850–73, 1876; Colby, 1850; Brown, 1852–61, 1864–78, 1887; Tufts, 1856; Lafayette, 1858; North Carolina, 1852–68, 1885; Michigan, 1858; Rensselear Polytechnic, 1865; Bowdoin, 1868; Virginia, 1868–82, 1885; Cornell, 1869; California; Toronto, 1879; Columbia, 1880; McGill, 1883; Yale, 1888; Leland Stanford, Jr., 1892. Zeta Psi owns buildings at Williams, Rutgers, Pennsylvania, North Carolina, Cornell, Yale, Michigan, and Leland Stanford, Jr. The fraternity is Eastern in its sympathies. White is the color of the fraternity. There are about 4,500 members, among whom are William P. Pepper, the former Provost, and Charles C. Harrison, the present Provost of the University of Pennsylvania. Ex-President Harrison E. Webster, of Union; Ex-President William T. Reid, of California; Professors Albert H. Gallatin, Henry G. Piffard, and Alfred L. Loomis, of New York University; Professors James M. Van Vleck, of Wesleyan, W. L. Wells and E. C. Mitchell, of Pennsylvania; Professors Truman H. Safford, James B. Greenough, Bennett H.

BADGE OF ZETA PSI

16

Nash, and Henry B. Hill, of Harvard; Lucien A. Wait, of the Cornell Faculty; Professor Henry Johnson, of Bowdoin; Alfred Reed of the Supreme Court of New Jersey, and Addison C. Niles of that of California; Judges R. L. Larremore and G. M. Van Hoesen of New York; Ex-U. S. Senator P. W. Hitchcock; Representatives in Congress Horatio Bisbee, Nelson Dingley, G. T. Garrison, James T. Jones, J. E. Leonard, C. E. Phelps, G. D. Robinson, and C. A. Sumner; Seldon Connor, formerly Governor of Maine, and James H. Budd, now Governor of California; Isaac Newton, Chief Engineer U. S. N.; Joseph Nimmo, Jr., Chief of the Bureau of Statistics; A. D. Hazen, formerly Third Assistant Postmaster General; Robert Garrett, Jr., late President of the Baltimore & Ohio R. R.; Rodney Welch of the *Chicago Times*; and the Rev. C. De W. Bridgman, of New York.

VIGNETTE OF ZETA PSI.

To Liberty Emery Holden who had been a member of Zeta Psi at Waterville College (now Colby University) is due the origin of the Michigan branch of this fraternity. Having entered as a junior at Ann Arbor in the autumn of 1856, he became acquainted with James Franklin Spalding of the freshman class, and the two laid plans for the establishment of a chapter. Holden began correspondence with the Waterville Zeta Psi, while Spalding interested certain of his classmates and friends in the project. The negotiations with Zeta Psi were not at first successful, and the little band which Spalding had gotten together decided that some organization was necessary to keep their membership intact, and to form a nucleus for accessions to their numbers. Accordingly, in the spring of 1858 they met at the house of James F. Spalding, and organized themselves into a local society, which they named Alpha Psi. A ritual was prepared, and pins so made that they could easily be changed into Zeta Psi badges were procured from New York jewellers. When the necessary authority had been obtained Mr. Holden initiated four other students, who, with himself, thus became the founders. On Commencement Day, June 23, 1858, the presence of Zeta Psi in Ann Arbor was announced by the appearance on the campus of fifteen members wearing the new badge. The membership increased to twenty-seven in 1859–60, but in the following year differences of opinion led to the withdrawal of twelve members, and the Civil War still further emptied the ranks, so that only two members, seniors, were left in college in the autumn of 1861. Fraternal zeal and activity overcame all obstacles, as they did in 1869–70 when the attendance was sadly reduced, and still later after Commencement in 1883, when only one undergraduate remained. The chapter's name, originally Beta, was changed to Xi in April, 1861. From 1879 to 1883 the Millen property on Washtenaw avenue was occupied as a chapter house. Other houses were rented and occupied until, in the summer of 1890 the society purchased for $6,000 the Hunt property, 512 South State street, directly facing the southwest corner of the campus. It is the intention to replace at an early date the present frame structure with an imposing edifice of stone and brick.

Especially prominent among the Michigan alumni of Zeta Psi are the following: Liberty E. Holden, '58, of the *Cleveland Plain Dealer*; Lewis McLouth, '58, President of the South Dakota Agricultural College; William J. Beal, '59, Professor of Botany in the Agricultural College at Lansing; General William H. H. Beadle, '61, of the South Dakota Normal School; Capt. James E. Eastman, '62, of the United States Army; Judge James E. Hawes, '62, of Xenia, Ohio; Dr. Lewis S. Pilcher, '62, of Brooklyn, N. Y.; Henry H. Swan, '62, Judge of the Federal District Court; William R. Bates,'66, United States Marshal for Eastern Michigan; Cornelius A. Gower, '67, formerly Superintendent of Public Instruction; Leander W. Pilcher, '67, Missionary to China; Isaac M. Weston, '67, recently mayor of Grand

CHAPTER HOUSE OF ZETA PSI.

Rapids; William K. Anderson, '68, now Consul at Hanover; Judge Aaron V. McAlvay, '68, now of our law department; Circuit Judge Frank Emerick, '70, of Alpena; John Eisenmann, '71, the Cleveland architect; Henry T. Thurber, '74, President Cleveland's Private Secretary; Frank H. Culver, '75, of the Chicago Bar; Jerome C. Knowlton, '75, Professor in our Law Department; Ben T. Cable, '76, Representative in Congress; Austin E. Wing, '77, recently National Bank Examiner for Michigan; Henry G. Sherrard, '92, teacher in the Detroit High School; and Lawrence A. McLouth, '87, Pomeroy Ladue, '90, and Frank W. Pine, '94, of the Faculty of New York University. In athletic sports not a few Zeta Psi men at Ann Arbor have been prominent. On the baseball nine have played W. R. Roberts, '77, DeForest Kendall, '82, and A. D. Welton, '89. The football elevens of Michigan have been strengthened by the following members: W. R. Roberts, '77; C. S. Mitchell, '80, E. H. Barmore, '82, F. B. Wormwood, '83, F. L. Smith, '90, and T. L. Chadbourn, Jr., '94.

A list of the members of the Xi of Zeta Psi follows:

'58 Horace Halbert, B. S.,
" Liberty E. Holden, A. B.,
" *Henry A. Humphrey, A. B.,
" Lewis McLouth, A. B.,
'59 William J. Beal, A. B.,
" *James M. Edmunds, A. B.,
" *John G. Everett, A. B.,
" Fayette Hurd, A. B.,
" Daniel Satterthwaite, A. B.,
" John P. Stoddard, A. B.,
'60 Osgood E. Fuller, A. B.,
" *Henry B. Northrop,
" Caleb Parkinson, A. B.,
" James F. Spalding, A. B.,
'61 *Amos W. Abbott,
" William H. H. Beadle, A. B.,
" *Ephraim G. Hall, A. B.,
'62 *John H. Beadle, A. B. '67,
" *l* James M. Burlingame, LL. B.,
" James E. Eastman, A. B.,
" James E. Hawes, LL. B. '62,
" Lewis S. Pilcher, A. B.,
" Henry H. Swan,
'63 David F. Fox,
" *l* *John H. Keep,
" *Henry W. Stevenson, LL. B. '69,
'64 *A. Frank Chaffee, A. B.,
" Nathan P. Cochran,
" *m* *George W. Dudley,
" *l* *Claude Hollywood,
" *l* *Augustus S. McAllister, LL. B.,
" William B. Slemons,
'64 *John P. Swan,
" *Lorison J. Taylor,
" Homer L. Wright,
'65 *m* Jonathan L. Lambert,
" George E. Smith,
'66 *l* William R. Bates,
" *Egbert Bogardus,
" James E. Chambers,
" *l* Johnson N. High, LL. B.,
" George W. Hunt,
" *l* Frank W. Merrick, LL. B.,
" *Benjamin F. Stage, LL. B.,
" *l* Robert L. Warren, LL. B.,
'67 *John O. Andrews, B. S.,
" *l* Daniel G. Cash, LL. B.,
" J. Monroe Darnell, B. S.,
" Cornelius A. Gower, A. B.,
" *m* Isaac W. Heysinger,
" *l* Francis A. Hoffman, Jr., LL. B.,
" Louis P. Judson, C. E.,
" Thomas Parker, Jr.,
" *John G. Pearce,
" *Leander W. Pilcher,
" Isaac M. Weston,
'68 *Arthur A. Abbott,
" Charles H. Allen,
" William K. Anderson, A B.,
" Noah W. Gray,
" Willard A. Kingsley, B. S.,
" Aaron V. McAlvay,
" David R. Murray,
" Rollin J. Reeves, C. E.,

68 Richard B. Robinson,
" William A. Underwood,
69 *l* *Russell H. Bishop, LL. B.,
" John G. Brooks,
" *Julian M. Case,
" Gordon N. Chipman,
" Henry G. Hull,
" Joel S. Kelsey,
" John B. Moore,
" *Harry D. Standart,
'70 *Sherman S. Avery,
" Frank Emerick,
" *l* William G. Howard,
" *l* Marshall L. Howell, LL. B.,
" Clark Olds, B. S.,
" Lloyd Selby,
" *Charles M. Underwood,
" Frank H. Van Cleve,
'71 Elroy McK. Avery, Ph. B.,
" *Emir J. Coon,
" *m* Joseph H. Cowell, M., D.,
" John Eisenmann, C. E.,
" Roy R. Hathaway,
" *Morton W. Latson, A. B.,
" *Edward C. Smith,
" Clarence H. Walker,
'74 *Charles T. Burton, LL. B. '72,
" John E. Ensign, B. S.,
" *William L. Otis,
" *m* *Arthur McD. Ransom,
" John S. Richardson, B. S.,
" Henry T. Thurber, A. B.,
'75 Frank H. Culver, Ph. B.,
" H. Clark Ford, B. S.,
" *l* *Harry H. Francis, LL. B.,
" *L. Wells Keller,
" Jerome C. Knowlton, A. B.,
" *l* William S. Mears,
'76 Ben T. Cable, B. S.,
" *Burton B. Campbell, B. S.,
" *l* Frank W. Chase, LL. B.,
" Louis H. Evans,
" Lester H. Strawn, C. E.,
'77 Charles A. Bosworth, A. B.,
" R. Byron Cardwell,
" Willis R. Roberts, Ph. B.,
" Austin E. Wing,
'78 *John H. Black,
" Charles M. Daugherty, A. B.,
" Harry Dewar,
" *l* Frederic G. Ingersoll, LL. B.,
" *p* Lucius W. Moody, Ph. C.,
" Stuart D. Walling, A. B.,
" George H. Wyman, Jr.,
'79 W. Burton Alderson,
" *William Livingston Axford, Ph.B.,
" *p* *Robert F. Mull, Ph. C.,
" Richard T. Robinson,
'80 *l* William Lamond Axford, LL. B.,
'80 John M. Brewer, A. B.,
" Sam H. DuShane, LL. B. '81,
" John A. Green, Jr., A. B.,
" William W. Lowrey,
" Charles S. Mitchell, Ph. B.,
'81 Charles T. Brace, A. B.,
" Robert P. Clarke,
" *l* William S. Davis, LL. B.,
" Frank A. Foster,
" Charles H. Hutchins,
" *m* Addison Morgan, M. D.,
" *l* William H. Scudder, Jr., LL. B.,
'82 Frank E. Baker, A. B.,
" Edmond H. Barmore,
" DeForest Kendall,
" *Wallace Massie,
" Thornton W. Sargent, A. B.,
" Henry G. Sherrard, A. B.,
" *Robert D. Stephens, M. D. '83,
'83 James W. Harsha,
" Leavitt K. Merrill, A. B.,
" Ralph Metcalf, A. B.,
" Arthur T. Packard, A. B.,
" John T. Winship, A. B.,
" Frank F. Wormwood,
'84 Harry F. Forbes, B. S.,
" *Ralph Kuechler,
" Edward C. Pitkin,
'85 Seward L. Merriam,
'86 Henry S. Tibbits, A. B.,
'87 Thomas J. Ballinger, Ph. B.,
" *m* Miles H. Clark, M. D.,
" Frank D. Jenks,
" Lawrence A. McLouth, A. B.,
" John E. Mills,
" Myron W. Mills, B. L.,
'88 Wait Talcott,
" George J. Waggoner, M. D.,
'89 Willis J. Beckley, Ph. B.,
" Frank W. Hawks, Ph. B.,
" *William P. Morgan,
" Arthur D. Welton,
" *m* Melvin L. Wines, M. D.,
'90 David B. Hempstead, A. B.,
" Pomeroy Ladue, B. S.,
" Harry R. Seager, Ph. B.,
" Frederic L. Smith, Ph. B.,
" Ashley J. Vantine,
'91 Follett W. Bull,
" Rufus C. Thayer, Ph. B.,
" Thaddeus H. Walker, M. D.,
,92 Henry E. Candler, B. S.,
" George G. Prentis, B. L.,
" Harry C. Reiner,
" Frederic L. Sherwin, Ph. B.,
'93 Paul M. Day, Ph. B.,
" Henry H. Denham, B. S.,
" Walter A. Forbes,
" *p* Carlyle E. Latta,

'93 William S. Miller, B. S.,
" *l* Hiram Powers, LL. B.,
" Charles W. Stratton, Ph. B.,
'94 Thomas L. Chadbourne, Jr.,
" Clarence N. Church,
" Marion T. Hyatt,
" Walter L. Maas,
" Frank W. Pine, A. B.,
" George T. Tremble, Ph. B.,
'95 Josiah W. Begole, Jr.,
" Lewis H. Bridgman,
" George V. D. Candler,
" Rex R. Case, LL. B. '94,
" Clark C. Hyatt,
" Benjamin F. McLouth, B. S.,
" Captain Frank Merrill,
" William T. Phillips,
" John A. Stevens,
'96 James H. Bement, Ph. B.,
" *l* Allan Greeley,
" Herbert W. Landon,
" Harry S. McAlvay,
" Lloyd C. Whitman, A. B.,
'97 Edwin J. Bement, Ph. B.,
" Marquis B. Eaton,
" Arthur E. Maas,
" Alexander F. Maitland,
" *m* Harry A. Newkirk,
" *p* Walter Scotten,
" Benjamin R. B. Townsend,
" Sidney B. Tremble, B. L.,
'97 Raymond C. Turck,
" Arthur B. Turner,
" Roland D. Whitman, A. B.,
'98 Don A. Baxter,
" Albert J. Bradner,
" Lewis W. McCandless,
" Schuyler S. Olds, Jr.,
" Paul M. Pilcher,
" George C. Stone,
" *l* Dwight J. Turner,
'99 Edgar N. Church,
" William A. Comstock,
" William A. Gilchrist,
" Robert Grinnell,
" Robert W. Norrington,
" Walter R. Seavey,
'00 Bret Nottingham,
" Walter S. Penfield,
" Thomas L. Robinson,
" Harry M. Sedgwick,
'01 Clarence W. Aird,
" Frank H. Bement,
" Lewis Buckingham,
" Matthew Davison, Jr.,
" Eugene Field, Jr.,
" Harry H. Hughson,
" David W. Mills,
" John L. Pierce,
" Eugene W. Scott,
" William M. Swan,
" Harold E. Zook.

The following Zetes, students in our professional schools, are not enrolled in the Xi Chapter:

'77 *m* Albion A. Andrews, M. D.,
'82 *p* Henry A. Fairbank,
'83 *l* Howard Hovey,
'84 *l* Preston W. Charles, LL. B.,
" *h* Charles Hawley.

Psi Upsilon owes its origin to seven undergraduates of Union College by whom it was founded on the 24th of November, 1833. Four of the founders are still living. The society is chiefly indebted for the rapidity and success of its early extension to the Hon. William E. Robinson, Yale, '41, recently deceased. This is peculiarly an Eastern order; it has steadfastly refused to start branches in the South, and has selected from the Western institutions those only which are most closely associated with the colleges of New England and New York. The names, colleges, and birth-dates of the twenty-two chapters are as follow: Theta, Union, 1833; Delta, New York, 1837; Beta, Yale, 1839; Sigma, Brown, 1840; Gamma, Amherst, 1841; Zeta, Dartmouth, 1842; Lambda, Columbia, 1842; Kappa, Bowdoin, 1843; Psi,

BADGE OF PSI UPSILON.

Hamilton, 1843; Xi, Wesleyan, 1843; Alpha, Harvard, 1850–57, 1870–72; Upsilon, Rochester, 1858; Iota, Kenyon, 1860; Phi, Michigan, 1864; Omega, Chicago, 1869–86, 1897; Pi, Syracuse, 1875; Chi, Cornell, 1876; Beta Beta, Trinity, 1880; Eta, Lehigh, 1884; Tau, Pennsylvania, 1891; Mu, Minnesota, 1891; and Rho, Wisconsin, 1896. All of the branches are in active operation except the Alpha at Harvard, which was discontinued because of the predominance of local clubs, and which the society has declined to revive. Garnet and gold are the fraternity colors. Buildings are owned by all of the twenty-one active chapters excepting those at New York, Dartmouth, Columbia, Bowdoin, Chicago, and Minnesota. Fully four-fifths of the members reside in the Northern States from Maine to Minnesota, the alumni representation in each of the chief cities of that region being very large. Among those who were members of Psi Upsilon during their college lives elsewhere than at Michigan the following may be named: the late Chester A. Arthur, President of the United States; William C. Whitney, formerly secretary of the Navy; the late Amos T. Akerman, Attorney-General of the United States; Frederick W. Seward, sometime Assistant-Secretary of State; Samuel G. Arnold, Charles H. Bell, Orris S. Ferry, William P. Frye, Joseph R. Hawley, Anthony Higgins, James W. Patterson, and George P. Wetmore, all United States Senators; Galusha A. Grow, formerly Speaker of the National House of Representatives; the late Benjamin F. Prescott, Governor of New Hampshire; Daniel H. Chamberlain, Ex-Governor of South Carolina; Andrew D. White, Ambassador to the German Empire; the late William W. Phelps, Minister to Austria; the late Eugene Schuyler, Minister to Greece; Walbridge A. Field, Charles B. Andrews, Charles Doe, Thomas Durfee, and Franklin J. Dickman, Chief Justices respectively of the Supreme Courts of Massachusetts, Connecticut, New Hampshire, Rhode Island, and Ohio; the Federal Circuit Judges Hugh L. Bond, LeBaron B. Colt, Walter H. Sanborn, and Willam H. Taft; Chauncey M. Depew,

ARMS OF PSI UPSILON.

recently President of the New York Central Railroad; Alexander Agassiz, President of the Calumet & Hecla Mining Company; the late Joseph W. Harper, the head of the firm of Harper Brothers; the Protestant Episcopal Bishops, Chauncey B. Brewster of Connecticut, J. H. H. Brown of Fond du Lac, Thomas F. Davies of Michigan, Abiel Leonard of Utah, A. N. Littlejohn of Long Island, I. L. Nicholson of Wisconsin, William S. Perry of Iowa, George F. Seymour of Springfield, J. F. Spalding of Colorado, Ethelbert Talbot of Central Pennsylvania, E. S. Thomas of Kansas, O. W. Whitaker of Pennsylvania, and G. Mott Williams of Marquette; Willard F. Mallalieu, Bishop of the M. E. Church; Dr. Morgan Dix, Rector of Trinity Church, New York; the Rev. Charles H. Parkhurst, of New York; the authors, Edmund Clarence Stedman, Charles Dudley Warner, William Allen Butler, James DeMille, Horatio Alger, Jr., and Poultney Bigelow; the college presidents, William J. Tucker of Dartmouth, Austin Scott of Rutgers, James B. Angell of Michigan, George E. Reed of Dickinson, James G. K. McClure of Lake Forest, Julian H. Seelye (formerly) of Amherst, and Charles E. Aiken (formerly) of Union; James O. Murray, Dean of Princeton University; William W. Goodwin, Professor of Greek at Harvard; and Henry S. Carhart, Francis W. Kelsey, George W. Patterson, Jr., and the late George S. Morris, of the Faculty of our University.

ARMS OF PHI OF PSI UPSILON.

Phi, the Michigan branch of Psi Upsilon, and the oldest but one of the five Western chapters of the fraternity, secured its charter in 1864, after ten years had been spent in persuading the society to place our University upon its roll of colleges. The fourteen charter-members comprised the entire undergraduate membership, one man excepted, of a society which had been established in the University nineteen years before. One member of the new chapter was initiated December 9, 1864, and the rest of the undergraduate petitioners were admitted January 26, 1865. Associated with the students in the change of fraternal relations were alumni of several classes prior to 1865. The chapter has had a full delegation in every class since its origin, and has graduated at least three men from the literary department at every Commencement. In 1875 a chosen body of alumni was incorporated under the laws of the state, and in 1879–80 the chapter house at the corner of State Street and South University Avenue was built upon ground which had been purchased in the summer of 1878. In the latter part of 1892 the building was reconstructed and greatly enlarged. Among the 378 members of the local chapter are the following: O. M. Barnes, '50, of Lansing; the late Professor James C. Watson, '57; Charles Kendall Adams, '61, President of the University of Wisconsin; Jonas H. McGowan, '61, sometime Regent and also Representative in Congress; Martin L. D'Ooge, '62, Professor of Greek in the University; Circuit Judge Orville W. Coolidge, '63; Dr. Henry M. Hurd, '63, Superintendent of the Johns Hopkins University Hospital; Schuyler Grant, '64, of Detroit; William H. Barnes, '65, formerly of the Supreme Court of Arizona; Henry W. Hubbard, '66, Treasurer of the American Missionary Association; Albert M. Henry, '67, of Detroit; George L. Maris, '67, Principal of the George School, Newton, Pa.; Professor Williard B. Rising, '67, of the University of California; Francis A. Blackburn, '68, Associate Professor of English in the University of Chicago; Oliver H. Dean, '68, of the Kansas City bar; Mark W. Harrington, '68, recently President of the University of Washington; H. H. C. Miller, '68, of the Chicago Bar; Edward L. Walter, '68, Professor of the Romance Languages in our University; Lawrence Maxwell, Jr., '74, of Cincinnati, recently Solicitor-General of the United States; Charles H. Aldrich, '75, of Chicago, formerly Solicitor-General; Dr. W. D. Miller, the well known dental surgeon of Berlin; the late S. V. R. Trowbridge, '76, Attorney-General of Michigan; Frederick L. Bliss, '77, Principal of the Detroit High School; Charles M. Gayley, '78, Professor of the English language and Literature in the University of California; George W. Knight, '78, Professor of History in the Ohio State University; Edward M. Brown, '80, Professor of the English Language and Literature in the University of Cincinnati; Benjamin L. D'Ooge, '81, Professor in the State Normal School; Dr. John J. Abel, '83, Professor in John Hopkins University; Louis M. Dennis, '85, Associate Professor of Chemistry in Cornell University; and Dean C. Worcester, '89, Assistant Professor of Zoology in our University. Upon the University baseball nine the Phi of Psi Upsilon has had these representatives: E. W. Gale, '68, J. A. Blackburn, '70, J. A. Mercer, '71, A. G. Tyng,

'73, W. R. Clark, '74, J. S. Ayres, '77, W. M. Thompson, '80, E. L. Webster, '80, F. W. Davenport, '82, A. H. Brown, Jr., '83, A. E. Miller, '83, C. C. Smith, '86, E. C. Best, '88, F. W. Mehlhop, '88, C. T. Miller, '88, W. B. Carpenter, '89, P. R. Gray, '90, E. R. Lewis, '91, J. T. Scott, '91, Frank Crawford, '93 *l*, W. D. McKenzie, '96, and H. S. McGee, '00. To the University football elevens this society has furnished C. H. Johnston, '81, R. T. Farrand, '90, E. W. MacPherran, '90, J. T. Scott, '91, E. L. Sanderson, '92, James VanInwagen, Jr., '92, S. C. Glidden, '93, and E. P. dePont, '94. The tennis championships at Ann Arbor have been awarded to the following members: L. M. Dennis, '85, Charles McClellan, '85, T. H. Gale, '88, C. T. Miller, '88, H. P. Dodge, '93, L. H. Paddock, '93 *l*, H. E. Chickering, '94, H. W. Suydam, '94, W. D. McKenzie, '96, L. M. Harvey, '98, W. D. Herrick, '98, and C. W. Seabury, '98.

CHAPTER HOUSE OF PSI UPSILON.

'50 Orlando M. Barnes, A. B.,
'57 *James C. Watson, A. B.,
'61 Charles K. Adams, A. B.,
" Edwin Hadley, LL. B.,
" Jonas H. McGowan, B. S.,
'62 Martin L. D'Ooge, A. B.,
'63 Orville W. Coolidge, A. B.,
" Henry M. Hurd, A. B.,
'64 *Arthur Everett, A. B.,
" Schuyler Grant, A. B.,
" *George C. Palmer, M. D.,
" Bluford Wilson,
'65 Abram J. Aldrich, A. B.,
" William H. Barnes, A. B.,
" James D. H. Cornelius, A. B.,
" *John B. Root, A. B.,
" John L. Turrel, LL. B.,
'66 Henry W. Hubbard, B. S.,
" Alfred E. Mudge, A. B.,
" *William B. Sager,
" *Henry H. Wines, M. D.,
'67 Albert McK. Henry, B. S.,
" Milton Jackson, B. S.,
" George L. Maris, A. B.,
" Willard B. Rising, M. E.,
'68 *p* George N. Bissell,
'68 Francis A. Blackburn, A. B.,
" *Adoniram D. Carter, A. B.,
" *Thomas Cresswell, LL. B.,
" Oliver H. Dean, A. B.,
" Edmund W. Gale, A. B.,
" Mark W. Harrington, A. B.,
" Humphrey H. C. Miller, A. B.,
" Galusha Pennell, A. B.,
" Lorenzo B. Potts, A. B.,
" Edward L. Walter, A. B.,
'69 *Byron A. Crane,
" William J. Darby, A. B.,
" Charles H. Hamilton, M. E.,
" John E. Hinman, A. B.,
" Edward A. Horton,
" J. Eugene Jackson,
" Marmaduke B. Kellogg, A. B.,
" Theodore F. Kerr, A. B.,
" Luther L. Mills,
'70 Arthur C. Adams, A. B.,
" Henry H. Barlow, A. B.,
" *Julius A. Blackbnrn, A. B.,
" Franklin Bradley, A. B.,
" Thomas C. Christy, A. B.,
" *Varnum B. Cochran,
" *Otis E. Haven, A. B.,

'70 *Frank H. Howe, A. B.,
" Arthur R. Simmons,
" *William Stagg,
" Lucius B. Swift, Ph. B.,
" Wallace W. Williams,
'71 Edward M. Adams, A. B.,
" Charles E. Gorton, Ph. B.,
" Henry C. Granger, A. B.,
" Earl Knight, A. B.,
" Joseph A. Mercer, A. B.,
" Charles A. Rust, B. S.,
" John W. Sleeper, A. B.,
" Eugene J. Weeks, Ph. C.,
'72 Charles G. Bennett, A. B.,
" Francis D. Bennett,
" Archer Brown, A. B.,
" *George E. Cochran, A. B.,
" Louis M. Iddings, Ph. B.,
" *Herbert H. Lyons, A. B.,
" John J. Mapel, A. B.,
" Homer Reed, A. B.,
" William T. Underwood, A. B.,
'73 Henry A. Adams,
" Sidney C. Eastman, A. B.,
" *James W. Ferry,
" James R. Goffe, Ph. B.,
" *Robert S. Gross, A. B.,
" Albert P. Jacobs, A. B.,
" George S. Johnson,
" Loyal E. Knappen, A. B.,
" George Rust, B. S.,
" Zar D. Scott, B. S.,
" Alexander G. Tyng, Jr.,
" Monroe Wheeler,
" Josiah W. Willis, C. E.,
" Kimball Young, A. B.,
'74 Isaac Adams, A. B.,
" Alpheus W. Clark, A. B.,
" George R. Gibson,
" Frank C. Hayman, A. B.,
" Theodore H. Johnston, A. B.,
" Lawrence Maxwell, Jr., B. S.,
" Charles A. Warren, Ph. B.,
'75 Charles H. Aldrich, A. B.,
" James M. Barrett, Ph. B.,
" *George A. Briggs, Ph. B.,
" William R. Clark, A. B.,
" Charles H. Jacobs, A. B.,
" Charles S. McDonald,
" Willoughby D. Miller, A. B.,
" Jonathan W. Parker, A. B.,
" William H. Potter, C. E.,
" Jacob C. Price, M. D.,
" Henry J. Robeson, A. B.,
" John J. Rust,
" Wesley E. Sisson,
" *Elliott H. Smith,
" S. Whedon Smith, A. B.,
'76 George S. Baker, A. B.,
'76 Frederick K. Gustin, A. B.,
" Myron H. Phelps,
" Charles W. H. Potter, A. B.,
" Edward H. Ranney, A. B.,
" *Stephen Van R. Trowbridge,
'77 *Joseph S. Ayres, A. B.,
" Frederick L. Bliss, A. B.,
" Granville W. Browning, B. S.,
" William H. Lightner, A. B.,
" Howell C. Moore, A. B.,
" William A. Satterlee, Ph. B.,
" William T. Smalley,
" Ernest F. Smith, Ph. B.,
" *Vernor J. Tefft, A. B.,
'78 Charles M. Gayley, A. B.,
" *Edward K. Hubbard, A. B.,
" George W. Knight, A. B.,
" Frank V. Luse,
" William A. Otis,
" James H. Raymond, Jr., A. B.,
" Douglass H. Stringham, A. B.,
" Theodore J. Wrampelmeier, A. B.,
'79 Oren Dunham, Ph. B.,
" John O. Henshaw,
" Horatio T. Morley, M. E.,
" Henry C. Post,
" Spencer R. Smith, A. B.,
'80 Orlando F. Barnes, A. B.,
" Edward M. Brown, Ph. B.,
" Charles W. Hitchcock, A. M.,
" P. Burr Loomis, Jr., A. B.,
" Charles E. Paddock,
" Augustus V. R. Pond, LL. B.,
" Edwin S. Sherrill, A. B.,
" Herbert W. Smith,
" Edward L. Webster,
" Charles C. Whitacre, Ph. B.,
'81 *Charles Belmont,
" Francis R. Day,
" Benjamin L. D'Ooge, A. B.,
" George H. Fletcher, A. B.,
" Thomas H. Hulbert,
" Collins H. Johnston, A. B.,
" Charles M. Lightner,
" Frank E. Roff,
" William M. Thompson, A. B.,
'82 *George L. Chubb,
" Charles L. Coffin, B. S.,
" *Frank W. Davenport, B. L.,
" Albert B. Hale, A. B.,
" James B. Herrick, A. B.,
" Louis H. Hyde, Ph. B.,
" William J. Miller, Ph. B.,
" Harrison Musgrave,
" Rollo B. Oglesbee, LL. B.,
" Harold Wilson, B. S.,
'83 John J. Abel, Ph. B.,
" Edward A. Barnes, A. B.,
" Addison M. Brown, A. B.,

'83 Austin H. Brown, Jr.,
" Clarence A. Lightner, A. B.,
" Edwin F. Mack, A. B.,
" Albert E. Miller, A. B.,
" John Morris, Jr., A. B.,
" Samuel B. Schoyer, A. B.,
" Edgar H. Scott, M. S.,
" Edwin N. Smith, A. B.,
" Charles H. Worden,
'84 Bestor G. Brown,
" Clarence Conely,
" John E. Cornell, A. B.,
" Leslie B. Hanchett, Ph. B.,
" Arthur A. Hinckley,
" Julian H. Tyler, A. B ,
" Louis B. Weaver,
'85 William E. Brownlee, A. B.,
" Louis M. Dennis, Ph. B.,
" Robert F. Eldredge, B. S.,
" Louis Gascoigne, A. B.,
" Charles McClellan, A. B.,
" Horace S. Oakley, LL. B.,
" Bowen W. Schumacher, A. B.,
" William P. Tyler,
'86 Herbert E. Boynton, A. B.,
" Charles E. Bruce, B. S.,
" Robert N. Dickman, A. B.,
" Joseph Ganahl, Jr., A. B.,
" Edward F. Harris,
" Josiah McRoberts, Ph. B.,
" Edward H. Mason,
" William M. Odell, Ph. B.,
" Russell M. Seeds,
" Clifford C. Smith, B. S.,
" Clyde Smith, A. B.,
" *Frederick B. Wixson, A. B.,
'87 Ephraim D. Adams, A. B.,
" James E. Ball, A. B.,
" Oliver H. Brush,
" James E. Milville, Ph. C.,
" Jerome B. Thomas, Jr., A. B.,
" Wallace W. Wemott,
'88 William G. Adams,
" Frank S. Arnett,
" Edgar C. Best,
" John N. Blair, A. B.,
" Thomas H. Gale, B. L.,
" Frederick W. Mehlhop, Ph. C.,
" Charles T. Miller, Ph. B.,
" Willard Pope, B. S.,
" Ralph M. Shankland, B. S.,
'89 Eugene N. Best, A. B.,
" Horace V. Birdsell, B. L.,
" John Greenshields, A. B.,
" William W. Harris, Ph. B.,
" George P. Hyde, Ph. B.,
" Elisha W. Kelly,
" Oscar F. Schmid, Ph. B.,
" Horace V. Winchell, B. S.,
'89 Dean C. Worcester, A. B.,
" Harry B. Wyeth,
'90 Charles T. Alexander, B. L.,
" Frank S. Bourns, B. S.,
" William B. Carpenter,
" Royal T. Farrand, M. D.,
" Paul R. Gray, A. B.,
" William W. Lovett,
" Edgar W. MacPherran, A. B.,
" William K. Maxwell, A. B.,
" *William B. Ramsay, A. B.,
" Leon J. Richardson, A. B.,
" John B. Warner,
'91 Frank R. Ashley, B. S.,
" Samuel S. Bradley,
" Leon H. Cooper,
" Daniel L. Dorsey, A. B.,
" Carl K. Friedman,
" Harry J. Hatch, B. S.,
" David L. Hyde,
" Edward R. Lewis, B. L.,
" *Willard L. Maris, B. S.,
" Samuel C. Park,
" *John T. Scott,
" Edward J. Woodworth, A. B.,
'92 Robert T. Holland, Ph. B.,
" William B. Larrabee, B. S.,
" Ralph S. MacPherran, B. S.,
" Wilhelm Miller, A. B.,
" William R. Murray, Ph. B.,
" Stephen H. Payne,
" William C. Quarles, Ph. B.,
" Edmond L. Sanderson, A. B.,
" William C. Smith,
" James VanInwagen, Jr.,
" Norman S. Waite,
" William E. Walter, A. B.,
" Philip B. Watrous,
'93 Earl D. Babst, Ph. B.,
" Cameron C. Burns, A. B.,
" Holbrook G. Cleaveland, A. B.,
" Frederick W. Davies,
" Henry P. Dodge,
" Stephen C. Glidden, M. D.,
" Leon M. Groesbeck, B. S.,
" John S. Hurd, A. B.,
" Frank W. Lightner, Ph. B.,
" *Albert L. Murray,
" Cyrenius A. Newcomb, Jr., B. S.,
" Ferdinand W. Peck, Jr.,
" Richard F. Rust,
" Gale Thompson,
" Arthur VanInwagen,
'94 George H. Angell,
" Howard E. Chickering, B. S.,
" Rudolph F. Flintermann, A. B.
" Harry C. James,
" Timothy D. Jerome,
" Robert E. Jones, A. B.,

'94 Edward P. dePont,
" Herman H. Sharpless,
" Horace W. Suydam,
" Edgar L. Watrous, B. L.,
'95 George E. Ball,
" Wallace W. Chickering, B. S.,
" Henry S. Crane, A. B.,
" Charles C. MacPherran,
" James K. Morgan,
" William H. Morley, Ph. B.,
" Harry T. Nightingale, Ph. B.,
" Franklin B. Spear, Jr., Ph. B.,
" Philip B. Spear, Ph. B.,
" William A. Spitzley, A. B.,
" Edward C. Weeks, Ph. B.,
" Robert M. Weidemann,
'96 Kirkland B. Alexander, Ph. B.,
" Henry E. Bodman, Ph. B.
" Burnham S. Colburn, B. S.,
" Frederick W. B. Coleman, A. B.,
" William F. Ford,
" Gaylord W. Gillis, B. L.,
" Edward M. Holland, A. B.,
" William D. McKenzie, A. B.,
" John S. Pratt,
" Joseph H. Quarles, Ph. B.,
" Walter Robbins, B. S.,
" Adrian D. Stevenson, B. S.,
" Duane R. Stuart, A. B.,
'97 Stephen C. Babcock, B. S.,
" Harry W. Cummings,
" James H. Flinn, B. L.,
" Edwin H. Humphrey, B. L.,
" John B. Keating, B. S.,
" Frank A. Ketcham,
" Otis H. Maclay,
" *Frederick C. Meisel,
" William W. Newcomb, B. S.,
" Ross A. Spence,
" Frederick R. Waldron,
'98 Standish Backus,
" Edward B. Caulkins,
" George W. Cottrell,
" Robert S. Cummings,
" William H. Emery,
'98 Greenleaf W. Gale,
" Leroy M. Harvey,
" Henry T. Heald,
" Walter D. Herrick,
" Stuart E. Knappen,
" Allen Loomis,
" *m* *William L. McCauley,
" Nathan S. Potter, Jr.,
" Charles W. Seabury,
" Richard C. Underwood,
'99 William G. Chesebrough,
" William L. Cooper,
" George E. Fay,
" *m* Clarence W. Mehlhop,
" Paul Oliver,
" Edward L. Quarles,
" Walter R. Weeks,
" Matthew B. Whittlesey,
'00 Ralph C. Apted,
" Frank Baumgardner,
" William Callan,
" Rufus W. Clark, Jr.,
" Frederick S. Colburn,
" Thomas G. Denby,
" M. Howard Foss,
" Harry S. McGee,
" Morris W. Montgomery,
" Roger S. Morris,
" Arthur W. Norton,
" Sidney J. Steele,
" Leigh M. Turner,
" *m* W. Douglas Ward,
" John J. Whittlesey,
'01 Aikman Armstrong,
" James G. Barada,
" Roger C. Butterfield,
" Fritz Goebel,
" William Grayson, Jr.,
" Gilbert S. Loomis,
" Carl F. Mehlhop,
" Carl F. Meyer,
" Stanley D. Montgomery,
" Arthur H. Richardson,
" Amasa M. Rust,
" Daniel F. Zimmerman.

Psi Upsilon has been represented in the University by the following members who, although temporarily affiliated with the Phi, are permanently enrolled with other chapters:

'68 *l* Justus B. Crane, LL. B.,
" *m* Rees Davis,
" *m* Henry R. Pratt, M. D.,
" *l* William O. Webster,
'69 *l* Henry C. Noyes, LL. B.,
" *l* Lewis L. Wood, LL. B.,
'70 *a* Austin Scott, A. M.,
'72 *l* Gustavus A. Florence,
'73 *l* Arthur M. Phinney,
'74 *l* Richard T. Colston, '74,
" *a* Eugene M. Robinson,
" *m* Baxter T. Smelzer,
'75 *m* John M. Lee,
'77 *l* William H. Fairchild, LL. B.,
'79 *l* Allen H. Sexton,
" *l* John DeW. Veeder,

'80 *l* Frank H. Shaffer, LL. B.,
" *l* Nathan S. Williams, LL. B.,
'82 *l* Henry P. Field, LL. B.,
" *l* Frederick H. Gile, LL. B.,
'83 *m* Henry E. Briggs,
" *l* Willis E. Noxon, LL. B.,
'84 *l* Frank Healy, LL. B.,
'85 *l* Charles E. Thomas,
'93 *l* Frank Crawford, LL. B.,
" *l* Lewis H. Paddock, LL. B.,
'94 *l* Arthur M. Lewald, LL. B.,
'96 *l* Charles R. Cary, LL. B.,
'97 *l* John P. Morse.

Phi Delta Theta was founded December 26, 1848, by six undergraduates of Miami University. Eighty-six chapters, of which twenty-three are extinct, have been instituted. The society is now represented at the following universities and colleges: Miami, Indiana, Centre, Wabash, Wisconsin, Northwestern, Butler, Ohio Wesleyan, Franklin, Michigan, Chicago, Ohio, Hanover, DePauw, Missouri, Knox, Iowa Wesleyan, Georgia, Emory, Mercer, Cornell, Lafayette, California, Virginia, Nebraska, Gettysburg, Washington and Jefferson, Vanderbilt, Mississippi, Alabama, Lombard, Alabama Polytechnic, Allegheny, Vermont, Dickinson, Westminster, Minnesota, Iowa, Kansas, Hillsdale, University of the South, Ohio State, Texas, Pennsylvania, Union, Colby, Columbia, Dartmouth, North Carolina, Central, Williams, Southwestern, Syracuse, Washington-Lee, Lehigh, Amherst, Brown, Tulane, Washington (Mo.), Leland Stanford, Jr., Purdue, Illinois, and the Case School. Buildings are owned by the chapters at Vanderbilt, University of the South, Amherst, Cornell, Lehigh, Gettysburg, Lombard, and Wisconsin. About 9,600 men have been admitted, among whom are the following: Ex-President Benjamin Harrison; Ex-Vice-President Adlai E. Stevenson; John W. Foster, former Secretary of State; W. F. Vilas, former Postmaster-General and United States Senator; J. B. Allen and J. C. S. Blackburn, United States Senators; J. A. Anderson, W. G. Brantley, L. J. Fenton, J. V. Graff, F. M. Griffith, J. M. Griggs, W. H. Hamilton, W. M. Howard, J. W. Lewis, C. L. Moses, T. M. Paschal, G. W. Prince, S. J. Pugh, J. C. Sherwin, and T. B. Ward, Representatives in Congress; E. H. Conger, sometime Minister to Brazil; J. S. Ewing, once Minister to Belgium; J. C. Black, formerly Commissianer of Pensions; G. M. Lambertson, Ex-Assistant Secretary of the Treasury; A. C. Melette, Ex-Governor of South Dakota; W. H. Ellerbe, Governor of South Caro-

BADGE OF PHI DELTA THETA.

lina; W. A. Woods, Federal Circuit Judge; J. F. Phillips, Federal District Judge; B. K. Elliott, Ex-Chief Justice of Indiana; W. B. Fleming, late of the Supreme Court of New Mexico; Norman Buck of the Idaho Supreme Court; the College Presidents, J. V. Logan of Central University, C. E. Nash of Lombard, J. P. Ashley of Albion, P. D. Pollock of Mercer, Alston Ellis of Colorado State, W. T. Stott of Franklin, and J. T. McFarland of Iowa Wesleyan; W. A. Keener, Dean of the Columbia Law School; L. W. Ross, sometime Dean of the Law Department of the University of Iowa; the Rev. W. G. Craig, D. D., of McCormick Theological Seminary; the Rev. Dr. David Swing, deceased; the late Eugene Field, poet and journalist; and the newspaper correspondents, H. V N. Boynton and Smith D. Fry. Blue and white are the colors of the fraternity, and its flower is the white carnation.

On the 28th of November, 1864, a charter was granted to three students of our University; but the existence of the society was not known outside until some months later, and the names of the members were not listed in The Palladium until 1866. In the spring of 1869 the chapter became dormant, having initiated only twelve men in the collegiate department, and only twenty-two in all. An attempted revival in 1877 failed, and in 1880 there was a brief period of *sub rosa* activity, after which Phi Delta Theta at Ann Arbor was quiescent until November 11, 1887. Since that time the chapter has lived without interruption. Among its alumni are Judge James L. Brown, 70 *l*; John M. Schaeberle, '76, of the Lick Observatary; Clarence G. Taylor, '81, Professor of Mechanical Practice in our University; William F. Edwards, '90, of the University of Washington; and Frank H. Dixon, '92, Assistant Professor of Political Economy at Michigan. Frank H. Decke, '93, was a member of the University football team of 1892. The local chapter has had 121 members, whose names follow:

VIGNETTE OF PHI DELTA THETA.

'65	Elbert L. Blakeslee, M. D.,	'68 *l*	William S. Harbert, LL. B.,
'66 *m*	William J. Elstun,	'68	*John C. Magill, A. B.,
"	George C. Harris, A. B.,	"	Henry C. Snitcher,
'67 *l*	Arthur D. Basnett, LL. B.,	"	Riley C· Storey, A. B.,

'69 *l* Theophilus T. Fountain,
'70 *l* James L. Brown,
" John L. Culley, C. E.,
" *m* Ervy L. Goodrich,
" *John W. Johnson,
" Darius C. Pennington, B. S.,
" *l* Palmer W. Smith, LL. B.,
" *m* Jonas Stewart,
" Leonard E. Stocking, Ph. B.,
" *m* Charles M. Taylor,
'71 Charles A. Cook, A. B.,
" Pembroke R. Flitcraft, A. B.,
" *Baron H. Pennington, C. E.
'72 Richard A. Moses,
'76 John M. Schaeberle, C. E.,
'81 Clarence G. Taylor,
'86 Erwin F. Smith, B. S.,
'86 *l* John B. Mecham, LL. B.,
" *Frank I. Muir, A. B.,
" Henry F. Shier, Ph. B.,
'89 Allen L. Colton, Ph. B.,
" *m* Willis C. Moore,
" Peter G. Sjöblom,
'90 *m* Edwin S. Antisdale, M. D.,
" William F. Edwards, B. S.,
" *m* George F. Keiper, M. D.,
" Henry A. Sanders, A. B.,
" William H. Stillhamer,
" *Oswald D. Vandersluis, A. B.,
" Robert H. Wolcott, B. L.,
'91 Theodore L. Chadbourne, B. S.,
" Erwin E. Ewell,
" Orville R. Hardy, B. S.,
" William L. Honnold,
" John T. Hoyt, B. S.,
" John P. Keyes,
'92 Gaylord H. Chilcote,
" Frank H. Dixon, Ph. B.,
" Arthur Frantzen, B. S.,
" Alexander B. Hardy,
" *George D. Mena,
" George F. Mulliken, A. B.,
" Adna C. Newell, B. S.,
" Arch S. Ralph,
" *George D. Sones, B. S.,
'93 Frank H. Decke, B. L.,
" Benjamin F. Hall, Jr., B. L.,
" Alfred W. Hookway, B. S.,
" Howard M. Raymond, B. S.,
'94 John D. Dunham, A. B.,
" William L. Dunn, B. S.,
" James C. Hallock,
" Farley D. McLouth,
" Harry B. Mulliken,
" John D. Neal,
" John A. Whitworth, A. B.,
'95 Charles W. Foster, B. L.,
'95 Richard K. Hoyt,
" Allan H. Kessler,
" Walter G. McCullough, B. L.,
" James H. Mallory, Jr., A. B.,
" William J. Melchers, B. S.,
'96 Fred E. Bradfield,
" Gail H. Chapman,
" Richard D. Ewing, B. S.,
" George K. McMullen, B. S.,
" Edward K. Preston,
" Leander W. Steketee.
" Hadley H. Walch. A. B.,
" Frank S. Whitman, B. S.,
" *Allan W. Wolcott,
" Samuel L. Wolcott,
'97 Frank C. Chesten,
" Edgar Crilley,
" Frank T. Faxon,
" Talbot H. France,
" Elmer B. Lane,
" Stanley M. Matthews, B. L.,
" Armand R. Miller, B. S.,
" Henry M. Smith, A. B.,
" Silvio H. von Ruck,
" Irving C. Woodward, B. S.,
'98 Oscar W. Gorenflo,
" Roy M. Hardy,
" George B. Lowrie,
" Ralph F. Palmer,
" Thomas Le Pollock,
" Charles M. Preston,
" Clarence W. Raynor,
" Howard P. Treadway,
" Ralph E. Waterman,
" Clinton H. Woodruff,
'99 Joseph M. Barr,
" George N. Blatt,
" Fred R. Hoover,
" Reginald D. Steele,
" Russell B. Thayer,
'00 Arthur J. Bleazby,
" William C. Brooks,
" Cornelins K. Chapin,
" Walter S. Foster,
" John W. Judson,
" John M. Paine,
" David D. Starr,
" Arlo R. Williams,
'01 Howell L. Begle,
" Ned C. Begle,
" Benjamin E. Dolphin,
" Floyd B. Hull,
" Frederick L. Lowrie,
" Pierre B. Pendill,
" Arthur M. Potter,
" Philip G. Young.

In addition to the roll of the Michigan Alpha Chapter Phi Delta Theta has had a long line of students at Ann Arbor. Doubtless the following list is not complete:

'66 *l* Charles K. Ladd, LL. B.,
'67 *l* Wickliff A. Cotton,
" *l* Thomas Speed,
'68 *l* John B. Allen,
" *m* David B. Floyd,
" *l* Theodore H. Ristine,
'70 *l* G. M. Overstreet, LL. B.,
'71 *l* Robert L. Lyons,
'72 *l* John B. Elam, LL. B.,
" *l* Elam Fisher, LL. B.,
" *m* Samuel E. Mahan,
" *l* Pliny W. Smith,
" *l* Samuel C. Stimson, LL. B.,
'73 Gilbert E. Bailey,
" *l* A. Dwight Baldwin, LL. B.,
'74 *m* James M. Logan,
" *l* Burnett M. Short, LL. B.,
'75 *l* James T. McClellan,
" *l* Albert M. Mackerly, LL. B.,
'76 *l* Holly R. Buckingham,
" *m* Warren M. Ristine,
'78 *l* Wilber F. Rudy, LL. B.,
" Charles C. Brown, C. E.,
'79 *m* Edwin L. Fosdick, M. D.,
" *l* *Edwin S. Palmer, LL. B.,
'80 *l* Frederick H. Austin,
" *m* Mason W. Gray, M. D.,
" *l* Samuel W. Haynes, LL. B.,
" *l* George W. Wilson,
" *l* Oliver R. Wood, LL. B.,
'81 *l* Charles R. Pence,
'82 *l* Frank J. Annis,
" *l* Ira W. Christian, LL. B.,
'82 *m* Albert B. Simonson,
" Guilford L. Spencer, M. S.,
'83 *l* Isaac Pearson, LL. B.,
'84 *l* William H. Bristol, LL. B.,
" *m* Daniel A. Capwell,
" *l* J. A. Follenwider, LL. B.,
" *l* Elmer O. Minnigh,
'85 *m* William O. McLean,
'86 Charles H. Perry,
'87 *p* Charles Baker, Ph. C.,
" *m* Edward S. Blair, M. D.,
" *m* John E. Brown,
" Albert B. Martin,
" *h* Edward H. Pond, M. D.,
" *m* Clement J. Olmstead,
'88 *m* Louis Becker,
" *l* John R. Calder,
" *m* Charles E. Stout,
" *p* Wilford C. Stryker,
'89 Henry C. Montgomery,
" *l* Samuel L. Thompson, LL. B.,
'90 *l* Anthony Bowen,
" *l* Joseph N. Tillett, LL. B.,
'91 Howard B. Beecher,
" *l* James L. Mitchell, Jr.,
" *h* Frank S. Tuthill,
'92 *m* Frank B. Miner,
'93 *l* Charles E. Sturtz,
'96 *l* John C. Munger,
'97 *d* Carey E. Jones,
" *l* John F. Wehrle,
'99 *m* John E. Burnett.

Kappa Phi Lambda.—This fraternity was founded in 1860–61 at Jefferson College. It had eleven branches, nearly all of them in Western colleges, and the last of them died in 1874. The Alpha of Michigan was instituted at Michigan in the autumn of 1865, by J. J. Belville, Jefferson '62, and George W. Andrews, another member of the order. An excellent society was built up at Ann Arbor, but when the college year 1868–69 opened only six men were on the ground, and the chapter disbanded, October 3. Five members joined Psi Upsilon, and one entered Alpha Delta Phi. Nearly all the members are well-known men. The roll is as follows:

BADGE OF KAPPA PHI LAMBDA.

'65 *l* George W. Andrews, LL. B.,
" *l* Jacob J. Belville, LL. B.,
'67 Allen M. Hurty,
'67 Henry A. Wise,
'68 Wickliffe W. Belville, A. B.,
" Oliver H. Dean, A. B.,

'69 Edward S. Jenison, C. E.,
" Henry S. Jewett, A. B.,
" Homer Reed, A. B.,
" James D. Smith,
'70 Henry H. Barlow, A. B.,
" Charles F. Burton, A. B.,
" Delos A. Chappel,
" Henry W. Lake,
'70 Zuinglius K. McCormack,
" B. T. K. Preston,
'71 John J. Mapel,
" John C. MacPherson,
" Samuel G. Milner, A. B. '72,
" Charles A. Rust, B. S. '72,
" Eugene J. Weeks.

Delta Tau Delta was founded in December, 1859, by seven students of Bethany College. The early extension of the society into Pennsylvania and Ohio was soon followed by establishments in the colleges of Indiana, Illinois, Michigan, and Iowa. In later years chapters have been organized in Southern and Northern states. Following is the list of the colleges now occupied by this society: Washington and Jefferson, Ohio, Allegheny, Ohio Wesleyan, Hillsdale, Indiana, DePauw, Illinois, Wabash, Stevens Institute, Lehigh, Michigan, Indianapolis (Butler), Albion, Rennselaer Polytechnic, Iowa, Kenyon, Georgia, Emery, Western Reserve, Minnesota, University of the South, Colorado, Mississippi, Vanderbilt, Wisconsin, Tufts, Massachusetts Institute, Tulane, Cornell, Northwestern, Leland Stanford, Jr., Nebraska, Ohio State, Washington and Lee, Brown, Pennsylvania, and California. Of the sixty-seven branches thirty-eight survive, twenty-one of which are in the West, ten in the East, and seven in the South. The fraternity colors are purple, gold, and white, and the pansy is the fraternity flower. About 5,700 men have been enrolled. The society is remarkable for the large number of its men living in the middle West; the four states of Ohio, Michigan, Indiana, and Illinois being credited with nearly 2,000. Prominent among those who wore the badge of this order in their college days are Senator John N. Wilson, of Washington State; Richard Blue, William H. Butler, Eugene J. Hainer, Albert J. Hopkins, John A. McDowell, and James R. Mann, Representatives in Congress; George W. Atkinson, Governor of West Virginia; Washington Gardner, Michigan's Secretary of State; William K. McAllister of the Supreme Court of Tennessee; Circuit Judge William L. Carpenter of Detroit; Joseph W. Mauck, President of the University of South Dakota; Charles L. Ingersoll, late Chancellor of the University of Nebraska; Dr. James N. Martin, Emory B. Lease, Albert W. Dorr, and Warren W. Florer, now or formerly of the Faculty of our University; Wilson M. Day, President of

BADGE OF DELTA TAU DELTA.

Cleveland's Chamber of Commerce; the Rev. Dr. J. Reed Stuart, of Detroit; Will M. Carleton, author and editor; and the late Brigadier-General Louis S. Thompson of the Confederate Army. To these should be added, from the Michigan branch, Professor Rolla C. Carpenter, '75, of Cornell University; Paul H. Hanus, '78, of the Harvard Faculty; George Horton, '78, American Consul at Athens; O. E. Angstman, '77 *l*, Frank E. Robson, '78 *l*, Byron S. Waite, '80, Alvah G. Pitts, '85, and Frank A. Rasch, '87 *l*, of the Detroit Bar, and Circuit Judge Norman W. Haire, '80. Delta Tau Delta has chapter houses at the University of the South and Leland Stanford, Jr., University.

STAR BADGE OF DELTA TAU DELTA.

As early as 1866 members of this society entered the professional departments of the University, and began to lay plans for the starting of a Michigan branch. In the college year 1870–71 nine or ten sophomores and freshmen were preliminarily organized into a chapter called the Xi; but other fraternities learned of the movement, and by drafting four of the members caused the rest to abandon the enterprise. In 1874, however, George W. Smith, a law student who had been a Delta Tau at Hillsdale College, succeeded in launching the Delta Chapter. Late in 1876 internal dissensions—fostered by unfriendly fraternities—led to a surrender of the charter; but the suspension did not last for long. As in the original establishment, so also in the revival of the chapter, an initiate from Hillsdale was the moving spirit; eight charter members were secured from the ranks of the "Independents"; and a reorganization was effected February 20, 1880. Admission to the pages of The Palladium was not allowed until 1883, but in the meantime the new chapter published a neat four-page account of itself with the names of its members. From 1891 to 1896 the well-known Winchell mansion in North University Avenue was occupied by the chapter, and at one time the purchase of the property was planned. The society has been represented upon the University baseball nine by J. F. Gallaher, '82, C. F. Lawson, '88, and F. D. McDonell, '88. Following is the roll of the 155 members of the Delta Chapter, which includes forty-five members initiated by other branches:

'74 Wilbur F. Reed, A. B.,
'75 *m* Hiram W. Austin, M. D.,
" Rolla C. Carpenter, C. E.,
" Charles R. Hume,
" Silas B. McManus,
'76 Anson P. DeWolf, A. B.,
" *Lewis C. Donaldson, C. E.
" John C. Floyd, B. S.,
" Joseph Ripley, C. E.,
" Franklin D. Shaver, A. B.,
" Alonzo J. Tullock, C. E.,
'77 *l* Oscar E. Angstman,
" *John S. Crombie, A. B.,
'78 *Franklin Garrison, A. B.,
" Paul H. Hanus, B. S.,
" George Horton, A. B.,
" Horace G. Myers, B. S.,
" Jay J. Reed, B. S.,
" Albert W. Ryan, A. B.,
'79 Chauncey F. Cook, A. B.,
" *p* Channing T. Gage, Ph. C.,
" Newton McMillan, A. B.,
" Charles G. Van Wert, Ph. B.,
'80 *l* William W. Cook, A. B.,
" Charles L. Dubuar, A. B.,
" Goorge L. Fisher, C. E.,
" Norman W. Haire, A. B.,
" Byron S. Waite, B. L.,
'81 Henry J. Butler, A. B.,
" *Thomas C. Tate, B. S.,
'82 Horace C. Alexander,
" Frederick Betts, A. B.,
" James F. Gallaher, A. B.,
" Arthur M. Gelston, A. B.,
'83 Henry H. Bradley,
" *m* John J. Encke, M. D.,
" Henry A. Fitzsimmons, A. B.,
" Walter B. Garvin, A. B.,
" Henry C. Gould,
" *m* William C. Marsh, M. D.,
" *l* Edgar E. Moss, LL. B.,
" *d* Byron S. Palmer, D. D. S.,
" *l* Frank E. Robson, LL. B.,
" Ferdinando A. Walker, A. B.,
" John F. Wilkinson,
" *Charles D. Willard, A. B.,
'84 Willis Baldwin, A. B.,
" James L. Callard, B. S.,
" Otto Landmann, Ph. B.,
" Adam H. Meeker,
" Samuel W. Norton, A. M.,
" *m* Wilson B. Paine,
" Allen G. Paul,
" Charles C. Walmsley,
'85 Frank W. Bishop,
" Franklin M. Cook,
" *l* Robert B. Milroy,
" *l* Walter J. Milroy,
" Alvah G. Pitts, A. B.,
'85 Frank A. Smith,
" Samuel A. Smith,
" *l* Williamson S. Summers, LL. B.,
" Ezra J. Ware, Ph. C., '88,
'86 *l* John I. Breck, LL. B.,
" Nathan E. Degan, A. B.,
" James G. Hays, A. B.,
" Edward E. Hughes,
" George E. Hunt,
" William A. McAndrew, A. B.,
" William A. McDonald, LL. B.,
" Edwin F. Saunders, Ph. B.,
" John C. Shaw, LL. B.,
" Lewis A. Springer, LL. B. '85,
" *m* James B. Tedrow, M. D.,
'87 *l* Albert D. Elliot, LL. B.,
" Frederick W. Guild,
" Guy L. Kiefer, A. B.,
" Charles C. Landon,
" John A. McDonald,
" William W. McNair,
" Charles H. Prescott, Jr.,
" *l* Elvin Swarthout, LL. B.,
'88 Hannibal G. Coburn, LL. B. '90,
" Charles H. Hatch, B. S.,
" Charles F. Lawson,
" Armin O. Leuschner, A. B.,
" Frank D. McDonell,
" Frank A. Rasch, LL. B.,
" Chester H. Rowell, Ph. B.,
" John H. Shaper, M. D.,
" Frank C. Wintrode,
'89 *d* Charles C. Cherryholmes, D. D. S.,
" Charles K. Eddy, Ph. B.,
" Julius W. Hegeler, B. S.,
'90 *l* *Henry W. Baird, LL. B.,
" William R. Cook,
" John R. Kempf, B. S.,
" William S. McArthur,
'91 *l* Daniel R. Anthony, Jr., LL. B.,
" *William J. Hinkson,
" Glenn Woolsey Holmes,
" Alfred C. Lewerenz, A. B.,
" Edward R. Loud,
" *p* Ernest J. Sanderson,
'92 William P. Borland, LL. B.,
" Franklin W. Callam, LL. B.,
" *m* Charles D. Colby, M. D.,
" James S. Downard,
" Abram L. Free, LL. B.,
" Samuel M. Trevellick,
" Charles G. Wicker, Jr.,
'93 Arthur P. Beardsell,
" Samuel F. Dibble,
" George A. Mansfield,
" Henry C. H. Porter,
'94 *l* Frederick W. Ashton, LL. B.,
" *l* Sewell L. Avery, LL. B.,
" *l* *George J. Bunday, LL. B.,

'94 Claude R. Corbusier,
" Herman J. Dowds,
" *l* Cyrus W. George, LL. B.,
" Frederick M. Gund,
" Benjamin F. Hall, Jr., B. L.,
" *l* Ralph W. Hartzell, LL. B.,
" James L. McKibben,
" Albert B Robbins,
" Charles F. Vaughn,
'95 *l* Edward B. Baker, LL. B.,
" Harry B. Cragin,
" *m* Harry A. Haze, M. D.,
" Fredland H. Parsons,
" Hervey M. Porter, LL B.,
" George R. Slater,
" James M. Swift, A. B.,
" Adolphus W. Wier, LL. B.,
'96 John C. Igenmann,
" George F. Greenleaf, Jr., B. S.,
'96 *m* Charles W. Hartloff,
" *l* Max Koehler,
" *l* Harry H. Wait, LL. B.,
'97 Gilbert V. Carpenter,
" Rollind I. Gillmer,
" Dewitt C. Huntoon, B. L.,
" *m* Hugh M. J. Mulheron, M. D.,
" Bernard A. Parsons,
'98 Rudolph R. Best,
" *d* Lyman S. Brown,
" William R. Carpenter,
'99 Mark B. Beattie,
" Douglas B. Burnett,
" *l* William H. Caley,
" *l* George F. Firestone,
" *m* James W. McEwan,
" Dewey D. Rockwell,
'00 *l* Edmund J. Mautz.

Besides the members of Delta Chapter, the following, initiated by Delta Tau Delta at other colleges, have studied at Ann Arbor:

'68 *l* James P. Elliott, LL. B.,
" *m* William H. Kirk, M. D.,
'69 *p* Robert G. Rex, Ph. C.,
'72 *l* Weller D. Bishop, LL. B.,
'73 *p* James P. Boyd, Ph. C.,
" *p* John G. Brown, Ph. C.,
" Walter M. Keenan, A. B.,
'74 *p* Charles G. Duncan, Ph. C.,
'75 *l* George W. Smith,
'76 *l* John P. Finley,
" *l* Harry R. Lewis, LL. B.
" *l* Edward W. Porter, LL. B.,
'77 *l* Calvin C. Staley, LL. B.,
'78 *m* William W. Ballard,
" *l* William L. Carpenter, LL. B.,
" *m* Lowell M. Gates, M. D.,
" *l* Henry A. Haigh, LL. B.,
" *h* William Watts, M. D.,
'79 *l* Cass E. Herrington, LL. B.,
'80 *l* Newberry J. Howe, LL. B.,
" *m* Lovais F. Ingersoll, M. D.,
'81 *l* Samuel D. Brosius,
" *l* Albert Dodge, LL. B.,
" *l* Fremont C. Hamilton, LL. B,
" *l* James F. Winn, LL. B.,
'82 *m* Charles H. Baker, M. D.,
" *l* Samuel W. Mangerum, M. D.,
" *m* William C. Marsh,
" *l* Martin Meeker, LL. B.,
'82 *l* Smith McF. Pence,
" *l* Henry S. Slaughter, LL. B.,
" *l* Irvine Watson, LL. B.,
" *l* Charles R. Wheeler, LL. B.,
'83 *l* *George E. Breck,
" *l* Albert De Camp, LL. B.,
" *m* James N. Martin, M. D.,
" *m* Jay S. Mead, M. D.,
" *d* Byron S. Palmer, D. D. S.,
" *l* *Elmer H. West,
'85 *m* Ervin D. Brooks, M. D.,
'87 *m* Grant S. Hicks, M. D.,
" *l* Lebbeus J. Knapp,
'89 *l* Ernest R. Keith, LL. B.,
'90 Willliam C. McCollough, A. M.,
" *l* Edward C. Mason, LL. B.,
" *l* Lambert Sternberg, LL. B.,
'91 *l* James A. Park, LL. B.,
" *l* Charles B. Warren,
'92 Gauin E. Swarthout, A. M.,
'94 Ned Abercrombie, LL. B.,
'95 *Clarence H. Perry, B. S.,
'96 Walter T. Peirce, A. M.,
" *l* Earl D. Reynolds, LL. B.,
" Charles H. Vaughan, B. S.,
'97 Clinton G. Stewart, A. B.,
'99 *m* Elihu A. Martindale,
" *l* Frederick R. Miller,
" *m* Thomas K. Moore.

Sigma Chi.—Founded at Miami University, December 24, 1855, by seven students, six of whom had been members of D. K. E., Sigma has spread into seventy-two colleges, and it now has fifty living chapters in the institutions following: Miami, Ohio Wesleyan, Mississippi, Indiana, DePauw, Dickinson, Virginia,

Gettysburg, Columbian, Bucknell, Washington and Lee, Butler, Denison, Northwestern, Hanover, Roanoke, Hampden-Sidney, Randolph-Macon, Purdue, Michigan, Pennsylvania, Centre, Illinois, Ohio State, Cincinnati, Beloit, Massachusetts Institute, Nebraska, Illinois Wesleyan, Wisconsin, Texas, Kansas, Tulane, Albion, California, Lehigh, Minnesota, North Carolina, Southern California, Cornell, Pennsylvania State, Vanderbilt, Leland Stanford, Jr., Hobart, Kentucky, Dartmouth, West Virginia, Columbia, Missouri, and Chicago. Buildings are owned at Hanover, Albion, Northwestern, Gettysburg, Hobart, and Cornell. Blue and gold are the society's colors, and the white rose is the fraternity flower. There are about 6,000 members, among the more prominent of whom are Presidents Harris of Bucknell University and White of Purdue University; William F. Elliott, of the Indiana Supreme Court; Ex-Governor J. T. Hamilton, of Illinois, Lieutenant-Governor T. A. Hanna, of Indiana; G. W. Cooper, J. M. Jordan, J. H. O'Neall, Lafe Pence, W. G. Stahlnecker, and E. C. Venable, Representatives in Congress; the Rev. Wallace Radcliffe, of Washington, D. C.; General Benjamin P. Runkle, of Cincinnati; and Fred M. Taylor, Junior Professor of Political Economy at Michigan.

BADGE OF SIGMA CHI.

A chapter of Sigma Chi called Psi was instituted at Michigan in 1874, with T. D. Cone, '76, and others as charter members, but it soon expired. Late in 1877, under the leadership of Orville S. Brumback, who had been a member at Wooster and Princeton, a chapter of Sigma Chi was formed in our law school, the literary department being thought to be fully supplied with fraternities. Theta Theta, as the new branch was called, was instituted December 12, 1877, with twelve law students as members. After an existence of nearly seventeen years the chapter was closed by the fraternity at large, which had not looked with favor upon a branch confined to prospective lawyers. In the winter of 1896–97 Theta Theta was revived as a regular academic fraternity. Among the prominent members of this charge of Sigma Chi are the following: Orville S. Brumback, '79 *l*, of the Toledo Bar; D. S. McClure, '80 *l*, Probate Judge; George D. Meiklejohn, '80, sometime Representative in Congress and now Assistant Secretary of War; and Orla B. Taylor, '87, of the Detroit Bar. Upon the University baseball team Sigma Chi has been represented by H. B. Krogman and W. W. Pepple, both '94, and of the members of the football team the society claims F. G. Higgins, '86 *l*, Fred Townsend, '88 *l*, B. J. Boutwell, '90 *l*, J. R. Sutton, '90 *l*, J. L. Morrison, '94 *l*, H. L. Dyer, '95 *l*, and J. E. Egan, '99. The tennis player R. S. Danforth, '98, is a member. While it was a law school society the chapter admitted to honorary membership President Grover Cleveland and the late Governor Alpheus Felch. Of the 226 regular members of the chapter 162 are law matriculates. The entire roll follows:

'76 Thomas D. Cone,
'78 *l* *Jeremiah W. Gladish, LL. B.,
" *l* Thomas C. Logan, LL. B.,
" *l* Eugene E. Prussing, LL. B.,
'79 *l* Henry E. Baker, LL. B.,
" *l* William L. Brackenridge, LL. B.,
" *l* Orville S. Brumback, LL. B.,
" *l* William J. Davis,
" *l* Thomas A. Dickson, LL. B.,
" *l* Jude E. Dunlap, LL. B.,
" *l* *John V. Eustace, Jr., LL. B.,
" *l* Henry C. Hanna, LL. B.,
" *l* Frank S. Hastings,
" *l* George Haywood, Jr., LL. B.,
" *l* Dana S. Lander, LL. B.,
" *l* Elbridge E. Lewis, LL. B.,
" *l* William B. McGrorty, LL. B.,
" *l* George M. Orr,
" *l* Winslow S. Pierce, LL. B.,
'80 *l* Samuel M. Brenneman, LL. B.,
" *l* Walter G. Cleveland,
" *l* Kirke H. Field, LL. B.,
" *l* *Frederick J. Haines,
" *l* Clarence A. Kenyon, LL. B.,
" *l* James P. Logan, LL. B.,
" *l* Isaac T. McCarty, LL. B.,
" *l* D. Stuart McClure, LL. B.,
" *l* Matthew M. MacMillan, LL. B.,
" *l* George D. Meiklejohn, LL. B.,
" *l* Bion De V. Meredith,
" *l* Mortimer C. Miller, LL. B.,
" *l* George F. Peabody, LL. B.,
" *l* Henry A. Smith, LL. B.,
" *l* Lynn T. Sprague, LL. B.,
'81 *l* James H. Atterbury, LL. B.,
" *l* Benjamin F. Berry,
" *l* Frederick H. Borradaile, LL. B.,
" *l* A. F. Allen Brown, LL. B.,
" *l* William F. Elliot, LL. B.,
" *l* George P. Graver, LL. B.,
" *l* Florence C. Miller,
" *l* James S. Negley, Jr.,
" *l* William C. Smith, LL. B.,
" *l* Willet B. Stickney, LL. B.,
'82 *Eugene L. Clark,
'82 James H. Clark,
" Walter Clark,
" Horace L. Combs,
" *l* Cyrus E. Davis, LL. B.,
" *l* Charles Hartzall,
" *l* Walter H. Hughes, LL. B.,
" *l* Taylor D. Kelley,
'83 *l* William B. Anderson, LL. B.,
" *l* Betrand D. Conklin,
" *l* Nathaniel P. Conrey, LL. B.,
" *l* Abner J. Easton,
" *l* Edwin R. Elliot,
" *l* Charles D. Etnyre,
" *l* Frank M. Gilmore, LL. B.,
" *l* Henry H. Hosmer, LL. B.,
" *l* Frank W. Hull, LL. B.,
" *l* Robert Matheny,
" *l* Horatio H. Nelson,
" Theodore Royer, Jr., A. B.,
" *l* William H. Savidge, LL. B.,
" *l* George E. Shaw, LL. B.,
" *l* Russell E. Shepherd, LL. B.,
" *l* Frank G. Warden, LL. B.,
" *l* Newton Wyeth,
'84 *l* Thomson Arnold,
" *d* Rowland W. Bailey, D. D. S.,
" *l* Lemuel G. Dafoe,
" *l* Reuben W. Edwards,
" *l* Albert L. Eliel,
" *l* John P. Elkins, LL. B.,
" *m* Charles O. Munns,
" Joseph K. Persons, LL. B.,
" Edson M. Rowley, LL. B.,
" Cassius A. Shafer,
" *m* J. Frederick Watts,
" John H. Yoell, LL. B.,
'85 *l* Charles J. Bocher,
" *l* John W. Bennett, LL. B.,
" *l* Elizur W. Goodrich,
" *l* Richard A. Haste,
" *l* George D. Tunnicliff, LL. B.,
" *l* Thomas Van Buskirk, LL. B.,
'86 *l* George Z. Dimmitt, LL. B.,
" *l* Elmer E. Halsey,
" *l* Francis G. Higgins, LL. B.,

'86 *l* Willet E. McMillan,
" *l* William L. Mason, LL. B.,
" *l* Frederick B. Shepherd, LL. B.,
" *l* John E. Sullivan, LL. B.,
" *l* Thomas B. White, LL. B.,
'87 *m* Walter S. Blaisdell,
" *m* Elmer E. Cary,
" *l* John B. Childe,
" *l* Hamilton Douglas, LL. B.,
" *l* Joseph H. Ingwersen, LL. B.,
" *l* Charles W. Kuhne, LL. B.,
" E. E. Ramsdell,
" *l* Francis G. Shumway, LL. B.,
" *l* Lyman B. Sullivan, LL. B.,
" *l* Orla B. Taylor, LL. B.,
'88 *l* Charles Alling, Jr., LL. B.,
" *l* Clarendon B. Eyer, LL. B.,
" *l* Frank M. Mather, LL. B.,
" *l* George H. Murdoch, Jr.,
" *l* Fred Townsend, LL. B.,
" *l* John E. Young,
'89 *l* Abraham Benedict, LL. B.,
" *l* James N. Edmonson, LL. B.,
" *l* Louis W. Holladay,
" *l* Samuel R. Ireland, LL. B.,
" *l* James A. Muir, LL. B.,
" Frederick L. Prentiss, A. B.,
" *l* Crawford S. Reilly, LL. B.,
" *l* Morton E. Stevens, LL. B.,
" *l* Charles W. Vermilion, LL. B.,
'90 *l* Benjamin J. Boutwell, LL. B.,
" *l* Leonard G. Cox,
" Dudley H. Doe,
" *l* Tolman T. Gelder,
" *l* Walter C. Parmenter, LL. B.,
" *l* George B. Shattuck, LL. B.,
" *l* James S. Shortle,
" *l* Edmund E. Sullivan, LL. B.,
" *l* John R. Sutton, LL. B.,
" *l* Percy A. Walling, LL. B.,
" *l* John F. Ziegler,
'91 *l* Pliny W. Andrews,
" Allan B. Bevans,
" James L. Bevans,
" *l* Asa H. Danforth, LL. B.,
" *l* Walter R. Dedrick, LL. B.,
" *l* Sam E. Low, LL. B.,
" *l* Charles W. Munger, LL. B.,
" *l* George L. Nye, LL. B.,
" *l* Eli R. Sutton, LL. B.,
" *l* Henry D. Wood, LL. B.,
'92 *l* James F. Burke, LL. B.,
" *l* Frank Combes, LL. B.,
" *l* George O. Crane, LL. B.,
" *l* Franklin H. Gale, LL. B.,
" *l* Frank L. Grant, LL. B ,
" *l* Walter M. Harvey, LL. B.,
" *l* George J. Reiner, LL. B.,
" *l* Joseph Sears, Jr., LL. B.,
'92 *l* *Arthur E. Sweet,
" *l* Boynton H. Van Derwent,
" *l* Arthur Webster, LL. B.,
'93 *l* Ross Beale,
" *l* Bernard F. Brough, LL. B.,
" *l* Ronoldo M. Cooper,
" *l* Herbert H. Cowen,
" *l* John H. James, LL. B.,
" *l* Ernest W. Marland, LL. B.,
" *l* George W. Nattinger,
" *m* Daniel A. Pelton,
" *l* Charles F. Roehrig, LL. B.,
" *l* Gideon M. Sipe, LL. B.,
'94 *l* Richard Apperson, LL. B.,
" *l* William H. Burtner, Jr., LL. B.,
" *l* Frank Crozier, LL. B.,
" Luther B. Freeman, LL. B.,
" *l* Edwin C. Henning, LL. B.,
" *l* Lott R. Herrick, LL B.,
" Warren W. Holliday, LL. B.,
" *l* Jerauld J. Ingle, LL. B.,
" *l* Isaac T. Jones,
" Herbert B. Krogman, B. L.,
" Dwight O. Miller, B. L.,
" *l* James L. Morrison,
" *l* Charles D. Orear, LL. B.,
" *l* Worth W. Pepple, LL. B.,
" *l* Hugh C. Smith, LL. B.,
" *l* Lewis A. Stoneman, LL. B.,
'95 *l* Richard J. Barr, LL. B.,
" *m* Robert J. Bunyan,
" *p* Arthur F. Calerdine,
" *l* Ira R. Carter, LL. B.,
" *l* James A. Cotner, LL. B.,
" *l* Robert B. Crane, LL. B.,
" *l* Horace L. Dyer, LL. B.,
" *l* Maurice E. Fitzgerald, LL. B.,
" *l* Joseph W. Kimberlin, LL. B.,
" *l* Charles O. Willits,
'96 *m* Norman L. Harris,
" *m* Saxe W. Mowers, M. D.,
" *d* Wilber Townsend, D. D. S.,
" *l* Henry J. Witbeck,
'97 Lewis B. Alger, Ph. B.,
" Louis W. Anderson,
" *m* Albert M. Carr,
" Harold O. Comstock,
" Carl H. Cooper,
" *m* James Long,
" Albert H. Stoneman, A. B.,
'98 Robert S. Danforth,
" J. Wistar Harris,
" Paul P. Ingham,
" Carl S. Kennedy,
" William L. Love,
" Ard E. Richardson,
" Morey A. Wood,
" Arthur R. Wren,
'99 Frank S. Bachelder,

'99 Charles F. Delbridge,
" Charles A. LaFever,
" Hugh Lane,
" Arthur D. Stansell,
" Clarence W. Whitney,
'00 Ebbie G. Beuret,
" George E. Granger,
" Burton O. Greening,
" Le Roy Webster,
'00 Lloyd A. Wilson,
'01 Waldo B. Bach,
" Chester O. Jordan,
" William W. Kittleman, Jr.,
" George W. Magly,
" Frederick C. Mellish,
" Walter H. Mills,
" Howard Richardson,
" Jesse J. Ricks.

The following members of Sigma Chi, elsewhere initiated, and not permanently affiliated with the local chapter, have attended the University:

'62 Jonathan W. Newman, B. S.,
'64 *l* John H. O'Neall, LL. B.,
'71 *l* Luther Short, LL. B.,
'72 *l* Julius W. Youche, LL. B.,
'73 *l* Edson B. Bauder, LL. B.,
'77 Holland W. Baker, C. E.,
" *l* D. Darwin Hughes, LL. B.,
" *l* Charles B. Moores, LL. B.,
" Elbert Sadler,
'81 *l* Jay J. Jennings, LL. B.,
" *m* Joseph A. Bennett,
'87 *m* Frank M. Kerry, M. D.,
'88 *l* William W. Baylor, LL. B.,
" Fred M. Taylor, Ph. D.,
'91 *m* James O. Ballard, M. D.,
'93 Frank H. Loomis,
'98 *l* Jacob M. Blake,
" *l* George Kingsley, Jr.,
" *m* Horace Newhart,
" *m* Solomon S. Lee,
" *m* Horace Newhart,
" *l* Matthias B. Pittman,
'99 *m* Wilber H. Cooper,
" *l* Thomas R. Dean,
" *l* John E. Egan,
" *l* Harry A. Fenton,
" *m* James M. Hervey,
'01 *h* Edgar C. Dunning.

Delta Upsilon.—The germ of this fraternity was an anti-secret society organized at Williams College in 1834, and which united with similar societies in other colleges to form the "Anti-Secret Confederation". In 1858 the present monogram badge was adopted; in 1864 Delta Upsilon was formally declared to be the name of the fraternity; and in 1880 the society became simply "non-secret." Besides six chapters which formerly existed at Vermont, Wesleyan, Washington and Jefferson, Miami, Trinity, and the College of the City of New York, Delta Upsilon has 31 branches at Williams, Union, Hamilton, Amherst, Adelbert, Colby, Rochester, Middlebury, Bowdoin, Rutgers, Brown, Colgate, New York University, Cornell, Marietta, Syracuse, Michigan, Northwestern, Harvard, Wisconsin, Lafayette, Columbia, Lehigh, Tufts, DePauw, Pennsylvania, Minnesota, Massachusetts Iustitute of Technology, Swarthmore, Leland Stanford, Jr., and California. The chapters at Williams, Hamilton, Amherst, Rutgers, Colgate, Cornell, Rochester, Syracuse, and Michigan, own buildings. Blue and gold are the colors. The membership is aobut 6,500. Particularly prominent among the alumni are the late

BADGE OF DELTA UPSILON.

President James A. Garfield; Daniel S. Lamont, late Secretary of War; former Attorney-General W. H. H. Miller; Ex-Solicitor-General Orlow W. Chapman; Charles G. Dawes, Comptroller of the Currency; Bartlett Tripp, Ambassador to Austro-Hungary; J. C. Caldwell, Ex-Minister to Uruguay; Representatives in Congress W. G. Donnan, E. P. Loring, S. E. Payne, Jarvis Rockwell, J. S. Smart, Horace B. Smith, C. W. Stone, and B. A. Willis; Brigadier-General Cyrus Hamlin; Ex-Governors Austin Blair of Michigan and M. S. Stearns of Florida; Justice Stephen J. Field of the Federal Supreme Court; U. S. Circuit Judge L. S. B. Sawyer; Ex-Chief Justice R. P. Boies of Oregon; E. G. Hamlin, formerly of the Supreme Court of Minnesota; the writers David A. Wells, Rossiter Johnson, W. E. Griffis, Homer Greene, and William Swinton; Presidents E. B. Andrews of Brown, David S. Jordan of Leland Stanford, Jr., Francis H. Snow of Kansas, J. E. Tuttle of Wabash, R. C. Flagg of Ripon, Jeremiah White of Lombard, George Washburn of Roberts College (Constantinople), and Daniel Bliss of the Syrian College at Beirut; and the Rev. Drs. Arthur T. Pierson of London, Hiram C. Haydn of Cleveland, and Nehemiah Boynton of Detroit.

CHAPTER HOUSE OF DELTA UPSILON.

The Michigan Chapter of Delta Upsilon was organized April 10, 1876, with four Sophomores and four Freshmen. In May, 1887, the society bought for $5,000 the house 522 Monroe street which it now occupies. Among the members of the chapter are Professor J. W. Jenks, '78, of Cornell University; W. A. Greeson, '79, and George N. Carman, '81, of the Lewis Institute, Chicago; the late Professor Carl W. Belser, '82, of the University of Colorado; Jacob E. Reighard, '82, J. H. Drake, '85, and C. L. Meader, '91, of the Michigan Faculty; and Professors C. W. Dodge, '86, of Rochester, F. C. Hicks, '86, of Missouri, and F. C. Clark, '87, of Leland Stanford, jr. The late Professor Edward Olney, of our University, was an honorary member. The society at Ann Arbor has been represented upon the University baseball nine by

R. M. Dott, '84, and upon the football teams by D. N. De Tar, '78, C. S. Henning, '79, E. E. Beach, '84, R. M. Dott, '84, H. G. Prettyman, '85, G. C. Schemm, '85, R. W. Beach, '86, and J. A. LeRoy, '96. Following is the roll of the 176 members of the Michigan branch of Delta Upsilon:

'78 David N. DeTar, A. B.,
" Watson D. Hinckley, Ph. B.,
" Jeremiah W. Jenks, A. B.,
" William L. Jenks, A. B.,
" John B. Johnson, C. E.,
" Ossian C. Simonds, C. E.,
'79 Charles S. Beadle, C. E.,
" Fred S. Bell, Ph. B.,
" James S. Bishop,
" Isaac C. Goff,
" William A. Greeson, A. B.,
" LeRoy Halsey, A. B.,
" Charles S. Henning, C. E.,
" Edward W. Jenney, A. B.,
" Jesse F. Millspaugh, A. B.,
" *Wilmot S. Pennington,
" *Lyman B. Sailor,
'80 *Harry S. Bangs,
" Arthur W. Burnett, A. M.,
" James T. Eaglesfield,
" *Thomas C. Green, Ph. B.,
" *William K. Jones, A. B.,
" Frank P. Secor,
'81 George N. Carman, A. B.,
" David Felmley, A. B.,
" Frederick H. Goff, Ph. B.,
" *Arthur G. Hall, A. M.,
" Charles Hutchinson, Ph. B.,
" William A. Locy, B. S.,
" Charles E. St. John,
" John G. Schurtz, A. M.,
" Asa D. Whipple, A. M.,
'82 Franklin C. Bailey, B. L.,
" *Carl W. Belser, A. B.,
" Clarence H. Childs, Ph. B.,
" Jacob E. Reighard, Ph. B.,
'83 Howard Ayres,
" Alfred M. Huycke,
" Robert G. Morrow, Ph. B.,
" Frank L. Osborne, A. M.,
" Alden H. Potter,
" Carman N. Smith, Ph. B.,
" James M. Thompson,
" Job Tuthill, B. S.,
" Samuel C. Tuthill, A. B.,
" Willard D. VanTuyle,
'84 Elmer E. Beach, A. B.,
" Henry D. Burnett, B. S.,
" Eugene A. Byrnes, A. B.,
" Emile C. Caleyron, A. B.,
" Charles W. Carman,
'84 Winthrop B. Chamberlain, A. B.,
" William C. Clark, B. S.,
" Richard M. Dott, LL. B.,
" Avon S. Hall, A. B.,
" Henry W. Hawley, Ph. B.,
" Arthur W. Stalker, A. B.,
" *Albert C. Stanard, B. L.,
'85 Robert N. Burnett, A. B.,
" Joseph H. Drake, A. B.,
" Alexander F. Lange, A. M.,
" Samuel L. Prentiss,
" Horace G. Prettyman, A. B.,
" Elias F. Schall,
" George C. Schemm, A. B.,
'86 Albert L. Arner, B. L.,
" Raymond W. Beach, B S.,
" Nathan D. Corbin, B. S.,
" Charles W. Dodge, B. S.,
" Frederick C. Hicks, A. B.,
" Chauncey A. Wheeler, A. B.,
'87 Arthur L. Benedict, A. B.,
" Clarence Byrnes, A. B.,
" Fred C. Clark, B. S.,
" Will F. Hathaway,
" Joseph M. Kramer,
" John C. Richter, Jr., LL. B. '86,
'88 Charles U. Champion, LL. B.,
" Elmer E. Clark, LL. B.,
" Oliver G. Frederick,
" James MacNaughton,
" Henry M. Morrow, LL. B.,
" Clayton A. Read, B. L.,
" William H. Turner, LL B.,
'89 Charles E. Decker,
" Charles A. Green, Ph. B.,
" Richard Khuen, B. S.,
" Frederick H. Loveridge, B. S.,
" Clyde V. Nafe, A. B.,
" Ernest B. Perry, B. S.,
" Will H. Sherzer, B. S.,
" Philip R. Whitman, B. S.,
'90 *Joseph L. McAllister,
" Irving G. McColl, B. L.,
" Arthur McNeal, A. B.,
" Edmund S. C. May, B. S.,
" Arthur D. Mott,
" Harry N. Quigley, A. B.,
" George H. Snow, Ph. B.,
" Charles A. Wheat, B. L ,
'91 James H. Harris, A. B.,
" Clarence L. Meader, A. B.,

'91 Charles W. Middlekauff,
" Reuben R. Moore, A. B.,
" William D. Plant, A. B.,
" Gabriel C. Tuthill, B. S.,
" Charles D. Warner,
" Eugene C. Warriner, A. B.,
'92 Charles C. Benedict, A. B.,
" Irving W. Durfee, LL. B. '94,
" Herbert Fox, Ph. B.,
" Fred H. Jerome,
" Richard D. Merrill, B. L.,
" Carl D. Perry, A. B.,
" Homer E. Safford, Ph. B.,
" Paul H. Seymour, B. S.,
'93 Truman P. Gaylord,
" Samuel B. Grubbs, A. B.,
" Harrison M. Randall, Ph. B.,
'94 William C. Conant, B. S.,
" Walter W. Drew, A. B.,
" Nathaniel Holmes,
" Arthur L. Hubbard, A. B.,
" Oscar Romel,
" Carlton R. Rose, Ph. B.,
" Lewis G. Seeley, A. B.,
'95 John A. Bendinger,
" Albert E. Greene, Ph. B.,
" Reynolds C. Mahaney,
" Edward G. Matter,
" Frederic B. Richardson, B. L.,
" Cassius E. Wakefield, B. S.,
'96 Harry O. Burkert,
" William A. Caldwell, Jr., B. S.,
" Raymond L. Coffin,
" John J. Crain,
" Will E. DeWitt,
" John H. Dietz,
" Hobart B. Hoyt, A. B.,
'96 James A. LeRoy, A. B.,
" Carl C. Parsons, A. B.,
" Louis A. Pratt, A. B.,
" Louis C. Walker, B. S.,
'97 John R. Crouse, A. B.,
" Chauncey W. Penoyer,
'98 George H. Allen,
" Clarence H. Brand,
" Harold D. Corbusier,
" Merritt M. Hawxhurst,
" Frederick M. Loomis,
" Frederick A. McVay.
" William P. McVay,
" Henry W. Nichols,
" Archibald W. Smalley,
" Charles C. Wallin,
" Samuel H. Warriner,
'99 Francis M. Bacon,
" Laurence L. T. Driggs.
" Arthur J. Farmer,
" Donald Fuller,
" Thomas S. Gray,
" Arthur M. Hyde,
" Clifford G. Roe,
" James H. Sawyer,
" Edward Schreiner,
" Nelson W. Thompson,
" Allen H. Zacharias,
'00 Norman S. Atcheson,
" Stephen P. Cobb,
" Charles H. Reynolds,
" Harrison S. Smalley,
'01 Emerson Davis,
" Ernest E. Freeman.
" Walter Gradle,
" Edward W. Kiefer,
" E. Sprague Pratt.

In addition to the foregoing these members of Delta Upsilon have attended our University:

'68 *m* Thomas H. Stewart, M. D.,
'73 *m* Charles R. Dryer,
" *l* Jacob P. Winstead, LL. B.,
'74 Francis E. Arnold, A. B.,
'75 *m* Samuel G. Moore,
'76 *m* John W. Mack,
'81 *l* Charles E. McKinney,
'83 *l* William F. Denfield,
" *m* J. S. Van Vechten, M. D.,
'87 *l* Elmer E. Brooks, LL. B.,
'92 *l* Fenton W. North, LL. B.,
'96 *p* Harold White,
'00 *m* Card H. Lund,
" *m* George K. Tinker.

Phi Kappa Psi.—Charles P. T. Moore, afterwards a member of the Supreme Court of Appeals of West Virginia, and W. H. Letterman, founded Phi Kappa Psi at Jefferson College, in February, 1852. Fifty-seven institutions have had branches of the fraternity, which is to-day represented in thirty-nine colleges and Universities, viz.: Washington and Jefferson, Virginia, Washington and Lee, Allegheny, Bucknell, Gettysburg, Hampden-Sydney,

Mississippi, Dickinson, Franklin and Marshall, Ohio Wesleyan, Northwestern, DePauw, Chicago, Wittenberg, Iowa, Columbian, Cornell, Lafayette, Indiana, Wabash, Columbia, Wisconsin, Kansas, Michigan, Pennsylvania, Johns Hopkins, Ohio State, Beloit, Syracuse, Minnesota, Colgate, Swarthmore, West Virginia, Leland Stanford, Jr., Brooklyn Polytechnic, Nebraska, Amherst, and Dartmouth. Buildings are owned at Gettysburg, Colgate, Cornell, Michigan, Beloit, Minnesota, Syracuse, Kansas, and Amherst. Lavender and pink are the fraternity colors. Laurel and ivy are the botanical preferences of the society. Of the 7,300 members the following are perhaps the most prominent: Presidents Fisher of Hanover, McKnight of Gettysburg, and Ort of Wittenberg; Professors John W. White of Harvard, James R. Weaver of DePauw, Edgar F. Smith of Pennsylvania, and Amos E. Dolbear of Tufts; Joseph B. Foraker, United States Senator; F. E. Beltzhoover, H. H. Bingham, W. T. Campbell, P. H. Dugro, G. W. Faris, C. S. Hartman, C. L. Henry, G. A. Jenks, E. L. Martin, W. H. Perry, S. R. Peters, J. E. Watson, Boyd Winchester, and S. H. Yocum, Representatives in Congress; E. P. C. Lewis, formerly Minister to Portugal; E. C. Little, sometime Consul-General at Cairo; Judges C. P. T. Moore of West Virginia, J. W. Phillips of Tennessee, W. W. Smith of Arkansas, and M. L. Buchwalter, of Cincinnati; Governor Lloyd Lowndes of Maryland; Charles C. McCabe, Bishop of the M. E. Church; the Rev. E. M. Stires, Rector of Grace Church, Chicago; Ex-Lieutenant-Governor D. B. Penn of Louisiana; and the Confederate Major-General James A. Walker of Virginia.

BADGE OF PHI KAPPA PSI.

The Michigan Alpha of Phi Kappa Psi was instituted at Ann Arbor in December, 1876, by William Yost, Monmouth '76, then studying in our law school. Like him, the other charter members were professional students; but representatives from the literary department were secured subsequently, and the chapter now confines its initiations to that branch of the University. Thirteen years ago the Millen property in Washtenaw Avenue was leased for a chapter house, and in April, 1893, it was bought by the society. Among the members at Ann Arbor are Judge J. W. McKinley, '79, of Los Angeles; Arthur S. Parker, '79 *p*, recently a member of the Detroit Board of Park Commissioners; Frank B. Leland, '82, of the Detroit Bar; Frank H. Hodder, '83, Professor of History at Kansas; Lewis A. Rhoades, '84, Professor of German at Illinois;

Professor J. V. Denney, '85, of Ohio State; Walter S. Holden, '89, and G. Fred Rush, '89, of the Chicago Bar; J. R. Effinger, Jr., '91, Instructor in French at Michigan; and James H. Prentiss, '96, Secretary of the Alumni Association of our University. Among the chapter's prominent athletes have been the baseball players W. C. Malley, '90, G. W. Denney, '91, and C. B. Smeltzer, '94, and the football men W. C. Malley, '90, and J. W. F. Bennett, '98. The chapter has enrolled 161 men. Their names follow:

CHAPTER HOUSE OF PHI KAPPA PSI.

'77 *l* Francis G. Carpenter, LL. B.,
" *l* William T. Coad, LL. B.,
" *l* Clement M. Hammond, LL. B.,
" *d* Marion Holland, D. D. S.,
'78 *l* Robert B. Brown,
" *l* James W. Johnston, LL. B.,
" *l* *Syrus T. D. Phelps, LL. B.,
" *m* George W. Spencer, M. D.,
" *l* William Yost, LL. B.,
'79 *l* Almon F. Hanson, LL. B.,
" *l* Samuel D. C. Hayes,
" James W. McKinley, B. S.,
" *p* Arthur S. Parker, Ph. C.,
'80 *Ralph A. Angell,
" *m* Frank D. Baker, M. D.,
" Archie W. Banks,
" John W. Dorst, C. E.,
" Frank P. Satterlee, M. E.,
'81 Claude R. Buchanan, A. B.
" Festus C. Cole, Ph. B.,
" Arthur B. Cook,
" William S. Hill, A. B.,
" Herbert M. Pelham, Ph. B.,
" *l* John R. Richards,
'82 John C. Chynoweth,
" Frederick G. Coldren, A. B.,
" *l* Walter F. Cooling, LL. B. '84,
" Harris B. Dahl,
" Frank B. Leland, A. B.,
" *p* Frederick L. Wilson, Ph. C.,
'83 James C. Dunning,
" Frank H. Hodder, Ph. M.,
" John H. Jennings, A. B.,
" Henry G. Ohls, Ph. B.,
'83 Frank L. Webster,
'84 George E. Mosher,
" Lewis A. Rhoades, A. B.,
'85 Caleb D. Arner,
" Edward M. Darrow,
" Joseph V. Denney, A. B.,
" Charles H. Harvey, A. B.,
" E. L. Hollingsworth,
" Victor E. Loughridge,
" Samuel C. Parks, A. B.,
" Everett T. Schuler,
" James B. Sheean, A. B.,
'86 Walter B. Bliss, A. B.,
" Fred B. Hollenbeck, A. B.,
" John N. James, A. B.,
" Edward L. Parmenter, Jr., B. L.,
" Henry A. Reynolds, A. B.,
" G. Byron Swisher, A. B.,
" Frank T. Wright, A. B.,
'87 Joseph Halsted, B. S.,
" Kendal W. Hess, B. S.,
" Charles Hudson,
" Clarence J. Miner,
" Robert E. Park, Ph. B.,
'88 Clarence G. Campbell, Ph. B.,
" David C. Christopher,
" Rossetter G. Cole, Ph. B.,
" Walter J. Hamilton, Ph. B..
" George F. James, A. M.,
" Frank G. Plain, A. B.,
" Ebenezer F. Walbridge, B. S.,
" Edwin E. Washburn, Ph. B.,
'89 Henry T. Bannon, B. L.,
" Walter S. Holden, A. B.,

'89 Henry Hudson,
" Frederick S. Loomis, A. B.,
" Robert B. Preble, A. B.,
" George F. Rush, A. B.,
" Robert B. Wilcox,
'90 Glenn M. Averill,
" Grant M. Ford, A. B.,
" William C. Malley, LL. B.,
" William W. Stevens,
'91 George W. Denney,
" John R. Effinger, Jr., Ph. B.,
" James B. Smalley,
'92 Mortimer O. Bigelow,
" Ralph R. Bradley,
" William H. Cole,
" William M. Johnstone, B. S.,
" Philip L. Marshall,
" Eber C. Preble,
" Wallace B. Rogers,
" Frank C. Smith, A. B.,
" Cyrus C. Warren,
'93 Ira C. Belden, Ph. B.,
" William J. Currer, B. S.,
" Philip S. Gardiner, B. S.,
" Valentine S. Ives, B. S.,
" Joseph J. Morsman, B. S.,
" Samuel C. Parks, Jr.,
" John Van Nortwick,
'94 Fred W. Colegrove,
" Hiram G. Effinger,
" Walter H. Kirk,
" Edgar M. Morsman, Jr., Ph. B.,
" Carlin Philips, Ph. B.,
" Andrew J. Purdy, B. L.,
" Charles P. Richardson,
" Charles B. Smeltzer, Ph. B.,
" William S. Smith, B. S.,
" Fred H. Staudt,
" Ernest H. Warren, B. L.,
'95 George A. McCollum,
" Charles H. Morse, Jr., B. S.,
" Charles H. Parkes,
" Henry A. Rice,
" Charles W. Sencenbaugh, B. L.,
" Bertram S. Varian,
" Carl B. Williams,
'96 Lewis H. Burton,
'96 Arthur G. Cummer,
" Waldo E. Cummer,
" Charles F. Drake, Ph. C. '95,
" Percy H. Evans,
" William B. MacHarg,
" James H. Prentiss, B. L.,
" David Whiting,
" Henry W. Williams,
'97 Harry A. Cole, B. L.,
" Robert L. Dean, B. L.,
" Herbert R. Gates,
" Fred S. Gerrish,
" Dan G. Swannell,
" John R. Tiernan,
" Miles G. Varian,
'98 J. Walter F. Bennett,
" James C. F. Bradley,
" James C. Chase,
" Bartlett C. Dickinson,
" Harry N. Hosick,
" Ward Hughes,
'99 Clarence Baum,
" Charles B. Hole,
" Lemuel H. Hole, Jr.,
" Eugene R. Lewis,
" William L. Mack,
" Thomas A. Neal,
" James T. Noble,
" Hurlbut H. Pinney,
" Charles B. Rider,
" Russell M. Simmons,
'00 George E. Baldwin,
" John H. Bartelme,
" George C. Davis,
" Thomas W. Flournoy,
" Grattan Foley,
" Gordon Grey,
" John D. Kilpatrick,
" George R. Sims,
" Joseph J. Walser,
" William W. Wood,
'01 Herbert Campbell,
" Harry K. Crafts,
" Fred Loomis,
" Frank M. Morseman,
" Frederick H. VanAllen.

The following members of Phi Kappa Psi, not permanently enrolled in the local chapter, have attended the University of Michigan:

'64 *m* James P. Hassler, M. D,
'67 Amos E. Dolbear, M. E.,
" *l* Nathan W. Fitzgerald,
" *l* Samuel R. Peters, LL. B.,
'69 Morris L. Buchwalter,
'70 *l* Amos Wolfe, LL. B.,
'71 *l* Edward Hutchinson,
'72 *l* John A. Pickler, LL. B.,
" *l* Festus Walters, LL. B.,
'74 *l* Charles G. Canfield, LL. B.,
" *l* John G. Woolley,
'75 *m* John W. McMillen,

'76 *l* Samuel R. Bell,
" *l* Alfred G. Carpenter, LL. B.,
" *l* John A. Moninger, LL. B.,
" Jonathan C. Sheppard, C. E.,
'78 *m* Samuel C. Buchan,
" *l* Joseph B. Connell, LL. B.,
'80 *m* James D. Hillis, M. D.,
'81 *l* Eddy M. Campbell, LL. B.,
" *l* *Frederick W. Lord, LL. B.,
'82 *l* Harvey Musser, LL. B.,
" *p* George H. M. Palmer, Ph. C.,
" *l* William F. Reed, LL. B.,
" *l* Charles F. Teter, LL. B.,
" *l* Ralph E. Twitchell, LL. B.,
'83 *l* Albert T. Cooper,
" *l* Woodfin D. Robinson, LL. B.,
" *m* James B. Siggins, M. D.,
'84 *m* Horace S. Davis,
" *m* William M. Edwards, M. D.,
" *m* Louis E. Tieste,
'85 *m* William K. Cherryholmes,
'86 *m* Frederick A. Swartwood, M. D.,
'87 *l* John A Fairchild, LL. B.,
'88 *l* Philip K. Buskerk,
" *l* Lewis C. Dennett, LL. B.,
'88 *l* Perley F. Gosbey, LL. B.,
" *l* Leander T. Turner, LL. B.,
'89 *p* Warner P. Cary,
" *l* James S. McCreery,
" *m* De Witt C. R. Miller,
" *l* James C. Needham, LL. B.,
" *l* Henry Warrum,
" *l* Noble Warrum, Jr.,
'90 *l* Laurence V. Buskirk,
" *l* William C. Malley, LL. B.,
" *l* George Shriber,
'91 *m* George R. Curran,
" *m* Robert B. Preble,
'92 *l* William H. Alexander,
" *l* William A. Beasly, LL. B.,
'93 *l* Campbell M. Voorhees, LL. B.,
" *l* Edwin A. Wilcox, LL. B.,
'95 *l* Charles B. Henderson, LL. B.,
" *l* Edward M. McCullough,
'96 *l* Daniel M. Glasscock, LL. B.,
" *l* Harry Y. Saint, LL. B.,
" *l* Merrill C. Slutz,
'98 *l* Edward E. Hindman,
'99 *l* Henry L. Goodbread.

Phi Alpha.—This fraternity is said to have been founded at the College of the City of New York in 1878, and to have had chapters in Rochester and Toronto. The badge was changed once or twice, but a monogram was the accepted form. A chapter existed at the University from 1882 to 1885. General A. L. Bresler '85, of Detroit, is one of the graduates. The roll of members which follows has been prepared from a list published in the Palladium for 1883, on page 112:

'83 *l* Oliver N. Downs, LL. B.,
" *l* Edgar H. Eckert, LL. B.,
" *l* Edward T. Noonan, LL. B.,
" *l* Eugene A. Roby, LL. B.,
" *l* Charles Sawyer,
'84 *l* Edward M. Bailey, LL. B.,
" *l* Charles E. Buroker, LL.. B.,
'84 *d* Louis R. Esau, D. D. S.,
" *d* Roy Nance,
'85 Arthur L. Bresler, A. B.,
" Thomas J. Peach, B. S.,
'86 John M. Opsahl, LL. B.,
— L. D. Taylor.

Chi Phi.—The Chi Phi fraternity is the result of the union in 1867 and 1874, of three different societies, each of which was named "Chi Phi," and the oldest of which was instituted at Princeton College in 1854, by John Maclean, Jr. Of the 45 branches accredited to Chi Phi, nineteen survive. These, in the order of age, are situated in the colleges following, viz.: Virginia, Rutgers, Hampden-Sidney, Franklin and Marshall, Georgia, Cornell, Emory, Wofford, Lehigh, Massachusetts Institute, Amherst, Lafayette, California, Sheffield (Yale) Scientific, Rennselaer Polytechnic, Ohio State, Vanderbilt, Stevens Institute, and Texas. Buildings are owned by the society at Amherst, California, Cornell, Rutgers, and the Yale Scientific School. Scarlet and blue are the colors of this order. Of the 3,800 members the most distinguished are U. S. District Judge Emory Spear, the late Henry M. Grady of Georgia, President George Winston of the University of Texas, General Lucius H. Warren of Philadelphia, and the Rt. Rev. F. R. Graves, Missionary Bishop of Shanghai. In 1882 a branch was instituted in the University of Michigan, the charter being entrusted to four students in the professional schools who had been Chi Phi men elsewhere. The chapter lived two years, never appeared in The Palladium, and had the following members:

BADGE OF CHI PHI.

'83 *m* Benjamin D. Bond, M. D.,
'83 *l* William A. Griffith, LL. B.,
" *m* Nathaniel P. Hunter,
" *l* Rawson T. Lovell, LL. B.,
" *l* Francis H. Register, LL. B.,
'84 *m* Charles A. Peterson,
" *l* Edward E. Rowe,
'84 *l* Leon H. Wadsworth, LL. B,,
" *h* Washington Wilson,
'86 Jacob J. Bernhardt,
" Frank M. Bingham,
" Negley D. Cochran,
" Alpheus E. Doe, LL. B.,
" Thomas A. Pool.

Chi Phi has also been represented in our University by the following members, initiates of other chapters:

'76 *l* James L. Humphreys,
" *l* Theodore Winningham, LL. B.,
'78 *Walter S. Abell, M. E.,
" *l* Charles N. Lauman, LL. B.,
'79 *m* Edwin L. Fosdick, M. D.,
'81 *l* Charles C. Black,
" *l* John D. White,
'82 William G. Elliot,
" *l* John P. Knowles, Jr.,
'86 *m* Frank W. Martin, M. D.,
'87 *l* Frank P. Whiteley, LL. B.,
'88 *m* Robert P. Gilbert,
'90 W. P. Morgan.

Phi Gamma Delta.—This fraternity was founded in May, 1848, by six students at Jefferson College. It has entered seventy-one different colleges, and is now represented in forty-five, viz., Washington and Jefferson, North Carolina, Marietta, DePauw, Bethel, Gettysburg, Virginia, Allegheny, Hanover, College of the City of New York, Wabash, Columbia, Illinois Wesleyan, Roanoke, Knox, Hampden-Sidney, Washington-Lee, Ohio Wesleyan, Kansas, Wooster, Lafayette, Wittenberg, Denison, William-Jewell, Lehigh, Colgate, Pennsylvania State, Cornell, Richmond, Minnesota, Tennessee, Johns-Hopkins, Leland Stanford, Jr., Worcester Polytechnic, New York, Wisconsin, Trinity, Union, and Amherst. Buildings are owned by the branches at Gettysburg and Pennsylvania State. Of the

BADGE OF PHI GAMMA DELTA.

members the following may be named: Presidents James C. Moffatt of Washington and Jefferson, C. H. Dabney of the University of Tennessee, W. F. McDowell of the University of Denver, J. D. Dreler of Roanoke College, Leslie Waggener of the University of Texas, H. M. Brown of the University of Nevada, and John M. Coulter, formerly of Lake Forest University, now Professor of Botany in the University of Chicago; J. C. Ridpath and Maurice Thompson, the authors; the Rt. Rev. W. E. McLaren, Bishop of Illinois; the Presbyterian clergymen James Woodrow and J. H. Shedd; Cyrus L. Pershing of the Supreme Court of Pennsylvania; W. H. Goodlove, Ex-Minister to Belgium; U. S. Senators Z. B. Vance and Charles W. Fairbanks; Representatives in Congress J. H. Hopkins, Morton C. Hunter, A. G. Jenkins, W. W. McClelland, T. M. Patterson, H. Y. Riddle, and E. M. Wilson; and Ex-Governor J. A. Copper of Colorado. Royal purple is the fraternity color, and the heliotrope is the fraternity flower.

ARMS OF PHI GAMMA DELTA.

Alphi Phi, the Michigan branch of Phi Gamma Delta, was installed December 8, 1885, by twelve students, five of whom had been admitted at other colleges. Internal dissensions led to a return of the charter in the spring of 1895. Edwin A. Blakeslee, '91, of the Michigan Senate, Dr. Aldred S. Warthin, '91 *m*, of our Medical Faculty, and A. A. Pearson, '94, the founder of The Michigan Alumnus, are included in the roll of seventy-five members, which reads thus:

'86 Jonathan Heaton, A. B.,
" *m* Edward B. Patterson, M. D.,
" Edwin D. Peifer, A. B.,
'87 Frank E. Beeman, A. B.,
" Charles E. Grove, A. B.,
" Otto Negelspach, M. D.,
" Alphonso G. Newcomer, A. B.,
" *l* James B. Owens, LL. B.,
" *l* Charles M. Stephens,
'88 Henry H. Brown, A. B.,
" *l* Andrew R. Cunningham,
'88 David Decker, LL. B.,
" Ellsworth T. Derr, A. B.,
" Preston M. Hickey, A. B.,
" *Charles B. Stevens,
" Elmer G. Willyoung, B. S.,
'89 Andrew M. Brown, B. S.,
" *l* Charles C. Chandler,
" Charles H. Dodge,
" *l* John M. Ormond, LL. B.,
" Harmon B. St. Clair, B. L.,
" James Wilson,

'89 Samuel A. Wilson,
" James B. Wood, B. S.,
'90 John S. Alexander, B. S.,
" Charles J. Greenstreet, B. S.
" Jacob L. Haner, A. B.,
" Forest G. Sweet, Ph. B.,
" Milford Wade,
'91 Edwin A. Blakeslee,
" Harry B. Carter,
" *l* Harry F. Downing, LL. B.,
" Walter S. Drew,
" *l* George Hefferan, LL. B.,
" Robert B. Lederle,
" *l* Amos C. Maple, LL. B.,
" *l* Janes S. Martin,
" *l* Enoch J. Price, LL. B.,
" William F. Ryburn,
" *m* Aldred S. Warthin, M. D.,
'92 Thomas E. Barnum, B. S.,
" Edwin H. Cheney, B. S.,
" Frederick P. Hoffman,
" Frederick P. T. Waterhouse,
'93 William E. Cullen, Jr., A. B..
" Stephen A. Douglas,
" *l* Charles K. Friedman, LL. B.,
" *m* Andrew M. Harvey,
" Charles A. Pratt,
'93 *l* Charles I. Stouffer,
" *l* Condit Voorhees,
" John P. Whiting,
'94 William H. Charnley, Ph. B.,
" Edward P. Childs,
" Norman T. Harrington,
" Alvick A. Pearson, B. L.,
" Frederick L. Searing, A. B.,
'95 *l* Walter R. Clayton, LL. B.,
" Harry De Y. Mills, B. S.,
" Isaac Sheets,
" Emmet P. Updergraff,
" Arthur J. Waldron,
" Elba E. Watson, B. L.,
'96 Barlow C. Dickey,
" *l* Charles A. Gridley, LL. B.,
" *l* Bertrand Lichtenberger, LL. B.,
" Charles E. Skinner, B. L.,
" Dandridge Spotswood,
'97 Edward W. Guitteau,
" Charles D. Webster, B. S.,
" Horatio E. West,
" Fred H. Winter,
" Wesley J. Wuerfel,
'98 George R. Harper,
" William P. Kavanaugh.

In addition to the official roll of the local chapter, Phi Gamma Delta has been represented at Ann Arbor by the following:

'71 *l* John M. Howard, LL. B.,
'78 *l* Morris C. Baum, LL. B.,
" *l* Herman H. Osthaus, LL. B.,
" *l* Benjamin F. Smith, LL. B.,
'79 *l* Joseph F. McNaught,
'82 George O. Curme, A. B.,
'83 *h* Morton C. Reeves, M. D.,
" *m* Frederick K. Smith,
'91 *l* Harold Taylor, LL. B.,
'93 *l* Alonzo J. Falknor, LL. B.,
" *l* James B. Nelson, LL. B.,
'94 *l* Ernest L. Finley,
" *l* Arthur J. Waldron,
'96 *l* Chester G. Browne,
" *l* Arthur Miller, LL. B.

Alpha Tau Omega was founded in the city of Richmond, Virginia, September 11, 1865, by a recent graduate and two seniors of the Virginia Military Institute, where, consequently, the mother chapter was placed. Until 1881, the growth of the fraternity was confined to the South, but since April of that year charters have been granted to many colleges in the North and West. Of the seventy chapters instituted by the society forty-three are in active operation. These are located at the following colleges: Washington and Lee, Cumberland, Virginia, Trinity (N. C.), University of the South, Columbian, Georgia, North Carolina, Alabama Polytechnic, Mercer, Pennsylvania, Emory, Muhlenburg, Adrian, Mount Union, St. Lawrence, Lehigh,

BADGE OF ALPHA TAU OMEGA.

Southwestern, Gettysburg, Wittenberg, Southern Alabama, Tulane, Vermont, Ohio Wesleyan, Cornell, Hillsdale, Georgia School of Technology, Wooster, Albion, Vanderbilt, Marietta, Maine, Leland Stanford, Jr., Ohio State, Colby, Tufts, Rose Polytechnic, Southwestern Baptist, Brown, Austin, Illinois, and Texas. Twenty of the living branches are in Southern colleges, eleven in Northern, and twelve in the Western. There are about 4,400 members, prominent among whom are the late Erskine M. Ross, Federal Circuit Judge; H. H. Dinwiddie, late President of Texas A. and M. College; Professor E. P. Lewis of the University of California; Professor F. M. Page of the University of Pennsylvania; J. H. Acklen, H. H. Carlton, R. P. W. Morris, Andrew Price, F. M. Simmons, Zachary Taylor, and T. S. Wilkinson, Representatives in Congress; Clifton R. Breckinridge, former Ambassador to Russia; the Rt. Rev. T. F. Gailor, Assistant Bishop of Tennessee; the Rev. Otis A. Glazebrook of Elizabeth, N. J., and William Fitts, Ex-Attorney General of Louisiana. Sky-blue and old-gold are the colors, and the white tea-rose is the fraternity flower. A chapter named Beta-Lambda was instituted in our University, December 8, 1888, when several law students were initiated as charter members. In 1893–94 the chapter ceased to exist, after having built up a roll of forty-nine members, whose names follow:

'89 *l* Joseph L. Glover, LL. B.,
" *l* Charles M. Hammond, LL. B.,
" *l* Frederick A. Sabin, LL. B.,
" *l* LaVergne B. Stevens, LL. B.,
" *l* Oscar R. Zipf, LL. B.,
'90 *l* John B. Chaddock, LL. B.,
" George M. Hosack,
" *l* Rodolphus W. Joslyn, LL. B.,
" *l* Wesley L. Mutton,
" *m* John D. Riker, M. D.,
" *m* Curtis C. Williams, M. D.,
" *m* Henry M. Woolman, M. D.,
'91 *d* Joseph H. Billmeyer, D. D. S.,
" William C. Johnson,
" *l* James W. Freeman,
'92 William S. Chandler,
" *l* Herbert W. Childs, LL. B.,
" Frank B. Graves,
" Asa H. Hankerson,
" Russell H. Helmley,
" George M. Hosack,
" George T. Jordan,
" Willard D. Norton,
" *m* Clyde P. Platts,
" *l* Abram L. Riker, LL. B.,
'92 George A. Robinson,
" Darius P. Shuler,
'93 *l* Frederick R. Barney, LL. B.,
" *l* Zeph G. Dunn, LL. B.,
" Will J. Fisher, B. S.,
" Walter G. Stark,
" Maurice C. Wright, A. B.,
— Roy H. Spencer,
'94 *m* Frederick W. Heysett, M. D.,
" Moulton J. Hosack,
" Oscar J. Larson, LL. B.,
" Edward F. LeGendre,
" *d* Robert B. Mackenzie, D. D. S.,
" *m* Edwin A. Murbach, M. D.,
" Harry L. VanTuyl, B. S.,
" *l* Winfred J. Wallace,
— Janson E. Hammond,
'95 George F. Key,
" LeRoy C. Yeoman,
'96 *m* Chester B. Bliss,
" Charles E. Driggs,
" Thomas J. Elliott,
" William W. Keer,
— H. Walter Booth.

Sigma Alpha Epsilon.—Founded by seven students at the University of Alabama, March 9, 1856, this fraternity was until 1883 confined to Southern colleges. It has had eighty-six branches, thirty-one of which are inactive; and it is now represented at Alabama, North Carolina, Virginia, Bethel, Cumberland, Georgia, Mississippi, Southwestern Baptist, Washington and Lee, Furman, Mercer, Alabama A. & M. College, Southern, Tennessee, University of the South, Emory, Southwestern Presbyterian University, Central, Davidson, Vanderbilt, Missouri, Texas, Mt. Union, Wofford, Adrian, Allegheny, Ohio Wesleyan, Michigan, Simpson, Cincinnati, Georgia School of Technology, Dickinson, Colorado, Cornell, Denver, Franklin, Leland-Stanford, Jr., Pennsylvania State, Boston, Washington (Mo.), Ohio State, Trinity, Massachusetts Institute, Harvard, Purdue, Nebraska, Bucknell, Worcester Polytechnic, Arkansas, Northwestern, California, St. Stephen's, Columbia, Tulane, and Louisiana. Chapter houses are owned at the University of the South, Leland Stanford, Jr., and Michigan. Purple and gold are the colors of the fraternity, and its flower is the violet. The number of members is about 5,000. Prominent among those who have worn the badge in college life are Postmaster-General William L. Wilson, now President of Washington and Lee University; Representatives in Congress, N. N. Clements and George P. Harrison of Alabama, Henry Jackson and Thomas E. Watson of Georgia, W. A. Harris of Kansas, J. W. Stokes of South Carolina, J. C. Hutcheson of Texas, and T. H. B. Brownie and J. W. Lawson of Virginia; Governor W. Y. Atkinson of Georgia; Ex-Governor Vernon H. Vaughn of Utah; Supreme Court Judges E. G. Simmons of Georgia, and Louis Hillard of North Carolina; Walter Acker of the Court of Appeals of Texas; and Harvey Johnson, Consul at Antwerp. Michigan Iota-Beta was instituted in our University with five charter members, January 12, 1889, "the entire Adrian branch coming up

BADGE OF S. A. E.

CHAPTER HOUSE OF S. A. E.

to give zest to the ceremonies." In 1893 the chapter established itself in a house built for it in Hamilton Park at an expenditure of $12,000. The football players W. I. Aldrich and R. W. E. Hayes, both of '95, are members of this society. Following is the roll of members 99 in number:

'91 Fred G. Cadwell, A. B.,
" Alfred S. Calkins, B. S.,
" Albert Z. Horning,
" Frederick E. King,
" *l* Stephen B. Monroe, LL. B.,
" David W. Spence, C. E.,
'92 Frederick R. Angell,
" Charles J. Barr, Ph. B.,
" George P. Cheney, B. L.,
" *l* George M. Harton, LL. B.,
" Charles W. Heywood, A. B.,
" *l* Ira A. Leighley,
" Edward C. Nichols, B. L.,
" *l* Horton C. Rorick, LL. B.,
" *l* Nobusobwro Sekurai, LL. B.,
" Oscar W. Swift,
" Pitt Townsend, A. B.,
" *l* Takenosuke Turnya, LL. B.,
" Arthur J. Tuttle, Ph. B.,
" Frederick E. Wood, A. B.,
'93 William Hunter, A. B.,
" Harry R. King, B. S.,
" George C. McDiarmid, B. S.,
" Charles C. Starr,
" William H. Wilson, B. S.,
'94 William W. Cook,
" William W. Hurd, Ph. B.,
" Samuel C. Irvin,
" Leroy L. Janes, Jr.,
" *l* Lewis B. Lindsay, LL. B.,
" *l* John B. Newman, LL. B.,
'95 William I. Aldrich,
" Eugene B. Binford, LL. B.,
" William E. Bolles,
" T. Edwin Gray, A. B.,
" Ralph W. E. Hayes, Ph. B.,
" Herman F. Hoch, Ph. B.,
" Louis G. Hupp,
" George C. Keech,
" Edwin H. Kelley,
" John B. Newman,
" Pearl O. Robinson,
" *p* Wilber J. Teeters, Ph. C.,
" Charles L. Wolf,
'96 *l* Clarke E. Baldwin, LL. B.,
" Harry J. Bond,
" J. Earl Brown,
" Frederick G. Candee,
" Hiram A. Emery,
" Norman Flowers, LL. B.,
'96 George E. Foerster,
" Adam H. Gentzler,
" *l* James D. Kennedy, LL. B.,
" *g* Will L. Lowrie,
" *d* Charles L. Sherwood,
" *l* Bradshaw H. Swales, LL. B.,
" Charles G. Towar,
" Richard H. Watts,
'97 Frederick S. Atwood,
" George J. Baker,
" Edward H. Decker,
" Walter Gray,
" Arthur D. Jackson,
" Harrison C. Jackson, B. L.,
" William C. Johnson,
" Roy M. Rogers,
" Osmund H. Tower,
'98 Wallace E. Brown,
" Charles G. Church,
" *l* Corry C. Ferrell,
" Albert L. Hayes,
" Forest S. Hayes,
" *l* William D. Kilpatrick,
" Charles E. Mudge,
" *l* Julius T. Muench,
" *l* Harvey Yeaman,
'99 Frank E. Baker,
" *l* Clifford W. Crandall,
" Jerome B. Harrington,
" Albert H. Keith,
" Charles W. Kent,
" Byron H. Knapp,
" Samuel K. McLeod,
" John T. Mountain,
" Joe C. Osborn,
" Frederick R. Sherman,
" Clyde I. Webster,
" Hugh White,
" Lucien A. Wittenmeyer,
'00 *l* Otis D. Allen,
" *l* Frederic E. Carlatt,
" *l* Matthew A. Foster,
" *l* Louis C. Ling,
" *l* Ralph Parker,
" *l* James Symington,
'01 Samuel L. Chambers,
" Joseph H. Harris, Jr.,
" Adrian S. Houck,
" Parvin N. Patterson.

Theta Delta Chi.—Founded at Union College in 1847 by six members of the class of '49, Theta Delta Chi has visited thirty-eight different institutions, and now exists in twenty-one, viz., Rennselaer Polytechnic, 1853-70, 1885; Brown, 1853-77, 1886; Bowdoin, 1854-64, 1872; Harvard, 1855-60, 1885-87, 1892; Tufts, 1856; Hobart, 1857; Hamilton, 1867; Lafayette, 1868; Dartmouth, 1869; Cornell, 1870; Boston, 1876; College of the City of New York, 1881; Columbia, 1883; Lehigh, 1884; Amherst, 1885; Sheffield (Yale) Scientific, 1887; Michigan, 1889; Williams, 1891; Minnesota, 1892; Wisconsin, 1895; Columbian, 1896. The fraternity is essentially Eastern in character as in origin. Buildings are owned at Tufts, Hamilton, Hobart, Amherst, and Cornell. Black, white, and blue are the colors. The membership is about 3,900. Among the prominent alumni are the following: John Hay, Ambassador to Great Britain; W. W. Thomas, Minister to Sweden; George H. Bridgman, Minister to Bolivia; J. L. Rathbone, Ex-Consul-General; John W. Griggs, Attorney-General of the United States, and recent Governor of New Jersey; W. D. Bloxham, Governor of Florida; H. C. Brockmeyer, Ex-Governor of Missouri; the late Nathan F. Dixon, United States Senator; D. U. Lockwood, C. H. Sinnickson, F. C. Stevens, and Henry R. Gibson, Representatives in Congress; George W. Smith, President of Trinity College; Elmer H. Capen, President of Tufts College; the Episcopal Bishops, M. N. Gilbert of Minnesota, A. M. Randolph of Southern Virginia, and J. H. D. Wingfield of Northern California; Arthur L. Brown of the Federal District Court; George B. Young, sometime Chief-Justice of Minnesota; Thomas Smith, Chief-Justice of New Mexico; the late W. K. Logie, Brigadier-General; and William Smith, Paymaster-General of the United States. Gamma Deuteron, the Michigan branch of Theta Delta Chi, was instituted December 13, 1889, with five charter members from '91 and two from '92. In the autumn of 1891 the chapter rented a house, and it is now domiciled at 1008 Cornwell Place. Among the graduates are George Rebec, '91, Instructor in Philosophy, and Charles H. Gray, '95, Instructor in English, both in our University. William F. Holmes, '96 *h*, catcher of the University baseball nine and member of the football team, and Frank J. Sexton, '98 *m*, and C. E. Wehrle, '99, both of the baseball nine, belonged to this society. The members, sixty-one in number, follow:

BADGE OF THETA DELTA CHI.

'91 Augustus S. Butler,
" Wolcott H. Butler, Ph. B.,
" George H. Conklin,
" Clarence E. DePuy, B. S.,
" George Rebec, Ph. B.,
" Lyman B. Trumbull, Ph. B.,
" Edward D. Warner, B. L.,
'92 Lawrence T. Cole, A. B.,
" George T. McGee,
'93 Edwin R. Cole,
" Ernest J. Dennan, A. B.,
" Henry G. Field, B. S.,
" Harvey R. Gaylord,
" Hugh F. McGaughey, B. S.,
" Arthur H. Veysey, A. B.,
'94 Ernest N. Bullock, A. B.,
" Edward L. Gedney,
" Harry W. LeClear,
" Ross C. Whitman, A. B.,
" *l* Percy Wilson, LL. B.,
" *l* Walter W. Woodbury, LL. B.,
'95 Frank Briscoe, A. B.,
" Howard M. Cox, B. S.,
" Augustus S. Gaylord,
" Charles H. Gray, B. L.,
" Frank F. VanTuyl, B. S.,
'96 James B. Hamilton,
" *h* William F. Holmes, M. D.,
" John A. Kreis,
" Thomas D. McColl, B. S.,
" Horace H. VanTuyl, Ph. B.,
'96 *l* Guy V. Williams, LL. B.,
" *l* Paul D. Wright,
" William W. Young,
'97 Ralph H. Collamore, B. S.,
" Richard H. Sutphen, A. B.,
" C. Ross Tatem,
'98 Granville M. Cox,
" Walter M. Dean,
" Norman H. Hackett,
" Richard M. Heames,
" Robert W. Hyde,
" L. Alvin Kreis,
" William K. Maxwell,
" Frank N. Savage,
" *m* Frank J. Sexton,
" Henry E. Wilkinson,
'99 Frank J. Arbuckle,
" Carl M. Green,
" Martin C. Huggitt,
" Charles R. Morey,
" *d* Philip R. Thomas,
" Charles E. Wehrle,
'00 John B. Hitchcock,
" Frank P. Llewellyn,
" R. Roy McPeek,
" J. Walter Wood,
'01 Forest H. Lancashire,
" Frederick C. Nash,
" Herman C. Stevens,
" William W. Talcott.

To complete the roll of Theta Delta Chi at Ann Arbor the following initiates of other branches should be added:

'80 *l* George F. Weeks, LL. B.,
'87 *l* William A. Carter,
'91 *l* William L. Miller,
" *l* John H. Winans,
'92 *m* Lorenzo Burrows,
'94 *l* Willis C. Belknap,
" *d* Edward L. Gedney, D. D. S.
" *l* James B. Beckett.

Kappa Sigma was founded in 1867 at the University of Virginia. There have been sixty-nine chapters in all, of which twenty-two are inactive. The living branches, in the order of their establishment are these: Virginia, Trinity (N.C.), Washington and Lee, Mercer, North Carolina, Vanderbilt, Lake Forest, Tennessee, University of the South, Southwestern Presbyterian, Hampden-Sidney, Texas, Centenary, Randolph-Macon, Purdue, Southwestern, Maine, Louisiana State, Cumberland, Swarthmore, Tulane, William and Mary, Arkansas, Davidson, Illinois, Pennsylvania State, Pennsylvania, Michigan, Columbian, Southwestern Baptist, U. S. Grant, Cornell, Vermont, Wofford, Bethel, Kentucky, Wabash, Bowdoin, Ohio State, Georgia School of Tech-

BADGE OF KAPPA SIGMA.

nology, Millsaps, Bucknell, Nebraska, William-Jewell, Brown, Richmond, and Missouri. Thirty-one of the forty-seven active chapters are in Southern colleges. The latest catalogue was published in 1897, but as it contains no biographical notes there is difficulty in ascertaining who of the 3,000 members have become distinguished. Perhaps Leon G. Tyler, President of William and Mary College, is as prominent as any. Maroon, peacock-blue, and old-gold are the colors, and the lily-of-the-valley is the fraternity flower. The Alpha-Zeta (Michigan) Chapter was instituted February 23, 1892, and is the fifty-first in age of the branches of Kappa Sigma. Until the present college year it was exclusively a law-school society at Ann Arbor, although elsewhere the fraternity is chiefly academic in character. Of the ninety-one members all but ten have been connected with the law department. The chapter holds a lease of the house 914 Hill street. Following is the Michigan roll:

'92 *l* William H. Giltner, LL. B.,
" *l* Richard A. Hall, LL. B.,
" *l* Julian A. Padgett, LL. B.,
" *l* Jesse E. Roberts, LL. B.,
" *l* Fred A. Sheldon, LL. B.,
" *l* Frank M. Wells, LL. B.,
" *l* Daniel W. Yancey, LL. B.,
'93 *l* Albert M. Ashley, LL. B.,
" *l* Ernest P. Bennett, LL. B.,
" *l* Charles E. Dedrick, LL. B.,
" *l* Ernest E. Ford, LL. B.,
" *l* Yate H. V. Gard,
" *l* Lyman O. Grundy, LL. B.,
" *l* John E. Johntz, LL. B.
" *l* Marshall Lamer, LL. B.,
" *l* Richard F. Purcell, LL. B.,
" *l* George F. Rich, LL. B.,
" *l* Anson D. Rose, LL. B.,
" *l* Mark A. Sands, LL. B.,
" *l* Byron C. Thorpe, LL. B.,
" *l* Harry K. Wolcott,
'94 *l* Joseph E. Barrell, LL. B.,
" *l* Charles A. Denison, LL. B.,
" *l* George W. Fuller, LL. B.,
" *l* Jesse Huber,
" *l* Allen G. Mills, LL. B.,
" *l* John W. Powers, LL. B.,
" *l* Guy L. Reed, LL. B.,
" *l* Frederick W. Smith, LL. B.,
" *l* McKenzie R. Todd, LL. B.,
" *l* Henry W. Trask,
" *l* Julius C. Travis, LL. B.,
" *l* Charles E. Ward, LL. B.,
'95 *l* Henry B. Anderson, LL. B.,
" *l* Willis S. Clark, LL. B.,
" *l* P. Percy B. DeChampagne,
" *l* Charles L. DeVault, LL. B.,
'95 *l* Frank L. Edinborough, LL. B.,
" *l* William A. Finch, LL. B.,
" *l* Henry G. Hadden, LL. B.,
" *l* Lindley G. Long, LL. B.,
" *l* LeRoy Palmer,
" *l* Glenn B. Roseberry, LL. B.,
" *l* Wilbur R. Thirkield, LL. B.,
" *l* Warren W. Travis,
" *l* Wilson K. Vance, LL. B.,
" *l* Edward M. Walsh, LL. B.,
" *l* Henry M. Zimmerman, LL. B.,
'96 *l* William T. Apmadoc, LL. B.,
" *l* Thomas M. Benner, Jr., LL. B.,
" *l* Henry W. Conner, LL. B.,
" *l* John C. Crapser, LL. B.,
" *l* Peter J. Crosby,
" *l* John C. Davies, LL. B.,
" *l* Alvan S. Hopkins, LL. B.,
" *l* August A. Huseman, LL. B.,
" *l* Philemon S. Karshner, LL. B.,
" *l* William C. Manchester, LL. B.,
" *l* Arthur A. Meeker, LL. B.,
" *l* E. Guy Ryker, LL. B.
" *l* Angus R. Shannon, LL. B.,
" *l* Joseph H. Short, LL. B.,
" *l* William H. Simons, LL. B.,
" *l* Olney S. Williams, LL. B.,
'97 *l* Grant C. Bagley, LL. B.,
" *m* Rolla J. Baldwin, M. D.,
" *l* Walter E. Dorland,
" *l* Archibald Stevenson, LL. B.,
" *l* Charles E. White, LL. B.,
'98 *l* A. J. Edgerton, Jr.,
" *l* Charles H. Ewing,
" *l* George R. Fox,
" *l* Edwin H. Gordon,
" *l* William B. Hice,

'98 Norman K. McInnis,
" *l* Gifford B. McKay,
" *l* Wallace D. Scott,
'99 *p* LeRoy Campbell,
" *p* Alex D. Gundry,
" *l* William R. Oates,
" *l* Frank R. Sweasey,
" *l* Lee J. Ullman,
'00 *l* Raymond B. Alberson,
'00 *l* Herbert B. Buster,
" *d* Travis Dailey,
" *m* Robert B. Griffith,
" *d* Hugh T. Gundry,
" *l* Clay W. Kelly,
" *d* Donald M. McCall,
'01 James R. Henry,
" Edwin McGinnis.

The following matriculates of the University are members of fraternities which never have had chapters here:

'76 *l* E. W. Wilson, LL. B., Κ Τ Χ,
'77 E. A. Halsey, A. B., Δ Ψ,
'78 *m* Edward S. Bell, Δ Ψ,
'79 *l* L. B. Winsor, LL. B., Φ Γ Π,
'80 *l* J. D. Hamrick, LL. B., Δ Β Φ,
'81 *l* Alfred K. Brown, Κ Κ Κ,
" G. S. Fuller, Δ Ψ (Vermont),
" *m* A. A. Gillette, M. D., Δ Ψ,
'83 *m* N. M. Dorms, Φ Χ (Vermont),
" *l* F. M. Gilmore, Κ Κ Κ,
" *l* William Snearer, Jr., LL. B., Φ Κ Σ,
'84 *m* Frank F. Smith, Κ Κ Κ,
'88 *m* Alexander C. Smith, Δ Ψ,
'89 Perlee R. Bennett, Ε Χ,
" *m* W. H. Dodge, M. D., Δ Ψ,
" *l* G. H. Wood, Berzelius,
'91 *m* R. E. L. Rogers, Ι Κ Α,
'94 *l* A. P. Cady, LL. B., Φ Γ Π,
" *l* T. G. Crothers, LL. B., Σ Ν,
" *l* W. R. Harvey, LL. B., Κ Α (Southern),
" *l* D. T. Mason, LL. B., Σ Ν,
" *l* A. C. Melchior, LL. B., Δ Ψ,
" *l* R. L. Motley, LL. B., Κ Α.,
" *l* V. H. Ringer, LL. B., Σ Ν,
'95 *l* Victor J. Obenauer, Φ Α Π,
" *l* Charles Zollinger, LL. B., Σ Ν,
'96 *l* W. W. Thayer, LL. B., Κ Α,
'98 *l* Oliver A. Ludlow, Κ Α,
'99 *l* Arthur G. Andrews, Α Σ Π,
" *l* Ellis G. Soule, Φ Κ Σ.

Initiations have been made among the matriculates of the collegiate department of our University by twenty-one different fraternities, all of which originated elsewhere than at Michigan. Six of these societies, Delta Phi, Kappa Phi Lambda, Phi Alpha, Chi Phi, Phi Gamma Delta, and Alpha Tau Omega, are not now represented here by chapters; and four of the others have not lived uninterruptedly in Michigan. The aggregate membership of the twenty-one fraternities is 3544, divided thus: Alphi Delta Phi, 413; Psi Upsilon, 378; Delta Kappa Epsilon, 352; Chi Psi, 292; Beta Theta Pi, 289; Zeta Psi, 244; Sigma Chi, 226; Sigma Phi, 216; Delta Upsilon, 176; Phi Kappa Psi, 161; Delta Tau Delta, 155; Phi Delta Theta, 121; Delta Phi, 104; Sigma Alpha Epsilon, 99; Kappa Sigma, 91; Phi Gamma Delta, 75; Theta Delta Chi, 61; Alpha Tau Omega, 49; Kappa Phi Lambda, 21 (six of whom belong to other societies); Chi Phi, 14; and Phi Alpha, 13.

Death has sadly broken the ranks of the older fraternities. Chi Psi has lost 73 of its 292 men, Alpha Delta Phi has lost 70 out of 413 members, and from the 352 men of D. K. E. 64 have departed. As regards number of living members Psi Upsilon stands first with 344, Alpha Delta Phi second with 343, and Delta

Kappa Epsilon third with 288. Of the 3544 members of the Michigan branches of the regular collegiate fraternities, 435, nearly an eighth, have died.

In the early days of the University several medical students were admitted by each of the three fraternities then at Ann Arbor, but Alpha Delta Phi soon adopted the rule of confining itself strictly to the literary department. Chi Psi, however, never has recognized any limitation in this respect, and during its long career has initiated 49 professional-school undergraduates. Zeta Psi at several periods in its existence has drawn somewhat heavily from the non-collegiate schools, as is shown the by fact that 36 matriculates of the latter now appear upon its rolls. Twenty of the 104 members of the defunct chapter of Delta Phi were law or medical students. Sigma Phi has admitted fifteen professional-school men, apparently for a special reason in each case. Three pharmacy students and one medical student are carried upon the long roll of Delta Kappa Epsilon; and among the 378 members of Psi Upsilon are three medical matriculates—brothers or nephews of other members—and one student in pharmacy who was initiated thirty years ago. Most of the fraternities of Western origin gained footholds at Ann Arbor through the law department, from which they ceased to draw members when the necessity therefor had passed. As has been said, Sigma Chi was strictly a law-school society for seventeen years, so that of its 226 members only 51 were admitted from the literary department. Delta Tau Delta's list of 155 men includes 38 professional-school matriculates. Phi Kappa Psi, originally organized in the law-department, has sixteen non-collegiate initiates. Beta Theta Pi has seven, Phi Delta Theta thirteen, Sigma Alpha Epsilon 24, Alpha Tau Omega 25, and Phi Gamma Delta 26. All but three of Kappa Sigma's 91 members were taken from the professional-schools, which have furnished to the fraternities 572 members.

Of the 2,618 members of the fraternities in the literary classes from '45 to '97 there have been graduated 1,392, nearly half of whom—to be exact, 653—belong to one or another of three societies, Alpha Delta Phi, Psi Upsilon, and Delta Kappa Epsilon, the respective figures being 237, 220, and 196. Beta Theta Pi has 131, Delta Upsilon 100, Chi Psi 85, Zeta Psi 82, Sigma Phi 82, Delta Tau Delta 55, Phi Kappa Psi 58, Phi Delta Theta 45, Phi Gamma Delta 26, Delta Phi 20, Theta Delta Chi 20, Sigma Alpha Epsilon 19, all others 16. Psi Upsilon has the largest number of living collegiate graduates.

The 265 fraternity men in the present undergraduate literary classes are divided thus: Psi Upsilon 34, Alpha Delta Phi 28, Sigma Chi 23, Zeta Psi 21, Beta Theta Pi 21, Phi Delta Theta 21, Phi Kappa Psi 21, Delta Upsilon 20, D. K. E. 19, Theta Delta Chi 16, Sigma Phi 15, Sigma Alpha Epsilon 11, Chi Psi 10, Delta Tau Delta 3, Kappa Sigma 3. Compared with the figures of twenty-five years ago Chi Psi shows a decrease of one, and D. K. E. a loss of five, while Alpha Delta Phi has gained three, Sigma Phi three, Zeta Psi ten, and Psi Upsilon six.

ARMS OF BETA THETA PI.

Fifty years ago two-thirds of the students were members of secret societies. In 1859–60 those organizations claimed 149 of the 234 undergraduates—nearly two-thirds. Only 125 of the 349 academic students belonged to fraternities in the year 1869–70, and although the close of the ensuing decade showed a slight increase, yet at the present writing only 265 out of nearly four times that number of literary and engineering students are connected with societies. The proportion of fraternity men has declined in forty years from two-thirds to one-quarter. A similar decrease appears in the proportion of fraternity men in the graduated classes. Of the eleven men who received diplomas with the class of '45 six are on the rolls of the secret societies; but of the 155 graduated with '97 only 30—less than one-fifth—were members of fraternities. Among the 145 men graduated in the first ten classes, '45 to '54, there were 83 Greek-letter initiates, 57 per cent. of all, and of the 353 graduates in the classes from '55 to '64 there were 212 society men, or 60 per cent. of the entire list. The fraternities claim 573 of the 1,267 male graduates from 1865 to 1884, about 45 per cent.; and the 513 Greek-letter initiates graduated 1885–97 constitute only 34 per cent. of the 1,489 men who received diplomas. Of the 3,255 male graduates of the literary department, 1,392, or 42 per cent., are members of the fraternity chapters here located. To the number of Greek-letter academic graduates should be added eight men who belong to fraternities that never have been represented by branches at Michigan, or that were not so represented when the members in question were graduated.

Certain characteristics are common to all or to nearly all of the fraternities. All are "four-year" organizations, that is, membership in each begins or may begin early in freshman year and continues until the member leaves college. The danger of admitting to membership students who have not been in college long enough to enable a correct judgment to be passed upon them is really not great in the case of the older societies, most of whose initiates are the sons, the brothers, or the friends, of older members. Members are not infrequently drawn by the fraternities from the upper undergraduate classes.

Toward the close of October each of the leading societies initiates its freshman delegation, the members of which may have been pledged for a year or more. In recent years certain fraternities have occasionally introduced into their initiations various absurd or dangerous features which were untirely unknown in early Greek-letter days, and which have been borrowed from the Harvard "Dickey Club" or from the now defunct freshman societies at Yale. With perhaps one exception the leading societies confine themselves to dignified forms in which the candidate is subjected neither to risk nor to humiliation. Most of the newspaper tales of what occurs at the annual initiatory exercises are grossly exaggerated or wholly false. Once admitted the new members are entitled to all the rights and privileges of their older brothers; but one of their number must go to the postoffice for the chapter mail week-day evenings and Sunday mornings, and if the door-bell of the chapter-house rings it is to be answered by a freshman if one is at hand. Contrary to what is sometimes said in the daily papers a recent initiate is not asked to go upon errands for older members, and "fagging" is unknown.

No matter what his class every member of a fraternity is required to wear the badge. This index of membership may cost from four to seventy-five dollars according to the extent to which precious stones are used in the ornamentation of it; and it is not good form to wear it upon the necktie or upon the coat lapel, as used to be the fashion among enthusiastic members. Now the badge is pinned in an inconspicuous place upon the waistcoat. Members elect wear "pledge buttons" which display the colors or some of the distinguishing emblems of the society.

Transfers of allegiance are comparatively rare. There have been about seventy in all at Ann Arbor. Occasionally a student becomes thoroughly dissatisfied with his fraternity and leaves it, or his society may become so displeased with his conduct as to dismiss him; in either of these cases the weight of opinion and the established practice seems to be that he may accept an election to some other coterie. So, too, when a chapter has been dissolved, any of its members may join another fraternity.

The usages of the fraternities at Michigan differ in no important respect from those in vogue at Brown, Dartmouth, Williams, Trinity, Union, Cornell, and other Eastern colleges where the four-year system obtains; and they are more formal and more dignified than those which characterize the Western colleges. At the University of Minnesota the members of a new society are "bounced," that is tossed in the air in a friendly way by the adherents of older organizations. This objectionable custom is not likely to find acceptance here, nor has the vulgar abbreviation "frat" for "fraternity" gained more than a limited circulation in this cultured community.

At few colleges was the chapter-house system introduced earlier than at Michigan. Nearly a quarter of a century ago one of the fraternities set up its household gods in a rented house; now the most costly and certainly the most interesting of Ann Arbor residences are the buildings owned by the Greek-letter orders. Ten societies — Delta Kappa Epsilon, Psi Upsilon, Alpha Delta Phi, Sigma Phi, Zeta Psi, Beta Theta Pi, Phi Kappa Psi, Delta Upsilon, Sigma Alpha Epsilon, and Chi Psi, — own the houses which they occupy, although, in the case of one of the newly acquired houses, nothing more than a contract interest is supposed to be held. Delta Kappa Epsilon has a secret lodge or temple as well as a house. The values of the different holdings are perhaps best indicated by the official ratings for taxation, it

ARMS OF SIGMA ALPHA EPSILON.

being premised that realty in Ann Arbor is assessed at two-thirds of its actual value. The figures are as follow: Delta Kappa Epsilon, house $13,500, lodge $2,500, total $16,000; Psi Upsilon, $15,000; Alpha Delta Phi, $15,000; Chi Psi, $9,000; Phi Kappa Psi, $9,000; Sigma Alpha Epsilon, $8,000; Beta Theta Pi, $7,500; Sigma Phi, $5,000; Delta Upsilon, $5,000; Zeta Psi, $4,000. Of these buildings, the chapter houses of Psi Upsilon and Zeta Psi face the campus, and very near them are the residences of Alpha Delta Phi, D. K. E., and Beta Theta Pi. Sigma Phi's place is north of the campus and overlooks the river, while the abode of Sigma Alpha Epsilon is situated perhaps less favorably than any of the others, being on low ground three-fourths of a mile south of the campus. Phi Kappa Psi has a picturesque site in Washtenaw avenue. Chi Psi and Delta Upsilon occupy pleasant and convenient, though not commanding positions. The buildings of Delta Kappa Epsilon, Alpha Delta Phi, and Psi Upsilon were built by the societies themselves on sites previously bought, and the abode of S. A. E. was erected for the society by the proprietor of the park in which it stands. All the other houses were purchased from earlier owners, and some of them will soon give way to finer edifices. Phi Delta Theta, Theta Delta Chi, Sigma Chi, and Kappa Sigma, occupy rented houses.

The expenses incident to membership vary considerably in the different societies. Of course one cannot go into details; and perhaps it is enough to say that in hardly any of the fraternities are the charges such as to exclude persons of moderate means. In one of the largest establishments a reduction in expenses has been effected, and the graduates have taken steps to prevent the dues from being onerous.

Much of the influence wielded by the chief societies at Michigan is due to the alumni members. The latter are frequent visitors at Ann Arbor; they recommend their relatives and friends to join the fraternities with which they themselves are connected; and by their contributions costly chapter houses are erected and maintained. Exactly in proportion to the number and character of its graduates, and to the extent of their interest, does a society flourish. It is customary to send to the alumni formal notices of the regular initiation in the autumn and of the annual reunion at Commencement, and it is supposed that every society informs its retired members concerning the principal events of the college year.

All of the older societies have alumni associations in Detroit and Grand Rapids. In the former city, as early as 1873, Delta Kappa Epsilon began to hold an annual reunion of its alumni. Psi Upsilon began to do the same thing in 1876, and a few years later Alpha Delta Phi followed. Nearly all of the important fraternities now hold annual dinners in Detroit, the undergraduate members of the Michigan chapters being invited and expected to attend. From recent publications it appears that D. K. E. and Psi Upsilon have each nearly one hundred alumni resident in the chief city of Michigan, and the membership of Alpha Delta Phi is not less than fifty, while Chi Psi, Sigma Phi, Zeta Psi, Beta Theta Pi, and Delta Tau Delta are represented by from forty to fifty graduates apiece.

An account of the college fraternities at Michigan would be defective did it omit to speak of the influence which the local chapters have exerted upon their respective orders. The Alpha Epsilon of Chi Psi was for many years the westermost bulwark of that society, and to it was due the institution of the flourishing branches at Minnesota and Wisconsin. During half a century, the Peninsular Chapter of Alpha Delta Phi has stood at the head of the western wing of the order, holding a high place in the general councils of the society, and becoming responsible in later years for the new branches at Minnesota and Chicago. Omicron of D. K. E has heen the most successful and in many respects the most influential of the four-year chapters of the fraternity to which it belongs. The Michigan Zeta Psi furnished the founder of the important chapter at Cornell, and a member from Ann Arbor successfully reinstituted the dormant branch at Harvard. Psi Upsilon's Michigan representative has always been recognized throughout the fraternity as one of the leading chapters, and notwithstanding the persistent opposition of the branch at Columbia, it has been able to secure the location of associate chapters in Wisconsin and Minnesota. Doubtless the abolishment of branches in the Agricultural College and at Hillsdale is attributable to the Ann Arbor exponents of Phi Delta Theta and Delta Tau Delta. Beta Theta Pi is understood to have regained its old superiority in the fraternity at large. The Michigan Alpha of Phi Kappa Psi is not merely the most important chapter of that order, but it is largely responsible for the increased prestige of the society throughout the country. With the possible exception of Cornell, Michigan is the most important stronghold of the fraternities.

Although the legal right of the secret societies to exist here was established half a century ago, those organizations have not at any time been exempt from severe criticism. The old charges that they tend to idleness and frivolity, that they encourage immorality, that they are hostile to religious influences, that they are expensive, exclusive, and aristocratic, and that they furnish the means for unfair combinations in college politics, are ever pending. Doubtless some of these accusations are well grounded, especially if they are confined to certain societies. Taken all in all, however, the workings of the fraternity system cannot fairly be held injurious to their members. This appears from the achievements of the latter in college and in after life. It is impossible to present scholarship records, because such have not been kept here; but it should be noted that the percentage of fraternity men who have received diplomas is somewhat greater than that of the neutrals. In the classes from '67 to '77, of the 134 Commencement appointments made by the faculty, 69 were received by the 295 members of societies and 65 were distributed among the 436 independents. More than half of the holders of the Jones Classical Fellowship have been fraternity men.

It must be conceded that the high character of their alumni bears strongly in favor of the Greek-letter orders. If the latter really are schools of idleness and dissipation, the pupils trained in them seem not to have profited by the instruction received. The 1,400 Greek-letter fraternity men, although hardly more than two-fifths of the 3,255 male academic graduates, include the four Senators of the United States, eleven of the fifteen Representatives in Congress, all the Cabinet Ministers and Assistant Secretaries at Washington, all the Ambassadors, foreign Ministers, and Consuls-General, the two Solicitors-General of the United States, nearly all the Governors and Lieutenant-Governors, almost all the members of State Supreme Courts, eleven of the seventeen Michigan Circuit Judges, all of the Presidents of important colleges, and nine of the eleven Regents of the University who have been graduated from the literary department. Upon the present faculty of Michigan the Greek-letter alumni are represented by Acting-President Hutchins, and by Professors D'Ooge, Walter, Pattengill, Herdman, Thompson, Knowlton, McLaughlin,

PRESIDENT ANGELL.

Reighard, Angell, Worcester, McAlvay, and Drake, while the non-society men include Professors Hudson, Demmon, Spalding, J. B. Davis, Hempl, Lane, Campbell, Novy, Scott, Newcombe, and Levi. In Faculties elsewhere the societies have a far stronger proportional representation than at home.

The chapter houses are assailed by the same class of persons as attacked the fraternities before the latter were equipped with buildings. All of the society houses are not free from objectionable features, nor, for that matter, are all of the town lodging-houses; but that the manners and the morals of the members of college societies have changed for the better since the chapter-house system was introduced cannot be questioned. Personal responsibility for the welfare of fraternity and chapter may be trusted to eliminate injurious incidents of chapter-house life. A society which, because of its evil reputation, fails to secure two or three desirable men, soon sets out to win a good name. It is, however, absurd to expect that the inmates of fraternity houses will rise to higher levels than obtain in their own homes, or in the social circles of the large cities from which they come.

That some of the societies are, after their own fashion, exclusive, must be admitted. Just why college boys should be debarred from the privilege—exercised by all other persons—of choosing their intimate associates, never has been explained. However, the stern necessity of living has compelled not a few of the fraternities to be quite democratic. To be a "society man" at Ann Arbor one need not be rich, or high-born, or handsome, or well-dressed. If two or three of the societies exact some or all of these qualifications, the other orders do not. Nor can it be said that the spirit of exclusiveness is growing. Most of the societies have more members than they had thirty years ago. The fact that the fraternities, although more numerous and influential than ever before, include a smaller proportion of the entire undergraduate attendance is explicable on other grounds. The expenses of society membership are necessarily greater than they used to be, and the increase in the number of available men has not kept pace with the increase in the undergraduate attendance. Then, too, membership in certain societies is so much more desirable than affiliation with others that not a few students remain outside of fraternities altogether simply because they have not opportunities of joining the organizations they prefer. Not many elections are refused on account of objections that would be applicable to all of the fraternities; but on the other hand the number of students who decline to join particular orders is known to be large. When one considers that in each of the societies a single negative vote means exclusion, and that such a vote may not be based upon the merits or demerits of the candidate but simply upon personal dislike or jealousy, it is readily understood that failure to receive an invitation from one or all of the few really desirable fraternities does not even suggest ineligibility. In fact the leading societies omit every year men who would be very valuable and useful members, and whose absence is regretted by the large majority of the fraternity which passes upon them. Hence it follows that some of the best men in each class are not members of any Greek-letter coterie, and it also follows that at Michigan—whatever may be the case elsewhere—it is not discreditable to be a "neutral". The term "fraternity man" is really misleading, because it implies that a dividing line is drawn between those who wear badges and those who do not. Except occasionally, and then only for political purposes, such a line is not marked. The members of the leading fraternities form a class by themselves, and in that class the fact that a particular student belongs to one of the other societies is not regarded as giving him a higher social status than he would deserve were he an "independent". It is by no means certain that the disadvantages attendant upon membership in certain fraternities are not greater than the corresponding advantages. At any rate, the term "society man" has not now-a-days great significance, although membership in any one of several fraternities that might be named is a valuable privilege.

Superficial observers of the society system regret that three-fourths of the students lack fraternity privileges, and fear that the zeal and activity of the non-society alumni will not meet the needs of the University. Accordingly they have suggested the formation of more fraternities; an expedient more plausible than practicable. For nearly all of the fraternities of the first class are now represented at Ann Arbor, and the three not now here are too shrewd to plant young chapters in the face of long-established rivals. Nor is it to be supposed that any of the Southern fraternities not already on the ground could ever command the attention of Michigan students. Whatever rank they hold elsewhere they have neither prestige nor influence in this region. Separated from sister branches and without the support of alumni a chapter of any fraternity not now here would soon die. A purely local organization could not live long enough to secure the strength necessary for one autumnal campaign. Exaggerated as are the advantages of intercollegiate affiliations, they are indispensable to-day unless for a local fraternity that has existed thirty or forty years. Then, too, a new society, whether intercollegiate or local, requires money for a chapter house and for many other purposes. Not having alumni the requisite funds must be contributed by undergraduates who as a rule are poor. So it is clear that it is easier to suggest than to found and maintain new societies at Michigan. In fact certain chapters now here are far from flourishing, and would be withdrawn were it not for the conviction entertained by their "grand lodges" that representation at Michigan is necessary to the good-standing of every fraternity.

That every undergraduate should belong to a Greek-letter order does not follow any more than that every citizen of Detroit or Chicago should belong to a club. Many a student is personally disqualified for the intimate association that the modern chapter house implies. Besides very many of the undergraduates are so poor as to be unable to meet the financial demands of fraternity membership. No matter how carefully a society is managed it cannot properly be conducted without money. It is idle to say that one's expenses when a member of a fraternity will be no higher than before. Nothing valuable in this world is to be had without paying for it, and membership in a society of the first class (none but second-rate men care to belong to any other) involves an expense that is not beyond the reach of students of moderate means, but that excludes—unless special provision is made for them—persons who are in straightened circumstances. Poverty has its disadvantages in college as well as in the world outside.

Although many of the students for one reason or another, are not members of fraternities, membership would not be regarded as an invidious distinction, nor would non-membership work discontent or lessen enthusiasm for the University, if the initiates of the societies would refrain from political and social combinations, and would not advertise the possession by themselves of certain supposed privileges which their fellow-students do not enjoy. One regrets that the Yale rule of absolute secrecy does not prevail here. The societies are in evidence altogether too much. They were not intended to be political machines, and it is not well for the University that they should intervene directly or indirectly in the social functions of the students. That their relative numerical strength is declining is really a good thing for the stronger fraternities, because political combinations are more difficult, and thus brilliant men in the societies are not as likely as they were of yore to be excluded from class offices and from the editorships of college periodicals. It is to be hoped that the time is near at hand when the influence of societies as such will not be felt in outside matters, and when all students, whether members of fraternities or not, will stand on the same footing in matters of general interest. For example, offices should not be bestowed or withheld by reason of fraternity affiliations or the lack of them; nor should committeeships be parcelled out among the fraternities, nor should the societies as such contribute to the funds raised for athletic or college purposes. The fraternities should conduct themselves and should be treated as strictly private clubs, concerning which it is not good form to speak in the presence of persons not members.

THE SCHOOL OF MUSIC.

CHAPTER XII

PROFESSIONAL-SCHOOL FRATERNITIES

For years the professional departments remained without fraternities of their own. Occasionally the academic societies drew upon the law-school, and less often students of medicine were initiated; but nearly all students outside of the pale of the literary department,—except those who had in other colleges become members of fraternities—remained ignorant of society life. A forerunner of the Greek-letter organizations which now throng our professional schools was the Alpha Phi, a local society in the law-school from 1864 to 1866. Excepting one other, that society was the earliest of its kind in the country. In 1869 the now influential and prosperous Phi Delta Phi, oldest of existing professional school fraternities, was founded in our law department. Nu Sigma Nu, the first fraternity to confine its attention to schools of medicine, was instituted here in March, 1882, and in the same month and year Michigan students organized Delta Sigma Delta, the original dental-school society. Phi Chi was founded in our school of pharmacy in 1883, and in 1889 the homœopathic Mu Sigma Alpha, also a Michigan product, appeared. Phi Delta Phi had a short-lived rival in Phi Chi, a medico-legal society, 1872–75, and from 1877 until 1894 a chapter of Sigma Chi exercised considerable influence in the law school. At present Delta Chi and Kappa Sigma (the latter of which now has members in all the departments), both organized in 1892, are opponents of Phi Delta Phi, while a newly-started branch of Phi Rho Sigma is beginning to do battle with Nu Sigma Nu. Delta Sigma Delta has a rival in Xi Psi Phi, which dates from 1889. Neither Phi Chi nor Mu Sigma Alpha has as yet met with organized opposition. There is in the professional departments one society of women, the Alpha Epsilon Iota, which was founded in 1889 by members of the regular school of medicine.

It is somewhat remarkable that while none of the fraternities or sisterhoods in the literary department is indigenous with us, nearly all of the societies of the professional schools have been founded here. These same fraternities are also the oldest and largest of their kind.

Alpha Phi.—This society, which was founded in the law school in 1864, was the first society of its kind in our University. It lived two years, called itself the Alpha Chapter, had a badge formed of the two letters of its name, and made but one appearance in The Palladium. Among its members were Probate Judge Allan M. Stearns, '65; William R. Bates, '66, United States Marshal for Eastern Michigan; James L. High, '66, well-known as a law writer; and Circuit-Judge W. I. Wallace, '66, of Missouri. Following is its roll:

'65 *l* George W. Ready, LL. B.,
" *l* George W. Seevers, LL. B.,
" *l* Allan M. Stearns, LL. B.,
" *l* George M. Walker, LL. B.,
'66 *l* William R. Bates,
" *l* Charles C. Dawson, LL. B.,
" *l* Henry S. Dow,
" *l* Parke D. Fay, LL. B.,
" *l* Lloyd F. Hamilton,
" *l* James L. High, LL. B.,
" *l* Lucius Hubbard, LL. B.,
" *l* Loftus N. Keating, LL. B.,
" *l* Robert B. Murray,
" *l* *William A. Palmer, LL. B.,
" *l* Augustus H. Salisbury,
" *l* Milo P. Smith, LL. B.,
" *l* James C. Taylor,
" *l* W. Irving Wallace.

Phi Delta Phi was founded in the Law School of our University December 13, 1869. Most of the members ascribe the origin of the fraternity to John M. Howard of the law class of '71, who had come to Ann Arbor commissioned to organize a chapter of the Phi Gamma Delta, an order whereof he had been a member at Monmouth College. Not finding suitable material he abandoned the idea of starting a rival to the powerful societies of the collegiate department, and from time to time during the fall of 1869 he discussed with a few friends the advisability of instituting a fraternity which should be composed exclusively of law-students and lawyers. Having learned that such a fraternity was not in existence in the older law schools of the Eastern States, Howard and six associates—Winfield S. Beebe, '70, Alfred E. Hawes, '70, James E. Howell, '70, Arthur M. Monteith, '70, John B. Cleland, '71, and Joseph D. Ronan, '71—set about establishing one for themselves. It was determined that the chapters of the new society should be named after distinguished jurists, statesmen, and lawyers, and that membership should be of two classes, regular, composed of undergraduates, and honorary, drawn from lawyers or from the faculty. Judge Thomas M. Cooley was the first honorary member. The parent chapter was called Kent. We are told in the printed history of the society that no attempt at extension was made until 1875, when the Sharswood Club, a local

FORMER BADGE OF PHI DELTA PHI.

organization of good standing in the Law School of the University of Pennsylvania, was admitted under the name of the Sharswood Chapter. The members, however, returned their charter shortly afterwards, for the alleged reason that the prescribed initiation ceremony was unsatisfactory. In 1878 the Illinois Wesleyan University was made the seat of a chapter called Benjamin, the charter of which was withdrawn ten years later. Booth Chapter was established at the Union College of Law in Chicago in May, 1880, and in December of the year following Story Chapter was instituted in the Columbia Law School. Other branches have been put forth as follows: Cooley, St. Louis Law School, Washington University, 1882; Pomeroy, Hastings College of the Law, University of California, 1883; Marshall, Columbian University, 1884; Jay, Albany Law School, 1884–93; Webster, Boston Law School, 1885; Hamilton, Cincinnati Law School, 1886; Gibson, University of Pennsylvania, 1886; Choate, Harvard Law School, 1887; Conkling, Cornell University, 1888; Tiedeman, University of Missouri, 1890; Dillon, University of Minnesota, 1891; Daniels, Buffalo Law School, 1881; Chase, University of Oregon, 1891; Harlan, University of Wisconsin, 1891; Swan, Ohio State University, 1893; McLain, University of Iowa, 1893; Lincoln, University of Nebraska, 1895, Osgoode Law School of Upper Canada, Toronto, 1896; Fuller, Chicago College of Law, 1896; Miller, Leland Stanford, Jr., University, 1897; Green, University of Kansas, 1897. The first national convention was held at Ann Arbor, March 3, 1892. At this conclave the shield-shaped badge of the order was exchanged for a monogram. Claret-red and pearl-blue are the colors of the society, and the forget-me-not is its flower. This fraternity does not assume a stringent air of secrecy. Though the motto, the grip, and the passwords are not communicated to outsiders, no especial mystery enshrouds its constitution or policy. It is not exclusive of the collegiate fraternities, although at least two of the latter at Ann Arbor now prohibit their men from joining it. According to the seventh edition of the catalogue, which appeared late in 1897, the total number of members is 3972. Of these 186 are honorary. Among the most prominent of the regular members of the Michigan Chapter are the following: George H. Hopkins, '71, of Detroit, formerly Collector of Internal Revenue; United States Circuit Judge William B. Gilbert, '72; William J. Stuart, '72, formerly Mayor of Grand Rapids; George Whitney Moore, '73, and DeForest Paine, '73, well-known lawyers of Detroit; John

C. Watson, '73, Acting-Governor of Nebraska in 1896; Charles C. Hopkins, '76, Clerk of the Supreme Court of Michigan; Russell C. Ostrander, '76, Ex-Mayor of Lansing; Clarence W. Ashford, '80, formerly Attorney-General of Hawaii; and Edward E. Wilson, '81, Representative in Congress. From other chapters are Theodore Roosevelt; Frank C. Partridge, late Minister to Venezuela; Richard C. Shannon, and George N. Southwick, Representatives in Congress; Professor Walter F. Willcox of Cornell University, Walter F. Freer, of the Supreme Court of Hawaii; and Professor Isidor Loeb of the University of Missouri. Phi Delta Phi at Michigan has been represented upon the University baseball team by Frank Crawford, '93 *l*, and E. C. Shields, '96 *l*, and upon the football team by G. H. Wood, '89 *l*, Frank Crawford, '93 *l*, D. B. Ninde, '95 *l*, Edwin Denby, '96 *l*, E. C. Shields, '96 *l*, and T. C. Teetzel, '00 *l*. The tennis player, A. S. Brown, '93 *l*, was a member. Kent Chapter occupies the handsome and commodious house 803 South State street.

BADGE OF PHI DELTA PHI.

The honorary members of the Kent Chapter, thirty-one in number, are the following: Associate Justices Henry B. Brown, John M. Harlan, and Samuel F. Miller, of the Federal Supreme Court; William H. Taft, of the United States Circuit Court; Henry H. Swan of the Federal District Court; John W. Champlin and Thomas M. Cooley, formerly of the Supreme Court of Michigan, and Claudius B. Grant, the present Chief Justice; Thomas F. Bayard, formerly Ambassador to England; Levi L. Barbour, Charles S. Draper, and Chas. R. Whitman, formerly Regents of the University; Acting-President Harry B. Hutchins; Henry Wade Rogers, President of Northwestern University; Edwin F. Conely, Levi T. Griffin, Charles A. Kent, and the late Charles I. Walker and William P. Wells, all of the Detroit Bar, and formerly of the Law Faculty at Michigan; Nathan D. Abbott, sometime Professor, and Thomas A. Boyle, Elias F. Johnson, Otto Kirchner, Jerome C. Knowlton, Aaron V. McAlvay, Floyd R. Mechem, Frank F. Reed, Bradley M. Thompson, and Horace L. Wilgus, present Professors in our Law Department; Melville M. Bigelow, the law author; and Circuit Judge E. D. Kinne. Following is the roll of the 441 regular members of the Michigan branch, all of whom, of course, belong to the law-school classes:

'70 Eugene E. Allen, LL. B.,
" Winfield S. Beebe, LL. B.,
" Alfred E. Hawes, LL. B.,
" James E. Howell, LL. B.,
" Ezra D. Lewis, LL. B.,
" Arthur McA. Monteith, LL. B.,
" John L. Starkweather, LL. B.,
" Frederick F. Wendell, LL. B.,
'71 Frank Butterworth, LL. B.,
" Henry Clark,
" John B. Cleland, LL. B.,
" Warren C. Dewey, LL. B.,
" *William E. Edgar, LL. B.,
" Daniel B. Hibbard, Jr., LL. B.,
" Robert J. Hill, LL. B.,
" George H. Hopkins, LL. B.,
" John M. Howard, LL. B.,
" *James Y. Marshall, LL. B.,
" *Martin Morris, LL. B.,
" *Willard H. Perley, LL. B.,
" *Joseph D. Ronan, LL. B.,
" *John W. Shepherd, LL. B.,
" Charles M. Swallow, LL. B.,
" Charles S. Thomas, LL. B.,
'72 Louis Blitz,
" *Charies W. Derr, LL. B.,
" Jacob L. Flickinger, LL. B.,
" William B. Gilbert, LL. B.,
" Edwin M. Irish, LL. B.,
" *Joseph D. Johnson, LL. B.,
" William J. Stuart, LL. B.,
" Festus Walters, LL. B.,
" James H. Winters, LL. B.,
" Charles D. Wright, LL. B.,
'73 Arthur A. Birney, LL. B.,
" John H. Campbell, LL. B.,
" George W. Cass, LL. B.,
" Will A. Chamberlain, LL. B.,
" Francis E. Hamilton,
" Samuel E. Kemp,
" George W. Moore,
" Henry A. Neal, LL. B.,
" Joseph T. O'Neal, LL. B.,
" DeForest Paine, LL. B.,
" James B. Peter,
" Hiram Smith, Jr., LL. B.,
" Alonzo S. Stephens, LL. B.,
" Charles E. Thornton, LL. B.,
" John C. Watson, LL. B.,
'74 John M. Brooks,
" Charles G. Canfield, LL. B.,
" Daniel B. English, LL. B.,
" Charles B. Gates, LL. B.,
" James Greenwood, Jr.,
" Howard E. Henderson,
" Thomas E. Knox,
" Joseph W. Martin, LL. B.,
" *Willis Merritt, LL. B.,
" *Louis E. Morris, LL. B.,
'74 Simeon T. Price, LL. B.,
" Seth C. Randall, LL. B.,
" *Martin S. Taylor,
" *Thomas A. Taylor, LL. B.,
" Albert Wassell, LL. B.,
" Elisha B. Wood, LL. B.,
'75 *Cornelius M. Burgess, LL. B.,
" *Joseph C. Coffman, LL. B.,
" John M. Eaton, LL. B.,
" George A. Gary,
" William B. Given, LL. B.,
" Edward J. Kennard, LL. B.,
" James T. McClellan,
" Mark W. Phelps, LL. B.,
" *George E. Putnam, LL. B.,
" Alexander Sampson, LL. B.,
" Rutus Sarlls,
" Perley K. Scott, LL. B.,
" George C. Squires,
" Gilbert M. Stark, LL. B,
'76 Ernest L. Allen, LL. B.,
" John L Burleigh, LL. B.,
" Jacob P. Dunn, LL. B.,
" William A. Fraser, LL. B.,
" Charles L. Frederic, LL. B.,
" Clarence M. Hill,
" Charles C. Hopkins, LL. B.,
" Eneshia Meers, LL. B.,
" *John O. Moffatt, LL. B.,
" John A. Moninger, LL. B.,
" Russell C. Ostrander, LL. B.,
" George W. Poland, LL. B.,
" Oscar M. Seward, LL. B.,
" Marion Steele, LL. B.,
" Frank W. Waring, LL. B.,
" Theodore Winningham, LL. B.,
'77 Truman E. Ames, LL. B.,
" Thomas B. Buckner, LL. B.,
" Silas H. Callender, LL. B.,
" Harry C. Davis,
" Stephen O. Foster, LL. B.,
" *Walter S. Judy, LL. B.,
" Edward L. Lemert,
" *Medary D. Mann, LL. B.,
" Nathan A. Mann, LL. B.,
" *Thcmas E. Morey, LL. B.,
" Calvin C. Staley, LL. B.,
" Louis F. Stifel, LL. B.,
" George F. White, LL. B.,
'78 Charles A. Barnes, LL. B.,
" Morris C. Baum, LL. B.,
" Burroughs F. Bower, LL. B.,
" John O. Garrett, LL. B.,
" Harry P. Hancock, LL. B.,
" Henry Hoffman, LL. B.,
" John C. Keith, LL. B.,
" J. Robert McGuffin, LL. B.,
" Charles C. Nelson, LL. B.,
" Edward Z. Perkins, LL. B.,

'78 D. Wilbur Reardon,
" Daniel C. Remick, LL. B.,
" Thomas Rinaker, LL. B.,
" Herman Ritter, LL. B.,
" *Edward P. Rose,
" Frank F. Rozzelle, LL. B.,
" Samuel W. Vance, LL. B.,
" Myron H. Walker, LL. B.
" *John S. Whitford, LL. B.,
" Henry Wollman, LL. B.,
'79 Gustav C. Bartels, LL. B.,
" James H. Blood, LL. B.,
" Walter P. Butler, LL. B.,
" Levy Chamberlain, LL. B.,
" Edward G. Embler, LL. B.,
" Carl E. Epler, LL. B.,
" Charles G. Fowler, LL. B.,
" *John P. Gale, LL. B.,
" John A. Mansfield, LL. B.
" Fritz Morris, LL. B.,
" Joseph F. McNaught,
" John C. Slayback,
" George A. VanDyke, LL. B.,
" John De W. Veeder,
" William H. H. Williamson, LL. B.,
'80 Clarence W. Ashford, LL. B.,
" Alfred J. Babcock, LL. B.
" John B. Booth,
" *Alexander Camp, LL. B.
" Lucian F. Easton, LL. B.,
" John H. Glade, LL. B.,
" Frank H. Hyatt,
" William H. Loomis, LL. B.,
" Alfred F. Maynard, LL. B.,
" William L. McKay, LL. B.,
" *Arthur P. Mitchell, LL. B.,
" Walter B. Scaife, LL. B.,
" William A. Weeks, LL. B.,
'81 Lorenzo C. Brooks,
" Frank A. Davis, LL. B.,
" *Gideon S. Fuller, LL. B.,
" Walter R. Hinckley, LL. B.,
" Gilbert M. Hitchcock, LL. B.,
" Frederick F. Huntress, LL. B.,
" John McCandless,
" Charles E. McKinney,
" Charles S. Smith, LL. B.,
" Buffon S. Walker, LL. B.,
" Frank P. Williams,
" Edward E. Wilson,
'82 Louis F. Bartels, LL. B.,
" William S. Bemis, LL. B.,
" John C. F. Bush,
" Morris L. Courtwright,
" Thomas G. Fitch, LL. B.,
" Lawrence Heiskell,
" Richard B. Latham,
" Charles G. Lawrence, LL. B.,
" *Henry W. McArthur, LL. B.,
'82 Mason J. Niblack, LL. B.,
" Oliver E. Pagin,
" Curtis E. Pierce, LL. B.,
" James W. Remich, LL. B.,
" Willis A. Rogers, LL. B.,
" Otto E. Sauter, LL. B.,
" Charles E. Temple, LL. B.,
" Edward F. Tierney, LL. B.,
" Horace B. Wing,
'83 David M. Alston, LL. B.,
" Arthur C. Denison, LL. B.,
" Charles P. Doolittle,
" James R. Downs,
" Rufus I. Eaton, LL. B.,
" Charles W. Franklin, LL. B.,
" Claus J. Gunderson, LL. B.,
" Austin Hawley, LL. B.,
" James S. Heaton,
" Willard F. Keeney,
" Harry H. Lockwood, LL. B.,
" Charles D. Long,
" Elmer W. Parkhurst, LL. B.,
" Willis B. Perkins, LL. B.,
" Charles T. Ralston,
" Elmer E. Richards,
" William Snearer, Jr., LL. B.,
" *Herbert M. Snow, LL. B.,
" Albert E. Stevenson,
'84 Herbert W. Baird, LL. B.,
" Eckstein Case, LL. B.,
" Anson Dill,
" Frank Healy, LL. B,
" John H. Holmes, LL B.,
" Richard H. Johnson, LL. B.,
" Thomas H. Loller, LL. B.,
" George B. McLane, LL. B.,
" Carroll H. Parmelee, LL. B.,
" William T. Perkins, LL. B.
" Fred Reynolds, LL. B.,
" Issie J. Ringolsky, LL. B.,
" Wayland W. Sanford,
" Edward T. Taylor, LL. B.,
" Samuel K. Woodworth, LL. B.
" *Edgar B. Wright, LL. B.,
" Richard Yates, LL. B.,
'85 Lemuel M. Ackley, LL. B.,
" George C. Cook, LL. B.,
" Howard W. Dickinson, LL. B.
" Henry C. Flower, LL. B.,
" Frank M. Goddard, LL. B.,
" Joseph F. Greene, LL. B.,
" Richard W. Groom, LL. B.,
" Adam H. Meeker, LL. B.,
" Charles W. Taylor, LL. B.,
" Ralph L. Aldrich, LL. B.,
" James H. Beal,
'86 William H. Brunson, LL. B.,
" Charles Dresbach, LL. B.,
" Charles H. Dudley, LL. B.,

" Benjamin C. Garrison,
" Ambrose E. B. Helmick, LL. B.,
" Charles M. Murphy, LL. B.,
" Norman T. Mason, LL. B.,
" Walter S. Meeker, LL. B.,
" John T. Moffit, LL. B.,
" Granville A. Richardson, LL. B.,
" Allen Showman, LL. B.,
" James G. Smith, LL. B.,
" James C. Work,
'87 William A. Carter,
" Fred I. Chichester, LL. B.,
" Albert D. Elliot, LL. B.,
" John A. Fairchild, LL. B.
" Thomas P. Fenton, Jr.,
" Charles G. Hurds, LL. B.,
" Austin M. Keene, LL. B.,
" George C. Manly, LL. B.,
" Charles S. Pierce,
" Charles Reed, LL. B.,
" James N. Saunders, LL. B.,
" Samuel I. Slade, LL. B.,
" John W. M. Stewart, LL. B.,
" George B. Watson,
" Frank L. Wean,
'88 John R. Calder,
" Lodowick F. Crofoot, LL. B.,
" Perley F. Gosbey, LL. B.,
" Harry A. Lovett,
" William H. Moore, LL. B.,
" John A. Murphy, LL. B.,
" Wilbur Owen, LL. B.,
" William L. Parmenter, LL. B.,
" Samuel L. Philbrick, LL. B.,
" Walter T. Smith,
" George B. Stewart, LL. B.,
" John Q. Van Swearingen, LL. B.,
" George B. Yerkes, LL. B.,
'89 Alfred J. Adams,
" Armand Albrecht, LL. B.,
" Arthur W. Brady, LL. B.,
" David K. Cochrane,
" Matthew C. Fleming,
" William W. Griffin, LL. B.,
" Volney O. Hildreth, LL. B.,
" Ernest R. Keith, LL. B.,
" John McF. Ormond, LL. B.,
" George J. Stoneman, Jr., LL. B.,
" Samuel L. Thompson, LL. B.,
" George H. Wood,
'90 *Henry W. Baird,
" Laverne Bassett, LL. B.,
" William F. Carter, LL. B.,
" Linton A. Cox, LL. B.,
" Brode B. Davis, LL. B.,
" Walter S. Holden,
" George A. Katzenberger, LL. B.,
" Edgar F. Koehler, LL. D.,
" Edward C. Mason, LL. B.,
'90 Arthur E. Pratt, LL. B.,
" George F. Rush,
" Lawrence VanBuskirk,
" Orlando G. Volkmor, LL. B.,
" Archie E. Watson, LL. B.,
'91 Daniel R. Anthony, Jr., LL. B.,
" Frederick W. Benz, LL. B.,
" Edwin A. Blakeslie,
" Charles W. Burt,
" Charles C. Butler, LL. B.,
" Ora E. Butterfield, LL. B.,
" Wilson S. Doan,
" Olen L. Everts, LL. B.,
" *James G. Foard,
" Williams C. Harris, LL. B.,
" Frederick A. Henry, LL. B.,
" Henry A. Hickman, LL. B.,
" John C. Huntoon, LL. B.,
" George S. Johnson, LL. B.,
" James S. Martin,
" Richard L. Melton,
" Norman A. Phillips, LL. B.,
" Harold Taylor, LL. B.,
" Duncan M Vinsonhaler, LL. B.,
" William H. Wadley, LL. B.,
'92 James H. Adams, LL. B.,
" William A. Beasley, LL. B.,
" Patrick A. Berry, LL. B.,
" Fenton W. Booth, LL. B.,
" John R. Effinger, Jr.,
" William H. Eichhorn,
" Victor M. Elting, LL. B.,
" John S. W. Holloway, LL. B.,
" Francis T. Hord, LL. B.,
" George E. Howes, Jr., LL. B.,
" Pomeroy Ladue,
" Elliott Northcott,
" Melvin B. Parmely, Jr., Jr., LL .B.,
" Charles S. Witbeck,
'93 Charles C. Benedict,
" Albert S. Brown,
" Edwin C. Caldwell,
" Oliver H. Carson, LL. B.,
" Frank Crawford, LL. B.,
" James W. Good, LL. B.,
" Edwin B. Harts, LL. B.,
" Milton Johnson, LL. B.,
" James B. Nelson, LL. B.,
" Jonathan Palmer, Jr., LL. B.,
" George G. Prentis, LL. B.,
" Henry A. Reese, LL. B.,
" Charles P. Richardson, LL. B.,
" John S. Ronntree, LL. B.,
" Frank C. Smith, LL. B.,
" Robert F. Thompson, LL. S.,
" Campbell M. Voorhees, LL. B.,
" Edwin A. Wilcox, LL. B.,
" Edward H. Williams, LL. B.,
'94 Alfred F. Bissell, LL. B.,

'94 George V. D. Candler,
" Henry E. Candler, LL. B.,
" Holbrook G. Cleaveland, LL. B.,
" Walter S. Fulton, LL. B.,
" William R. Hervey, LL. B.,
" J. Stanley Hurd, LL. B.,
" Gordon N. Kimball,
" Frank C. Kuhn, LL. B.,
" Samuel Medbury,
" William G. Ramsey, LL. B.,
" Hedley V. Richardson, LL. B.,
" Lindsay Russell, Jr., LL. B.,
" James J. Sheridan, LL. B.,
" John G. Stone, LL. B.,
" Luther O. Wadleigh, LL. B.,
" Percy Wilson, LL. B.,
" Harry F. Worden, LL. B.,
'95 Elmer L. Allor, LL. B.,
" Ira C. Belden,
" Harry C. Bulkley, LL. B,
" John S. Burnett, LL. B.,
" Leigh R. Crawford, LL. B.,
" Henry H. Cushing, LL. B.,
" Robert W. Dunn, LL. B.,
" Harry I. Dunton,
" Allan P. Gilmour, LL. B.,
" Frank P. Graves, LL. B.,
" Charles B. Henderson, LL. B.,
" Hugh G. Keegan, LL. B.,
" Rufus G. Lathrop, LL. B.,
" Charles S. McDowell, LL. B.,
" Edgar M. Morseman, Jr., LL. B.,
" Daniel B. Ninde, LL. B.,
" Victor J. Obenauer,
" Gilmore D. Price, LL. B.,
" Edward S. Rogers, LL. B.,
" Charles Zollinger, LL. B.,
'96 John B. Archer, LL. B.,
" Franklin E. Bump, LL. B.,
" Edwin Denby, LL. B.,
" Charles W. Foster, LL. B.,
" Benjamin A. Gage, LL. B.,
" Warren W. Guthrie, Jr., LL. B.,
" John T. Harrington, LL. B.,
'96 Alfred H. Hunt, LL. B.,
" Nathaniel H. Kennedy, LL. B.,
" Robert W. Manly, LL. B,
" Herbert R. Marlatt, LL. B.,
" John C. Munger,
" Harry Y. Saint, LL. B.,
" Edmund C. Shields, LL. B.,
" Oliver L. Spaulding, Jr., LL. B.,
" Wade W. Thayer, LL. B.,
" Frederick W. Winkler,
'97 Freeman Field, LL. B.,
" Ransom F. George, LL. B.,
" Clare H Stearns, LL. B.,
" Edward F. Wehrle, LL. B.,
'98 Norman T. Bourland,
" Charles G. Cook,
" Luman W. Goodenough,
" Oliver A. Ludlow,
" Lester E. Maher,
" Rufus P. Ranney,
" Errol H. Y. Spicer,
" Francis E. Stevens,
" Dwight J. Turner,
" Orestes H. Wright,
'99 Arthur G. Andrews,
" Armin W. Brand,
" Charles P. Davis,
" Frederic Harry,
" Paul C. King,
" Stanley M. Matthews,
" Samuel I. Motter,
" Morris H. Reed,
" Philip W. Seipp,
" Wallis C. Smith,
" Ellis G. Soule,
" Francis L. Wurzburg,
'00 William B. Davies,
" Edmund J. Mautz,
" Harry W. Paddock,
" Clayton T. Teetzel,
" Russell B. Thayer,
" McLane Tilton, Jr.,
" James F. Yeager.

Phi Chi, a local medico-legal fraternity (not to be confounded with the pharmaceutic Phi Chi) was formed in 1872 as a rival of Phi Delta Phi. It styled itself the Alpha, and its badge was a monogram of *Φ* and *X*. Excluded from The Palladium this society published The Sapphire in 1873. Phi Chi seems to have lived until some time in 1875–76. Theobald Otjen, '75 *l*, now a Representative in Congress, was a member, and the roll included the following, possibly other, names:

'74 *l* Irving R. Fisher, LL. B.,
" *m* *Rufus H. McCarty, M. D.,
'75 *l* *Myron E. Bishop, LL. B.,
" *m* George L. Graham,
" *l* Theobald Otjen, LL. B.,
'75 *m* Phil Porter,
" *l* Charles O. Tattershall,
" *m* John E. Weaver,
'76 *l* Leonard C. Reynolds.

Delta Chi.—This is a fraternity exclusively devoted to law schools. It was founded at Cornell University in 1890, and has the following additional chapters: New York University, Michigan, Minnesota, Dickinson, Chicago College of Law, University of Buffalo, Osgoode Hall (Toronto), and Northwestern. The Michigan chapter, founded with fourteen charter members, May 25, 1892, has been very successful. It occupies the beautiful building 733 South State street, and has the following honorary members: Professor Herman V. Ames, Benjamin Butterworth, Professor John B. Clayberg, J. P. Dollivar, Judge Victor A. Elliott, Marshall D. Ewell, Judge William G. Ewing, James L. High, Ex-President Benjamin Harrison, Robert T. Lincoln, Judge Samuel Maxwell, and Roger Q. Mills. The well-known baseball players is A. W. Jefferis, '93 *l*, and S. C. Spitzer, '94 *l*, were Delta Chi men. The roll of the 87 regular members follows:

BADGE OF DELTA CHI.

'93	Marvin E. Barnhart, LL. B.,	'96	T. Myron Westover, LL. B.,
"	Robert L. Campbell, LL. B.,	'96	Federick W. Bacorn, LL. B.,
"	Miner L. Davis, LL. B.,	"	Oliver R. Barrett, LL. B.,
"	Willim C. Fitzer, LL. B.,	"	Luther G. Beckwith, LL. B.,
"	Edgar M. Hall, LL. B.,	"	Edward S. Ferry, LL. B.,
"	Metcalf B. Hatch, Jr., LL, B.	"	Frederick H. Gaston, LL. B.,
"	Otis E. Hungate,	"	Forrest M. Hall, LL. B.,
"	Albert W. Jefferis, LL. B.,	"	Laurence R. Hamblen, LL. B.,
"	Edwin L. Johnson, LL. B.,	"	William W. Kerr. LL. B.,
"	Harvey T. Lovett, LL. B.,	"	Bertrand Lichtenberger, LL. B.,
"	John H. Park, LL. B.,	"	Allen C. MacCaughan,
"	George J. Parker, LL. B.,	"	George R. Miller, Jr., LL. B.,
"	Charles F. Parsons, LL. B.,	"	Stuart H. Perry, LL. B.,
"	George C. Stewart, LL. B.,	"	Edward E. Spear, LL. B.,
"	Howard A. Thornton, LL. B.,	"	Evan Stevenson,
'94	Milton E. Blake, LL. B.,	"	Myron R. Sturtevant, LL. B.,
"	Robert C. Chapman, LL. B.,	"	Daniel R. Williams, LL. B.,
"	Charles W. Chapman, LL. B.,	"	David B. Woodworth, LL. B.,
"	Charles O. Duncan,	'97	Chester G. Brown,
"	Willis V. Elliott, LL. B.,	"	Thomas A. Berkebile, LL. B.,
"	Robert B. Mitchell, LL. B.,	"	Frederick B. Stanley, LL. B.,
"	Charles A. Park, LL. B.,	'98	Duane D. Arnold,
"	Harry H. Patterson, LL. B.,	"	William R. Blackburn,
"	Sherman C. Spitzer, LL. B.,	"	Jacob M. Blake,
"	Charles I. Stouffer,	"	William H. Feindt, Jr.,
'95	Frank W. Ballenger,	"	Carl L. Flood,
"	Arthur C. Bartels, LL. B.,	"	Daniel W. Fishell,
"	Philo G. Burnham, LL. B.,	"	Hugh H. Hart,
"	Llewellyn B. Case, LL. B.,	"	Maurice E. Harvey,
"	Thornton Dixon, LL. B.,	"	Frank G. Mason,
"	Walter M. Ellett,	"	Howard I. Shepherd,
"	Thomas S. Hayden, Jr., LL. B.,	"	J. Sterling St. John,
"	Edward Horskey, LL. B.,	'99	John C. Ammerman,
"	Schuyler C. Hubbell, LL. B.,	"	Earle V. D. Brown,
"	Harry H. Parsons, LL. B.,	"	John Campbell,

'99 Henry Catron,
" Harry L. Chapman,
" Harold H. Emmons,
" John E. Harding,
" Charles A. Klotz,
" Robert D. Magill,
" Warren Mullett,
" George Smith,
" Albert D. Stevens,
'99 LeRoy A. Wilson,
'00 Basil B. Adams,
" Joseph Chamberlain,
" Harry A. Converse,
" William L. Day,
" Clarence C. Dutch,
" Leonard Masters,
" Thomas G. Masters.

Nu Sigma Nu.—This medical-school fraternity, the oldest of its kind, was founded at our University March 2, 1882, by five members of the class of '83. April 20, 1882, seven pins were worn in public, and the existence of the fraternity was openly announced. Uniform prosperity has attended the order at Ann Arbor and elsewhere. The roll of chapters is as follows: Alpha, Michigan; Beta, Detroit College of Medicine; Delta, Western University of Pennsylvania; Epsilon, Minnesota; Zeta, Northwestern; Eta, Illinois (Chicago College of Physicians and Surgeons); Theta, Ohio Medical College; Iota, Columbia; Kappa, Chicago; Lambda, Pennsylvania; Mu, Syracuse; Nu, University of Southern California. There are about 700 members. Garnet and white are the colors. The local chapter occupies the house 114 North Division street, and is represented in the Faculty by G. Carl Huber, '87 *m*, Simon M. Yutzy, '91 *m*, J. R. Arneill, '94 *m*, J. T. McClymonds, '94 *m*, R. N. Gorden, '97 *m*, William A. Spitzley, '97 *m*, George B. Wallace, '97 *m*, and W. H. Waite, '98 *m*. To this fraternity belonged the baseball player W. W. Pearson, '93 *m*, and the football men, E. E. Hagler, '90 *m*, R. T. Farrand, '92 *m*, S. C. Glidden, '93 *m*, W. W. Pearson, '93 *m*, and L. C. Grosh, '96 *m*. The Alpha chapter has eighteen honorary members, most of whom are now or have been members of the Medical Faculty at Ann Arbor. Their names follow: Doctors John J. Abel, Flemming Carrow, Walter S. Christopher, Arthur R. Cushny, Cyrenus G. Darling, George Dock, Corydon L. Ford, George E. Frothingham, George A. Hendricks, Henry F. Lyster, W. A. MacGugan, Donald Maclean, J. P. McMurrich, W. L. Moore, Charles B. Nancrede, Frederick G. Novy, Thomas J. Sullivan, and Victor C. Vaughan. The list of the regular members of the parent chapter, 135 in number, follows:

BADGE OF NU SIGMA NU.

'83 Frederick C. Bailey, M. D.,
" Charles M. Frye, M. D.,
" William J. Mayo, M. D.,
" *Robert D. Stephens, M. D.,
" Benjamin G. Strong, M. D.,
'84 Sidney H. Culver, M. D.,
" Charles W. Dodd, M. D.,
" John D. Gish, M. D.,
" George S. Hatch, M. D.,
" George A. Haynes, M. D.,

'84 William W. Johnson, M. D.,
" Frederick W. Main, M. D.,
" Herman Ostrander, M. D.,
'85 James M. Postle, M. D.,
" Charles E. Rankin, M. D.,
'86 Edward L. Bower, M. D.,
" Henry H. Dawson,
" William C. Riddell, M. D.,
" Charles H. Waterhouse,
" Scott P. Woodin, M. D.,
'87 Walter H. Allport,
" Oliver E. E. Arndt, M. D.,
" Miles H. Clark, M. D.,
" Walter A. Cowie, M. D.,
" James W. Dalby,
" Albert G. Dunaway,
" Leonard F. Hatch, M. D.,
" G. Carl Huber, M. D.,
" Wilmot F. Miller, M. D.,
" John A. Prince, M. D.,
" Albert F. Schafer, M. D.,
'88 Frank Chaffee, M. D.,
" Arthur H. Coe, M. D.,
" James L. Halsey,
" Frederick S. Heller, M. D.,
'89 Carroll O. Boyce, M. D.,
" William S. Connery, M. D.,
" William H. Dodge, M. D.,
" William W. Haworth,
" John L. Irwin, M. D.,
" Lewis H. Kemble, M. D.,
" Charles McGregor, M. D.,
" Wadsworth Warren, M. D.,
'90 John A. Barnett, M. D.,
" Elmer E. Hagler, M. D.,
" Napoleon D. Kean, M. D.,
" John J. Marker, M. D.,
" Chester W. Merrill,
" Benjamin F. Parrish,
" Francis M. Phillips, M. D.,
" R. E. L. Rodgers,
" George H. T. Sparling,
'91 Nelson Abbott, M. D.,
" *James C. Ballard, M. D.,
" Edward C. Davidson, M. D.,
" William H. Fisher, M. D.,
" William J. Furness, M. D.,
" Walter J. Green,
" Thomas A. R. Jones, M. D.,
" John H. Kimble, M. D.,
" Samuel S. Lindsey, M. D.,
'91 Donald Macrea, Jr., M. D.,
" John Rebur,
" George L. Renaud,
" William G. Rice, M. D.,
" Cassius D. Silver, M. D.,
" Will P. Walter,
" Simon M. Yutzy, M. D.,
'92 George H. Brash, M. D.,
'92 Arthur P. Burroughs,
" John H. Dent, M. D.,
" Royal T. Farrand, M. D.,
" Henry M. Joy, M. D.,
" Peter D. McNaughton, M. D.,
" Richard R. Smith, M. D.,
" Henry C. Valentine, M. D.,
'93 William W. Pearson, M. D.,
'94 Alonzo Andrews, 2d,
" James R. Arneill, M. D.,
" James F. Breakey, M. D.,
" Calvin R. Elwood, M. D.,
" Joseph Foster, M. D.,
" Stephen C. Glidden, M. D.,
" Charles T. McClintock, M. D.,
" Julian T. McClymonds, M. D.,
" George E. McKean, M. D.,
" Edwin A. Murbach, M. D.,
" George P. Wintermute,
'95 Thomas M. Cooley, M. D.,
" Harry A. Haze, M. D.,
" John R. Rogers, M. D.,
'96 Chester B. Bliss, M. D.,
" Allen N. Borden, M. D.,
" Frank S. Bourns, M. D.,
" Harry L. R. Crummer,
" Gilbert S. Furness, M. D.,
" Lawrence C. Grosh, M. D.,
" Saxe W. Mowers, M. D.,
" Homer E. Safford, M. D.,
" Harry E. Sauer,
" James W. VanDusen, M. D.,
'97 Ralph N. Gorden, M. D.,
" Howard A. Ijams, M. D.,
" John H. Kincaid, M. D.,
" Frederick P. Lawton, M. D.,
" William B. Lunn, M. D.,
" George D. Perkins, M. D.,
" William A. Spitzley, M. D.,
" George B. Wallace, M. D.,
" Harry C. Watkins, M. D.,
" Robert D. Wilson,
'98 Thomas S. Burr,
" Norton D. Coons,
" John D. Covert,
" A. Ernest Gale,
" Clarence A. Good,
" Park Howell,
" Mark S. Knapp,
" Will MacLake,
" Herbert H. Waite,
'99 Philip D. Bourland,
" Willis G. Cook,
" Willard D. Hutchins,
" John V. Keogh,
" Clarence W. Mehlhop,
" Frank W. Nagler,
" Samuel Schultz,
" Frederick T. Wright,

'00	Harold M. Doolittle,	'00	John Stoddard,
"	Theodore A. Hoch,	"	Bert K. VanNaten,
"	George B. Lowrie,	'01	Alfred C. Bartholomew.
"	Carl H. Lund,		

Phi Rho Sigma, a medical-school fraternity, was founded in 1892 at the Northwestern University, and in addition to the parent (Alpha) Chapter has these branches: Beta, Chicago College of Physicians and Surgeons; Gamma, Lake Forest University; Delta, University of Southern California; Epsilon, Detroit College of Medicine; and Zeta, University of Michigan, established in June, 1897. The local chapter occupies the house No. 538 Church street. It has enrolled the following men, among them Corydon F. Heard, '98*m*, of the University baseball nine of 1897:

BADGE OF PHI RHO SIGMA.

'94	George M. Reese, M. D.,	'98	Archie A. Swinton,
"	Carleton D. Morris, M. D.,	"	Charles H. Williams,
"	Frederick W. Palmer, M. D.,	'99	Roy B. Canfield,
'97	Albert A. Church, M. D.,	"	William P. Harlow,
"	Herman R. Dewey, M. D.,	"	Downey L. Harris,
"	Stowell B. Dudley, M. D.,	"	Cabot Lull, Jr.,
"	Charles B. Gauss, M. D.,	"	Thomas K. Moore,
"	Benjamin W. Kelley, M. D.,	"	Martin A. Mortensen,
"	John A. Mapes, M. D.,	"	Hiram W. Orr,
'98	Howard B. Baker,	"	Andrew L. Swinton,
"	John M. Craig,	"	Wesley E. Taylor,
"	Corydon F. Heard,	'00	William A. Coventry,
"	William S. Jackson,	"	Joseph B. Palmer,
"	Jesse K. Marden,	"	Herbert E. Peckham,
"	Horace Newhart,	'01	Herbert B. Horton,
"	Joseph C. Scarborough,	"	Herbert S. Olney.

Phi Chi, a society in the School of Pharmacy, was organized in 1883, and now has a branch in the Northwestern University. At Ann Arbor it occupies as a chapter house the dwelling 344 South Division street. Professors Albert B. Prescott, Victor C. Vaughan, Alviso B. Stevens, and David L. Davoll, Jr., are honorary members, and the society has already one regular member, Professor J. O. Schlotterbeck, '87, in the Faculty. Following is the roll, as compiled from the successive issues of The Palladium:

BADGE OF PHI CHI.

'84	Charles E. Bond,	'84	Herbert W. Snow, Ph. C.,
"	Franklin H. Frazee, Ph. C.,	"	Azor Thurston,
"	Llewellin H. Gardner, Ph. C.,	"	Albert T. Waggoner, Ph. C.,
"	Calvin P. Godfrey, Ph. C.,	'85	Frank M. Clark, Ph. C.,
"	*Adolph G. Hoffman, Ph. C.,	"	DeLagnel Haigh, Ph. C.,
"	Arthur G. Hopper, Ph. C.,	"	Benjamin J. Lauer, Ph. C.,
"	Charles Hueber, Ph. C.,	"	Samuel J. North, Ph. C.,
"	*George P. Leamon, Ph. C.,	"	Willard F. Pett, Ph. C.,

'85 Arthur S. Rogers, Ph. C.,
" Hugh Scott,
" Albert W. Smith, Ph. C.,
" Henry M. Spencer, Ph. C.,
" Laird J. Stabler, Ph. C.,
" Edward A. Tupper, Ph. C.,
'86 Gordon A. Bowdish, Ph. C.,
" Andrew J. Buckham, Ph. C.,
" *Edward W. Clark, Ph. C.,
" Charles T. Haigh, Ph. C.,
" Charles L. Stinchcomb,
" Edwin R. Stivers, Ph. C.,
" William A. Zimmer,
'87 Herman L. Barie, Ph. C.,
" Louis A. Dryfoss, Ph. C.,
" Richard S. Dupont, Ph. C.,
" Jacob J. Haarer,
" Samuel S. Hance, Ph. C.,
" Fred J. Henning, Ph. C.,
" Jennings Pemberton,
" Julius O. Schlotterbeck, Ph. C.,
" Charles G. Shubel, Ph. C.,
'88 Dorsey P. Horine, Ph. C.,
" Charles F. Lawson,
" Henry Levy, Ph. C.,
" John H. Shaper, Ph. C.,
" John A. Wesener, Ph. C.,
" J. Burgess Whinery, Ph. C.,
" Frank D. Wiseman, Ph. C.,
89 Henry A. Allshouse, Ph. C.,
" Frank B. Ambler,
" Warner P. Cary,
" Starr K. Church, Ph. C.
" William S. Lockwood, Ph. C.,
" Firdinand E. Parkinson, Ph. C.,
" George E. Steketee,
" George L. VonKleine,
'90 C. Wilson Baker, Ph. C.,
" F. Wilford Baker, Ph. C.,
" William E. Collins, Ph. C.,
" Joseph M. Gries,
" Theophil Klingmann, Ph. C.,
" Otto P. Meyer, Ph. C.,
" Wallace C. Palmer, Ph. C.,
" O. Clayton Reed,
" John G. Steketee,
'95 Henry J. Bowerfind, Ph. C.,
" Henry A. Herzer, Ph. C.,
'95 Carl W. Jones,
" John N. Judy, Ph. C.,
" James W. T. Knox, Ph. C.,
" Ernest G. Reese, Ph. C.,
" Wilbur B. Scott,
" Edward E. Washburn, Ph. C.,
'96 James W. Ames, Ph. C.,
" Ernest L. Curtis,
" Joseph M. Drew,
" Edward P. Graves, Jr.,
" Frank C. Hitchcock, Ph. C.,
" Walter A. Parker,
" Edward L. Schmitt, Ph. C.,
" Burton A. Sweet,
" Roland B. Taber, Ph. C.,
" Henry W. Taylor, Ph. C.,
" Miles L. Trowbridge, Ph. C.,
" Milton L. Trowbridge, Ph. C.,
" Elisha B. Williams, Ph. C.,
'97 Ursa S. Abbott,
" Fred J. Austin, Ph. C.,
" Fred J. Baringer, Ph. C.,
" George W. Beisel,
" Arthur L. Green,
" P. Willis Hickman,
" Frederic J. Klein,
" William H. Noll, Ph. C.,
" Harry S. Stoddard, Ph. C.,
'98 John N. Adams,
" Carl J. Biehl,
" John A. Coram,
" Mark B. Hawes,
" Leroy E. Minot,
" Leonard Short,
" Philip Schaupner,
" Will E. Sullivan,
" Herbert E. Taber,
" Sam H. Zimmerman,
'99 Lyman Barlow,
" Lavern O. Cushing,
" Charles A. Duerr,
" George Eckel,
" Ralph Hicks, Jr.,
" Philip Kephart,
" Olney R. Morse,
" William B. Saladin,
'00 Henry C. Hitchcock,
" Burton A. Sweet.

Delta Sigma Delta.—The Alpha Chapter of this, the earliest fraternity of dental students, was founded at Michigan in 1882. The sister branches are: Beta, Chicago College of Dental Surgery; Gamma, Harvard University (Dental Department); Epsilon, University of Pennsylvania (Department of Dentistry); Zeta, University of California (College of Dentistry); Eta, Northwestern University Dental School; Theta, University of Minnesota (College of

Dentistry); Iota, Detroit College of Medicine (Dental Department); Kappa, Vanderbilt University (Dental Department); Lambda, Western Reserve University (Dental Department); Mu, Boston Dental College; Nu, Kansas City Dental College. There are also "Auxiliary Chapters" in Detroit, Chicago, Boston, Minneapolis, Cleveland, and Philadelphia. The total membership of the society is about 1,600. A quarterly magazine called Desmos is published by the order. Turquoise-blue and garnet are the colors. The chapter at Ann Arbor occupies the house 624 Packard street, and is accumulating a fund for building. Upon its membership roll are the following honorary initiates: Doctors Calvin S. Case, James Cleland, William H. Dorrance, George H. Field, James W. Gale, C. H. Harroun, Nelville S. Hoff, Joseph Lathrop, Sr., William Mitchell, Edward L. Moore, and Fred S. Whitslar. Among the graduates are many well known dental surgeons, of whom William Cleland, '84 *d*, of Detroit, and Louis P. Hall, '89, of our Dental Faculty, are types. Upon the University baseball and football teams the fraternity has been represented by F. R. Carson, '84 *d*, E. V. Deans, '96 *d*, A. H. Kinmond, '98 *d*, and H. E. Lehr, '98 *d*. A roll of the 156 regular members of Alpha Chapter follows:

BADGE OF DELTA SIGMA DELTA.

'84 Franklin R. Carson, D. D. S.,
" William Cleland, D. D. S.,
" Lyndall L. Davis, D. D. S.,
" Clarence J. Hand, D. D. S.,
" Charles W. Howard,
" Louis M. James, D. D. S.,
" Ezra L. Kern, D. D. S.,
" *Donald D. Magill, D. D. S.,
" Louis J. Mitchell, D. D. S.,
" Francis W. Temple, D. D. S.,
" Charles P. Weinrich, D. D. S.,
'85 Louis P. Bethel, D. D. S.,
" Francis E. Cassidy,
" E. Johnson Galbraith, D. D. S.,
" George B. Haught, D. D. S.,
" Henry C. Merrill, D. D. S.,
" Willoughby B. Smith, D. D. S.,
" Will H. Whitslar, D. D. S.,
'86 DeWitt C. Bacon,
" Edmund K. Clements, D. D. S.,
" William A. Courtney, D. D. S.,
" Harry W. Davis, D. D. S.,
" Henry A. Dawley, D. D. S.,
" George J. Dennis, D. D. S.,
" Frank F. Douds, D. D. S.,
'86 William A. Hering,
" Sandy H. Houston,
" Clifford F. Snyder, D. D. S.,
" George H. Watson, D. D. S.,
" Benjamin F. Yates, D. D. S.,
'87 Frank C. Babcock, D. D. S.,
" Edward L. Dillman, D. D. S.,
" Elmer L. Drake, D. D. S.,
" David A. Harroun, D. D. S.,
" William A. Wright, D. D. S.,
'88 *Clarence W. Berry, D. D. S.,
" Rollin E. Drake, D. D. S.,
" Arthur N. Hart, D. D. S.,
" Elmer B. Hause, D. D. S.,
" Egbert T. Loeffler, D. D. S.,
" Charles E. Meerhoff, D. D. S.,
" Irvin Myers, D. D. S.,
" Harry C. Nickels, D. D. S.,
" Homer E. Parshall, D. D. S.,
" Sherman F. Stauffer, D. D. S.,
'89 Edwin C. Clow,
" Louis P. Hall, D. D. S.,
" Horace N. Holmes, D. D. S.,
" Jacob W. Jungman, D. D. S.,
" *Reuben J. Kirk, D. D. S.,

'89 Frank E. Morey, D. D. S.,
" Charles F. Noyes, D. D. S.,
" Arthur M. Potter, D. D. S.,
" DeWitt Spalsbury, D. D. S.,
" Will S. Taylor,
'90 Ernest Catt, D. D. S.,
" George H. Copp, D. D. S.,
" William C. Herbert,
" John B. Keesing, D. D. S.,
" Melville W. Mason,
" George Northcroft, D. D. S.,
" William H. Siebert, D. D. S..
" Fred S. Sizelan, D. D. S.,
" John H. Waterhouse, D. D. S.,
'91 Frederick W. Fleming, D. D. S.,
" *Frank S. Henry, D. D. S.,
" Alfred L. Sickler, D. D. S.,
" Charles F. Stone, D. D. S.,
" Jonathan R. Taft, D. D. S.,
'92 Archibald W. Diack,
" George Dilworth, D. D. S.,
" Allison W. Haidle, D. D. S.,
" Edward B. Spalding, D. D. S.,
'93 Charles W. Adamson, D. D. S.,
" Frank W. Boyer, D. D. S.,
" Charles A. Church, D. D. S.,
" Herman Kreit, D. D. S.,
" Greenbury A. Rawlings, D. D. S.,
" William H. Van Iderstine, D.D.S.,
" William H. Van Deman, D. D. S.,
" Milton T. Watson, D. D. S.,
" Will L. Webster, D. D. S.,
'94 Frederick H. Codding, D. D. S.,
" James K. Douglas, D. D. S.,
" Calvin R. Elwood,
" Homer F. Hussey, D. D. S.,
" George W. Kenson, D. D. S.,
" Allen H. Kessler, D. D. S.,
" Joseph Lathrop, Jr., D. D. S.,
" Walter C. McKinney, D. D. S.,
" Benjamin F. Pearce, D. D. S.,
" Charles T. Whinery, D. D. S.,
'95 Douglas Anderson, D. D. S.,
" Lewis E. Coonradt, D. D. S.,
" Fred E. Dodge, D. D. S.,
" John B. Dowdigan, D. D. S.,
" Edmond Dnbuis, D. D. S.,
" Albert L. LeGro, D. D. S.,
" Frank E. McLaughlin, D. D. S.,
" Henry P. O'Connor,
" Harry B. Respinger, D. D. S.,
" Clifford P. Sweny, D. D. S.,
" George McA. Tyng, D. D. S.,
'95 Frederick von Widekind, D. D. S.,
'96 Clarence H. Bailey, D. D. S.,
" Edwin V. Deans, D. D. S.,
" Charles A. Devlin, D. D. S.,
" Stanford J. Farnum, D. D. S.,
" Stanley A. Farnum, D. D. S.,
" Fred J. Hale, D. D. S.,
" Burton T. Hunt, D. D. S.,
" Raymond L. Williams, D. D. S.,
'97 James C. Blair, D. D. S.,
" Frank R. Fletcher, D. D. S.,
" Frank W. Howlett, D. D. S.,
" Wendell H. Johnson, D. D. S.,
" Frederick M. Joslin, D. D. S.,
" Frederick H. Leland, D. D. S.,
" William R. Purmort, D. D. S.,
" Alfred J. Reed, D. D. S.,
" Delmer W. Stoup, D. D. S.,
" Edward L. Vaile, D. D. S.,
" James N. Vodrey, Jr., D. D. S.,
" Harry D. Watson, D. D. S.,
'98 Edward J. Anderson,
" Roy Archbold,
" Lyman S. Brown,
" Wilton J. Hardy,
" Alexander H. Kinmond,
" Herbert E. Lehr,
" Harry B. McMillan,
" Edwin K. Medler,
" Fred C. Miller,
" Clarence E. Pease,
" Joseph B. Stewart,
" Fred G. Titus,
" Thomas B. Van Horne,
'99 Hilen D. Aldrich,
" Arthur E. Alther,
" Carroll F. Chase,
" George M. Freeman,
" Paul R. Furlong,
" Claude E. Hathaway,
" James C. Lowrie,
" Clair G. Meseroll,
" Edgar E. Nelson,
" Philip R. Thomas,
" Benjamin W. Wells,
'00 Carl Bonham,
" Bert G. Coggin,
" Artemas B. Gray,
" Eugene P. Hall,
" Carlos J. Light,
" Lorne Moodie,
" Percy S. Peck.

Xi Psi Phi.—This dental-school fraternity was founded at our University in 1889, and has spread into the following institutions: New York College of Dentistry, Philadelphia Dental College, Baltimore College of Dental Surgery, University of Iowa, University of Cincinnati, University of Maryland, Indianapolis College of Dental Surgery, University of California, Chicago College of Dental Surgery, and Ohio Medical University. These branches are named in the regular order of the Greek alphabet. There are about 1,000 members. Alpha, the chapter at Michigan, occupies the house 408 East Washington street. It was incorporated March 31, 1892. The following list of members was compiled from the successive issues of The Palladium and The Michiganensian:

BADGE OF XI PSI PHI.

'93 Frank I. Ball, D. D. S.,
" Herbert J. Burke, D. D. S.,
" *William J. Clark, D. D. S.,
" Otis DeUrfae,
" Jesse J. McMullen, D. D. S.,
" Thomas B. Mercer, D. D. S.,
" Charles L. Mitchell,
" Mason Moyer, D. D. S.,
" Fred M. Prettyman, D. D. S.,
" Milton R. Stimson, D. D. S.,
'94 Gerald W. Collins, D. D. S.,
" Frank B. Dawley, D. D. S.,
" Alfred W. Hall, D. D. S.,
" George E. Hathaway, D. D. S.,
" John L. Hoover, D. D. S.,
" Beaumont H. Kaighn,
" Thomas A. McIndoe, D. D. S.,
" Robert B. McKenzie,
" Frank L. Stow,
" Harvey A. Sturdevant, D. D. S.,
" Charles R. Vanderbelt, D. D. S.,
" James Whiting,
'95 Joseph H. Billmeyer, D. D. S.,
" J. Austin Bucknall, D. D. S.,
" George F. Fiddyment, D. D. S.,
" C. VanGarratt, D. D. S.
" Arche G. Hicks, D. D. S.,
" Arthur S. Kennedy, D. D. S.,
" Jad H. F. Kuyper, D. D. S.,
" Clarence F. Piper, D. D. S.,
" Charles S. Preston,
" Andrew R. Thorpe, D. D. S.,
" Christian L. Thuerer, D. D. S.,
'96 Robert R. Buckthorpe, D. D. S.,
" George F. Burke, D. D. S.,
" James N. Clarke, D. D. S.,
" Frank Day, D. D. S.,
" Charles F. Fitch, D. D. S.,
'96 Charles A. Phillips, D. D. S.,
" Will H. Roper, D. D. S.,
" Frank J. Sheldon,
" Charles E. Slagle, D. D. S.,
" Morley P. Templar, D. D. S.,
" Ralph L. Williams, D. D. S.,
" Percy B. Wright, D. D. S.,
'97 William Bruce,
" Ernest E. Bubb,
" Albert J. DuBois, D. D. S.,
" Samuel W. Hussey, D. D. S.,
" Cary E. Jaynes,
" Frederick J. Klein, D. D. S.,
" Frank D. Loomis, D. D. S.,
" Roland S. Mitchell, D. D. S.,
" Samuel K. Scharlott, D. D. S.,
" Arthur M. Schurtz, D. D. S.,
" Luman R. Slawson, D. D. S.,
" Daniel Templar,
" Albert J. Wildanger, D. D. S.,
'98 Arthur A. Baker,
" James R. Davis,
" D. Willard Flint,
" Percy R. Glass,
" Claude C. Goodes,
" Chalmers J. Lyons,
" Gail H. McFarland,
" Don C. McKinney,
" Guy R. Palmer,
" Leslie W. Platt,
" Lester G. Platt,
" Thomas C. Reed,
" Ralph J. Roper,
" Ollie W. White,
'99 Arthur L. Baker,
" Will C. Butler,
" Wilfred D. Kirk,
" Fred C. Orvis,

'99 Harry C. Orvis,
" George M. Richardson,
" Samuel C. Sims,
" Charles F. Steinbauer,
" Clifford F. Stepp,
'00 Earl M. Brown,
'00 Archie W. Cook,
" Albert R. Hervey,
" Ray A. Horning,
" Marvin Houghton,
" Charles Lord,
" Robert P. Roe.

Mu Sigma Alpha.—This homœopathic-medical fraternity was organized late in 1888, but did not make its formal appearance in public until Monday, February 4, 1889. There were eight founders. It has prospered in correspondence with the school which it represents. It has neither rivals nor chapters. Doctors Hugo R. Arndt, Charles A. Gatchell, Wilbert B. Hinsdale, Charles S. Mack, Daniel A. McLachlan, Henry L. Obetz, Charles F. Sterling, and James C. Wood, are honorary members of this order, which numbers among its regular graduates Professors Roy S. Copeland, '89, and Charles W. Ryan, '94. The following are known to be members:

BADGE OF MU SIGMA ALPHA.

'89 Roy S. Copeland, M. D.,
" Walter N. Fowler, M. D.,
" James A. McLachlan, M. D.,
" Charles A. Macrum, M. D.,
'90 Ernest A. Clark, M. D.,
" Andrew B. Nelles, M. D.,
'91 Arthur W. Burdick, M. D.,
" John H. Harvey, M. D.,
" Guert E. Wilder, M. D.,
'92 Ernest F. Gamble, M. D.,
" Lewis B. Gardner, M. D.,
'93 George F. Clark, Jr., M. D.,
" John L. Ireland,
" F. Clifton Laur, M. D.,
" Henry M. Northam, M. D.,
" Frank Rich, M. D.,
" Milton T. Watson, D. D. S.,
" Harvey G. Young, M. D.,
'94 Charles A. Critchlow, M. D.,
" Charles W. Ryan,
" Glenn G. Towsley, M. D.,
'94 Burt D. Walker, M. D.,
'95 William H. Atterbury, M. D.,
'97 Albert J. Elliott, M. D.,
'98 Charles Montague,
" Clarence A. Schimansky,
" S. Porter Tuttle,
'99 S. Newton Babcock,
" Robert T. Johnson,
" William W. Jungels,
" Dean W. Myers,
" Hardy M. Piper,
" Paul Thompson,
" Tisdale S. Walker,
" Charles E. Wehrle,
'00 Paul E. N. Greeley,
" Scott F. Dodge,
" Harry D. Obert,
" Harley A. Haynes,
" Arthur S. Moore,
" George R. Owen.

CHAPTER XIII

CLASS SOCIETIES

Many causes have operated to prevent the development in our University of a system of class societies similar to that which is the characteristic feature of student life at Yale. As the early classes with us were very small, the fraternities planted at Ann Arbor in 1845 became of necessity four-year affairs; whereas the same or similar Greek-letter fraternities at Yale from 1837 to 1844, and there preceded by senior-class secret societies, naturally confined themselves sooner or later to the junior class, which always afforded them plenty of material. Not before 1870 were Michigan's classes large enough to ensure the continued prosperity of an order limited to one delegation; but by that time the four-year fraternities had grown so strong that they could not be reduced to a subordinate plane. That the so-called "Owl" came very near to permanent success is true, yet the very fact that after living ten years it was compelled to yield to the opposition of the Greek-letter societies shows how hard it is for an order of its kind to survive at Ann Arbor.

BADGE OF KAPPA SIGMA EPSILON (YALE).

As for freshman or sophomore societies they never have a serious excuse for being where four-year fraternities exist. At Dartmouth and at Amherst the lower-class orders imported from Yale were successful so long only as the regular fraternities were wholly or largely confined to the upper classes; and so with us membership in the stronger and more honorable organization precludes attention to one of less importance. If the fraternities would refrain from initiating new men until the opening or the middle of sophomore year, there would be room for several under-class societies; and the latter, if decently conducted, would be useful factors in college life. But when composed of men who owe allegiance to the full-course fraternities a freshman or a sophomore society has no special field.

BADGE OF DELTA KAPPA (YALE).

The Owls.—This senior-class society was founded in 1860 by members of the class of '61. It is said to have been suggested by Andrew D. White, Yale '53, then Professor of History in the University, and to have been modelled by him after the plan of the Skull and Bones of Yale. Fifteen men were to be chosen in each class, but this number was reached in '61 and '63 only, and there were but ten men in '66. Among the members were Ex-Ambassador Uhl; Ex-Regent Barbour; Judges Swan, Coolidge, and Kinne; Representative in Congress Snover; Ex-President Harrington of the University of Washington; Professors D'Ooge and Walter of Michigan, Hurd of Johns Hopkins, Campbell of Dartmouth, Blackburn of Chicago, and Rising of California; Messrs. Utley, Grant, and Hart of Detroit; and many other distinguished graduates.

VIGNETTE OF THE OWLS.

Both because it hurt the feelings of the non-elect, and because it threatened vested interests, the society was violently attacked. The following extract from the University Magazine for March, 1862, shows how the Owl was regarded by part of the student body.

"There appeared in our midst last year a Secret Society in the Senior Class. It was composed of members of different societies. It was not noticed much, until it was noised around that the members called themselves the best men in College. Each man, it seemed, was a committee to extol and praise every member except himself . . . . . . This year it has appeared again . . . . . . By the aid of dashes and names of men who do not belong to the College, it makes the sacred fifteen. They style themselves variously '555's', 'Owls', and 'Sons of Minerva'. They like the latter appellation best, however. It places them above the vulgar rabble and on a footing with gods . . . . . . The spirit of their constitution is, to elevate themselves at the expense of others. It is a mutual admiration fraternity; a you-tickle-me-and-I'll-tickle-you-society. This is its plan. Its members come from the different secret societies. These secret societies are not supposed to be very friendly to one another. Hence a member of one society can easily praise certain members of another with an apparent show of fairness. For instance, a Beta Thet. sticks his impertinant phiz in any place he gets a chance, and says that there are only three or four Delta Kaps who know anything at all, the rest are all asses. A Delta Kap says the same of the Beta Thets; an Alpha Delt. speaks in this way of Delta Kaps and Beta Thets; and so it goes on in the rogues' circle . . . . . In the class it is a clique that sneers and scoffs at all honest merit outside of its own organization".

As the "555" began to gain something of the prestige and influence of its Yale prototype, the Greek-letter orders grew uneasy. Sigma Phi expelled two men for joining it; Alpha Delta Phi stood aloof after 1866; and although D. K. E. and Psi Upsilon remained friendly, more than half of the '69 delegation was supplied by the so-called neutrals. Men were secured from '70 and also from '71, but the names of the members in those classes were not recorded in the Palladium. Indeed, the last appearance of the order in the annual mentioned was in 1869, after which date the career of the Owls is shrouded in mystery even deeper than that which characterized its earlier life. No elections were conferred upon the class of '72, and the order became dormant in June, 1871. It is remarkable for the affection with which its members regard it. Following is the roll, from which are omitted the delegations in '70 and '71:

'61 *Frederic Arn,
" William H. Beadle,
" Samuel M. Billings,
" Benjamin F. Blair,
" Charles H. Denison,
" William E. Crume,
" Isaac H. Elliott,
" Edward S. Jackson,
" John C. Johnson,
" Henry B. Landon,
" John S. Lord,
" Samuel R. B. Lord.
" Moses K. Rosebrugh,
" Henry M. Utley,
" *Thomas B. Weir,
'62 H. Austin Burt,
" Charles Chandler, Jr.,
" *John E. Colby,
" Martin L. D'Ooge,
" Edward A. Fay,
" *H. Dewey Follett,
" *Theodore H. Hurd,
" *Aaron C. Jewett,
" *W. Eugene Nelson,
" *Albert Nye,
" Moses K. Rosebrugh,
" Henry H. Swan,
" Edwin F. Uhl,
'63 J. Clement Ambrose,
" Levi L. Barbour,
" *Levi J. Brown,
" Orville W. Coolidge,
" *C. Stuart Draper,
" Lincoln T. Farr,
" Clark Gray,
" William S. Harroun,
" Henry M. Hurd,
'63 Conway W. Noble,
" George P. Peck,
" Delos Phillips,
" Stephen Powers,
" James L. Taylor,
" *George S. White,
'64 George S. Albee,
" *William S. Brewster,
" *Arthur Everett,
" William A. Ewing,
" Schuyler Grant,
" Joseph C. Hart,
" Zina P. King,
" Edward D. Kinne,
" Herbert A. Lee,
" Henry D. Smith,
" S. Consider Stacy,
" Shubael F. White,
" *Clarence E. Wilbur,
'65 Abram J. Aldrich,
" Oscar P. Bills,
" Gabriel Campbell,
" Charles A. Dudley,
" William J. Maynard,
" Homer C. Powers,
" William H. Barnes,
" *Edward C. Boudinot,
" James D. H. Cornelius,
" Sanford B. Ladd,
" *Samuel R. McLean,
" *Delos Phillips,
" *J. Barnes Root,
" Charles A. Sanford,
'66 James K. Blish,
" Gabriel W. Crutcher,
" William C. Frew,
" Henry W. Hubbard,

'66 *Edwin D. Kelley,
" A. Eugene Mudge,
" John W. Remington,
" *James M. Scott,
" Henry Smith,
" George S. White,
'67 William H. Brown,
" Wellington Carleton,
" George E. Church,
" *Isaac N. Elwood,
" Lester O. Goddard, Jr.,
" Milton Jackson,
" George L. Maris,
" *Isaac N. Otis,
" Joseph H. Reid,
" Willard B. Rising,
" John A. Rollins,
" *James Steel,
" Edward W. Wetmore,
'68 William K. Anderson,
" Wickliffe W. Belville,
" Francis A. Blackburn,
" Edward C. Burns,
'68 Oliver H. Dean,
" Mark W. Harrington,
" Edward L. Hessenmueller,
" Edward S. Jenison,
" Willard A. Kingsley,
" *John C. Magill,
" Humphrey H. C. Miller,
" Galusha Pennell,
" Rollin J. Reeves,
" Edward L. Walter,
'69 Sidney Brownsberger,
" William J. Darby,
" Samuel Hayes,
" J. Eugene Hinman,
" Allen M. Hurty,
" Theodore F. Kerr,
" *George B. Lake,
" Benjamin L. C. Lothrop,
" Charles E. Otis,
" Horace G. Snover,
" Thomas C. Taylor,
" *John Whiting,
" Alfred E. Wilkinson.

Sigma Tau was a society founded in 1867 and confined to the class of '70. "The initiations and the disorders of exercises cannot be described", said the chronicler of the class.

Delta Sigma Phi was a senior society which began and ended with thirteen members of the class of '90, not all of whom, by the way, were actually seniors when the society was founded. These were the members, most of whom were from Alpha Delta Phi, D. K. E., or Psi Upsilon:

'90 Charles T. Alexander,
" James R. Angell,
" William D. Ball,
" Dugald Brown,
" Benjamin P. Bourland,
" Frederick W. Crane,
" Royal T. Farrand,
'90 Edwin F. Gay,
" Paul R. Gray,
" Walter L. Mann,
" William L. Page,
" William B. Ramsay,
" John R. Rogers.

The Satyrs, another senior-class society, was started by men of '94, and it ended with them. Of its ten members three belonged to D. K. E., two to Sigma Phi, two to Zeta Psi, two to Psi Upsilon, and one to Alpha Delta Phi. The society was received with great disapprobation by one of the leading fraternities, and steps were taken to prevent further accessions to it from that source. Following is the roll of members:

'94 Thomas B. Bradfield,
" George J. Cadwell,
" William R. Canfield,
" Robert F. Hall,
" Alfred H. Hunt,
'94 Robert E. Jones,
" Frank W. Pine,
" Henry M. Senter,
" George T. Tremble,
" Edward L. Watrous.

Omicron Phi was a junior-class society, which was founded in 1889–90 for the purpose of uniting in social intercourse sixteen fraternity men of the junior class, and of giving an occasional german. Only two delegations were received into the order. Of the members Alpha Delta Phi had nine, Psi Upsilon seven, D. K. E. five, Sigma Phi five, Zeta Psi four, and Phi Kappa Psi three. A small monogram of *Ο Φ* of gold was worn as a badge by the members, whose names follow:

'91 Frank R. Ashley,
" George P. Codd,
" Thomas B. Cooley,
" James M. Crosley,
" John R. Effinger, Jr.,
" Carl K. Friedman,
" Theodore H. Hinchman, Jr.,
" John A. Jameson, Jr.,
" Chancey R. Lamb,
" Harrison B. McGraw,
" Loyal L. Munn, Jr.,
" Samuel C. Park,
" Frederick S. Richmond,
" Edward H. Smith,
" Rufus C. Thayer,
" Edward J. Woodworth,
'92 Fitzhugh Burns,
" Harry E. Chandler,
" James E. Ferris,
" William M. Johnstone,
" David W. McMorran,
" William R. Murray,
" Frederic S. Porter,
" George G. Prentis,
" Alfred D. Rathbone, Jr.,
" Frederic L. Sherwin,
" Frank C. Smith,
" Richard R. Smith,
" James VanInwagen, Jr.,
" William E. Walter,
" Carl C. Warden,
" Edward D. Wickes.

Cord and Magnet.—This was a sophomore social club, which had for a badge a tiny horseshoe of gold encircled by a cord. The society had sixteen members in the class of '93, divided thus: Alpha Delta Phi five; D. K. E. and Psi Upsilon each four; Chi Psi, Beta Theta Pi, and Phi Kappa Psi one apiece. Following are the names:

'93 William H. Andrews,
" Edward S. Beck,
" Henry P. Dodge,
" Frank R. Gilchrist,
" Frank P. Graves,
" Samuel S. Harris,
" George E. Howes, Jr.,
" Rufus G. Lathrop,
'93 John C. Loomis,
" Dwight C. Morgan,
" C. A. Newcomb, Jr.,
" Edward L. Sanderson,
" Arthur VanInwagen,
" John VanNortwick,
" Laurence J. Whittemore,
" Edwin C. Wilkinson.

Theta Nu Epsilon.—This sophomore fraternity was founded at Wesleyan University in 1870. A Beta Chapter was instituted at Syracuse in 1874, and a Gamma at Union in 1876. Many other branches have been established elsewhere, but not a few of them have fallen through Faculty displeasure. The chief manifestations of the society are elaborately absurd initiations, and midnight pranks of an exaggeratedly sophomoric type. Upsilon, the Michigan branch, was organized in 1892 under the auspices

T.N.E. BADGE

of students who had been initiated at other colleges. About twenty members were admitted from each college class, all the initiates being fraternity men, and D. K. E. having a large representation. Psi Upsilon refused to allow its members to join "T. N. E." Toward the close of 1894–95 the chapter became dormant, although it is said, four men were initiated in 1897. The names of the initiates, as far as can be ascertained, are these:

'94 Elmer E. Beal,
" Thomas P. Bradfield,
" Vincent R. Dwyer,
" Hiram G. Effinger,
" James S. Henton,
" Alfred H. Hunt,
" Marion T. Hyatt,
" Carlin Phillips,
" Frank W. Pine,
" Hiram Powers,
" Charles W. Sencenbaugh,
" Dietrich C. Smith, Jr.,
" Fred H. Standt,
" George T. Tremble,
" Lloyd J. Wentworth,
" Ernest H. Warren,
" Harry F. Worden,
'95 Josiah W. Begole,
" Philip D. Bourland,
" Rex R. Case,
" John C. Condon,
" Charles C. Conrad,
" Stuart E. Galbraith,
" Clark C. Hyatt,
" Fred King,
" Harry L. L. Lyster,
" Robert W. Manly,
" Samuel Medbury,
" Frank C. Merrill,
'95 Charles H. Morse, Jr.,
" Earle Munson,
" James O. Murfin,
" Charles H. Parkes,
" William H. Perkins,
" George B. Russel,
" Bertram S. Varian,
" Stewart E. White,
" Carl B. Williams,
'96 Norman T. Bourland,
" Harry A. Cole,
" Arthur G. Cummer,
" Waldo E. Cummer,
" Charles P. Davis,
" Charles F. Drake,
" Dexter M. Ferry, Jr.,
" Raynor S. Freund,
" Edmund R. Harrington,
" Herbert W. Landon,
" William B. MacHarg.
" George A. Marston,
" Frank E. Miller,
" Harry G. Nicol,
" Henry B. Otis,
" Frank H. Petrie,
" William T. Phillips,
" Ben C. Rich,
" Albert W. Russell,
" Lloyd C. Whitman.

Gamma Kappa Epsilon, originally a freshman society, and afterwards a four-year affair, but always addicted to innocuous diabolism, was founded in 1876 by nine freshmen, Allen, Ambrose, Deacon, DuShane, Mitchell, Parker, Reynick, Thompson, and Webster. Its men were drawn quite evenly from Chi Psi, D. K. E., Sigma Phi, Zeta Psi, and Psi Upsilon. It seems to have passed away unlamented after the graduation of '83. Following is the list of members:

'80 J. S. Ambrose,
" A. S. Deacon,
" S. H. DuShane,
" C. S. Mitchell,
" C. J. Reynick,
" E. L. Webster,
'81 F. G. Allen,
'81 C. T. Brace,
" Samuel Chandler,
" C. H. Kumber,
" F. C. Mandell,
" D. L. Parker,
" H. C. Richardson,
" W. M. Thompson,

'82 F. E. Baker,
“ B. P. Brodie,
“ C. L. Coffin,
“ C. S. Collins,
“ R. M. Cooley,
“ F. W. Davenport,
“ W. L. Loveland,
“ J. H. Norton,
“ F. A. Robinson,
“ T. W. Sargent,
“ H. G. Sherrard,
“ F. D. Weeks,
“ F. G. Whiting,
“ G. B. Whitney,
'83 E. A. Barnes,
“ *l* T. J. Lynch,
“ H. A. Mandell,
“ W. C. Marsh,
“ L. K. Merrill,
'83 Ralph Metcalf,
“ *l* C. M. Sherman,
“ E. C. Strong,
“ C. T. Wilkins,
“ J. T. Winship,
“ T. F. Wormwood,
'84 W. J. Abbott,
“ F. L. Beeson,
“ B. G. Brown,
“ Clarence Conely,
“ H. O. Crane,
“ H. F. Forbes,
“ L. B. Hanchett,
'85 F. K. Ferguson,
“ C. H. Hills,
“ H. S. Oakley,
“ C. F. Pettibone,
“ R. M. Seeds,
“ Delos Thompson.

Omega Nu.—This was a freshman society, founded in 1890. It kept up an existence more or less active through the four years spent by '94 at Ann Arbor, and it gave no elections to the class of '95. There were sixteen members:

'94 G. H. Angell,
“ T. P. Bradfield,
“ C. N. Church,
“ G. S. Crane,
“ V. R. Dwyer,
“ H. G. Effinger,
“ A. H. Hunt,
“ M. T. Hyatt,
'94 H. C. James,
“ W. L. Maas,
“ S. F. Mason,
“ Carlin Phillips,
“ D. L. Quirk, Jr.,
“ B. C. Robinson,
“ C. W. Sencenbaugh,
“ D. C. Smith, Jr.

CHAPTER XIV

COLLEGIATE SISTERHOODS

Only a few days after the admission of women into the University occurred the foundation, in an Indiana college, of Kappa Alpha Theta, the prototype of the Greek-letter sisterhoods. This was in January, 1870. Five years later some of the young women at Ann Arbor were asked to join in forming a chapter of the society mentioned; but they declined on the ground that a secret order would lead to dissention among the exponents of co-education. This argument lost its force as the number of female students increased; The Chronicle of November 23, 1878, mentioned as in circulation a report that "the co-eds are to have a secret society after the manner of the boys"; and, toward the close of 1879, the Eta of Kappa Alpha Theta made its appearance. Thereupon The Chronicle of December 20, 1879, declared that "Since the advent of the new secret society the boys have only one remaining advantage over the co-eds, and that is the possession of the back seats in Psychology; but without doubt this last prerogative will soon be wrested from them". The new movement was so quiet and unostentatious that it at first attracted little attention. Before long the stage of ridicule was reached. "It is reported", says one of the town papers of the time, "that on moonlight nights a large Maltese cat can be seen frolicking about in a certain section of the city. It is tailless, and has its fur so clipped as to leave in bold relief on its back the Greek letters *Κ Α Θ*. Whence came the animal?" "Last Saturday evening", says a veracious college journal, "two new members were introduced into the mysteries of the Kappa Alpha Theta. Pussy-wants-a-corner was one of the games".

Despite ridicule, perhaps because of it, the original feminine sodality of Michigan grew and flourished. A rival, the Gamma Phi Beta, appeared in 1882; and another, Delta Gamma, was organized in 1885. In the latter year the Michigan members of Kappa Alpha Theta became dissatisfied with the fraternity at large, and, having surrendered their charter, they became in 1886 the collegiate branch of the New York Sorosis. In 1888 a fifth sisterhood, the Michigan Beta of Pi Beta Phi, was instituted in the University. This was followed by Kappa Kappa Gamma in 1890, by Alpha Phi in 1892, and by Delta Delta Delta in 1894. In 1893 Kappa Alpha Theta was reëstablished; and as all the others have lived uninterrupted lives there are now among the women of the academic department eight societies, seven of which are chapters of secret Greek-letter orders elsewhere founded. Sorosis is nominally non-secret, and is strictly local. A description of each of the women's societies follows.

Kappa Alpha Theta.—This, the earliest Greek-letter society of women, was founded at Asbury (now DePauw) University, January 27, 1870, by Bettie Locke (Hamilton), '71, Alice Allen (Brant), '71, Bettie Tipton (Lindsey), '71, and Jennie Fitch (Shaw), '73. It has had in all thirty-two chapters of which twenty-one are active, and are in the following institutions: DePauw, Indiana, Wooster, Michigan, Cornell, Kansas, Vermont, Allegheny, Hanover, Nebraska, Northwestern, Minnesota, Syracuse, Wisconsin, California, Leland Stanford, Jr., Swarthmore, Ohio State, Illinois, Women's College of Baltimore, and Brown. The eleven dormant branches were at Moore's Hill College, Butler, Illinois Wesleyan, Ohio, Simpson, Albion, Ohio Wesleyan, Wesleyan, Southern California, Toronto, and University of the Pacific. The total membership is somewhat more than 2,000 Black and gold are the colors, the pansy is the society flower, and a magazine called *The Kappa Alpha Theta* is issued quarterly. Eta Chapter, the pioneer of the feminine orders at Ann Arbor, was instituted December 10, 1879, with six charter members, Carrie C. Parrish, Alice Van-Hoosen, Jane Eyer, Charlotte L. Hall, Hattie M. Collier, and Laura Hills. In 1885–86 the undergraduates, with the co-operation of certain alumni, gave up their charter, and the Eta remained dormant until, at the general convention of the society held at Chicago in July, 1893, nine Michigan students who had united for the purpose of reviving the chapter were initiated as charter-members. Miss Katharine E. Coman, '80, Professor of Political Economy in Wellesley College; Mrs. Minnie Clark Dennis, '87, wife of Professor Dennis of Cornell; and Mrs. Henry C. Adams, '88, of Ann Arbor, are among the members of the local chapter. Its "patronesses" are Mesdames M. L. H. Walker, J. H. Brewster, and Floyd R. Mechem. The chapter-house is 1008 Hill street. Following is the Michigan roll:

BADGE OF KAPPA ALPHA THETA.

'76 Louise M. Reed (Stowell), B. S.,
'77 M. Louise Hall (Walker), Ph. B.,
'80 Katherine E. Coman, Ph. B.,
" Carrie C. Parrish, A. B.,
'81 Jane Eyer (Smoot), A. B.,
'82 *Hattie M. Coliier,
" Laura Hills (Norton), Ph. B.,
'83 Lee Bird (Barron),
" Linda E. Harris,
" Florence May Lyon,
" Carrie C. Smith (Curme),
'84 Bessie P. Hunt,
'85 *Fanny L. Wassall,
'86 Emma P. Stephenson (Marble),
'87 Minnie O. F. Clark (Dennis), A.B.,
'88 Bertha H. Wright (Adams), A. B.,
'92 Mamah B. Borthwick, A. B.,
'93 Martha H. Chadborne, Ph. B.,
'94 Jessie I. Beal,
" Jessie Harris,
" Gertrude Hull,
'95 Winnifred R. Craine, B. L.,
" Fanny A. Gale,
" Mabel G. Gale,
" Lina K. Gjems, Ph. B.,
" Louise M. Harris, Ph. B.,
" Myra M. Post, B. L.,
'95 Alice E. Wadsworth, B. L.,
'96 Kate A. Landfair,
" Bertha Hull,
" Nellie E. McCaughan.
" Grace McNoah,
'97 Edna L. Paddock, B. S.,
" Minerva B. Rhines, B. L.,
" Dorotheo Roth,
" Mary R. Swope,
" Harriette C. Waller,
'98 Irene M. Blanchard,
" Editha L. Dann,
" Matilda A. Harrington,
" Susan F. Patterson,
" Maud Philips,
" Edith L. Rice,
" Clara Wilson,
'99 Louise R. Gibbs,
" Anna L. Harris,
" Carrie B. Mowry,
" Mary L. Reid,
'00 Jeannette Blanchard,
" Katherine E. Veit,
" Charlotte H. Walker,
'01 Margaret Jones,
" Grace L. Moore,
" Jane V. Pollack.

Anna H. Adams, Ph. B. '90; Arletta L. Warren, now a graduate student; and Kate M. Johnson, '00 *m*, are members of other chapters of Kappa Alpha Theta.

Gamma Phi Beta.—This sisterhood was founded in 1874 at Syracuse University by Helen M. Dodge, '76, Frances E. Haven, '77, E. Adelaid Curtis, '78, and Minnie A. Bingham, '78. It was favored from the outset by Chancellor Haven, who gave to the society its open motto. The chapters are: Alpha, Syracuse; Beta, Michigan; Gamma, Wisconsin; Delta, Boston; Epsilon, Northwestern; Zeta, Baltimore; Eta, California; and Theta, Denver. There are about 550 members. Light-fawn and seal-brown are the colors, and the society flower is the carnation.

BADGE OF GAMMA PHI BETA.

Beta, the Michigan branch, instituted in 1882, is the oldest of the women's societies at Ann Arbor if continuous existence be considered. The chapter house is 720 S. State street. Mrs. Isadore T. Scott, '84, wife of Professor F. N. Scott, is one of the alumni. The entire roll, which includes nineteen classes and 101 members, follows:

'83 Grace Darling (Madden), Ph. B.,
" Clara Weir (Stockley), Ph. B.,
'84 *Elizabeth G. Cornell (Stebbings), B. L.,
" Jane Emerson (Miller), A. B.,
" Myra Pollard, A. B.,
" Delia Rood (Doty),
" *Jenny Scranton, A. B.,
" Isadore Thompson (Scott), A. B.,
'85 Minnie Hamilton (Grosvenor),
" Mary B. Putnam, Ph. B.,
" Jessica T. Washburn,
'86 Nettie C. Daniels, A. B.,
" Dennie G. Dowling,
" Alice Parks (Hinshilwood), A. B.,
" Sarah Satterthwaite (Leslie), A. B.,
" Loraine Westbrook,
'87 Estelle L. Guppy, A. M.,
" M. Ruth Guppy, B. S.,
" Violet D. Jayne, A. B.,
" Gertrude Stevens (Lewis), B. S.,
" Ruth Sunderland (Hodge),
'88 Alice M. Hosmer (Preble), A. B.,
" Achsa S. Parker, A. B.,
" Honta B. Smalley, A. B.,
'89 Isabella M. Andrews (Talley), A.B.,
" Helen M. Fallows,
" Mabel L. Randall,
'90 Faith Helmer (Parks), Ph. B.,
" Margaret M. Hunt, A. B.,
" Edith Stevens)Fitzgerald),
" Anna Yeaton (Miller),
'91 Frances Atkins,
" Emma M. Ballentine (Hinchman), A. B.,
" Mary Harnard,
" Mary E. Sanborn, Ph. B.,
'92 Gertrude Bundy (Parker), A. B.,
" Mary A. Ford (Armstrong),
" Ada Gilbert (Close), B. L.,
" Louise Randolph (Gay), A. B.,
" Cornelia Steketee (Hulst),
'93 Rosetta Anderson,
" Alice Beckwith (Thompson),
" Maude B. Bedell, A. B.,
" Mary Carpenter, Ph. B.,
" Margaret Cahill (Bartholomew),
" Mary C. Colver (West), B. L.,
" Augusta H. Durfee (Flintermann), A. B.,
" Grace Ford (Todd),
" Jennie B. Sherzer, Ph. B.,
" Mary Eloise Walker, A. B.,
'94 Frill G. Beckwith,
" Sara den Bleyker (Van Deman), B. S.,
" June Carpenter (Greeley), Ph. B.,
" Maude Hicks,
" Annah M. Soule, B. L.,
" Anna M. Wiley,
'95 Elsie G. Anderson,
" Marie L. Goodman, Ph. B.,
" Cora F. Reilly (Beck), B. L.,
" Helen Randall (Kidder),
" Esther Rich, B. L.,
" Lillian Thompson,
'96 Grace L. Collins, Ph. B.
" Helen L. Douglas, Ph. B.,
" Rob Hanson (Hyde),
" Edith M. Kimball, Ph. B.,
" Bessie B. Larrabee, A. B.,
" Emma J. MacMorran, Ph. B.
" Georgien E. Mogford, A. B.,
" Harriet S. Taylor,
" Isabella Hosie,
'97 Martha W. Bancker,
" Margaret A. Douglas (Bement),
" Edna M. Holbrook, B. S.,
" Abigail Hubbard,
" Zayde Spencer (Molitor),
'98 Esther Braley,
" Lillian J. Cole,
" Josephine Daniels,
" Emelie A. Flintermann,
" Grace F. Goodman,
" Eva J. Hill,
" Esther Kinne,
" Erma Wheeler,
" Mary E. Young,
'99 Katherine E. Ballentine,
" Winnifred A. Hubbell,
" Frances L. Petit,
'00 Edna Burington,
" Ruth Burington,
" *m* Caroline B. Colver,
" Sadie A. Platt,
" Lorette Sherman,
'01 Lucy C. Davis,
" Ida Louise Holden,
" Jessie M. Horton,
" Mabelle Leonard,
" Mabelle F. Randolph,
" R. Winifred Sunderlin.
" Constance E. B. Webber,
" Leonora Yeager.

Delta Gamma owes its origin to four students who founded it in 1872 at the University of Mississippi. The parent chapter was called Psi, and became dormant in 1889. Branches now exist in Buchtel, Wisconsin, Minnesota, Mt. Union, Northwestern,

Albion, Cornell, Michigan, Colorado, Iowa, Nebraska, Women's College of Baltimore, and Leland Stanford, Jr.; thirteen in all. Besides there are fourteen inactive chapters. The total membership is about 1200. Pink, blue, and bronze are the colors, and the pearl rose has been adopted as the fraternity flower. A quarterly magazine, the Anchora, represents the interests of the Society. Xi, the Michigan branch, was instituted in 1885. It rents and occupies the house 1309 Wilmot street, has enrolled as honorary members the late Mrs. Gayley Brown, Mrs. Henry S. Carhart, Mrs. Mark W. Harrington, Mrs. Charles B. Nancrede, Mrs. Albert B. Prescott, Mrs. Mortimer E. Cooley, and Mrs. Frank B. Lillie, and has the following list of regular members, seventy in all:

BADGE OF DELTA GAMMA.

'85 Mary E. Thompson (Stevens), A.B.,
'86 Clara V. Grover (Tappan), A. B.,
'87 Helen L. Lovell (Million), A. B.,
'88 Blanche Epler,
" *Fannie T. Mulliken (Thompson), Ph. B.,
" Lizzie H. Northup (Avery), B. L.,
'89 Clarissa S. Bigelow, Ph. B.,
" Bertha A. Joslyn (Burrows), B. L.,
" Josephine Milligan, M. D.,
" Lizzie I. Shiell (Hause), A. B.,
" Zada J. Wilson, Ph. B.,
'90 Florence E. Wilson (Hall), Ph.B.,
'91 Minnie T. Buick (Van Dusen), B.L.,
" Marie Fleming (Sullivan), A. B.,
" Ida Z. Hibbard (Everson), B. L.,
" *Harriet A. Lovell, A. B.,
'92 Katherine R. Carlisle,
" Martha F. Eddy, Ph. D.,
" Ernestine Krolik (Kahn), Ph. B.,
" Ada Zarbell, A. B.,
'93 Maude Parsons, A. B.,
" Florence H. Pope (Wolverton), Ph. B.,
" Mary F. Power, Ph. B.,
'94 Carolyn P. Adams (Griffith),
" Flora G. Barnes (Munger), Ph. M.,
" Katharine L. Angell,
" Rose E. Mills,
" Almira A. Prentice, A. B.,
" Gertrude Richardson (Carson),
" Stella L. Wood,
'95 Florence E. Barnard, A. B.,
" Anna R. B. Bayer,
" *Mabel Colton, A. B.,
" Bessie L. Hopkins, Ph. B.,
'95 Carlotta E. Pope, Ph. B.,
" Mae H. Purmost (McBratney),
" Lurene Seymour, Ph. B.,
'96 Susie H. Allen, Ph. B.,
" Artena M. Chapin, A. B.,
" Maud I. Cooley (Seeley), A. B.,
" Helen Dryer, A. B.,
" Elizabeth A. Eberle,
" Caroline M. Taylor,
'97 Sara S. Browne, Ph. B.,
" Agnes Burton,
" Bell Krolik, Ph. B.,
" Anna T. McLaughlan, A. B.
" Inez C. Perrin, A. B.,
'98 Julia M. Angell,
" Clara R. Bell,
" Gertrude A. Boynton,
" Mary E. DeVeny,
" Harriette Harlan,
" Margaret Thain,
" Cornelia A. Wilding,
'99 Anne M. Barnard,
" Laura Dolese,
" Elsa King,
" Helen M. St. John,
" Lucy H. Seeley,
" Ruth L. Smith,
" Marion Stickney,
'00 Genevieve L. Derby,
" Henriette Pagelson,
" Ruby Richardson,
" Ada M. Safford,
" Clara Scott,
'01 Katharine Hine,
" Frances Fugate
" Kate Young.

Sorosis.—In June, 1886, former members of the Eta (Michigan) Chapter of Kappa Alpha Theta, who had become dissatisfied with that intercollegiate sisterhood, accepted a charter from the New York Sorosis. Most of the alumni of '84 and '85 joined the undergraduates in their movement. Unembarrassed by branches in other and perhaps undesirable institutions, the Collegiate Sorosis (as it is called to distinguish it from its parent) is very flourishing. In 1896 an incorporation under the name of "The Sorosis Club of Michigan" was effected, and a building-site in Washtenaw avenue was purchased for $2,000. Yellow and white are the society colors. The emblem is the pineapple. Mrs. Jennie June Croly is an honorary member, and Mrs. James B. Angell, Mrs. George S. Morris, Mrs. P. R. B. de Pont, and Mrs. Victor C. Vaughan are associate members. The wives of Professors Pattengill, Patterson, Worcester, and Freer, were members during their college lives, as also was the wife of President Henry Wade Rogers of Northwestern University. There are in all 120 members, as follow:

BADGE OF SOROSIS.

'80 Alice Van Hoosen (Jones) A. B.,
'81 Charlotte L. Hall (Eastman),
'83 Carrie C. (Smith) Curme,
'84 Nellie M. Fishback (Wait),
" *Clementine L. Houghton (Lupinski), B. L.,
" Isabella H. Hull, A. B.,
" Lydia A. Mitchell (Creager),
" Francis M. Skinner (Winship),
" Bertha VanHoosen, A. B.
" *Jessie B. Wood,
'85 Caroline P. Bell (Stevens), A. B.,
" Nellie Borland, Ph. B.,
" *Emma D. Healey,
'86 Alice Borland,
" Harriet A. Chipman (Dewey) Ph. B.,
" Ella D. Cochran (Merrill),
" Portia Goodson, A. B.,
" Winnogene Ramsdell (Scott),
" Emma F. Stephenson (Marble),
" *Eliza P. Underwood, A. B.,
" Bessie E. West (Pattengill),
'87 Nellie B. Haire (Levinson), A. B.,
" Katherine M. West, A. B.,
'88 Katharine H. Gower (Hatch), A. B.,
" Martha P. Merwin, A. B.,
" Julia C. Skinner (Thompson),
" Laura E. Whitley (Moore) A. B.,
" Clara Wilson,
'89 Elizabeth M. Coffin (Gilbert),
" Belva M. Herron, B. L.,
'89 Florence E. Whitcomb (Welch), B. L.,
'90 Dora O. Bennett, A. B.,
" Flora Bennett, A. B.,
" Lydia C. Condon,
" Cora M. Rowell, Ph. B.,
" Merib S. Rowley (Patterson), A. B.,
'91 Lucy Coolidge, Ph. B.,
" Lillian W. Johnson, A. B.,
" Isabella Kellogg (Moore),
" Ruth W. Lane, A. B.,
" Nanon F. Leas (Worcester),
" Opal Robeson (Siegenfoos), Ph. B.,
" Emma (Winner) Rogers, B. L.,
" Marion I. Watrous (Angell), B. L.,
'92 Agnes M. Leas (Freer),
" Mary Plant,
" Alice M. Tryner,
" Gertrude S. Wade (Slocum),
'93 Katherine V. Camp, B. S.,
" Genevieve Cornwell,
" Maude E. Merritt (Drake). B. L.,
" Ida M. Muma, A. B.,
" Josephine L. Roberts (Bent), A. B.,
" Ednina L. Shaw (Obenauer),
" Caroline C. Sterling,
" Lillian L. Wattling,
" Grace C. Webb,
'94 Lora D. Ankeney,
" Mary R. Butts (Carson),
" Ida C. Evans (Tasker),

'94 Henrietta I. Goodrich, A. B.,
" Ada L. Skinner,
'95 Elise C. Bennett, Ph. B.,
" Elizabeth F. Camp, Ph. B.,
" Katharine L. Codd (Sexton),
" Mary B. Cooley,
" Annie D. Dunster, Ph. B.,
" Katherine S. Fletcher,
" Elizabeth C. Hench, Ph. B.,
" Margaret E. Hench (Gardiner),
" *Josephine J. Hyde,
" Elizabeth W. Moore,
'96 Bertha F. Bradley,
" Alice Brown, A. B.,
" Elizabeth L. Gardiner (Cox),
" Carlotta Goldstone (Glynn), A. B.,
" Mary W. Lewis,
" Mary E. Trueblood, Ph. B.,
" Ruth M. Tuttle, Ph. B.,
'97 Juliet M. Butler, B. S.,
" May M. Butler, B. S.,
" Grace G. Millard, Ph. B.,
" Julia L. Morey, Ph. B.,
" Julia Pike, Ph. B.,
" Louise B. Swift, A. M.,
" Sarah F. Wilcox, Ph. B.,
'98 *Helen M. Babcock (Dow),
" Helen S. Bennett,
" Alice Chandler,
" Harriet L. George,
'98 Annie Hegeler,
" Macy Kitchen,
" Sara L. McKenzie,
" Hellen E. Ramsdell (Dempsey),
'99 Amy A. Collier,
" Fannie Cooley,
" Florence G. Dillon,
" Lena Z. Hegeler,
" Marguerite Knowlton,
" Evangeline C. Land,
" Caroline E. Pattengill,
" Maude H. Thayer,
" Clara Turner,
" Lila Turner,
'00 Beatrice O. Belford.
" Bertha M. Goldstone,
" Olga K. Hegeler.
" Christine M. Lilley,
" Sybil M. Pettee,
" Marian S. Roberts,
" Lilian A. Steele,
" Jane O. Turner,
'01 Mary L. Clark,
" M. Marguerite Gibson,
" Florence W. Green,
" Vena L. Harris,
" Katharine G. Healy,
" Euphemia G. Holden,
" Rachel B. McKenzie,
" Grace E. Seekell.

Pi Beta Phi.—This, the fifth in age of the women's societies represented in our University, was originally called the I. C. Sorosiss, and was founded at Monmouth College in April, 1867, by eleven students. The name Pi Beta Phi, adopted in 1883 as a secondary title, has since 1888–89 been used as the sole designation of the society. So, while the order is older than any other intercollegiate sisterhood, it is far from being the oldest Greek-letter sisterhood. Of the forty collegiate branches chartered by this organization twenty-seven are in active operation, there colleges being these: Iowa Wesleyan, Lombard, Kansas, Simpson, Iowa, Knox, Colorado, Denver, Hillsdale, Franklin, Michigan, Columbian, Ohio, Indiana, Leland Stanford, Jr., Ohio State, Swarthmore, Northwestern, Boston, Middlebury, Bucknell, Illinois, Wisconsin, Nebraska, Syracuse, Newcomb (Tulane), Women's College of Baltimore, and Indianapolis. About 2,400 members have been enrolled. Wine-red and light-blue are the colors, and the carnation is the society flower. The periodical of the order is called *The Arrow*. The Michigan Beta was organized in 1888, and in addition to its four

BADGE OF PI BETA PHI.

honorary members—Mrs. Martin L. D'Ooge, Mrs. Albert A. Stanley, Mrs. Francis W. Kelsey, and Mrs. Israel C. Russell—it has had the following adherents at Ann Arbor:

'89	Minnie H. Newley (Ricketts), Ph. B.,
'90	Franc Arnold (Chaddock), Ph. B.,
"	Fanny K. Read, B. L.,
'91	Mary C. Bancker,
"	Sadie F. Paine,
"	Statia Pritchard (Oursler),
'92	Gertrude Clark (Sober), B. S.,
"	Lucy Parker (Huber),
"	Zuell Preston (Tyler), B. L.,
"	Nina M. Tobey (Coburn),
'93	Ada M. Bennett,
"	Etta L. Hulbert,
"	Frances L. Stearns, B. S.,
"	Mary B. Thompson (Reid), A. B.,
"	Elizabeth R. Wylie,
'94	Mary Bartol, A. B ,
"	Dora D. Elmer, A. B.,
"	Florence E. Wolfenden,
'95	Miriam Dunbar, B. S.,
"	Hattie L. Hasty,
"	Mary C Lewis, A. B.,
"	Susan W. Lewis, A. B.,
"	Thyrza McClnre,
"	Lucy A. Maris,
"	Alice Pierce,
"	Edith H. Purdum, B. L.,
"	Lois B. Rowe (Lewis),
"	Fanny E. Sabin, Ph. B.,
"	Annie S. Thompson, A. B.,
'96	Nina M. Bushnell,
"	Joanna K. Hempsted, B. L.,
"	Lelia I. Kennedy (Galpin),
"	Lida R. Le Maistre,
'96	Elizabeth Wallace,
'97	Nettie H. Bates,
"	Lelia M. Coolidge,
"	Frances A. Foster, B. L.,
"	Faith H. Gilbert, Ph. B.,
"	Jessie Keith, A. B.,
"	Mary A. Pyle (Davoll),
"	Katharine L. Rogers,
"	Jessie H. Smith, A. B.,
'98	Harriet E. Beard,
"	Laura H Bevans,
"	Rebecca E. Finch,
"	Florence L. Richards,
"	Madge G. Sibley,
"	Flora A. Sigel,
"	Laura P. Temple,
"	Helen G. Wetmore,
'99	Mary Anderson,
"	Edna Bevans,
"	Gertrude A. Edwards,
"	Ruth L. Smith,
"	Florence K. Wetmore,
"	Lida V. H. White,
"	Ethelberta Williams,
'00	Nancy M. Bentley,
"	Grace P. Hunt,
"	Mabel L. Parker,
"	Christine G. Robertson,
"	Mary Wilson,
"	Elizabeth Wylie,
"	Alma M. Zwerk,
"	Margaret Cousins,
"	Mabell S. Leonard,
"	Eva Nichols.

Kappa Kappa Gamma was organized at Monmouth College, in 1870, by four undergraduates. Anti-fraternity legislation killed the parent chapter in 1878; but in the meantime other branches had been started. There have been in all thirty-one chapters, of which twenty-seven survive at the following institutions: Indiana, Illinois Wesleyan, Wisconsin, Missouri, DePauw, Wooster, Buchtel, Butler, St. Lawrence, Minnesota, Hillsdale, Boston, Iowa, Northwestern, Adrian, Syracuse, Cornell, Kansas, Nebraska, Allegheny, Ohio State, Pennsylvania, Michigan, Barnard, Leland Stanford, Jr., Swarthmore, and California. The society has about 2,800 members. It publishes a quarterly magazine called the Key, and the colors are light blue and dark blue. Beta Delta, the branch at Ann Arbor, was established Friday, October 3, 1890, with six charter mem-

BADGE OF KAPPA KAPPA GAMMA.

bers. The chapter-house rented by the society is No. 326 Division street. Mesdames W. H. Pettee, W. J. Herdman, and Flemming Carrow, are the patronesses of the chapter, which has enrolled the following members :

'89	Blanche K. Barney, B. L.,	'96	P. Ernestine Robinson, B. L.,
'90	Alice H. Damon, A. B.,	"	Bessie M. Whitehead, B. L.,
"	Caroline C. Penny (Lange), A. B ,	'97	Lucy B. Green,
'91	Lucy D. Clarke, A. B.,	"	Florence R. Howland,
"	Bertha E. Pritchard, Ph. B.,	"	Mary E. Roueche,
"	Laura E. Sprague, Ph. B.,	"	Mabelle Turner,
'92	Maude McGregor (Vanderventer),	"	May VanHorn,
"	Jessica V. Penny, A. B.,	'98	Ruth G. Beckwith,
'93	Katharine S. Alvord, A. B.,	"	Alice M. Boutell,
"	Ruth G. Bagley, A. B.,	"	Helen Dunham,
" l	Mary S. Benson, LL. M.,	"	Charlotte E. Kennedy,
"	Mildred Hinsdale,	"	Erie M. Layton,
"	Katharine B. Ross, B. S.,	"	Susanne O. MacCauley,
"	Anna B. Skinner,	"	Elizabeth K. Toms,
"	Georgia Smeallie (Nims), B. L.,	'99	Isabel A. Ballou,
"	Lula B. Southmayd, A. B.,	"	Mabel E. Gillette,
'94	Katharine A. Crane, B. L.,	"	Florence E. McIntyre (Clark),
"	Achsah S. Hiller (Eddy),	"	Mary N. McKay,
"	Jessica M. McIntyre, Ph. B.,	"	Mildred L. Weed,
'95	Elizabeth W. Alexander,	"	Bertha Wright,
"	Belle L. Brewster,	'00	Genevieve I. Broad,
"	Belle Donaldson, A. B.,	"	Mary P. Herrick,
"	Anna S. Duncan,	"	Gertrude B. Kennedy,
"	Mildred T. Hinsdale, Ph. B.,	"	Margaret R. Layton,
"	Bouise A. McGilveay,	"	Lucile C. Morris,
'96	Bertha C. Barney, B. L.,	"	Laura M. Rinkle,
"	Harriet E. Bingham, B. L.,	"	Sophie R. St. Clair,
"	Daisy F. Evans,	"	Alice M. Thorne,
"	Florence M. Halleck,	"	Florence Walker,
"	Harriet Lake,	'01	Anna M. Rogers,
"	Nina H. Paddock, B. L.,	"	Olive J. Rouech.

Alpha Phi.—This collegiate sisterhood was founded in 1882 by ten students of Syracuse University. The Alpha Chapter, which built a house of its own in 1889, was followed nine years later by the Beta at Northwestern University. The other branches are: Eta, Boston University, 1883; Gamma, DePauw, 1887; Delta, Cornell, 1889; Epsilon, Minnesota, 1890; Zeta, Women's College of Baltimore, 1891; Theta, Michigan, 1892; aud Iota, Wisconsin, 1894. There are about 700 members. Silver-grey and bordeaux-red are the colors of the society, and its favorite flowers are lillies-of-the-valleys and forget-me-nots. There is a magazine called The Alpha Phi Quarterly. The building 126 North Division street is occupied by the chapter in our University. Mrs. Junius E. Beal, Mrs. Alfred H. Lloyd, Mrs. William H.

BADGE OF ALPHA PHI.

Wait, and Mrs. Robert M. Wenley are the "patronesses" of the local organization, which also has the following members:

'94 Gertrude Buck, M. S.,
" Winifred A. Higby (Rose), Ph.B.,
'95 Bertha Hine, A. B.,
" Nina M. Holden (Cummer), A. B.,
" Clara M. McOmber, Ph. B.,
" *Martha E. Orr, B. L.,
" *Allene Peck (Belknap),
" Flora M. Quigley (Will),
" Lillian M. Quigley (Agnew),
" Effie Lois Roberts, A. B.,
'96 Minnie A. Boylan (Beal), Ph. B.,
" Nina H. Denton, Ph. B.,
" Mathilde Hine, Ph. B.,
" Helen A. Kelley, Ph. B.,
" Jane Littlefield, (Kelley),
" Bertha Rose (Wakefield),
" Sadie E. Sheehan, A. B.,
" Bess B. Stevens, A. B.,
" Mary W. Wood,
" Elizabeth Wrenge (Humphrey),
'97 Myrtle M. Bruner, B. L.,
" Nellie M. Hayes,
" Lena L. Hine,
" Julia M. Hodge, Ph. B.,
" Susie L. McKee, A. B.,
" Agnes Morley,
" Edith H. Noble,
" Carolyne M. Putnam,
" Katharyne G. Sleneau, A. B.,
" Lillian M. Tompkins, A. B.,
" Stella Westcott, A. B.,
'98 Anna L. Decker,
" Julia E. Gettemy,
" Mable E. Holmes,
" Jessie M. Mack,
" Gertrude Savage,
" Jeannette Smith,
" Winnifred Smith,
" Gertrude L. Springer,
" Adda L. Stevens,
'99 *m* Florence E. Allen,
" Ruth A. Bartley,
" Mary L. Bunker,
" Grace S. Flagg.
" Anne W. Howe,
" Anne McOmber,
" Margaret D. Mason,
" Winnie J. Robinson,
" Louise Shepard,
" Grace B. Ward,
'00 Irene K. Goddard,
" Florence M. Hall,
" Juliet Grace Horton,
" Nina M. Howlett,
" Marian C. Kanouse,
" Marian H. Larsen,
'01 Genevieve Decker,
" Jessie A. Howell,
" Maude Hudson,
" Mable Mead,
" Frances E. Terwilliger,
" Edith A. Wheeler.

Delta Delta Delta.—This is the youngest, both as a general society and at Ann Arbor, of the women's collegiate orders. It was founded at Boston University, by four undergraduates, who in 1889 associated themselves as the Alpha Chapter. A Delta Chapter, formed in the Iowa Agricultural College, in 1889, soon perished, and its placed was taken by the Delta Deuteron Chapter at Simpson College. Somewhat later, but still in 1889, the Epsilon was formed at Knox College, and these earlier branches have been followed by

BADGE AND EMBLEMS OF DELTA DELTA DELTA.

the following: Gamma, Adrian; Beta, St. Lawrence; Zeta, Cincinnati; Eta, Vermont; Theta, Minnesota; Iota, Michigan; Kappa, Nebraska; Sigma, Wesleyan; Omicron, Syracuse; Nu, Ohio State; Lambda, Baker University; Upsilon, Northwestern. A new chapter has just been formed in the University of Wisconsin. The total membership is about 600. A magazine called *The Trident* is issued by the fraternity.

The members of the local chapter, which was instituted in 1894, include Mrs. Lizzie F. Millen, an honorary initiate, and the following graduates and undergraduates:

'96 Nell Kempf (Close), Ph. B.,
" Almerene M. Orsborn, Ph. B.,
" D. Zena Thomson, B. L.,
'97 Harriette A. Brown,
" Effie L. Danforth, Ph. B.,
" Nellie M. Walters, B. L.,
'98 Harriet T. Averill (Haas),
" Gertrude M. Brown (Tower),
" Ruth W. Butterworth,
" Elizabeth A. Dugdale,
" Leonore Loxley,
" Josephine P. Powell,
" Lucile A. Shelley,
" Blanche M. Young,
'99 Nellie A. Brown,
" Emma D. Burke,
" Charlotte L. Reichmann,
'00 Katheryne F. Bateman,
" Elizabeth Boulsom,
" Ingeborg S. Fredlund,
" Belle H. Goldsmith,
" Eva A. Hillman,
" Elizabeth J. Lobb,
" Florence McHugh,
" Florence P. Mildon,
" Edith M. Popkins,
" Alvena D. Reichmann,
'01 Lillian M. Haadsten.

Excluding their honorary and associate members, the eight sisterhoods of the literary department have had a total membership of 564, distributed thus: Sorosis, 120; Gamma Phi Beta, 101; Delta Gamma, 70; Pi Beta Phi, 66; Kappa Kappa Gamma, 62; Alpha Phi, 62; Kappa Alpha Theta, 54; Delta Delta Delta, 28. Beginning with the class of '80, and including all classes except those now in college, the total membership is 556, of which number 207 have been granted literary degrees by the University. As the number of women graduated 1880–97 is 680, of which total the societies claim 207, it follows that society privileges have been enjoyed by about 30 per cent of the ladies who have finished their literary studies.

BADGE OF ALPHA EPSILON IOTA.

Alpha Epsilon Iota.—This medical sisterhood was founded at the University of Michigan, February 3, 1890, by five undergraduates. It did not appear in the students' annual until 1897. *The Chronicle* of May 9, 1891, reported that the society had added to its ranks "three illustrious women, Emily Blackwell (Dean of the Women's Medical School, New York City), Mary Putnam Jacobi, and Sarah Hackett

Stevenson". It has also acquired as honorary members, Dr. Frances E. White, of Philadelphia, Dr. Frances Huson, of Detroit, and Miss Eliza M. Mosher, M. D., '75, Women's Dean of the University. Mrs. V. C. Vaughan, Mrs. W. J. Herdman, and Mrs. W. A. Campbell are the "patronesses" of the society at Ann Arbor, which makes its home at 307 North State street, and calls itself the Alpha Chapter. In January, 1898, a Beta Chapter was instituted at the Women's Medical College of Northwestern University; and a Gamma Chapter was established in February, 1898, at the Laura Hills Memorial College, Cincinnati. Following is the roll of the Michigan initiates, forty-one in all:

'90 Lotta R. Arwine, M. D.,
" Minnie A. Howard, M. D.,
" Lily MacGowan (Eellows), M. D.,
'91 Elizabeth D. Bayer, M. D.,
" Ada F. Bock, M. D.,
" Anna W. Croacher, M. D.,
" May B. Stuckey (Reynolds), M.D.,
" Mary W. Williams, M. D.,
'92 Henrietta A. Carr, M. D.,
" Jeanne C. Solis, M. D.,
'93 Katherine R. Collins, M. D.,
'95 Florence A. Amidon, M. D.,
" Jean M. Cooke, M. D.,
" Harriet L. Hawkins, M. D.,
'96 Elizabeth Campbell,
" Gertrude D. Campbell, M. D.,
" Eleanor S. Everhard, M. D.,
" Penelope M. Flett, M. D.,
" Jennie J. Hall, M. D.,
" Maude L. Hassard, M. D.,
" Frances Hulbert, M. D.,
'96 Anna L. Preston, M. D.,
'97 Anna W. Locke, M. D.,
" Marion Nute, M. D.,
" Georgia Smeallie (Nims), M. D.,
'98 Annie M. Stevens,
'99 Helen A. Affeld,
" Felecie von Autenreid,
" Frances E. Barrett,
" Blanche M. Butler,
" Mary L. Cook,
" Susan B. Jarrett,
" Mary M. McArthur,
" Mary C. McKibbin,
" Elizabeth Rindlaub,
" Alice G. Snyder,
'00 Harriet V. Baker,
" Alice M. M. Chesley,
" Helen T. Cleaves,
" Minta P. Kemp,
'01 Georgia O. Robertson.

BADGE OF OMEGA PSI.

Omega Psi, a sophomore society, a sort of feminine Theta Nu Epsilon, was instituted here in 1896 with thirteen charter-members drawn from Gamma Phi Beta, Delta Gamma, and Alpha Phi. It is a branch (the Beta) of the organization of the same name founded in 1894 at the Northwestern University. The Michigan members are:

'98 Esther Braley,
" Lillian Cole,
" Josephine Daniels,
" Mary J. DeVeny,
" Grace S. Flagg,
" Eva J. Hill,
" Jessie M. Mack,
'98 Gertrude Savage,
" Winnifred Smith,
" Adda L. Stevens,
" Margaret Thain,
" Lilian M. Tompkins,
" Mary E. Young.

INDEX OF SUBJECTS

INDEX OF ILLUSTRATIONS

ROEHM & SON, JEWELLERS

184 and 186 Woodward Avenue

DETROIT, MICHIGAN

Reverently preserved in the archives of the older Greek letter societies are some of the badges devised and worn by the founders of those associations sixty or more years ago. One of these emblems was constantly carried by its possessor from the night of his initiation until his death, a period of nearly half a century. Another, after having lain for twenty years in a grove where it had been lost, was found by the owner's son, who in the meantime had himself become a member of the fraternity which it typified. Still another of these old pins was handed down as an heirloom from father to son and from son to grandson, so that it did duty for three generations of college men.

BADGE OF DELTA PSI.

Precious as are these venerable jewels for the associations which cluster round them, they are hardly to be compared in point of beauty with the badges produced by the artists of to-day. Messrs. Roehm & Son have transformed Phi Beta Kappa's token—anciently called at Union, from its somewhat clumsy shape, the "stoneboat"—into a badge of real elegance, while still preserving the original design. They are also manufacturing the watch-key of that ancient and exclusive fraternity, the Kappa Alpha, which, with six Eastern chapters, represents the men by whom at Union College seventy-three years ago the Greek-letter system of societies was originated. Of course the symbols of the Kappa Alpha key remain as the founders originated them; but by ingenious workmanship, effectiveness has been added to what was before one of the most beautiful of college badges.

To the fraternities which were organized in Yale College during the earlier half of the present century, is due much of the influence now exerted by the Greek-letter orders throughout the country. The founder of the Psi Upsilon at Yale was also the organizer of branches at Brown and Amherst; and the Yale Chapter of Delta Kappa Epsilon is the mother of that powerful and extensive fraternity. When the chapter of Alpha Delta Phi at Yale, upon the completion of its costly stone temple, resumed after an interval of twenty-three years its old place as a junior society, Messrs. Roehm & Son were awarded the order for the badges to be donned by the first Junior delegation under the new arrangement. It is also noteworthy that the Executive Council of the Psi Upsilon, in selecting an official badge for use throughout the fraternity, unanimously adopted in preference to many other exhibits, the "Yale" badge furnished by the firm above mentioned.

SEAL OF ALPHA DELTA PHI AT HARVARD.

Roehm & Son were also makers of the beautiful badge set with diamonds which was presented by the Sigma Alpha Epsilon fraternity to President McKinley, one of its honorary members, and which was worn by the chief magistrate on the day of his inauguration.

The records kept by Roehm & Son show that they make goods for more than half the chapters of most of the oldest and largest fraternities, and in some cases the percentage of chapters runs over eighty.

While encouraging trade from societies requiring all classes of work, Roehm & Son exert their main efforts for new business in directions where the highest grade of workmanship is desired.

BADGE OF SOUTHERN KAPPA ALPHA

During the senior year of '73 a freshman bought from one of Ann Arbor's bookdealers several packages of envelopes bearing the flamboyent seal of that class. The youth remarked that the articles purchased were the neatest thing in the way of fraternity envelopes he had seen that year.

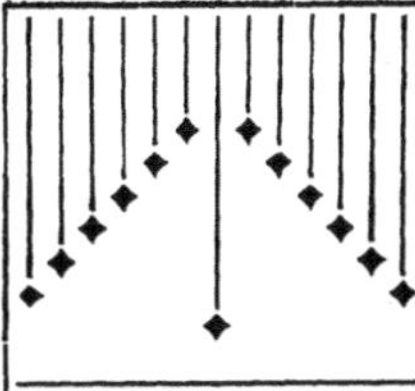

Wadhams, Ryan & Reule

Clothiers
and
Furnishers

200-202 South Main Street, . . . ANN ARBOR

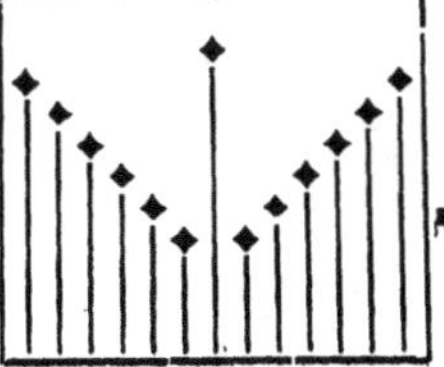

IT is said that Edward Bulwer, Lord Lytton, once received a proposal of marriage from a young girl, and that, years afterwards, when he had experienced innumerable infelicities from an alliance with another, he declared he had gone further and had fared worse. Doubtless this would be the self-accusing comment of the Michigan student, who passing by the well-supplied furnishing house of Messrs. Wadhams, Ryan & Reule, should travel to Detroit or Toledo and there purchase at higher prices goods less satisfactory than could be procured at the establishment mentioned. Whether the alumnus or the undergraduate seeks a new suit or a new umbrella, whether he wants a necktie or a pair of gloves, a mackintosh or collars and cuffs, he can obtain any or all of these at the south-west corner of Main and Washington Streets, as well as, and more cheaply than, in any of the shops in Chicago or Detroit.

A junior, unable to write German script, was told to use the Latin characters in writing his German exercise on the blackboard. Immediately he replied "I never studied Latin, Professor."

BADGE OF PI KAPPA ALPHA

MICHIGAN CENTRAL Passenger Station, ANN ARBOR, MICH.

MICHIGAN CENTRAL

FOR many years the only access by rail to Ann Arbor was furnished by the Michigan Central, and the handsome structure of stone which since 1886 has welcomed and has bid farewell to so many students, attests the special interest taken by the Company's officers in the University, of which not a few of them are graduates.

To quote from the Official Report of the State Railroad Commissioner's Inspection of the Michigan Central: "The main line is as near perfection in the way of construction, appointments, service, and able management as can be conceived in modern railroading. No skill or expenditure has been spared to make it the modern railroad of the country." The road is a first-class line for first-class travel between Ann Arbor and Chicago, and from Ann Arbor to Detroit and to New York. Graduates, old or young, professors and students, in fact all persons who have been or are connected with the University, have cause to regard the Michigan Central as an essential part of the institution itself, as much so as the walks around and through the campus.

When the entire scientific section of '74, in its freshman year, joined the Good Templars, the sophs. said they wished to get on good terms with one of their professors who was worthy chief and had conditioned a good many of them.

The sophomores of '76 were to use the words of The Chronicle, "Not half as big fools as some persons think." Their instructor in Mathematics required them to bring exercise II, page 28, Olney's Calculus, in on paper. They borrowed a nice solution and figure from a junior, had a photographer make 100 copies, and sent them in.

Sigma Nu, a fraternity not as yet represented at Michigan, was founded about thirty years ago in the Virginia Military Academy, and has many branches in the South and West.

RENTSCHLER

.. Photographer

Studio:
Cor. Main and Huron Sts.

RENTSCHLER'S NEW CABINETS
the most Artistic Photographs
ever made in Ann Arbor . . . . .